Johnson's
mother
& baby

CANADIAN EDITION

JOHNSON'S®
mother
&baby

Editor
Carol Cooper, MD

Canadian Editor
Anne Biringer, MD

Photography by Ruth Jenkinson

Senior editor: Jennifer Williams
Senior art editor: Glenda Fisher
Editor, Canada: Julia Roles
Project editors: Angela Baynham,
Corinne Asghar, Anne Esden
Project art editors: Alison Tumer,
Liz Brown, Edward Kinsey
DTP designer: Karen Constanti
Production controller: Heather Hughes
Managing editor: Anna Davidson
Managing art editor: Emma Forge
Art direction: Sally Smallwood
Jacket editor: Beth Apple
Jacket designer: Nathalie Godwin
Category publisher: Corinne Roberts

First Canadian Edition, 2004
04 05 06 07 08 10 9 8 7 6 5 4 3 2 1

Dorling Kindersley is represented in Canada by Tourmaline Editions Inc.,
662 King Street West, Suite 304, Toronto, Ontario M5V 1M7

JOHNSON'S® is a registered trademark of Johnson & Johnson

National Library of Canada Cataloging in Publication Data
Johnson's mother & baby/Carol Cooper, editor;
Anne Biringer, Canadian editor – Canadian ed.
Includes index.
ISBN 1-55363-033-5

1. Pregnancy. 2. Parent and child. I. Cooper, Carol 1947–
II. Biringer, Anne. III. Title: Johnson's mother and baby.

RG525.J66 2004   649'.122   C2003-903447-X

Reproduced by Colourscan Overseas Pte. Ltd., Singapore
Printed by Toppan Printing Co (HK) Ltd., Hong Kong

Discover more at
www.dk.com

A Message to Parents from *Johnson & Johnson*

The most precious gift in the world is a new baby. To your little one, you are the center of the universe. And by following your most basic instincts to touch, hold, and talk to your baby, you provide the best start to a happy, healthy life.

Our baby products encourage parents to care for and nurture their children through the importance of touch, developing a deep, loving bond that transcends all others.

Parenting is not an exact science, nor is it a one-size-fits-all formula. For more than a hundred years Johnson & Johnson has supported the healthcare needs of parents and healthcare professionals, and we understand that all parents feel more confident in their role when they have information they can trust.

That is why we offer this book as our commitment to you to provide scientifically sound, professionally reviewed guidance on the important topics of pregnancy, baby care, and child development.

As you read through this book, the most important thing to remember is this: you know your baby better than anyone else. By watching, listening, and having confidence in your natural ability, you will know how to use the information you have in your hands, for the benefit of the baby in your arms.

contents

baby and child care 81

introduction

From the moment you start to think about becoming parents, you are embarking on life's most amazing adventure. People have babies every day, but when it happens to you it is the most magical experience in the world, one that alters your perspective on life. As you welcome your baby as the newest member of your family, you can look forward to deep joy – and plenty of fun.

As your baby grows into a child and then matures into an adult, there will be many different influences on him, but you are the most important of all. The relationship you forge with your child forms the pattern for every one of his relationships throughout life. At the same time, you have a lot of practical matters to attend to, such as feeding and bathing your baby, and protecting him against illness.

There aren't hard-and-fast rules on how to bring up a baby, but there is a lot of information for new parents to absorb. This book aims to support and guide you on all the important issues of parenting so that you can be confident and make the most of family life. Much of the advice represents a fusion of my professional expertise as a family doctor and my personal experience as a mother.

how this book works

The book is divided into four main sections.

pregnancy takes you all the way from preconception and planning right through to the birth and recovery afterward. This is an exciting time and expectant women – and their partners – are fascinated by what's happening in the womb during the months of pregnancy. At each stage, words and pictures show you the changes taking place in your own body and how your baby is growing. There is plenty of helpful information on diet and exercise during pregnancy, what your prenatal care will involve, and reassuring advice on how to cope with common discomforts, and when to get medical help if conditions of concern arise.

baby and child care is fully illustrated and shows you how to look after a baby from birth until the age of three. This section, arranged chronologically to guide you as your child grows up, is where you can find information on feeding, weaning, bathing, dressing, sleeping, and more. There's down-to-earth advice on managing a crying baby, feeding and weaning, toilet training, and other issues that we know parents can find challenging. Throughout you'll notice that the emphasis is on making the most of the time you spend with your child, even if you're only carrying out a basic task such as changing your baby's diaper.

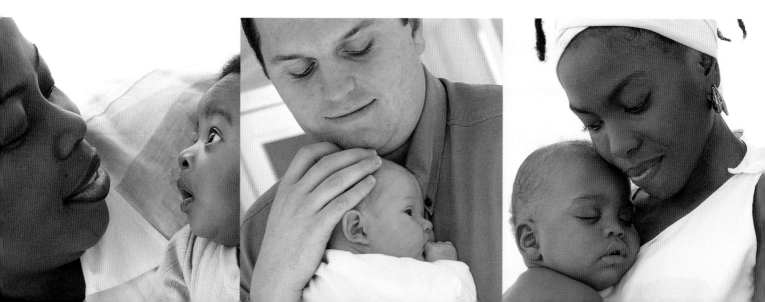

development covers a topic that is important to parents, but can be confusing. What your child can do at each age is a barometer of his growing understanding of the world. Reaching developmental milestones also provides parents and grandparents with some glorious moments. You will get a thrill from your baby's first smile, first sounds, and first steps. We hope this section will put development into perspective and help parents appreciate the wide range of normal behavior. Once again, the accent is on understanding a baby's and young child's development so that you can enjoy every moment, celebrate achievements, and help bring out the best in your child.

health gives valuable advice on ways to help protect your child from illnesses and accidents. Designed to be straightforward to use, it also includes a number of conditions that, though fairly common, are not always covered in childcare books – hand, foot, and mouth disease or Kawasaki syndrome, for example. While easy to assimilate, the information takes into account the latest medical thinking. Throughout, my aim is to give you the same advice and reassurance I give parents in my consulting room. I have also drawn on my own experiences as a parent to share with you my tips on caring for a baby or child who isn't feeling his best. At the end of this section there's advice on first aid. Although we hope you never need to put these procedures into practice, it is a good idea to read through this section and keep it as a handy reference if needed.

At the very end of the book you'll find a resource list, consisting of names and addresses of support groups, non-profits, and other organizations. These are divided into four categories to correspond with the four main sections of the book, and Internet addresses are included wherever possible.

the richness of family life

You will soon find out that parenting isn't a one-way process. Your moods and your child's moods will affect each other, and there will inevitably be highs and lows as your child grows up. This is completely normal. Becoming a parent may be natural, but it is not always a simple transition to make. This book is here to help you meet the challenges, and deal with the hopes and fears that are part of family life.

We recognize, too, that families come in all shapes and sizes, and that parents have important relationships other than the one with their child. That's why you will find there is something for everyone – whether you're a working parent, stay-at-home parent, single parent, or even a grandparent or caregiver. We hope you'll discover plenty in this book to guide you and stimulate you. As I have learned, raising children is a uniquely satisfying experience. We wish you great happiness and fulfillment as you set out on this amazing adventure.

Dr. Carol Cooper

pregnancy

The next nine months or so are an extraordinary time for you and your growing baby. Your body and your emotions will change as never before, while inside you your baby is developing faster than he will at any other time in his life. Soon, your tiny embryo will become your fully developed new baby. Don't worry if you have questions. This section will give you guidance on the choices available for prenatal care and labor. Before you know it, you'll be ready for the momentous process of birth and the many joys that lie ahead.

planning a baby

How wonderful! You've decided you'd like to have a baby. It's a big decision that is going to change your life forever – but in the nicest possible way. Trying to become pregnant can be an anxious time, but most couples do not experience problems. Don't expect it to happen immediately, but consider the possibility that, within a few months, you will be expecting your child.

lifestyle considerations

Before you start trying to have a baby, and once you are pregnant, it's worth taking a lifestyle check.

No one is expecting you to change radically, but there may be some adjustments that you and your partner can make to ensure that you're doing everything you can to safeguard your health and that of your child.

Diet

Healthy eating during pregnancy doesn't differ much from any other time: choose fresh fruit and vegetables, limit processed food, cookies, and cakes, and limit fat. Once you're pregnant, avoid undercooked meat; unwashed vegetables and salads; unpasteurized foods and cheeses (see page 27). You won't be sure you're pregnant until you're at least two weeks into the pregnancy, so you might want to avoid these foods when you start trying to conceive.

It's also recommended that you take a folic acid supplement (400 mcg) even before you start trying to get pregnant, and until you start prenatal vitamins, as this has been shown to reduce the incidence

of spina bifida and other neural-tube defects. The first step toward healthy eating is to look at the foods in your daily diet. Early in pregnancy, some women find that their appetite comes and goes. Try to eat a variety of foods each day. An average woman needs about 2,200 calories per day. When you are pregnant, you need about 300 calories more.

Smoking

Stop smoking before, during, and after pregnancy to avoid risking your health and the health of your baby. Each puff subjects you and the fetus to harmful chemicals such as nicotine, tar, and carbon monoxide. If you or anyone else smokes around the baby, the baby is

Menstrual cycle
The average menstrual cycle lasts 28 days, during which the uterus prepares itself for fertilization. The uterine lining (endometrium) thickens to receive a fertilized egg, then sheds if the egg is not fertilized. Follicle-stimulating hormone (FSH) causes an egg to mature, and luteinizing hormone (LH) triggers its release. Estrogen levels peak just before ovulation and the rise in progesterone stimulates the endometrium to thicken. Ovulation takes place around day 14, and the most fertile period is approximately day 12 to day 16.

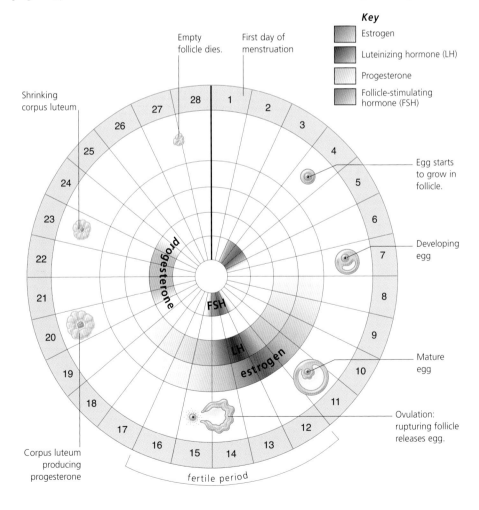

Key
- Estrogen
- Luteinizing hormone (LH)
- Progesterone
- Follicle-stimulating hormone (FSH)

Empty follicle dies.

First day of menstruation

Shrinking corpus luteum

Egg starts to grow in follicle.

Developing egg

Mature egg

Ovulation: rupturing follicle releases egg.

Corpus luteum producing progesterone

fertile period

trying **to become pregnant**

♦ Don't worry too much about timing sex with the day you're ovulating – research shows that couples who make love throughout the month tend to conceive most quickly. Just enjoy your sex life.

♦ At the same time, keep in mind that you are at your most fertile and most likely to conceive in the middle of your menstrual cycle (see diagram opposite).

♦ Cut down on coffee consumption – it can take longer to conceive if you're drinking more than three cups a day.

♦ If you have a hectic lifestyle, try to take things more calmly than usual. There's no real evidence that stress interferes with conception, but it certainly can't do any harm to reduce your stress level.

"Over the last 18 months we've talked more about starting a family, and now that it's happening, it's tremendously exciting. Finding out Jenny wasn't pregnant the first three or four months was quite a surprise. Then when we did conceive we hadn't expected to. We were amazed, as well as thrilled, when the test was positive."

SIMON NORTH, 30, HUSBAND OF JENNY, 8 WEEKS PREGNANT

exposed to the harmful effects of the smoke, so it is also vital that your partner and any other members of the household stop smoking.

Alcohol

It is unknown how much alcohol is too much during pregnancy, but research shows that it may cause a serious condition called Fetal Alcohol Syndrome (FAS). Heavy drinking can also increase the risk of miscarriage. To be safe, don't drink any alcohol during pregnancy.

Other considerations

When you decide you are ready to conceive, there are several important factors you should consider.

♦ Any medical condition for which you or your partner takes regular medication – talk to your doctor or midwife.

♦ Any genetic or congenital condition in your own or your partner's family – talk to your doctor and if, there are grounds for concern, ask for a referral to a geneticist before you start trying for a baby.

♦ Your rubella status. If you're worried you might not be protected against rubella (German measles, which if contracted during pregnancy can harm the baby) ask your doctor for a blood test. Have a vaccination at least three months before you conceive.

♦ Confirm your immunity to varicella, the virus that causes chicken pox.

Becoming parents
Creating a new life together is a unique way of expressing your love. Discuss your hopes and feelings before you start trying to conceive.

fertility **problems**

Although fertility problems have become more common in the last few years, don't worry, you are still unlikely to be affected. Nine out of 10 couples conceive during the first year of trying, and of the remainder, about half conceive in the second year.

Age makes a difference

If you're in your 20s you're less likely to have fertility problems, so don't rush off to your doctor if it's been three months and nothing has happened. If, on the other hand, you're in your late 30s or even your 40s, and you don't conceive within six months, it's worth seeing your doctor – if only to get some advice.

Many couples who fear they're having fertility problems find that just seeking professional advice seems to help, and they conceive easily at that point without the need for intervention.

Having a fertility problem investigated is a tough time for any couple, especially if – as is often the case – you're surrounded by pregnant friends and siblings.

Once you have decided to try to have a baby, it can be tempting to tell the world because you are excited. However, if you do you will probably get a lot of questions from well-meaning friends and family about whether you are expecting a baby yet, so you might want to consider keeping your decision private for a while.

Keeping life in perspective

Try not to let your attempts to have a baby become the focal point of your life. Plan treats and vacations and don't put things off "in case" you're pregnant. If you do conceive, you'll adjust your plans as you need to, and keeping a sense of perspective is very important right now.

conception

Oh my goodness – deep down you hadn't really believed it would happen to you, and the news that you have conceived might leave both you and your partner feeling a little uncertain. Finding out that you're expecting a baby is an incredibly exciting moment. Of course, it happens to thousands of people every day, but right now you probably feel as if you're the only ones it has ever happened to.

discovering you are pregnant

You can't be sure yet, but you strongly suspect that somewhere deep inside you there's a tiny bundle of cells that is going to change your life forever.

Some women "know" they're pregnant, but the vast majority don't realize until about 14 days after fertilization has taken place. Noticing your period is late is the number-one sign that you're probably pregnant.

However, it is possible to have bleeding when you are pregnant – although it is probably scantier than usual. If a pregnancy test is positive and you are bleeding, see your doctor.

Pregnancy tests

Most people buy a test from the supermarket or pharmacy and do it at home. You can, if you prefer, ask to have a test at your doctor's office – the ones they use are often very similar to home tests.

Pregnancy testing kit
Home-testing kits are simple to use and very accurate if you follow the instructions.

The basic pregnancy test checks your urine for a hormone called hCG (human chorionic gonadotropin). You urinate onto a stick and within a short time you see a color change in the window, indicating you are pregnant.

calculating your **delivery date**

The average pregnancy lasts for 266 days measured from conception. Because it can be difficult to know exactly when conception occurred, the delivery date is usually calculated from the first day of your last menstrual period (LMP). This means that your estimated delivery date, which obstetricians call your estimated date of delivery (EDD), will be 280 days from your LMP.

To calculate your EDD, find the date of your LMP in the left-hand columns of the chart opposite. The boldface date in the adjacent right-hand column is your EDD or "due date."

Remember that this is only an estimated date, and very few babies actually arrive on the date given. The delivery date is particularly difficult to predict if you do not have regular 28-day cycles. Doctors consider anything between 38 and 42 weeks to be a normal-length pregnancy.

Jan	Oct	Feb	Nov	Mar	Dec	Apr	Jan	May	Feb	Jun	Mar	Jul	Apr	Aug	May	Sep	Jun	Oct	Jul	Nov	Aug	Dec	Sep
1	8	1	8	1	6	1	6	1	5	1	8	1	7	1	8	1	8	1	8	1	8	1	7
2	9	2	9	2	7	2	7	2	6	2	9	2	8	2	9	2	9	2	9	2	9	2	8
3	10	3	10	3	8	3	8	3	7	3	10	3	9	3	10	3	10	3	10	3	10	3	9
4	11	4	11	4	9	4	9	4	8	4	11	4	10	4	11	4	11	4	11	4	11	4	10
5	12	5	12	5	10	5	10	5	9	5	12	5	11	5	12	5	12	5	12	5	12	5	11
6	13	6	13	6	11	6	11	6	10	6	13	6	12	6	13	6	13	6	13	6	13	6	12
7	14	7	14	7	12	7	12	7	11	7	14	7	13	7	14	7	14	7	14	7	14	7	13
8	15	8	15	8	13	8	13	8	12	8	15	8	14	8	15	8	15	8	15	8	15	8	14
9	16	9	16	9	14	9	14	9	13	9	16	9	15	9	16	9	16	9	16	9	16	9	15
10	17	10	17	10	15	10	15	10	14	10	17	10	16	10	17	10	17	10	17	10	17	10	16
11	18	11	18	11	16	11	16	11	15	11	18	11	17	11	18	11	18	11	18	11	18	11	17
12	19	12	19	12	17	12	17	12	16	12	19	12	18	12	19	12	19	12	19	12	19	12	18
13	20	13	20	13	18	13	18	13	17	13	20	13	19	13	20	13	20	13	20	13	20	13	19
14	21	14	21	14	19	14	19	14	18	14	21	14	20	14	21	14	21	14	21	14	21	14	20
15	22	15	22	15	20	15	20	15	19	15	22	15	21	15	22	15	22	15	22	15	22	15	21
16	23	16	23	16	21	16	21	16	20	16	23	16	22	16	23	16	23	16	23	16	23	16	22
17	24	17	24	17	22	17	22	17	21	17	24	17	23	17	24	17	24	17	24	17	24	17	23
18	25	18	25	18	23	18	23	18	22	18	25	18	24	18	25	18	25	18	25	18	25	18	24
19	26	19	26	19	24	19	24	19	23	19	26	19	25	19	26	19	26	19	26	19	26	19	25
20	27	20	27	20	25	20	25	20	24	20	27	20	26	20	27	20	27	20	27	20	27	20	26
21	28	21	28	21	26	21	26	21	25	21	28	21	27	21	28	21	28	21	28	21	28	21	27
22	29	22	29	22	27	22	27	22	26	22	29	22	28	22	29	22	29	22	29	22	29	22	28
23	30	23	30	23	28	23	28	23	27	23	30	23	29	23	30	23	30	23	30	23	30	23	29
24	31	24	1	24	29	24	29	24	28	24	31	24	30	24	31	24	1	24	31	24	31	24	30
25	1	25	2	25	30	25	30	25	1	25	1	25	1	25	1	25	2	25	1	25	1	25	1
26	2	26	3	26	31	26	31	26	2	26	2	26	2	26	2	26	3	26	2	26	2	26	2
27	3	27	4	27	1	27	1	27	3	27	3	27	3	27	3	27	4	27	3	27	3	27	3
28	4	28	5	28	2	28	2	28	4	28	4	28	4	28	4	28	5	28	4	28	4	28	4
29	5			29	3	29	3	29	5	29	5	29	5	29	5	29	6	29	5	29	5	29	5
30	6			30	4	30	4	30	6	30	6	30	6	30	6	30	7	30	6	30	6	30	6
31	7			31	5			31	7			31	7	31	7			31	7			31	7
Jan	Nov	Feb	Dec	Mar	Jan	Apr	Feb	May	Mar	Jun	Apr	Jul	May	Aug	Jun	Sep	Jul	Oct	Aug	Nov	Sep	Dec	Oct

explaining **fertilization**

Fertilization occurs when the sperm meets the egg, usually in the fallopian tube, and penetrates it. The sperm's body and tail then break off. Next, the head of the sperm joins forces with the nucleus of the egg – each contains half the number of chromosomes normally found in a human cell, which is 46. The 23 sperm chromosomes and the 23 egg chromosomes then pair up. This minuscule cell now contains every piece of genetic information that your baby needs to develop into the child, and beyond that the adult, you will come to know and love.

How gender is determined
You and your partner are each providing half the material to create this new human being – and your genes are now being rearranged in a totally unique way. The only difference between what your genes and your partner's do concerns sex determination: every egg a woman produces contains an X chromosome, because the genetic makeup of a female is XX. But sperm come in two different types: X sperm (which, when combined with an egg, will make a baby girl) and Y sperm (which will make a boy). Whether you're having a boy or a girl is therefore decided at fertilization, before you find out you're pregnant.

Twins
A twin fertilization occurs either when a fertilized egg divides into two at a very early stage, creating genetically identical twins who are the same sex, or when two separate eggs are fertilized by separate sperm, creating fraternal, or nonidentical twins, who may be the same or different sexes.

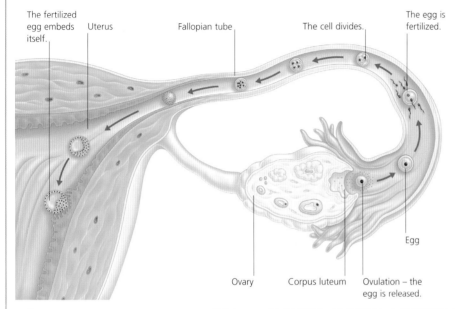

The fertilized egg embeds itself. | Uterus | Fallopian tube | The cell divides. | The egg is fertilized. | Egg | Ovulation – the egg is released. | Corpus luteum | Ovary

If no change occurs, the test is negative. Sometimes, especially if you're testing on the day your period is due, you may see just a faint color change. It is still a positive test, although you may want to repeat it in a few days to be certain. If the test is negative, but you still feel you might be pregnant, repeat the test a few days later. If there is a question, your doctor may perform a serum (blood) pregnancy test.

Other indications
Many women in early pregnancy don't feel any different. Some, though, do have other indications that they've conceived:
♦ needing to urinate more frequently
♦ feeling more tired by early evening
♦ a strange taste in the mouth – some women describe it as metallic
♦ feeling nauseous
♦ tender nipples that may be darker than usual.

"I thought my period had started so I told my husband I wasn't pregnant. But 24 hours later there was nothing so I did a test. I was amazed when it was positive. I phoned my husband right away and he couldn't believe it – we still can't, really. It's our secret, because we've decided we're not telling anyone else for a few weeks yet."

MARIA PEEL, 32, NEWLY PREGNANT

assisted **conception**

Fertilization fuses the genetic material of the egg and the sperm within a single cell. This is true whether your baby has been conceived entirely naturally or via an assisted reproductive technique. Often a failure to conceive is the result of a problem in the mechanism that brings the egg and sperm together (for example, the woman may have blocked fallopian tubes, or the sperm may not be mobile enough to swim to where it's needed).

How assisted conception works
Assisted reproductive techniques such as IVF (in vitro fertilization, in which the egg is fertilized outside the body) or the relatively new variation, ICSI (intracytoplasmic sperm injection), in which a single sperm is injected directly into the cytoplasm of a mature egg, and then transferred into the uterus after the egg has been fertilized, helping many couples to conceive.

prenatal care

What's available in terms of prenatal care differs from one region to another, and there are often more options available to you if you live in a city rather than a rural area. But wherever you live you should have some choice in the type of care you receive.

types of care

Before you choose the kind of care (and birth) you want, you must consider your health and understand all the possibilities.

Your choice of care may depend on the hospital or birth center with which your healthcare provider is affiliated, the recommendation of your doctor or friends, or a provider's flexibility about birthing options. Sometimes groups of healthcare professionals work together to provide care for pregnant women. These groups may include combinations of family doctors, midwives, nurse practitioners, and obstetricians.

♦ **Family physician** Approximately half of all Canadian babies are delivered by their family doctor, despite the fact that fewer family physicians are providing maternity care. There is wide variation between provinces and between locations within each province. The family doctor can provide continuity of care through preconception, pregnancy, and birth (for uncomplicated pregnancies) and then medical care for the baby. He or she will consult with an obstetrician if there are concerns during the pregnancy or birth.

♦ **Obstetrician** You may be referred to an obstetrician for complications in your pregnancy; however, many obstetricians also follow uncomplicated pregnancies. The obstetrician is specially trained to perform cesarean sections as well as difficult forceps or vacuum-assisted births.

♦ **Midwife** Midwives are licensed independent healthcare professionals in several provinces in Canada. This means that they function independently in providing prenatal and birth care. They are paid by the provincial health system and attend births both in the hospital and at home. They consult with a physician if there are complications. Midwives spend more time with you during labor than the average doctor and may be more flexible about birthing options.

♦ **Perinatal specialist** Your doctor or midwife may consult with, or refer you to, a perinatologist if your pregnancy is high risk.

your **first prenatal visit**

Your first prenatal appointment is an opportunity to assess your general health and the health of your baby. It is also a good time to ask your doctor or midwife questions about what to expect in the coming months. This initial visit is usually scheduled after you have missed a period.

What to expect

Your doctor or midwife will determine your due date, provide you with useful information about your baby's development, and perform first-trimester lab tests (such as urinalysis, pap smear, and blood work). You will be asked about your medical history, your partner's medical history, your menstrual history, and the date of your last period. Your weight will be measured and you will be given an internal exam (your uterus will be palpated to give your doctor or midwife an idea of how your baby is growing).

You may be offered an "early ultrasound" to confirm viability (life), the number of fetuses, if there are possible complications, such as bleeding, or if you have had a history of miscarriage.

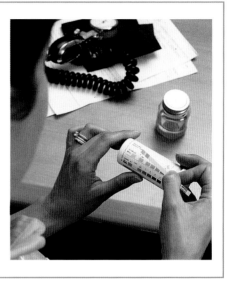

Regular checkups
At each appointment, your blood pressure will be tested and your urine checked for protein and glucose.

diagnostic and screening tests

In addition to the level II ultrasound (see page 39), you may be offered one or more of the tests listed below. Regional differences affect which tests are offered. Before having a test, discuss the implications with your partner and healthcare provider.

Although your healthcare provider may recommend certain tests, taking them is your choice alone. Always ask why you are being referred for a test, so you can make an informed decision. Keep in mind that screening tests can be abnormal even when the baby is perfectly healthy (this is called a false positive), but diagnostic tests are invasive and carry a slight risk of miscarriage. Talk this over thoroughly with your provider and partner. Think about whether you would consider a termination if the test result was positive.

These tests may also reveal the sex of your unborn child, so establish beforehand whether you want this information or not.

WHICH TEST?	AT WHAT STAGE?	HOW THE TEST WORKS
Early ultrasound	8–12 weeks	Ultrasound confims life and dating.
MSS (Maternal Serum Screen)	15–20 weeks	Uses a blood test to measure three or four hormones. Computer analysis of the hormone levels, considered with the mother's age and date of pregnancy, estimates the likelihood of neural-tube defects, Down syndrome, or other abnormalities.
NT (Nuchal Translucency)	11–14 weeks	Ultrasound measurement of the thickness of the skin of the fetal neck. Abnormalities are associated with Down syndrome, other chromosomal problems, or other abnormalities.
FTS (First Trimester Screening)	11–14 weeks	Computer analysis of the NT, mother's age, and two hormone levels estimates the likelihood of Down syndrome or other abnormalities.
IPS (Integrated Prenatal Scan)	11–14 weeks and 15–17 weeks	This combination of NT plus hormone levels done at 11–14 weeks and at 15–17 weeks estimates the likelihood of Down syndrome, neural tube defects, or other abnormalities.
Amniocentesis (diagnostic)	15–20 weeks	Involves taking a sample of amniotic fluid, and with it a few cells shed by the baby, via a needle. Results show whether your baby has Down syndrome or other chromosome disorders.
CVS (Chorionic Villus Sampling) (diagnostic)	10–12 weeks	Fragments of your placenta are analyzed to check for Down syndrome or other chromosome disorders.

rights and benefits

It is now easier than ever for Canadian mothers and fathers to access maternity and parental benefits. Under the federal Employment Insurance Act, all natural and adoptive parents are entitled to 35 weeks of parental leave, in addition to 15 weeks of funded maternity benefits for eligible employees.

knowing your rights

Investigate your company's policies on paid and unpaid leave before your baby is due. Many companies will "top-up" the government maternity benefits for a set period of time. Trade unions and enlightened employers are also starting to include paid paternity leave in their contracts.

It is important that you keep your employer informed of your plans. You must notify them in writing at least 30 days before your expected departure from work and keep them apprised of your plans after the baby arrives. You are entitled to certain rights regardless of how many hours you work, or how long you have been employed. For additional rights you must have fulfilled certain criteria (see below).

your **rights**

All employees are entitled to:

♦ working conditions that are safe for your unborn child

♦ time off work (without loss of salary) to attend prenatal appointments

♦ minimum maternity leave and pay.

If you have worked a minimum of 600 hours of insured work in the last 52 weeks, you are entitled to:

♦ at least 15 weeks funded maternity leave (55 percent of your average insured earnings up to a certain maximum)

♦ 35 weeks of parental leave.

Upon return to work:

♦ you must be restored to your original job or one with equivalent pay

♦ you cannot be penalized or fired for taking maternity or parental leave.

Working while you are pregnant

Working through a pregnancy, especially your first, can be a strange experience. When you're expecting a baby everything is different, and your priorities have obviously shifted: at the same time, you may feel very strongly that you're as committed to your work as ever, and no one should think otherwise.

You may feel compromised now that your colleagues know that you're about to change your life by becoming a mother. They will take their lead from you to some extent, so if you don't want to spend a long time at work talking about your happy event, resist the temptation to

discuss your pregnancy, unless you have to. However, be aware that you may need to make some adjustments to your life at work.

Keeping active helps your circulation and as you get bigger regular exercise makes you feel less weighed-down (psychologically at least) by your pregnancy.

Throughout your pregnancy, always listen to what your body tells you: this isn't the time to go for any medals for around-the-clock working, no matter what you do for a living.

Taking a break
Even if you usually work through your lunch hour, try to find the time to go for a walk or even a swim one or two days a week.

return-to-work plan

One of the most difficult decisions to make while pregnant, is whether to return to work after your baby is born. For many mothers, returning to work is a financial or career necessity. Other mothers may be able, and prefer, to stay home with their baby. Explore your options before your delivery. Look for solutions that work well for both you and your employer, and make sure your plans are flexible – you may have a change of heart.

♦ **Part-time work** With part-time work, what you gain in time with your child, often offsets what you lose in terms of benefits and career advancement. This solution also allows working mothers to keep their "foot in the door," and jump back into a full-time position when mutually agreed upon.

♦ **Telecommuting** Working from home eliminates the need to commute, saving you valuable time. This situation allows you to set your own schedule – within the

framework of a full-time job – and maintain full pay and benefits. You will, however, still need child care.

♦ **Job sharing** In this scenario, two workers split one job. The benefits include spending half your time at home with your baby without the worry of work piling up on your desk. Difficulties include finding a compatible work

partner and splitting benefits.

♦ **Freelance or temp work** A flexible schedule is often the top priority for those who freelance or do temp work; you choose when to work. Some jobs, though, cannot easily be apportioned out into freelance or temp work and the sporadic nature of this situation necessitates very flexible child care.

postpartum plan

In the weeks after delivery, many new mothers will need more support than friends and family are able to provide. Other options for at-home services may be covered under your insurance plan.

♦ A postpartum doula is trained to care for the new mother. Unlike baby nurses of the past, a doula allows you to focus on your new baby while she takes care of cooking, cleaning, and running errands.

♦ Breastfeeding assistance is vital for many new mothers. Lactation consultants may be covered. Non-profit organizations like La Leche League are free and will talk you through common breastfeeding problems.

FIRST TRIMESTER

| 1 | 2 | 3 | 4 | 5 | 6 | 7 | 8 | 9 | 10 | 11 | 12 |

SECOND TRIMESTER

| 13 | 14 | 15 | 16 | 17 | 18 | 19 | 20 | 21 | 22 | 23 | 24 | 25 | 26 | 27 |

THIRD TRIMESTER

| 28 | 29 | 30 | 31 | 32 | 33 | 34 | 35 | 36 | 37 | 38 | 39 | 40 |

weeks 0–8

It's finally sunk in that you're having a baby – and it's amazing how much is going on inside your body. By week eight, it's about four weeks since your period would have been due, but you're already two-thirds through the first trimester – even if you don't feel it.

your body changes

Many women don't feel or look any different at this stage – if that applies to you, don't worry, there IS a lot going on.

You are producing a lot of hormones to help establish the baby's life-support system, and your breasts are already beginning to prepare for feeding your baby.

Classic symptoms

If you feel different, it's likely to be fatigue and perhaps nausea that affect you most. The fatigue can be more draining than any you've ever experienced before: even women who are used to staying up late at night or working long hours are often surprised by having to go to bed much earlier than usual. Some say they even wake up feeling totally exhausted, and a few confess to needing a nap during the day. Nausea is the other classic early pregnancy symptom, commonly known as "morning sickness" (see opposite).

FACTS ABOUT **YOU**

♦ Your heart rate is increasing – possibly by about 10 beats per minute.

♦ Your breasts are getting bigger, and may feel a lot more sensitive than usual.

♦ Your metabolic rate is increasing by between 10 and 25 percent.

♦ You may have put on 2–3lb (900g–1.4kg). Only a tiny percentage of this is the baby; the rest is the weight of your growing uterus and its contents, and the newly formed placenta.

easing your **symptoms**

Dealing with fatigue
Don't try to beat fatigue – the only thing to do is listen to your body and, if possible, change your schedule so you can rest more.

If you are commuting to work, try to change your travel times so you're not in the car or on the train at the busiest times of the day, which is stressful and can really wear you out.

Nausea
Some women find dry toast and crackers help with nausea (for more tips see *managing morning sickness* opposite).

Mood changes
If you find you are experiencing lots of mood changes and swings, talk it over with your partner so he understands how you're feeling. Don't shut him out, keep communicating.

YOUR CHANGES   YOUR BREATHING RATE INCREASES • YOUR STOMACH FEELS BLOATED • YOU SOMETIMES FEEL FAINT • YOU MAY SUFFER FROM CONSTIPATION • YOU WILL NEED TO URINATE FREQUENTLY

your emotions

The first weeks of pregnancy are often a time of conflicting emotions. Although you may have longed for a baby, worries about the future, plus the hormonal changes going on inside your body, can be unsettling.

Adjusting to being pregnant

On the one hand, you're very excited – your life is about to be changed forever by the arrival of a baby. You may have longed for a baby, or maybe your pregnancy is a complete surprise. Either way, you are now looking forward to becoming a mother. You know this change is going to throw you and your partner into a new world – and it's a world you can't fully know until you're actually there. So there are also worries – about how it's going to change your life, your relationship, and your career. Hormonal changes can make you prone to mood swings, irritability, and tearfulness – some women compare this time to a prolonged period of premenstrual syndrome.

Common concerns

♦ **Am I really pregnant at all?** If you're not experiencing many physical symptoms this is often a worry, but you are not the only woman who has thought this!

♦ **Am I gaining too much weight?** Nausea can make a lot of women eat more than usual in the early weeks, and you might not want to put on extra pounds. Try to eat healthy snacks.

♦ **Am I going to miscarry?** Miscarriage is most common in the first trimester, but with each day and week that goes by your pregnancy is more established. If you've had any bleeding, or have any other reason to be especially worried, report your concerns to your doctor. An ultrasound may be performed.

What you can do

Talk over your concerns with your partner, but try to relax and be confident that, whatever challenges you may face as a couple, your lives will be enriched by the creation of this new life.

managing **morning sickness**

Pregnancy nausea is like no sickness you've ever experienced before – often it's a kind of gnawing emptiness and you feel you just have to have something to eat. The trouble is, eating doesn't necessarily help (or not for long) and may even make you vomit.

The term "morning sickness" is misleading. As many women experience nausea or vomiting in the evening as in the morning, and for the very unlucky it can go on throughout the day.

The positive side is that nausea is due to the increased amount of hormones circulating in your system – which is usually a sign of a healthy pregnancy.

A common concern is "Am I going to feel this awful for another seven and a half months?" If you're suffering badly from fatigue and nausea you may worry about this – but the answer, happily, is almost certainly no, and you should feel a lot better by week 13 or 14.

Diet and nutrition

Eat small meals frequently. Eating something before you get out of bed, such as crackers or ginger snaps, may be useful. Ginger supplements, acupuncture, or acupressure may also help. If vomiting is interfering with your ability to nourish yourself and your baby, speak to your doctor about prescribing a doxylamine/ pyridoxine combination since this has the greatest evidence to support its safety and efficacy.

Eating well
Bananas are rich in vitamin B6 and will help to prevent your blood-sugar levels from dropping.

"I've felt nauseous a lot, but distracting myself seems to help. If I keep busy, and I'm enjoying what I'm doing, I can keep the nausea at bay. Having plenty of snacks throughout the day also seems to help. I try always to have an apple in my bag, and a bottle of water, too."

KAREN SERGEANT, 26,
8 WEEKS PREGNANT

SEE ALSO   PRENATAL CARE pages 20–21 • EATING WELL page 27 • HAVING AN ULTRASOUND page 29
 • DENTAL CARE page 37 • A WORKING PREGNANCY page 41

your baby at 8 weeks

Although it's only six weeks since your baby was actually conceived (because pregnancy is dated from the start of your last menstrual period – see page 18), all the main internal organs are already in place. Of course, there's a lot of development ahead, but the rudiments of all the vital body parts are now present and correct.

Your baby's appearance

Although your baby is tiny (just under 1in/2.5cm long), he already has the beginnings of a recognizably human face, with nostrils, lips, and a mouth with a tongue. His head and face begin as the largest part and curve inward toward the tail, or bottom – at this stage, your baby looks a bit like a tadpole. Buds have already appeared and are beginning to develop into arms and legs – there are also nodules which are growing into hands and feet.

Your baby is covered in a thin layer of skin cells, but is still translucent. He weighs about as much as a grape, and has already started moving around inside your uterus – although, of course, it will be some weeks before you'll be able to feel the movements yourself.

Development

In the early weeks of life, your baby's body parts and internal organs are forming. Over the months ahead, they will become more specialized and complicated. Initially, there are three layers of cells that go on to create the different systems of his body.

The innermost layer develops into the heart, lungs, liver, thyroid gland, pancreas, and bladder. The middle layer becomes the skeleton, muscles, sex organs, blood cells, and kidneys. The outer layer becomes the skin, sweat glands, hair, nails, and tooth enamel. At eight weeks, all these cell types are busy creating the systems they will be responsible for, so deep inside you there is an incredible amount of activity going on.

As your baby is so busy developing, you can see why it is important to take care of yourself, and why you may at times feel very tired and nauseous during these early weeks.

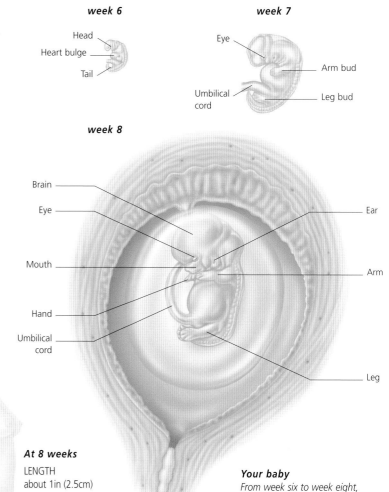

week 6
Head
Heart bulge
Tail

week 7
Eye
Arm bud
Umbilical cord
Leg bud

week 8
Brain
Eye
Mouth
Hand
Umbilical cord
Ear
Arm
Leg

At 8 weeks
LENGTH
about 1in (2.5cm)
Every baby is different and all the measurements given are averages at each stage.

Your baby
From week six to week eight, your baby develops from a tadpolelike creature to a baby with a recognizably human face.

your **growing** baby

♦ From week eight, your baby officially graduates from being an embryo to being described as a fetus. This literally means "little one."

♦ The little tail has almost completely disappeared by this stage.

♦ His heart has already started to beat, and this can now be seen on an ultrasound.

♦ This means his blood is already circulating around his little body, thanks to the pumping action of his own heart.

♦ His heart has four chambers, and beats at approximately 180 beats per minute, which is about double the speed of an adult's heart.

♦ The placenta, which will form the baby's life-support system, is developing fast and is becoming concentrated in one area of the uterine wall.

♦ The uterus, in which the baby is growing, is still only about the size of a tennis ball.

♦ Your baby's fingers and toes are beginning to develop, but these are still slightly webbed at week eight.

♦ Initially the arms develop faster than the legs – just as later, after birth, your baby will develop hand and arm control faster than leg control.

♦ Ten dental buds have formed in each jaw. These will become baby teeth.

eating well

A good diet will benefit both you and your baby throughout pregnancy. Your baby relies on you for all of his nutrients, and so it is important that you provide your body with the right foods to sustain you both.

Basic rules

A balanced diet is a major part of good health at all times of life. During pregnancy, diet is even more important. When you are pregnant, you need about 300 calories more a day than usual. Prenatal vitamins may be prescribed to assure adequate vitamins and minerals and are a good way to augment a healthy diet. Some women, however, find the added iron hard on the digestive system.

Eat plenty of fresh fruit and foods rich in fiber because constipation is often a problem in pregnancy. Cut down on processed foods because these are often high in fat and sugar and low in nutrients.

Cravings

It is common to develop a taste for certain foods during pregnancy. If you do, indulge yourself, but stick to the guidelines and don't eat excessively.

Foods to avoid

Although the chances of contracting an infection from food are low, it is best to avoid the following foods:

♦ unpasteurized dairy produce, especially soft and blue-veined cheeses

♦ raw fish such as sushi and certain cooked fish (check with your caregiver)

♦ undercooked eggs and poultry

♦ organ meats, such as liver

♦ undercooked meats and pâtés

♦ prepared meals, unless thoroughly heated. In addition, wash all fruits and vegetables before eating or cooking.

Vegetarian diets

These can be just as healthy as diets that include meat, and the extra vegetables will be beneficial. However, you may need iron and vitamin B12 supplements. Ask your caregiver for advice.

Eating between meals
Keep healthy snacks, such as fruit, available so that you do not get too hungry during the day. Eating small meals often keeps your blood sugar stable and can help prevent indigestion.

questions & answers

q **Is it safe for me to continue drinking alcohol?**

a Frequent, heavy, or binge drinking could seriously harm the development of your baby. The safest course of action is to avoid alcohol during pregnancy.

q **Should I avoid caffeine?**

a Caffeine, found in tea, coffee, carbonated drinks, and chocolate inhibits the absorption of iron. Excessive caffeine has been linked to miscarriage. Cut down to one cup a day, or eliminate it completely.

Chamomile tea
Try this instead of caffeinated drinks. Chamomile will also help you relax.

q **Are any medications safe to take during pregnancy?**

a If you have a medical condition that requires medication, discuss the situation with your doctor – ideally before you are pregnant, and certainly once you are. Medicines for some conditions may be continued. It's a question of weighing the risks to you if the drug is stopped, compared with the risk to the baby if the medicine continues to be taken. Sometimes, a different medication is safer.

Street drugs aren't a good idea at any time, but there are additional hazards if you're having a baby – some consequences, such as birth defects, premature birth, and placental bleeding, are very serious.

q **Surely an occasional cigarette won't harm my baby?**

a The evidence for not smoking during pregnancy is overwhelming. When you smoke, carbon monoxide and nicotine pass into your lungs and bloodstream. As a result, your baby receives a reduced amount of oxygen, and his heart beats faster.

If you smoke, or spend time in a smoky atmosphere (if your partner smokes, for instance), your baby is more likely to have a low birthweight, to be miscarried, or to be born prematurely, and is at greater risk of Sudden Infant Death Syndrome (see page 225). Children of smokers are also more likely to develop illnesses such as asthma.

Cigarette smoke makes many women feel queasy in the early weeks of pregnancy. If your partner smokes, too, make a pact to quit together. Quitting smoking is the first positive thing that you and your partner can do for your new baby.

week 12

Congratulations – you're officially pregnant! Not that nothing has been happening until now, of course – but this is the stage when a lot of couples decide to "make it official," to spread the good news and to celebrate with family and friends that there is a new baby on the way.

your body changes

You may have been looking forward to reaching this point in your pregnancy because getting this far dramatically increases the chances of everything going well. Your clothes may be beginning to feel slightly tight, but you probably still won't look pregnant, and it could be several weeks before you'll need maternity clothes.

Feeling better

If you have been suffering from fatigue and morning sickness, the good news is that from this week onward both are likely to diminish. Don't expect everything to be perfect from now on, but in the next week or two, if you're lucky you may find that two or three hours have gone by and you haven't felt nauseous. It's a breakthrough, and who knows, before long you might even be able to watch the late news without falling asleep!

By this stage you may have gained about 10 percent of your total pregnancy weight gain (about 3lb/1.3kg), although if you have lost weight from morning sickness, your gain may be less. Don't worry if this applies to you. You should be feeling better soon and you will catch up by eating a healthy diet. Speak to your caregivers if you are concerned.

FACTS ABOUT **YOU**

♦ Your placenta has taken over production of the hormones that are supporting the baby's growth. As a result, your risk of miscarriage drops.

♦ You may develop a hormone-related dark line, called the linea nigra, on your abdomen – this will fade after the birth.

♦ You may develop dark marks on your face called chloasma, or the "mask of pregnancy." These should fade after birth.

♦ Your uterus is the size of a grapefruit.

easing your **symptoms**

Bleeding gums
This is due to a hormonal change. Try not to brush or floss too vigorously, but be careful not to neglect your dental hygiene. Go for regular dental checkups.

Frequent urination
Lean forward when you urinate to empty the bladder fully since this may help reduce the number of times you need to go. Don't drink less water; you need more, not less, when you're pregnant.

Increased breast size
Buy a good quality bra, and have it professionally fitted (see page 33).

Skin problems
Increased hormones may result in acne. Wash your face often and increase your intake of fresh fruit, vegetables, and water.

YOUR CHANGES — YOU MAY DEVELOP A DARK LINE CALLED THE LINEA NIGRA ON YOUR ABDOMEN • ANY NAUSEA MAY BE JUST STARTING TO WEAR OFF • YOU MAY NEED TO URINATE FREQUENTLY

your emotions

You're probably feeling very relieved now that you've reached 12 weeks and the risk of miscarriage has dropped dramatically. But you may find yourself worrying about the prospect of screening tests.

What you can do

Some women welcome an early ultrasound as a chance to see the baby for the first time, but for others, the possible results are a source of anxiety. The fact is, every pregnant woman worries whether her baby is going to be healthy, but the chances are very high that all will be well.

Talk to your doctor or midwife about the various screening tests he or she recommends and those that may be optional. Some tests are invasive and some are not. Make sure you understand what each test involves (see page 21), and what the risks are. You and your partner may refuse any of the tests you are offered.

case **history**

SARAH ELLIS, 27
12 WEEKS PREGNANT

"I had my first prenatal checkup this week. My obstetrician examined me and took some blood and a urine specimen. She spent a lot of time with me and was easy to talk to. The whole thing was more comforting than I thought it would be – between the my obstetrician, and the midwife attached to her practice, I think most of my questions were answered."

"I also had to answer some questions, fill out a lot of forms, and think about how I want to have my baby – naturally or with painkillers. It was encouraging to hear my doctor explain all the choices I have. The possibility of having a natural delivery, if I felt it would be right for me, is a very exciting idea, and I do feel drawn to it. It's a lot to think about. So, I'm going to do some research on my own, discuss it with my partner, and talk some more with my obstetrician when I go back for my checkup next month."

having an **ultrasound**

Many patients will have one or more ultrasounds during their pregnancy. Often a provider will perform an ultrasound during the first prenatal visit (between eight and 12 weeks' gestation) to confirm the pregnancy or a multiple gestation. The doctors are looking at the size of the fetus to see if it is appropriate based on the last menstrual period, as well as to learn if the fetus has fetal-heart activity.

At this stage of pregnancy, ultrasound is usually carried out via a transvaginal probe, which gives the operator the clearest possible view inside your uterus. The scan usually takes about 10 to 30 minutes. If you have an external ultrasound, you will be asked to drink a lot of water to help provide a clear picture of the baby.

Having an ultrasound is not painful, nor is there any evidence of harmful effects. One of the benefits is seeing your baby for the first time – an unforgettable moment for both parents.

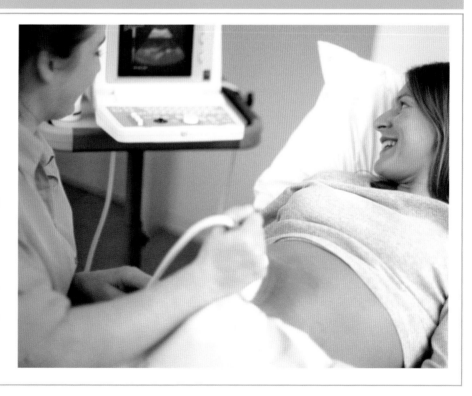

SEE ALSO   PRENATAL CARE pages 20–21 • RIGHTS AND BENEFITS pages 22–23 • MANAGING MORNING SICKNESS page 25 • EATING WELL page 27 • MATERNITY CLOTHES page 33 • DENTAL CARE page 37

your baby at 12 weeks

It's an extraordinary thing to contemplate, but by week 12 your baby is already a fully formed human being. From now on she will get bigger and the various body systems will mature, but the most amazing developments have already taken place, and there is a tiny, kicking baby deep inside you.

Your baby's appearance

The face you will see in a few months' time is taking shape rapidly. At just 12 weeks your baby has a chin, a high forehead, and a tiny nose. Her eyes have moved to the front of her head from their earlier position at the sides, although they are shut and still spaced far apart.

Your baby's ears have moved higher on her head and the external ears are well-developed. Improved muscular control means that she can purse her lips and wrinkle her forehead to form a frown.

The umbilical cord, which connects mother and baby, delivers vital supplies of oxygen-rich blood and nutrients. As her hands, which are already well-developed, begin to unfurl, the cord will become her first plaything as she reaches out and grasps it.

Development

The weeks from eight to 12 have been a particularly busy stage in your baby's development. The main organs are all present inside this tiny fetus, although they are not yet fully functional. The heart is pumping blood around the body; the stomach is forming and is linked to the mouth and the intestines.

The cells that will form the brain are multiplying rapidly and moving to the correct areas. At the same time the baby's head is enlarging to accommodate her developing brain.

If you could take a peek into your uterus right now, there would be no denying there is a baby in there. Even at this stage, the fetus is recognizably human – an awesome thought. She's still absolutely tiny, of course – about 2½in (6cm) long, which is about the size of a plum.

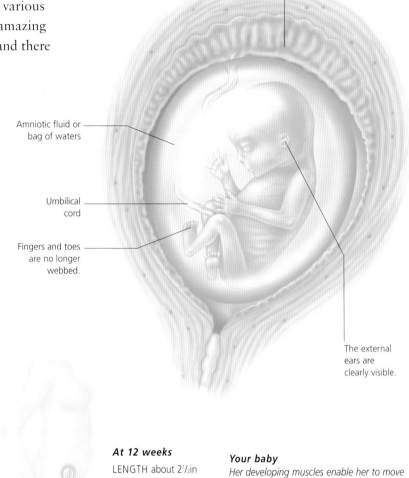

The placenta provides nutrients for your growing baby.

Amniotic fluid or bag of waters

Umbilical cord

Fingers and toes are no longer webbed.

The external ears are clearly visible.

At 12 weeks
LENGTH about 2½in (6cm) crown to rump
WEIGHT about ½oz (15g)

Your baby
Her developing muscles enable her to move around in the uterus, kicking and curling her newly formed fingers and toes.

your **growing** baby

♦ Although you can't yet feel it, your baby is quite active – she kicks and stretches inside the uterus.

♦ Her immediate environment is the amniotic fluid, and your baby is already swallowing minute amounts of it in preparation for swallowing milk once she is born.

♦ She can also pass urine, which becomes the amniotic fluid.

♦ Her arms are quite well-developed, and can already bend at the elbows.

♦ She has wrists and ankles.

♦ She has tiny fingernails.

♦ Her head is still very large, about half the length of her entire body.

♦ Her fingers and toes have now separated and are distinct.

♦ The external genitals are developing, although it is not yet possible to tell the sex of a baby visually on an ultrasound. Testes or ovaries have formed inside your baby's body.

♦ Eyelids have formed over the eyes, although they cannot open yet.

♦ She has earlobes.

♦ She can flex her fingers and toes and make a fist.

the placenta

By the time you reach week 12, the placenta has formed completely and is able to take over the all-important job of supporting the pregnancy. This is why the risk of miscarriage diminishes and the fatigue and nausea you may have experienced will begin to ease.

What is the placenta?

At this stage of pregnancy the placenta is a lot bigger than your baby. It is a thick, disk-shaped organ that is attached to one part of the uterus, usually in the upper half.

In the early weeks the placenta grows at a much faster rate than your baby to ensure that she is adequately nourished. From now on that changes, and by the time your baby is born, the placenta will weigh about a sixth of her weight and will be about the size of a dinner plate.

The placenta will be delivered after your baby at the birth. Take a look at it if you're given the opportunity because it is fascinating to see the organ that has quite literally sustained the life of your child (see page 73 for more on the third stage of labor).

How the placenta works

The placenta allows you to supply all your baby's needs from now until she is born. It produces the hormones necessary to support the pregnancy, maintain the health of the uterus, and even prepare the breasts for lactation. It is a sophisticated filtering system using your blood to deliver nutrients and oxygen to your growing baby. It also removes your baby's waste products.

What you can do

The placenta protects your baby from many toxins, but certain medicines and alcohol can still cross it, so it's important to limit your exposure to potentially harmful substances. Cigarette smoking diminishes the placenta's effectiveness and exposes your baby to toxins.

Pool of mother's blood

Fetal blood vessels (chorionic villi)

Umbilical cord

Maternal blood vessels

The structure of the placenta
The placenta allows the mother and baby to exchange fluids, nutrients, and gases, but does not mix maternal and fetal blood. Exchange takes place where the placenta adheres to the uterine wall.

questions & answers

q **Will the obstetrician be able to hear my baby's heart when I go for my first checkup?**

a Yes, if it is done at about 12 weeks or later. The obstetrician can use a handheld ultrasound device, which uses high-frequency sound waves to check the baby's heartbeat. You will be able to hear it clearly, too. This device doesn't harm the baby, and you'll find it reassuring, and probably very moving, to hear your baby's heart beating healthily.

Handheld Doppler device
This handheld device is a noninvasive method of checking the baby's heartbeat.

q **I'm going for an ultrasound this week – will the ultrasound technician be able to tell me at this stage whether I'm having a boy or a girl?**

a Although the genitals are developing, it will almost certainly be too early to tell if it's a boy or a girl. An ultrasound at this stage is really used to date the pregnancy accurately; to check whether you're having one baby or more; to see that the heart is beating properly.

q **I'm wondering whether to have screening tests. Are the chances high that I might be expecting a baby with Down syndrome?**

a The probability depends mostly on the age of the mother. A baby with Down syndrome can be born to a mother of any age, but the risk becomes greater the older

q **Can my baby sense the outside world?**

a She is beginning to respond to the world outside the uterus. If the mother's abdomen is pressed she may try to move away.

a woman is. In your 20s you have about a 1 in 1,000 chance; by 35 it's 1 in 350; by 40 it's 1 in 100 and by 45, it's 1 in 25. Think about what you would do if you found your individual risk factor was high. Would you want a diagnostic test (see page 21), and would you consider terminating the pregnancy? If the answer is no, you should discuss your options with your healthcare provider. However, if you would prefer to know your risk, it is worth taking the test.

FIRST TRIMESTER													SECOND TRIMESTER															THIRD TRIMESTER												
1	2	3	4	5	6	7	8	9	10	11	12	13	14	15	16	17	18	19	20	21	22	23	24	25	26	27	28	29	30	31	32	33	34	35	36	37	38	39	40

week 16

The fact that you're expecting a baby has really sunk in now, and hopefully the nausea and fatigue of early pregnancy have receded or even disappeared. What's more, you probably look pregnant now. This is the blooming phase of your pregnancy – enjoy it!

your body changes

This is when things start to increase rapidly – your appetite and your belly! Having said good-bye to the nausea of the first trimester, you may feel ravenous a lot of the time and your clothes may be a little tight. Pay attention to your body's needs.

Visibly pregnant

As your belly gets bigger, you are going to need a few larger items of clothing, and you'll get your money's worth if you start wearing them now (see opposite). Snack on fresh fruit and wholegrain cereals – these are more nutritious than processed food and sweets and will help alleviate the constipation you may be experiencing as a result of your digestive system's being more sluggish. Dried fruit is an excellent source of iron, and also helps alleviate constipation, which can be aggravated by iron supplements.

Your skin may become more deeply pigmented. Your nipples and the surrounding areola may also become darker.

FACTS ABOUT YOU

♦ Your uterus is getting five times the amount of blood pumped to it as it did before the pregnancy, in order to support your growing baby.

♦ Your kidneys are processing 25 percent more blood than usual.

♦ Your heart rate has increased, and its output is 30–50 percent above its pre-pregnancy level.

♦ You've probably gained about 5–10lb (2.25–4.5kg) in weight.

easing your symptoms

Tight clothing
Don't ignore any feelings of tightness in your clothing or underwear – invest in looser outfits now (see opposite).

Keeping active
Getting into an exercise routine now will help you keep fit as you get bigger. Find a pregnancy exercise class where the pacing is right. You can also try walking, swimming, yoga, or the stationary bike.

Constipation
Drink a lot of water and eat plenty of fresh fruit snacks throughout the day.

Recording your symptoms
Make a note of any symptoms you experience so you remember to discuss them with your doctor when you go for your prenatal checkup – it's all too easy to forget if you don't write them down.

YOUR CHANGES YOU'RE PROBABLY MORE ENERGETIC THAN IN THE EARLY WEEKS • YOUR BELLY MAY BE MORE VISIBLE • YOU MAY HAVE CONSTIPATION

your emotions

This is often the most exciting stage of pregnancy because you may have the pleasure of feeling your baby move inside you for the first time – a moment you will never forget.

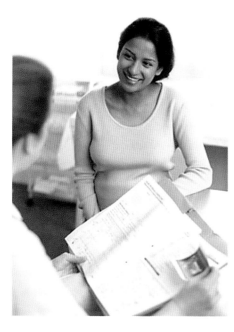

Feeling your baby move

You may feel your baby move any time now, especially if this is your second or subsequent child. Initially you won't be sure whether what you feel is your stomach rumbling or a genuine baby flutter, but over the next few weeks the sensation will get stronger and you'll soon be in no doubt at all. First-time mothers often don't notice movement until about 20 weeks or later.

Work worries

Telling people outside of your immediate circle of close friends and family can be exciting and you may be enjoying all the attention. However, making the pregnancy public can be a time of mixed feelings. At work you may fear that colleagues will think you're not so serious about your job any more, and you may wonder how you will cope if you plan to return to work after the birth. Talk to other mothers about how they managed, and you'll see that strategies to cope with being a working mother (if that's what you want, or will have to do) eventually emerge (see pages 114–115).

Thinking about childbirth classes

Popular classes get booked up quickly, so if you're interested in taking them, talk to your obstetrician at your next appointment about parenting education in your area, if you haven't already.

"My obstetrician wondered whether I was having twins. I'd had a lot of nausea in the early weeks, and she thought my uterus seemed big. My husband and I went for an ultrasound at week 15, and discovered that we were expecting two babies! I feel a little overwhelmed, but it's very exciting."

SARAH-JANE SIMPSON, 25,
16 WEEKS PREGNANT

maternity clothes

Maternity clothes don't have to be expensive. If you're working you may need to invest in a significant outfit or two. Some boutiques offer the latest styles, but think before you invest in an expensive outfit – you won't be wearing these clothes for long. If you are hoping to have more children, look for classics you can reuse in a couple of years' time. Secondhand maternity clothes stores can be very useful; parenting organizations can often give you details of what is available in your area.

Creating your own style

It is important to feel comfortable in your clothes, not just physically but emotionally as well. Choose clothes that make you feel attractive throughout your pregnancy. Fitted clothes are often more flattering to your new body shape than loose dresses and baggy sweaters, although you should choose maternity clothes that suit your own personal style and taste.

Underwear

You will need a comfortable bra (avoid underwires) that gives you good support. Since your breasts will be changing size throughout your pregnancy, it is a good idea to be measured professionally. Buy two at first, then more as your breasts grow. Look for a bra with a deep band under the cups, broad shoulder straps, and an adjustable back. You may find cotton bras most comfortable. Later in pregnancy you may want to wear a light-weight bra for support while you sleep.

If you are planning to breastfeed, you will need to buy at least two nursing bras, but you should wait until the 36th week of your pregnancy before you are measured for these to be sure to get the right size (see page 53).

SEE ALSO   RIGHTS AND BENEFITS pages 22–23 • EATING WELL page 27 • A WORKING PREGNANCY page 41 • EXERCISE AND POSTURE page 45 • CHILDBIRTH CLASSES page 49 • A LOVING RELATIONSHIP page 53

your baby at 16 weeks

You may not be able to feel it yet, but your baby is already moving around quite vigorously in your uterus. His eyelids are still closed, but this week or next he might hear his first sounds – which will be sounds from inside and outside your body.

Your baby's appearance

His limbs and features are formed, his legs are now longer than his arms, and he looks more in proportion than at 12 weeks. But he still looks very thin, with transparent skin through which the blood vessels are visible: the layer of fat under his skin hasn't been laid down yet, so he has yet to become the chubby baby you'll hold after the birth.

His external genital organs are now formed, and if you had an ultrasound at this stage the technician might be able to tell you whether you are having a boy or a girl (although this would depend partly on your baby's position in the uterus at the time).

Development

Although he's so tiny, your baby is already quite adept at movement. He can flex and extend his limbs and fingers, and he kicks and somersaults in the amniotic fluid. This is partly so he can tone his muscles and practice the movements he'll need to make to develop his coordination after he's born.

He is also trying out facial expressions because his facial muscles are already developed – although since the nervous system is still developing, these aren't fully under his control yet. The tiny bones in his ears are hardening, enabling him to hear your voice, your heart, and even your digestive system.

Amniotic fluid

Your baby's immediate environment is the amniotic fluid – for him, it's like being immersed in a warm swimming pool and trying out underwater movements. The umbilical cord is like a diver's breathing apparatus because it delivers essential oxygen via the blood cells. The amniotic fluid also cushions your baby from any knocks from outside the uterus.

Fundus

His head is still large in proportion to his body.

His neck has developed.

He has his own unique fingerprints.

Cervix

At 16 weeks
LENGTH about 4³/₄in (12cm) crown to rump
WEIGHT about 4¹/₂oz (130g)

Your baby
His facial features continue to develop as the facial bones form, and tiny fingers and toes can be seen.

your **growing** baby

♦ This is a period of rapid growth. In the last four weeks your baby will have almost doubled in length, and his weight will have increased to about 4¹/₂oz (130g).

♦ His fingernails and toenails are well formed. Some babies' nails grow so much in the uterus they need to be trimmed soon after birth.

♦ A girl baby has about two million eggs in her ovaries by this stage – the number first increases, and then diminishes during pregnancy so that by birth she has about one million, compared with 200,000 at age 17.

♦ His ears have moved from his neck, where they started to develop, to their correct position on the sides of his head.

♦ Your baby swallows some amniotic fluid, and his kidneys turn this fluid into urine – he empties his bladder approximately every hour into the amniotic sac.

♦ He yawns and stretches in the uterus from time to time.

♦ He has very small eyebrows and eyelashes.

♦ Fine, downy hair has formed on his face and body (lanugo).

♦ He may suck his thumb.

♦ His skeleton is beginning to develop, first in the form of flexible cartilage, then hard bones.

♦ Small respiratory movements can be seen.

twins

If you're carrying twins you will be feeling a lot bigger at this stage than a woman who's having a single baby. Although you've got two babies in there, each will be similar in size to a single baby.

Twin growth and development

Your babies may lie the same way, or one might be head up while the other is head down. By this stage, they will be aware of each other's presence in the uterus. You'll receive extra prenatal care if you're having twins, and your caregivers will want to check that each baby is growing properly.

There are some rare conditions in which one twin is a lot bigger than the other, and both babies can develop problems if this happens. Twins and multiples develop at the same rate as a single baby until about 30 weeks of pregnancy, but are often not as large at birth, especially because they are usually born earlier (see page 55).

Ultrasound showing twins
A twin or multiple pregnancy is confirmed using an ultrasound. The babies may be identical, formed from one fertilized egg that then divides, or fraternal, developing from two separately fertilized eggs.

questions & answers

q Can my baby control his movements?

a The development of the nervous system means that by week 16 he can flex and extend his limbs and fingers. All the connections between your baby's brain, nervous system, and muscles are established by this stage.

and these are potentially dangerous to your baby even in the latest weeks of pregnancy. Keep to the same food habits as before: wash all fruit, vegetables, and salad ingredients, especially well; avoid raw and undercooked meat and unpasteurized dairy products (see page 27).

q Do all babies develop at the same rate in the womb?
a No, they don't. In the early days and weeks development is at a very similar rate, but after 12 weeks there are a lot of differences, proving that every baby is unique. Try not to compare the size of your belly or your baby with that of other mothers. Your baby's growth, and the size he is when he is born, depends on a whole host of factors including his genes; whether he's your first baby or not (first ones tend

to be smaller); whether you have any underlying medical conditions such as preeclampsia; what you're eating and drinking, and whether or not you smoke (see page 47).

q If my baby's organ systems are already formed, do I still have to be careful about avoiding certain foods?
a Yes. Some of the foods considered dangerous carry the risk of causing bacterial infections such as toxoplasmosis and listeriosis,

q Can having sex harm our baby?
a Your baby is well-protected by the amniotic fluid, and so will not be harmed. When you have an orgasm, your uterus contracts and becomes harder, as it sometimes does at other times, too. The baby will be aware of this, but it won't be a problem. These contractions may feel like hugs to the baby. However, if you've had any bleeding or a history of miscarriages or premature labor, you may be advised to avoid sex (see page 53).

FIRST TRIMESTER												SECOND TRIMESTER															THIRD TRIMESTER												
1	2	3	4	5	6	7	8	9	10	11	12	13	14	15	16	17	18	19	20	21	22	23	24	25	26	27	28	29	30	31	32	33	34	35	36	37	38	39	40

week 20

There's no mistaking your pregnancy now – and congratulations, because you're half way there. Over the next few weeks your belly will continue to grow and your baby will become more active. As your baby grows, so will your unique bond with her.

your body changes

You're getting bigger, and you may be feeling a little breathless sometimes, but this is still the "blooming" phase. You are looking forward to the birth, but are still not too weighed down by the extra person you've got onboard.

Gaining weight

You may notice that it's not just your tummy that's getting bigger this month – the tops of your thighs and your buttocks may be larger, too. Don't worry about this: it's an entirely natural change because your body is laying down extra fat in pregnancy to call on when it's needed for breastfeeding.

Of course, you should stick to a healthy diet and not binge on processed or sugary food or you'll gain excess weight. Don't worry about being a bit larger all around. You should not diet at any point in pregnancy. You will lose the extra fat after the baby is born.

FACTS ABOUT **YOU**

♦ The top of your uterus, or fundus, reaches to about your belly button, and will continue to grow about 1/2in (1cm) a week.

♦ The pressure of the growing baby might make your belly button pop out and stay that way until after the birth.

♦ The weight of the baby might make you feel a bit unbalanced.

♦ You may develop stretch marks.

easing your **symptoms**

Feeling breathless
Take things easy. Ask your midwife or doctor if you need a blood test for anemia.

Stuffy nose and nosebleeds
Ease stuffiness with a little petroleum jelly in each nostril.

Heartburn
Avoid large meals, alcohol, and spicy food. Stretch your hands above your head to alleviate the symptoms. Antacid medication is useful and is generally safe to take in pregnancy. Talk to your doctor about which antacid might be right for you.

Itchiness
Try foods rich in B vitamins. Speak to your caregiver if symptoms persist.

Increased vaginal secretions
This is normal – however, if the discharge is very profuse, has an odor, or irritates, discuss it with your doctor.

YOUR CHANGES   YOUR BELLY IS GETTING STEADILY BIGGER NOW • THE BABY IS INCREASINGLY ACTIVE • YOU'LL PROBABLY BE SCHEDULED FOR AN ULTRASOUND AROUND THIS TIME

your emotions

As your body shape changes, it's normal to become a bit anxious about gaining weight, even though there's an entirely positive and natural reason for that right now.

Your new shape

We're conditioned from childhood to see "gaining weight" as a negative thing, and it's hard to shake off that feeling now.

Weight gain in pregnancy averages 25 to 35 pounds (11.5–16kg), with first-time moms gaining an average of 27½ pounds (12.5kg). About 20 pounds of the weight gain is baby weight: The rest is usually storage of fat.

Each person's weight gain will vary, depending on their prepregnancy weight. A very thin woman who is below her optimum weight may gain more than an overweight woman. If you eat well and are active, the amount of weight you gain should stay within the recommended boundries.

Massage
A massage can be wonderfully relaxing. Choose a practitioner who has experience working with pregnant women. Opt for unscented oils because some aromatherapy oils should not be used in pregnancy.

JULIE MILLER, 27
20 WEEKS PREGNANT

"I've told a couple of the classes I teach that I'm expecting a baby – some of the children thought I was just getting fat! I'm trying to go swimming after work, which is really good exercise. Now I have lots of energy and can even cycle to and from work – a six-mile (10-kilometer) round trip. I've been to my first childbirth classes, run by a midwife and an obstetric physiotherapist, on how to keep in shape. We are also planning a weekend away as a treat before the baby arrives."

dental **care**

You need to take special care of your teeth and gums while you are pregnant. Tell your dentist as soon as you know you are expecting a baby because you should avoid X rays unless absolutely necessary. Have your teeth checked regularly. Your dentist will advise you on the best way to take care of your teeth, and check for any signs of disease or infection.

Changes to your teeth and gums

Your increased blood supply during pregnancy and the higher-than-normal level of the hormone progesterone combine to soften all the tissues in your body, including your gums. This makes them spongy and more susceptible to infection.

The increased blood supply also puts pressure on the capillaries positioned around the gum line, making them more likely to bleed, especially while brushing or flossing.

What you can do

The best way to protect your teeth and gums is to be scrupulous about dental hygiene and to follow a healthy, balanced diet. Make sure you get plenty of calcium, protein, and vitamins B, C, and D. Dairy products and plenty of fresh fruit and vegetables will supply the required nutrients. Of course, you need to avoid sugary foods, so this is yet another reason not to indulge in too many sweets or carbonated drinks.

Have your teeth cleaned regularly by the dentist during your pregnancy to help prevent gum disease and infections, which are associated with premature birth. Talk to your dentist if you have any concerns.

Flossing
Cleaning between your teeth with dental floss is essential for healthy gums and teeth, but be very gentle because your gums are softer than before you were pregnant, and will bleed more easily.

SEE ALSO   RIGHTS AND BENEFITS pages 22–23 • EATING WELL page 27 • MATERNITY CLOTHES page 33
• RELAXATION TECHNIQUES pages 48–49 • SLEEP page 57 • COMMON COMPLAINTS pages 60–61

your baby at 20 weeks

Your baby's senses are developing fast, and she's becoming a lot more aware of her immediate surroundings. She's starting to move around more in the uterus, and is hearing the voices of those around her, through the uterine wall.

Your baby's appearance

She now measures about 6in (15cm) crown to rump, almost half the length she will be at birth. There's been a growth spurt during the last few days, but although she's lengthened, your baby is still tiny – about 9oz (270g) in weight. From now on her growth rate will be less dramatic, although it will be steady as she gains weight slowly and surely. She is covered with lanugo, a layer of ultra-fine, downy hair, which will have virtually disappeared by the time she is born. The exact function is not well understood – it might help regulate her body temperature, or it could help to keep the protective vernix (a thick, white, waxy coating) in place on her skin.

Development

Your baby now has the same number of nerve cells as an adult, and is increasingly sensitive and aware of what's going on around her. The sensory areas of her brain are developing quickly at the moment, and the nerves are being covered in a protective coating called myelin. Now messages can be passed from the brain to different parts of the body, which means that, increasingly, your baby's limbs are under her own control.

Taste buds have developed on her tongue, and she will soon be able to distinguish a sweet from a bitter taste. Her skin is becoming sensitive to touch, and if you touch her through your abdomen you will find she is aware of the sensation and may respond.

When she's born she'll soon start to play and explore, and that process is already starting within your uterus: she sometimes holds on to the umbilical cord or grasps her other hand as they brush together – these are her first playthings.

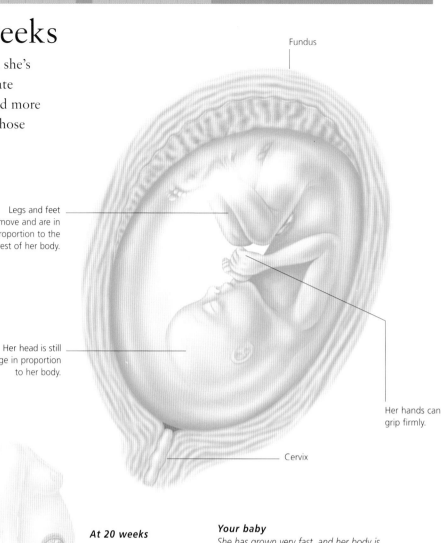

Fundus

Legs and feet move and are in proportion to the rest of her body.

Her head is still large in proportion to her body.

Her hands can grip firmly.

Cervix

At 20 weeks
LENGTH about 15cm (6in) crown to rump
WEIGHT about 270g (9oz)

Your baby
She has grown very fast, and her body is covered in fine body hair (lanugo). You may be able to feel her movements, even if this is your first pregnancy.

your **growing** baby

♦ Hair has started to grow on her scalp.

♦ She inhales amniotic fluid and practices shallow breathing movements.

♦ Her permanent teeth buds are developing behind her baby teeth buds.

♦ She has a primitive immune system and can already fight off some infections.

♦ A protective layer of "brown" fat, which helps in temperature regulation, is now starting to be laid down.

♦ If your baby is a girl, her vagina is beginning to develop at this stage; if a boy, the scrotum is still forming.

♦ In both girls and boys the nipples and mammary glands appear.

♦ She can grasp one hand with the other, and can also form fists.

♦ Her eyes are still shut, but she can move her eyes slowly from side to side.

♦ She has much more control over her movements due to the development of her muscles and nervous system.

♦ The nervous system is beginning to produce the myelin sheath, which coats the nerves that link muscles to the brain, allowing messages to be passed along.

♦ Her first teeth have formed in her gums.

♦ The bones in her ears are hardening, allowing her to hear the world outside the uterus.

what your baby can hear

Your baby's hearing is now well-developed, and she's getting to know your voice and that of your partner and anyone else in your household.

Sounds from outside the uterus

If there's a bang or a loud noise your baby may jump. She will also be aware of other noises outside the uterus, and some evidence suggests she may respond to certain types of music. Studies have shown that Vivaldi and Mozart tend to be the preferred composers for the as-yet-unborn: mothers have reported that the memory of music stays with their baby in the early weeks of life, and sometimes a crying baby can be comforted by the sound of music that was played to her before birth – it seems to "remind" her of her time in your uterus. You can enjoy talking and singing to your baby as you relax or have a bath, in the knowledge that your sounds really are getting through to her!

Your baby's response to sounds
Your baby responds to sounds by moving, or her heartbeat may alter momentarily. As your baby develops, and you become more aware of her movements, you may find she responds to your voice or certain pieces of music.

questions & answers

q **What happens during my second trimester scan?**

a The mid-term, or anatomic, scan is used to check on the baby's general development and the development of the major organs. The ultrasonographer – who may be a radiologist, an ultrasound technician, or an obstetrician – will look in particular at your baby's heart, kidneys, brain, and spine, and will measure the baby's head circumference and length of

the limbs. The location of the placenta will be determined to be sure that it isn't in danger of lying over the cervix at the time when you give birth.

q **I'm worried by reports that ultrasound can cause brain damage in babies. Should I have one?**

a Ultrasounds have been used in pregnancy for more than 30 years, so it's unlikely there are any serious problems that haven't been detected by now. Generally, doctors regard them as safe and a good way to detect fetal abnormalities. However, having these tests does not guarantee that your baby will not have any problems.

Seeing your baby
Since you discovered you were pregnant you have been getting to know your baby, but seeing her on the screen during a scan brings her closer to you than ever before.

q **What will happen if my scan shows something unusual?**

a If there's a suspicion that something is in any way unusual, you'll be referred for more tests. This usually includes more in-depth ultrasound, possibly carried out at a hospital with more specialized equipment and a more highly trained operator. Make sure that you speak to your doctor or midwife if you have any questions.

FIRST TRIMESTER												SECOND TRIMESTER															THIRD TRIMESTER												
1	2	3	4	5	6	7	8	9	10	11	12	13	14	15	16	17	18	19	20	21	22	23	24	25	26	27	28	29	30	31	32	33	34	35	36	37	38	39	40

week 24

Pregnancy is great right now. You're not so big that getting around is difficult, and you've got a lot more energy than you had in the early weeks. And although the birth still seems a long way off, at other times you're starting to feel really excited.

your body changes

This is the stage when people you don't know will start to guess you might be having a baby. Around this time you may have a growth spurt, so your belly becomes more noticeable.

Getting ready

Meanwhile, your uterus is having practice, or Braxton Hicks, contractions, getting ready for labor. When this happens, your abdomen may become hard for a few seconds. The uterus often contracts, whether you're pregnant or not, but now you are more likely to be aware of the muscles working.

Iron-rich foods are essential for the blood supply of the fetus and for you. Get as much iron as you can from your diet. Eat lean red meat, poultry, lentils, legumes, spinach, and other dark, leafy vegetables, and iron-rich cereals. Vitamin C helps to increase the absorption of iron.

FACTS ABOUT **YOU**

♦ The fundus (top of the uterus) is above your belly button.

♦ When the baby moves you may be able to make out a little foot or leg through the abdominal wall.

♦ Your breasts may be feeling very tender due to the hormonal changes in preparation for breastfeeding.

♦ Your body is retaining water, putting weight on your thighs and upper body.

♦ You may feel hot more often.

easing your **symptoms**

Urinary tract infections

These are more common during pregnancy. To help prevent them, drink lots of water every day – at least eight to 10 glasses. Water dilutes the urine, flushing out your urinary system and making infections less likely.

Indigestion

Progesterone makes the digestive system sluggish: food sits in the stomach longer and can make you uncomfortable. Avoid heavy meals – eat small, frequent meals.

Dry eyes

Dry eyes are common from about halfway through pregnancy. You may notice that your eyes have less moisture and are sensitive to light, particularly if you wear contact lenses. Ask your pharmacist to recommend a solution to add moisture, but mention that you are pregnant.

YOUR CHANGES YOU PROBABLY DON'T NEED TO URINATE AS OFTEN • YOUR WAISTLINE HAS VIRTUALLY DISAPPEARED • YOU MAY FIND YOU PERSPIRE MORE THAN USUAL

your emotions

Having a growing belly so that the world can see you are pregnant can be enjoyable. After all, having a baby is something to be very proud of.

Dealing with other people

Not everyone sees it that way, though, and even if you sometimes enjoy having a stranger ask you about your pregnancy, you might not always want to have a half-hour conversation with someone you don't know. When you're obviously pregnant many things you'd usually keep to yourself are clear to anyone you happen to meet. One, you're sexually active; two, you have (or recently had) a partner; three, you're going to be a mother in the not-too-distant future.

Some women find all this discussion annoying, and find it difficult to be polite to strangers who ask personal questions (was it planned? are you hoping for a boy or a girl? was it a natural or an assisted conception?) as though you were wearing a sign proclaiming: "Ask me anything you want." You may also find that people want to tell you lots of popular myths about pregnancy and birth, or reminisce about their own, or other women's, experiences of labor. Some people may even want to touch your tummy, including those you don't know very well!

What you can do

This can be infuriating, especially if you are feeling very tired, or are attempting to cope with uncomfortable physical symptoms, but try not to lose your temper with people. Remind yourself that people mean well: often, it's a case of the world rejoicing with you when you're pregnant. Take pride in the fact that people are interested in the new life inside you – soon everyone will be admiring your new baby, and you will be thrilled with the attention. Just think of the extra interest as early admiration of your baby. You already think your baby is wonderful, and so do they.

a working pregnancy

Managing a job and a pregnancy presents quite a challenge, and while many organizations are supportive of mothers-to-be, it is vital to listen to your body, understand your rights, and to establish a balance that is right for you. Don't be tempted to keep going just because another pregnant woman seems to be fine doing the same amount, or because of anecdotes from friends about how hard they worked when they were pregnant. Do what is right for you and your baby.

Know your rights

Try not to overdo things – listen to your body, pace yourself at work, and make sure your workstation is comfortable. Traveling to and from work can be

Striking a balance
A comfortable working environment is essential. Drink plenty of water throughout the day and be sure to stretch and walk around at regular intervals.

exhausting when you are pregnant, especially if you have to contend with heavy traffic or crowded public transportation. If you can, travel at less busy times or work from home for a couple of days each week. You are also entitled to information about possible exposures in the work environment. Work that involves exposure to toxins, radiation, or infections should be avoided. By working with your doctor and your employer, you should be able to avoid undue risk.

Prenatal appointments
Taking time off for prenatal care is important. Make sure to keep your appointment even when work gets busy.

Planning your future
Try not to get too hung up on decisions about what you will do once the baby has arrived: keeping an open mind is probably best at this stage. Concentrate on the present and discuss future plans once the baby is born.

SEE ALSO   RIGHTS AND BENEFITS pages 22–23 • EATING WELL page 27 • YOUR NEW SHAPE page 37 • RELAXATION TECHNIQUES page 49 • COMMON COMPLAINTS pages 60–61

your baby at 24 weeks

We think of babies as being chubby, but for most of the time your baby is developing in the uterus he's actually long and thin. But from about 24 weeks he starts to fill out, and looks more solid and babylike.

Your baby's appearance

Part of the reason for his more solid appearance is that his skin is no longer translucent, and he is losing the fragile look that has so far characterized his time in the uterus. The brown fat, which will be crucial in helping him to regulate his body temperature after birth, is still developing – as more of it appears your baby's bottom will fill out and become rounder.

His facial features are fully formed so that, if you could look inside and see him, he would already look like the baby you'll get to know in about 16 weeks, although his lean face means that his eyes bulge at this stage.

Development

Most of your baby's body systems are now fully formed and starting to function. The main organs are all working, apart from the lungs, which he won't use until he is born. They are still filled with amniotic fluid, although the alveoli (air sacs) are beginning to form.

The brain and nervous system are developing fast, and the cells that control conscious thought are forming, so your baby is becoming much more aware of his surroundings and of sounds and movement in the world outside your uterus.

The main purpose of the rest of his time in your uterus will be to fine-tune his systems and to lay down more fat, readying for the outside world. Even though you probably feel your pregnancy still has a long time to go, your baby would have at least a chance of survival if he was born this early, and this is an indication of how well-developed he really is at this stage.

Placenta

Eyebrows are forming.

His head is now in proportion to his body.

His eyes bulge.

Umbilical cord

Skin is now thicker, reddish, wrinkly, and covered with fine hair called lanugo.

His bottom is becoming more rounded.

At 24 weeks

LENGTH about 8in (20cm) crown to rump

WEIGHT about 1lb 6oz (625g)

Your baby
By this stage he still has room to move freely, and his movements are helping to build strength and dexterity.

your **growing** baby

♦ At the end of 24 weeks, your baby's eyes will have opened for the first time.

♦ His heart rate has dropped to about 140–150 beats a minute.

♦ He has fingers and toes, but these are still slightly webbed.

♦ He is still constantly swallowing and then excreting the amniotic fluid as urine.

♦ Within his intestines, the meconium, which will make up his first stool, is already beginning to form.

♦ Within his lungs, the small air sacs, or alveoli, are forming.

♦ Sweat glands are forming in your baby's skin.

♦ He is now able to cough and hiccup.

♦ The lanugo (downy layer of body hair) darkens. Beneath it, your baby's skin is reddish in color rather than translucent as before.

♦ He has a cycle of sleeping and waking, which you might become aware of over the next few weeks.

♦ As your baby grows, the placental blood vessels will respond by supplying him with more of the nutrients he needs.

are you carrying a boy or a girl?

You may not have wanted to find out at the ultrasound which sex your baby is, but many parents-to-be enjoy trying to figure it out through other means. It's natural for you and your partner to wonder what this new little baby will be like.

Guessing the gender

Here are a few traditional ways to determine the gender. They are not scientific, but you and your partner can have lots of fun trying them out.

♦ If the heartbeat is persistently above 140 it's a girl; below, you are carrying a boy.

♦ If you're carrying the extra weight out front, it's a boy; around the sides, it's a girl.

♦ Hang a needle on a thread over your abdomen – if it moves in circles, it's a boy. Side to side, it's a girl.

♦ If your belly is shaped like a basketball, it's a boy; like a watermelon, it's a girl.

Getting to know your baby
Thinking about and talking to the new baby inside will help you make the transition to parenthood, and may bring you and your partner closer together.

---

questions & answers

q How do I know if my baby is moving around enough?

a You'll soon get to know your baby's patterns. Some babies seem more passive than others, but no one knows whether babies vary in the amount they move, or if some women detect the baby's activity more than others. You may notice movements more when you are resting. The most important thing is that you feel some movements from now on, if not earlier.

Getting to know the baby
Feeling the baby move is exciting for the whole family, and may help older children form a bond with the new sibling.

q Why is my abdomen so much smaller than my friend's, even though our babies are due at the same time?

a Your baby is almost certainly about the same size as your friend's baby at this stage, but the size of your abdomen depends on more than the size of your baby. Don't forget your uterus also contains amniotic fluid, and some pregnancies have more of this than others. Also, the amount of space inside your abdomen is governed by your physical structure and overall size. In general, abdomens tend to be bigger in women who are petite than in women with a bigger build who have more space sideways. If it's not your first baby, your belly often gets bigger more quickly, which is the result of the uterus and abdomen having stretched in the past.

week 28

This week marks the official start of the third trimester, so you're in the homestretch now. Revel in your pregnancy as much as you can because when you look back, you'll find it amazing how quickly it all slipped by. In about three months' time you will meet your new baby.

your body changes

Week 28 is often the stage at which being pregnant starts to make a difference in your everyday life, as you become accustomed to maneuvering with your expanding belly.

Looking good

Many women spend hours at the mirror admiring their belly – and now your breasts are so much bigger than usual, you've probably got cleavage to be proud of.

Make the most of your new look – try wearing close-fitting maternity outfits, rather than tentlike garments, because you'll feel thinner (honestly!) and emphasizing your belly makes you feel sexy rather than simply sacklike. Good buys if you're looking for ways to lift your spirits are earrings, scarves, necklaces, and a great haircut. Borrowing maternity clothes from a friend is a practical way to have clothes for the last few weeks of your pregnancy.

FACTS ABOUT **YOU**

♦ From now on, you'll see your doctor or midwife every two weeks, then weekly from 36 weeks.

♦ Your breasts may leak colostrum (see page 86), although some women don't produce this until the baby is born.

♦ You may be short of breath because of the upward pressure of the uterus on your lungs and diaphragm.

♦ You may develop varicose veins because of the pressure on your legs.

easing your **symptoms**

Hemorrhoids
Drink plenty of water and eat lots of fruit. If iron supplements are making you constipated, which increases the risk of hemorrhoids, ask your caregiver for advice.

Leg cramps
These are common, especially at night. Straighten your leg, bend the ankle, and massage your calf. Avoid high heels.

Puffy hands and feet
Wear comfortable shoes, especially during the afternoon and evening when swelling in your feet is likely to be at its worst. You may have to remove any rings you wear before they become too tight.

Varicose veins
For some relief put your legs up when you can and lie down with your feet raised. Support stockings may be helpful.

YOUR CHANGES YOU MAY HAVE RIB PAIN CAUSED BY THE PRESSURE OF YOUR BABY • YOU MAY GET A CRAMPLIKE PAIN DOWN THE SIDE OF YOUR ABDOMEN AS YOU WALK • YOU'RE GAINING MORE WEIGHT

your emotions

Almost all women have anxieties and worries about having a baby, but these tend to stay below the surface most of the time. For many mothers-to-be it can be difficult to talk openly about their concerns.

Pregnancy dreams

Not surprisingly, it's often only when we're asleep that our fears are unleashed. Vivid dreams are very common in late pregnancy. Here are some of the most common pregnancy anxiety dreams.

♦ The baby is born with a disability or deformity – this is a worry every pregnant woman has at some stage.

♦ The baby is born when you're not ready and in desperation you try to put it back – the fear here is that you won't get everything finished before the birth.

♦ You go into labor, but there isn't a baby, or the baby doesn't survive – this isn't an omen that things won't go well, it's a sign that you have normal worries about the birth and becoming a parent.

"I'm doing pregnancy yoga. You meet other mothers-to-be and it's all tailored for women hoping for an active, natural birth, which is what I certainly want. There's a lot of talk about positions for first- and second-stage labor, for example. And the relaxation techniques are fabulous. I go swimming twice a week, which is really energizing."

Gemma Stone, 23, 28 weeks pregnant

exercise and **posture**

It's not a good idea to take up strenuous exercise for the first time when you're pregnant. But these exercises are excellent whether you've done them before or not – although you should always listen to your body and stop when you feel you've done enough. Speak to your provider before embarking on any exercise program.

Exercises to try

♦ Swimming is a great all-around exercise at any time of life, and when you're pregnant it's refreshing to feel weightless and unencumbered in the water.

♦ Walking is great. In the third trimester it's also good for positioning the baby for birth.

♦ Yoga is an excellent form of exercise and relaxation. Choose a class that's designed for mothers-to-be.

Kegel exercises

During pregnancy, increased progesterone levels soften the pelvic-floor muscles. These muscles run around the urethra, vagina, and anus, and are thickest at the perineum. The softening of the muscles and the pressure of the uterus can cause leaks of urine. Practice every day and resume as soon as possible after the birth (see page 79).

Good pregnancy posture

Stand tall with your back straight and your bottom tucked in, so your baby is supported by your thighs, buttocks, and stomach muscles. Well-toned muscles regain their shape more quickly after birth. Good posture will also aid digestion.

Pelvic tilt

This exercise is an excellent preparation for labor, strengthening the stomach and making the back and pelvis more flexible.

1 Kneel on all fours, making sure your back is flat. Keep your shoulders still.

2 Pull in your stomach and bottom. Gently tilt your pelvis forward while breathing out, so that your back arches upward. Hold for a few seconds, but keep breathing. Inhale and release. Repeat several times.

SEE ALSO   EATING WELL page 27 • MATERNITY CLOTHES page 33 • RELAXATION TECHNIQUES page 49 • COMMON COMPLAINTS pages 60–61

your baby at 28 weeks

If she were born now, your baby would stand an excellent chance of survival, but might need expert help from a neonatologist (premature-infant specialist) due to potential breathing problems. She's very active right now, and you are probably aware of her movements much of the time.

Your baby's appearance

Your baby's head is much more in proportion to her body now, and she looks very much like she will when she's born. She's getting chubbier all the time, and greasy vernix is now covering her body. This is to protect her skin, which is immersed the whole time in the amniotic fluid. When she is born she may still have some of this creamy substance on her body. Her skin continues to be wrinkled because she still has a lot of fat to lay down before she is fully developed. Her eyes open and close, and the color of the iris is now visible, although the color may change after birth.

Development

Your baby's lungs have developed greatly during the last few weeks. The alveoli (air sacs) are now almost completely formed, and a substance called surfactant is being produced by the lung cells. This is essential to keep the lungs open when breath is exhaled.

A lack of surfactant can cause respiratory symptoms in a premature baby. If a mother goes into premature labor, an injection of steroids may be offered to hasten surfactant production; this can reduce the chance of the baby needing mechanical breathing assistance after delivery in a birth before 34 weeks.

Her kidneys are fully working now, producing about a pint of urine each day, and your baby's bone marrow is responsible for the manufacture of her red blood cells.

Now that she is bigger, there is less fluid cushioning her from the outside world so you may be more aware of her moving. You might even see the outline of a hand or foot through your abdomen. This is a wonderful thing to share with your partner because it will be his first direct contact with his baby.

Her abdomen is fuller and rounder.

Bones begin to harden.

Her eyes can open.

She can hear well.

Hair may be growing all over her head.

At 28 weeks
LENGTH about 10in (25cm) crown to rump
WEIGHT about 2lb 7oz (1.1kg)

Your baby
The extra fat deposits mean that she looks like a small newborn. She can still change position easily and will be very active at this stage.

your **growing** baby

♦ Your baby gets hiccups from time to time, and you may be aware of them, too. These are probably caused by the baby "practicing" breathing movements.

♦ If he's a boy, his testes are descending.

♦ She may suck her finger or thumb some of the time.

♦ The placenta receives about 14fl oz (400ml) of blood from the mother's circulation every minute.

♦ Her muscles are now well-toned and in proportion to her body size.

♦ Her limbs are sometimes visible moving around under the skin of your abdomen.

♦ Her skin is still wrinkled, but fat is continuing to develop underneath, giving her a less lean appearance.

♦ She has an acute sense of taste, which is greater than it will be when she is born.

♦ Her brain is growing at a very rapid rate and the nervous system is developing so that messages can be passed from the brain to different parts of the body.

♦ She has a well-developed sense of touch.

♦ She is developing the ability to orient herself within her space.

♦ She responds to stimuli, such as light and sound.

how big will your baby be?

Most women are concerned about the size of their baby. You want her to grow healthily, but late in pregnancy you may worry about giving birth to a very large baby.

What affects your baby's size?

This is determined by a number of factors. The first consideration is genetics, so if you are small, the chances are that your baby will be as well. And if your first baby is particularly large or small, it's likely that subsequent babies will follow this trend. Your own size at birth can also be an indication of how big your baby will be. First babies are often smaller than their siblings, and boys tend to be heavier at birth than girls.

If you have a medical condition, such as diabetes or preeclampsia, this can affect the size of your baby; your pregnancy will be closely monitored if this is the case. Babies born to parents who smoke are often of a lower birthweight than those born to nonsmokers. Your nutritional status can affect your baby's size, but unless you are malnourished your baby should continue to grow. If there is any cause for concern, you may be referred for an ultrasound.

What you can do

Listen to your caregivers' advice, but don't become too obsessed with trying to guess how big your baby will be. All babies grow at their own paces.

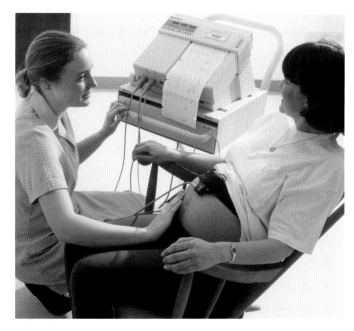

Checking your baby's progress
Your doctor or midwife will regularly check how your baby is growing and can also measure the fetal heartbeat using a handheld device. Electronic fetal monitoring (EFM) may be used later in pregnancy to assess fetal well-being, particularly if there are any concerns.

questions & answers

q Is my baby aware that my obstetrician is touching my tummy and listening to her heartbeat?

a Yes, your baby will be aware of your obstetrician's exam. Usually this will be noticeable when the heartbeat is checked because it will be faster than normal. You'll probably feel your baby move about in response to the obstetrician's palpations. The use of the ultrasound or doppler listening device, which will probably be used to check the heartbeat, may disturb the baby a little. Some doctors say babies tend to squirm more when the sound of the heartbeat is listened to.

q I've been told that my baby seems small for dates, what does that mean?

a It means your baby is smaller than would be expected at the stage of pregnancy you're at. Hearing your child is small for dates is worrisome, but in the majority of cases, there's nothing to be overly concerned about. Obviously, healthcare professionals are dealing with averages when they say something like this, and it's quite possible that your baby is simply not meant to be as big as other babies of the same age.

Another possible reason is that your dates are slightly inaccurate, and your pregnancy isn't as advanced as your estimated date of delivery (EDD) suggests. The main concern about a small-for-dates baby is that the placenta may not be functioning optimally, so your healthcare provider will take extra steps to watch the baby's growth. This is generally done using ultrasounds that are performed at intervals throughout the pregnancy.

q If I eat more, will my baby put on more weight?

a Probably not, unless your diet is severely short of vital nutrients. If you eat too much you will put on excess fat and will be at increased risk of gestational diabetes. On average, a non-pregnant woman requires 2,200 calories a day. When you are pregnant, you need about 300 calories more each day to stay healthy and help the fetus grow.

FIRST TRIMESTER													SECOND TRIMESTER															THIRD TRIMESTER												
1	2	3	4	5	6	7	8	9	10	11	12	13	14	15	16	17	18	19	20	21	22	23	24	25	26	27	28	29	30	31	32	33	34	35	36	37	38	39	40

week 32

There's no getting away from your big belly now, and although you feel it's already enormous, it is going to grow even more over the weeks ahead. The final weeks tend to fly by – soon it's going to be week 40, and you'll be wishing you had more time to get everything done!

your body changes

Your advanced state of pregnancy affects everything you do, from getting up in the morning to going to bed at night. Take things slowly and listen to your body.

Adjusting to late pregnancy

You're probably feeling tired again because of all the extra demands on your body. Rest when you can – put your feet up for an hour or two each day if possible.

Your pelvic joints are expanding now in preparation for the birth. This means that you may experience some aches and pains and feel a bit like a disjointed doll. Avoid sudden movements. When you get out of bed in the morning, keep your legs together and swing them around and onto the floor – this reduces the chance of damage to your pelvis.

Your baby is still moving around a lot, but you can tell his space is more limited now – his movements are more like whole-body shifts and jerks rather than the rippling movements you felt when he could still do complete somersaults in the uterus a few weeks ago.

FACTS ABOUT **YOU**

♦ You may not be sleeping very well at night, which in turn makes you feel even more tired during the day.

♦ Pressure on your bladder means you may need to get up at least once each night to urinate. You may also leak a little urine when you run, cough, sneeze, or laugh.

♦ Your pelvis may ache, especially when you have to stand or when you've been sitting with your legs crossed, because of the weight of the baby.

easing your **symptoms**

Cramps
Don't rush around; sudden movements increase the chance of cramplike pains and you'll become breathless quite easily.

Stretch marks
These will lighten after the birth, but until then an unperfumed body lotion will help to ease any itching and keep the skin moisturized. Do not scratch the marks.

Backache
This is often a problem in the final weeks. Stand tall, with your pelvis tucked under and your weight distributed between your heel and the ball of your foot.

Heartburn and indigestion
Eat several small meals a day, with plenty of fruit. If you can, avoid meals that are high in carbohydrates, sugars, and fats. Have your biggest meal earlier in the day.

YOUR CHANGES THE BABY IS MOVING AROUND A LOT • YOU MAY ALSO BE AWARE OF HIS HICCUPING INSIDE YOU • YOU MAY NEED TO URINATE FREQUENTLY

your emotions

Make sure you indulge yourself, just a little, by spending at least 20 minutes each day lying down, being in touch with your baby.

Bonding

"Bonding" isn't an event that happens after you've given birth, it starts from the moment you know you've got a baby inside you, and turning your attention to that baby, especially in the last few weeks, is a way of feeling close to him even before you've held him in your arms. If you have older children, it is easy to keep the focus on them, so making time for the baby is doubly important.

Relaxation techniques

Make sure the room you are in is warm enough for you to relax comfortably.
♦ Play some gentle music.
♦ If you're sitting up, concentrate on dropping your shoulders at the same time as breathing out slowly. This is also an excellent exercise to do before each breastfeeding.
♦ Try lying on your left side, with your right leg supported by a large cushion – stretch out your bottom leg and bend your top one.
♦ Focus on your breathing, especially on breathing out, keeping it even and controlled.
♦ Think about the baby inside you – imagine him curled up in your uterus, waiting to be born and being welcomed into your arms.

childbirth **classes**

By now you will be thinking more about the birth, so childbirth classes provide a great opportunity for you and your partner to learn more and discuss ideas and worries with a childbirth professional and other parents-to-be.

Getting ready

Most women – and their partners – attend childbirth classes toward the end of their third trimester. Childbirth classes are usually offered at the hospital or birthing center where the baby will be delivered, or at your local YMCA, YWCA, church, or synagogue. Classes provide information about labor and delivery, as well as suggesting techniques and exercises for managing pain during labor.

Options for delivery are discussed in detail and partners are given tips on how to support, assist, and participate in the birth of their child. Childbirth classes also provide a good opportunity for new

Sharing the experience
Childbirth classes can provide an oasis of time in which you and your partner can really focus on the pregnancy.

mothers-to-be to meet other women whose babies are due at about the same time.

Try to stay in touch with each other after the class is over so that you can compare labor and delivery notes and get together after your babies are born. It's never too soon to start building a support group.

SEE ALSO   EATING WELL page 27 • EXERCISE AND POSTURE page 45 • THINKING ABOUT THE BIRTH page 53
• COMMON COMPLAINTS pages 60–61 • PREPARING FOR THE BIRTH pages 64–67

your baby at 32 weeks

By week 32 your baby's facial features are well developed, and his face is a lot more filled out and wrinkle-free. He's possibly head-down in your uterus, and if he is he'll probably stay that way until the birth.

Your baby's appearance

Your baby's skin, which used to be red, is now normal flesh-color and less transparent, and he's looking very like the baby he'll be after the birth. This is due to the deposits of white fat he is continuing to lay down under his skin. Once he is born, these fat deposits will provide him with energy and allow him to regulate his temperature.

His arms and legs are now in proportion and he spends most of his time with his legs pulled up toward his chest. This is the most comfortable way for him to sit in your uterus, since he doesn't have as much space to move around as he did earlier.

Your baby will continue to kick and move his arms, so you should feel some movements, but as his space decreases over the next few weeks, they will feel less dramatic than before, which may make you feel more comfortable.

He's covered in a waxy vernix at this stage, which protects his skin, and hair is continuing to cover his head.

Development

Your baby's organs are continuing to mature, and many are already almost fully developed. The lungs are continuing to develop, although if he were born now a ventilator might still be needed to assist his breathing.

His brain and central nervous system are developing at a fast rate, but they still have a few weeks of fine-tuning to go. This is one reason why premature babies tend to have a poor sucking reflex.

As his eyes become more mature, his irises can dilate and contract, so he is able to react to, and differentiate between, light and dark.

Fingernails will have reached the ends of his fingers.

His eyes can react to light.

Wrinkles on his face are beginning to smooth out.

At 32 weeks
LENGTH about 12in (30cm) crown to rump
WEIGHT about 4lb (1.8kg)

Your baby
Your fully formed baby will have less room to move in the uterus than before. For the rest of the pregnancy, he will be developing fat supplies and preparing for the birth. This baby has moved into a good position, ready for birth.

your **growing** baby

♦ His movements peak around this week, so expect to have a lot of wakeful nights! From now on your baby may seem to move less because he is growing quickly, and space will be at a premium.

♦ His brain is growing a lot at this time.

♦ His bones are hardening, but his skull bones will remain unjoined so they can fit over one another during the journey through the narrow birth canal.

♦ His fingernails may be fully grown.

♦ His fine body hair disappears.

♦ His irises can now dilate and contract in response to light.

♦ He's aware of the practice Braxton Hicks contractions, which occur in your uterus, even if you don't notice them.

♦ He weighs about 4lb (1.8kg), but his growth from now on will be considerable, and he may double in size in the next month or six weeks.

♦ Ultrasounds of unborn babies from this stage show they sometimes have periods of REM, "dream sleep"; the cornea can be seen to move on a sonogram.

♦ He's surrounded by about 1½ pints (750ml) of amniotic fluid, but this will decline over the next few weeks as he grows.

your baby's position

By now your baby may be getting into position for the birth. It can be reassuring to know that your baby is head-down, although he may move again before the birth. Only about three to four percent of babies are breech, or bottom-down, by the due date.

Is he head-down?

By this stage of pregnancy many babies are already head-down, and will remain there until they're born. The "normal" presentation is known as cephalic, and means the baby's head is pointing down into the pelvis, with his bottom up under your diaphragm and his limbs curled up in front of his chest and tummy.

If, when you go for a prenatal checkup, your caregiver finds that your baby is still head-up in the womb, don't worry; many babies remain head-up until a couple of weeks, or even days, before the birth, and only three to four percent of babies are breech, or bottom-down, by the due date.

What you can do

If your baby does stay breech, some exercises may encourage your baby to turn to the cephalic position. Lots of walking may also help. An obstetrician can try to turn the baby externally, known as external cephalic version. This technique is usually done with an ultrasound and in a hospital in case the need for an emergency delivery arises. The procedure can be very successful, although babies can turn back to the breech position afterward. Ask your healthcare provider whether it would be appropriate for you and your baby.

Discussing the options

If your baby is in a breech position when you're 39 or 40 weeks, the most likely recommendation may be a cesarean section. The decision to attempt a vaginal delivery or have a cesarean section should be discussed thoroughly with your providers.

Encouraging a breech baby to turn
Resting with your head below your hips can encourage a baby in the breech position to turn. You may also try to visualize your baby turning.

questions & answers

q I've heard it's a good idea to start counting the baby's movements about now – is this right?

a You're thinking of something called a fetal-kick chart, which is a way a mother can reassure herself that her baby is moving often enough. There are various methods of doing this – some require you to check for a certain number of movements in a certain period of time, and then to write them down. But it's important to get the method you're using right before you start, so talk to your caregiver about whether it's a good idea to start yet, and exactly what you're looking out for.

q I get breathless a lot, especially when I'm climbing up stairs. Does this mean my baby isn't getting enough oxygen?

a Breathlessness is very common at this stage of pregnancy due to the demands of carrying the baby and his position in the uterus. Don't worry. Whether you are feeling breathless or not, oxygen will continue to be delivered to your baby efficiently via the placenta.

Protecting your baby
The uterus is a safe environment, but remember that some harmful substances can reach your baby via the umbilical cord, so avoid potential toxins.

q Does the placenta stop harmful substances from passing through to my baby?

a The placenta is very selective about what it does and doesn't let across to your baby. However, some potentially harmful substances can cross the placenta. Avoid drinking alcohol, because this passes through the placenta virtually unchanged. Most drugs cross the placenta, so check with your caregiver before taking any medicines.

FIRST TRIMESTER												SECOND TRIMESTER															THIRD TRIMESTER												
1	2	3	4	5	6	7	8	9	10	11	12	13	14	15	16	17	18	19	20	21	22	23	24	25	26	27	28	29	30	31	32	33	34	35	36	37	38	39	40

week 36

You probably feel you have been pregnant for ever, and can't wait to meet the little person who is growing inside you. Many women begin to wonder what sort of labor they will have and start to make preparations for the big day. Rest and relax as much as you can.

your body changes

Put your feet up and enjoy these last few weeks. You may feel fine, but your belly is now so large that it affects all your bodily functions, and your lower abdomen and back may ache if you walk a lot. Your hands and feet might be puffy, especially at the end of the day.

Engagement

From 36 weeks, your baby's head will drop lower into your pelvis. It is "engaged" when its largest diameter is lower than the brim of your pelvis. This may make your upper abdomen more comfortable, so you have less heartburn and indigestion, but you may have the urge to urinate more often. This is completely normal at this stage, but if you also feel burning when urinating, contact your midwife or doctor in case you have an infection.

FACTS ABOUT **YOU**

♦ The "nesting instinct" is often strong; you may feel the urge to do some spring-cleaning, but don't overdo it.

♦ If this is your first baby, heartburn, indigestion, and breathlessness should lessen once the head drops in the pelvis.

♦ Your bladder is under pressure, so you may want to urinate more often.

♦ You may tire easily, because of poor sleep and the extra weight of the baby.

♦ Braxton Hicks contractions may become more frequent and more intense.

easing your **symptoms**

Discomfort from kicking
Feeling your baby move is reassuring and exhilarating, but if you find that she is kicking repeatedly in one place and making you uncomfortable, changing your position frequently can help.

Fatigue
Rest every day with your feet up, preferably on your left side. This will help build your stamina as well as increase the blood flow to the placenta. Don't try to be too active at this stage.

Carpal tunnel syndrome
Symptoms are tingling, numb fingers caused by swollen tissues in your wrist as a result of pregnancy, creating pressure on a nerve. This usually gets better after delivery. Wearing a wrist splint and taking vitamin B6 daily may help.

YOUR CHANGES HEARTBURN, INDIGESTION, AND BREATHLESSNESS SHOULD LESSEN • YOU WILL NEED TO URINATE FREQUENTLY • HANDS AND FEET MAY BE PUFFY • YOU WILL FEEL TIRED

your emotions

Your world revolves around the birth and thinking about the changes that being a parent will make to your life. Such thoughts are normal, but can be disconcerting.

Talking it over

Remember that every woman experiences childbirth differently. Your doctor or midwife is the best person to advise you. If you feel impatient, pass the time reading or listening to music. Do things that will be difficult to do once the baby is born – plan an evening out with friends or your partner, go to a concert, or see a movie.

Buying a nursing bra
You can now be measured for your nursing bras. A bra with cups that can be opened individually in the front is essential. Some have cups that unzip, others unhook from the strap.

What you can do

♦ Think about parenting styles and discuss them with your partner. Don't worry about problems over which you have no control.

♦ Make all your practical arrangements for the birth so that you can relax. Pack your labor bag and make your birth plan (see page 67).

♦ Stock up on some instant meals for after the birth.

♦ Take things slowly. You will become tired and breathless more easily, and your ligaments are more relaxed now.

♦ Treat yourself to a haircut or a pedicure.

♦ Don't listen to scary stories about birth. Remember that people often exaggerate.

a loving **relationship**

It is natural to wonder about having sex during pregnancy. Are there risks? What is normal? Unless you have risk factors that preclude sex, you and your partner are free to define what a loving relationship means to you. The important thing is to keep talking about how both of you feel.

What is normal?

You and your partner may experience varying degrees of desire during your pregnancy – there is no such thing as a "normal" pattern of sex. Changes in your body during pregnancy, such as nausea, fatigue, and breast tenderness, may affect your interest level. On the other hand, the months leading up to delivery may feel like the ideal time to strengthen intimate bonds. Together, you and your partner will figure out what "normal" is.

When to abstain

If you have complications, your doctor or midwife may recommend that you abstain from sex. Sexual activity may pose a threat if you are at risk for, or have had a history of, miscarriage and preterm labor. You will likewise be advised to abstain if you have had vaginal bleeding during pregnancy or if you have placenta previa. You should abstain if you or your partner has a sexually transmitted disease such as herpes. In any case, you should abstain from sex after your water has broken. Ask your doctor or midwife if you have any of these risk factors.

What is safe?

Check with your doctor or midwife, but for most couples, sex during pregnancy is safe. Despite old wives' tales of infection, miscarriage, or endangering the baby, you can have sex all the way through a normal pregnancy – as long as you are comfortable. Your baby is protected – the amniotic fluid acts as a cushion, and the amniotic sac and cervical mucous plug act as a seal.

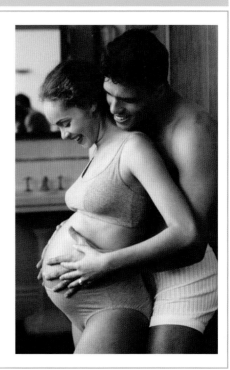

SEE ALSO   URINARY TRACT INFECTIONS page 40 • EXERCISE AND POSTURE page 45 • RELAXATION TECHNIQUES page 49
• CHILDBIRTH CLASSES page 49 • COMMON COMPLAINTS pages 60–61 • PREPARING FOR THE BIRTH pages 64–67

your baby at 36 weeks

Just two weeks from now, your baby would be officially "on time" if she were to be born. Although we usually count a pregnancy as 40 weeks, in fact anything from 38 to 42 weeks is considered normal.

Your baby's appearance

She's still a little bit on the thin side compared to a full-term baby, but otherwise she is identical to any other newborn you might encounter. She's got hair on her head – although not necessarily the same color as yours or your partner's, as hair color is notoriously difficult to predict. Her skin is beginning to smooth out, and her face is losing its wrinkled appearance. Her eyes are opening and closing a lot, and she can sense light changes through your abdomen.

The lanugo, or fine downy hair covering her body, is disappearing now – when she's born you might notice some of it left on her shoulders, but it will basically be gone. The lanugo and her top skin layer are shed into the amniotic fluid before birth. They are then ingested by the baby and form the solid mass of what will be her first bowel movement, known as meconium.

Development

Her lungs are now almost fully developed, and in preparation for a lifetime of breathing, she's started to "practice" breathing in and out, which involves inhaling small amounts of amniotic fluid into her lungs. Her kidneys are fully developed and her liver is able to process some waste products.

She's developed a cycle of activity and sleep that you're probably aware of. Unborn babies often sleep during the day while you're up, then wake up and move around when you lie in bed at night. This may predict sleep patterns when your baby is first brought home. The movements have a different feel now because there's less space, and she will not be able to move around as freely as before.

Soft nails have grown to the tips of her fingers and toes.

Most of the fine hair (lanugo) will be shed from her body.

Skin will become more smooth and soft.

Hair may have grown as much as 2in (5cm).

The baby's shape will be more rounded.

Your baby now opens and closes her eyes frequently.

Your baby's head may have engaged in your pelvis.

At 36 weeks
LENGTH about 13in (32cm) crown to rump
WEIGHT about 5lb 8oz (2.5kg)

Your baby
If this is your first baby, her head may have descended into the pelvis in preparation for birth. You will still feel her legs kicking and her arms moving.

your **growing** baby

♦ There's less amniotic fluid in the womb now that your baby is so much bigger.

♦ The weight of the uterus grows from 1–2oz (30–60g) to about 2.2lbs (1kg) at the end of pregnancy.

♦ The placenta is producing a hormone to stimulate your breasts to make milk for when the baby is born.

♦ The placenta is mature and the supply of nutrients from the placenta to the baby is at its greatest.

♦ The central nervous system is still maturing, with the baby's reflexes improving day by day.

♦ Ninety-nine percent of babies born at this stage of pregnancy survive, almost all without problems.

♦ Your baby is developing her fat supplies and putting on weight more quickly now, gaining about 5oz (140g) each week.

♦ By this stage if she's awake, her eyes will be open.

♦ If your baby is a boy, his testicles will have dropped down into the scrotum.

♦ If you move around a lot or press gently on your abdomen, your baby may wake. Eating a meal rich in carbohydrates may have the same effect.

getting ready for birth

If this is your first baby she's likely to engage, or move down into your pelvis for the birth, any time from now on.

Has she engaged?

Engagement occurs when the presenting part of your baby – usually the head – moves lower and slips into your pelvis. You may notice your baby is engaged as the pressure on your diaphragm eases, making it easier to breathe, or you may need to urinate more often as the baby presses on your bladder. Your doctor or midwife will check whether she is engaged in your pelvis by internal examination – to feel the presenting part – and then by palpating the head externally to determine if it is fixed in position or "floating free."

Once your baby is engaged, your doctor or midwife will check how far down into the pelvis she is by feeling how much of her head she can palpate. The location is measured by "station." A station of -3 means the baby's head is three centimeters above the midpelvis. A 0 station means the baby's head is in the middle of the pelvis, and at a +4 station, the head is at the vaginal opening.

Late engagement

In a second or subsequent pregnancy, the uterine muscles do not exert as much pressure on the baby as in a first pregnancy, so later engagement is not unusual. If this is your first pregnancy and the baby has not engaged, your doctor may want to check that your baby's head is not too large to fit into your pelvis.

Your baby's movements are more restricted, but you will still feel him kicking and moving his arms.

The soft bones of your baby's skull will compress during birth to fit through the birth canal.

Your baby's position in the pelvis
Once your baby's head is low inside the hollow of the pelvis, it is engaged, ready for birth.

twins

Twins are often considered "term" at 37 weeks, although it's not uncommon for them to be born as late as 40 weeks.

Giving birth to twins

♦ Exactly how labor is triggered isn't fully understood, but the size of the uterus does have a role to play and because it's been so stretched by a twin pregnancy, labor often starts earlier than 40 weeks.
♦ The type of delivery you have will in part be influenced by the babies' position in the womb. If they're both head-down you may go for a natural delivery, but if one or both are breech, you might decide to have a surgical delivery because there's a risk you'll need one to deliver the second baby, even after one vaginal delivery. Occasionally, one of the babies may be lying in a transverse position, across the uterus. If this is the case, you will need a cesarean section.
♦ Many multiple births proceed without complications. However, a twin birth, whether surgical or normal, almost always involves an obstetrician and often an anesthesiologist.

Cephalic twins
This is the most straightforward presentation.

Cephalic/breech
You may need a cesarean delivery for the breech baby.

Breech twins
Your obstetrician may recommend a cesarean section.

questions & answers

q Is it possible for a baby to lie across the uterus?

a It is rare for a baby to lie sideways (known as transverse), or diagonally (oblique). If your baby remains in this position when you go into labor, it's more likely you'll need a cesarean section to deliver her safely.

q How will I know if the head has engaged?

a Your belly may look lower than it did and you might not be kicked in the ribs as often as you were before. You may need to urinate more frequently. Engagement is also known as "lightening." Your doctor or midwife will confirm engagement by an external or internal examination.

q Do my twins share the same umbilical cord and amniotic fluid?

a Twins almost always have their own cords, even identical twins (these are formed from an early split in a fertilized egg and are genetically the same). Usually, twins (including identical ones) have their own amniotic sacs, too, so their amniotic fluid is separate. This means there is a thin membrane between them in the uterus. They may, however, share a placenta.

FIRST TRIMESTER												SECOND TRIMESTER															THIRD TRIMESTER												
1	2	3	4	5	6	7	8	9	10	11	12	13	14	15	16	17	18	19	20	21	22	23	24	25	26	27	28	29	30	31	32	33	34	35	36	37	38	39	40

week 40

A few months ago you thought this day would never arrive. In the next few days, your baby will finally be out in the big wide world and, more importantly, in your arms. It is a moment to cherish and the start of a whole new way of life, for you as well as the little person you're about to meet.

your body changes

The final few weeks of pregnancy see the greatest strain on your body, so it is important to get plenty of rest before the baby arrives.

The last few days

Your tummy is impressively large and you're also probably very tired. This is completely normal; you are carrying a ready-to-be-born person, so take it easy. Good posture is vital. Ease the pressure by standing tall and tucking your pelvis under as much as you can. This can help alleviate the backache and pelvic pressure you feel. Many women give birth between weeks 40 and 41, but if you're still pregnant next week, you'll probably see your healthcare provider and at least discuss the possibility of inducing your labor, although many providers don't advise it until about week 42 unless there are signs that the baby needs to be born (see page 75).

FACTS ABOUT **YOU**

♦ You'll now be having your prenatal checkups weekly, or even more frequently if there's any cause for concern.

♦ Your weight gain has slowed or stopped since about week 37. In fact, you may lose about 2–3lb (900g–1.4kg) in the last couple of weeks.

♦ The weight of the baby may be causing you to leak urine. Keep doing your pelvic-floor exercises (see page 45) right up to the birth, and start again as soon as you can after. They really do help.

easing your **symptoms**

Impatience
This is arguably the main complaint at this point. Try not to become too obsessed with your estimated date of delivery (EDD); it is just that, an estimate. As many as 40 percent of babies arrive more than a week after their EDD. Make the most of the time before the birth and get plenty of rest.

Anxiety
As the birth of your baby is now imminent, it is natural to experience some anxiety. Try to relax (see page 49) and focus on the new life that you are about to bring into the world.

Shortness of breath
This is pretty normal at this stage due to the size of the baby, especially when you exert yourself. You may have to limit some of your activities, but you can still swim and do pelvic-floor exercises. Keep feet and ankles moving when you can.

YOUR CHANGES YOU MAY HAVE SOME SIGNS OF ONSET OF LABOR, SUCH AS: ● A BLOODY SHOW — THE LOSS OF THE MUCOUS PLUG ● SLIGHT DIARRHEA ● CONTRACTIONS. REPORT THESE TO YOUR OBSTETRICIAN

your emotions

Excitement, nervousness, fear, anticipation, longing – you go through so many different mood swings in these last few days of a pregnancy.

Coping with concerns

You and your partner may be very close, aware of this big change you're about to go through together – or you may be so nervous that you're keeping your distance emotionally. Don't shut each other out at this vital time. Try to enjoy being just the two of you because it's going to be a long time before it's like this again.

Build in a few treats that are going to be less frequent in the weeks and months ahead – a night at the movies, perhaps, or dinner at a restaurant, or taking walks together.

♦ Your main concern at this point is probably impatience that it's all taking so long. Try to enjoy the final days of your pregnancy without getting too uptight about being "late" – in fact, don't think of yourself as late at all. Many babies arrive after their due date, and this is especially true of first babies.

♦ Making love at this time may encourage the onset of labor. The prostaglandins in semen are thought to ripen the cervix for labor.

♦ Go through your birth plan (see page 67) and make sure you are happy with all of your arrangements. The more confident you are, and the more you understand what is likely to happen, the less apprehensive you will feel.

♦ Everyone has concerns about the birth and about being parents. Try the relaxation techniques suggested (see page 49), and banish negative thoughts from your mind.

♦ Make sure you know the signs of labor (see page 68). If you are having contractions every 5–10 minutes, are in a lot of pain, having any vaginal bleeding, or think your water may be leaking or broken, call your caregiver.

case history

SAMANTHA WHITE, 26
40 WEEKS PREGNANT, SECOND BABY

"I have a real nesting urge at the moment, which hopefully means the baby will be here very soon. Last time I was pregnant my baby was 10 days overdue, and I got so fed up with people calling to check whether the baby had arrived. This time I told everyone (except my partner) that the baby is due a week after the actual due date – so I won't be under pressure. I have 30-day menstrual cycles, and my obstetrician told me that women with longer-than-average cycles often go to 41–42 weeks."

a good night's sleep

It is common to have trouble sleeping in the last four weeks of pregnancy, partly due to the size of your abdomen and partly because of the hormonal changes that are taking place. A good night's sleep may seem like an impossible dream, but there are steps you can take to improve your chances. A warm bath (not hot) before bed will relax you, as will a glass of milk or a bowl of cereal. There are a number of self-help methods you can try. Always consult a qualified practitioner and inform your doctor before trying any alternative therapies.

Diet and nutrition
A deficiency in B vitamins may contribute to your insomnia. If your blood-sugar levels fall during the night, you may wake because of hunger or nausea. Try foods rich in calcium, such as yogurt, milk, almonds, or sesame seeds, as evening snacks. Foods rich in vitamin B6, such as green leafy vegetables and wholegrains, may help you sleep.

Finding a good position
Avoid lying on your back once your pregnancy is advanced because this position will compress the main vein, which may make you feel faint, as well as reducing the blood flow to the baby through the placenta. Sleeping on your left side takes the weight off your back and allows an unrestricted blood supply to the placenta and the baby. Lie on your left side and support yourself with pillows under your top leg. You may also find it comfortable to place a pillow under your abdomen.

Sleeping comfortably
Lie on your side and support yourself with pillows. Don't sleep on your back because you may feel faint.

SEE ALSO   EATING WELL page 27 • EXERCISE page 45 • RELAXATION TECHNIQUES page 49 • COMMON COMPLAINTS pages 60–61 • PREPARING FOR THE BIRTH pages 64–67 • BIRTH PROCEDURES pages 74–75

your baby at 40 weeks

The big day is almost here (if it hasn't happened already) and your baby is about to get his first taste of life in a world he has glimpsed through the sounds and lights that have penetrated through your uterus. From the moment he's born, he'll begin to start making sense of it all.

Your baby's appearance

The average weight of a newborn baby at term is 7lb 8oz (3.4kg), although anything between 5lb 8oz (2.5kg) and 9lb (4kg) is considered a normal weight. He's probably fairly plump by now because in the last few weeks the fat deposits have built up under his skin, and consequently he's also less wrinkly. The lanugo has disappeared from his skin, although when he is born, you may still see some of the waxy vernix.

Your baby will have gray, brown, or blue eyes at birth. His true eye color will be evident as he gets a few weeks older.

Development

By 40 weeks your baby's body is in full working order, and his lungs and nervous system, which matured more slowly than other body systems, are functioning properly. His brain, of course, is the organ that has the most developing still to do – but there's always babyhood and childhood, not to mention the rest of his life, to take care of that.

His immune system is not fully mature yet. During your pregnancy, the placenta has provided your baby with some of the antibodies he needs. Breast milk also provides him with antibodies to protect him once he is born. His immune system will develop slowly over the first few years of his life. The myelin sheath that coats the nervous system also has some maturing to do, and will be complete when your child is about two years old.

He has more body fat.

All the organs are mature and fully functioning.

Skin will become more smooth and soft.

At 40 weeks

LENGTH about 14in (36cm) crown to rump

TOTAL LENGTH about 20in (50cm)

WEIGHT about 7lb 8oz (3.4kg)

Your baby

He is now ready to be born, and much more chubby than he was before. Over the last 40 weeks, he has grown from a tiny bundle of cells into the fully formed human being now inside you.

your **growing** baby

♦ At 40 weeks, 97 percent of babies are head-down in the uterus and will be born this way.

♦ The placenta at birth is roughly one-sixth of the size of the baby.

♦ The umbilical cord is about the same length as the baby.

♦ You may have lost a little weight in the final couple of weeks.

♦ In boy babies, the testes should have descended. In girls, the ovaries stay above the pelvic brim until after birth.

♦ Your due date is an estimation. Only about six percent of babies are born on

what was calculated to have been their due date. The majority are born between 38 and 42 weeks.

♦ It's now a very tight fit in the womb, and he has to curl into a tight ball.

♦ The amniotic fluid, which surrounds the baby until hours or even minutes before he emerges, has changed from a colorless liquid into a pale, milky consistency because of the lanugo (the fine downy hair that covered his body) that has been shed into it.

♦ There are about two pints (one liter) of amniotic fluid surrounding your baby.

choosing a name

Choosing your baby's name is another exciting job for you and your partner while you await the birth. Remember that you are choosing something that will be with your baby throughout his life.

Points to consider

♦ You need to think about how the name fits with your family name, and check to see if the initials will make a word when placed together.

♦ In some families it is traditional to pass on a name. If you are not happy with this, you could perhaps make it a middle name.

♦ An unusual spelling gives your child a name that is almost exclusively his, but think how annoying it could be for him to have his name misspelled or mispronounced throughout his life.

♦ Remember that a name that suits your tiny newborn baby needs to suit a fully grown adult as well.

♦ Choosing a name that reflects the country of origin of one of the parents or another member of the family has become very popular in recent years.

♦ You may find that you and your partner just cannot decide. If this is the case, wait until he's born and then see what he looks like. Even if you have chosen a name, sometimes it just doesn't seem right when you actually meet your baby.

♦ You might want to think about a name that in some way links the baby to the circumstances of his birth, such as a name that is local to the area in which he was born.

A joint decision
Fathers-to-be can feel a little left out in the final weeks, but deciding what to call the new member of your family is something you can both do for your baby before he is born. However, be prepared in case you want to change your minds once he arrives.

questions & answers

q What is the nesting instinct?

a Many women get a sudden surge of energy from about week 36, when they feel the need to clean the house, or repack their hospital bag, or reorganize the baby's room. This desire to make sure everything is ready is entirely natural, but take it easy! Avoid excessive fatigue.

q Can I be the first person to touch my baby after he is born?

a Discuss your wishes with your caregiver and your partner, and incorporate them into your birth plan (see page 67). Whether you will be the first person to make physical contact with the baby will depend on a number of factors, including your delivery position, and whether there are any concerns over the baby's health. If everything is straightforward, and especially if you are upright when you give birth, it should be possible for you to lean down immediately afterward and take your baby into your arms.

q When will the cord be cut after the birth?

a Again, this depends on the method and circumstances of the delivery. If it's a surgical or assisted birth, the cord will be clamped and cut immediately. If you have a natural, vaginal delivery you may want to ask the doctor or midwife if the cord can be left intact until it stops pulsating. Some people believe that the baby continues to benefit from the nutrients he receives from the placenta after the birth, and if you feel you would prefer this, talk to the doctor or midwife beforehand.

common discomforts

A few lucky women sail through pregnancy without so much as a stretch mark, but the majority experience the occasional ailment. Most are not serious, but they can be uncomfortable and unpleasant. You will want to avoid taking medications during pregnancy, and, fortunately, for most of the minor discomforts there are different remedies or therapies available that may help ease the symptoms.

dealing with minor ailments

Talking to other pregnant women, and women who've been pregnant recently, can be enormously helpful. Your doctor or midwife will also be an important source of useful ideas.

If something is bothering you, don't wait until your next scheduled appointment to ask for advice.

General advice

Most women are wary of taking medication while they are pregnant, but this does not mean suffering in silence. Minor ailments of pregnancy can often be eased by a small adjustment to your diet or lifestyle. Complementary therapies are increasingly popular with mothers-to-be, and some women have reported great success in treating their ailments. However, just because something is natural does not necessarily make it safe to use in pregnancy. For example, many herbs and some aromatherapy oils should not be used by pregnant women. Always consult a qualified practitioner with experience in dealing with pregnant women, and tell your caregiver before beginning any treatments.

Vaginal infections

Infections and increased vaginal secretions are quite common in pregnancy. Always consult your doctor or midwife if you have an unusual or heavy discharge, or if you are itching. It is important to check whether your symptoms are caused by a simple case of yeast or if you have another infection. The closer you are to term the quicker you should seek help because some infections, such as Group B streptococcus (GBS), can be contracted by your baby during delivery.

Eating well
A diet rich in fruit and vegetables is excellent for your general health, and that of your baby. It is also a good way of avoiding constipation.

Anemia

Anemia is much rarer than fatigue. It's caused by a reduced amount of hemoglobin in your red blood cells. This is the result of either a diet that doesn't contain enough iron, or the heavy demands of your pregnancy. If you think your fatigue could be caused by insufficient iron it's worth asking your doctor or midwife for a blood test to check your hemoglobin levels (this will be done at least once during your pregnancy as a matter of routine). Iron supplements can cause constipation, so if this is a problem a different brand or prescription may be better for you.

Backache

Carrying a baby places considerable stress on your frame, which is why backache is so common. It isn't inevitable, though, and the best way to keep it at bay is to be aware of your posture (see page 45). Don't make the classic pregnancy mistake of

Keeping up your fluid intake
Throughout pregnancy drink plenty of fresh water to avoid dehydration and improve your digestion.

arching your back and sticking out your abdomen: this taxes your back, and it's far better for your spine if you can pull your tummy in. Balance your body weight between your heels and the balls of your feet, and sit, when you can, with both feet on the floor instead of crossing your legs.

If you develop backache, seek help from a specialist. Your doctor can point you in the direction of someone helpful such as a physical therapist, an obstetric chiropractor, or an osteopath. Whoever you consult about your backache should be able to show you special exercises to help alleviate the discomfort.

Constipation

Again, this isn't an inevitable consequence of pregnancy so don't just assume you have to put up with it. Your digestive system becomes more sluggish during pregnancy, but you can counteract the effects by increasing the amount of water you drink (aim for eight glasses a day), and your intake of fresh fruit and vegetables (aim for at least five or six portions a day). Dried fruit is also good (it provides extra iron, too). Talk to your obstetrician about other methods of treating constipation. Some mothers-to-be have reported good results from reflexology and acupuncture.

Heartburn

This unpleasant condition is often worst in the evening: it's caused by pregnancy hormones relaxing the valve at the top of your stomach so that the acid contents are released upward, combined with physical pressure due to the enlarging uterus pushing the GI tract toward the upper abdomen. You feel bloated and have a burning sensation in your upper chest. Standing tall, with your arms raised above your head, can offer a bit of immediate relief, since it increases the amount of chest space. Eat small meals throughout the day rather than

Finding some time for you
Many minor discomforts can be eased by taking it easy and listening to your body's needs. Remember that even early in pregnancy, when you have little or no belly, your body is working much harder than usual to help your baby develop and grow.

one or two large ones. Avoiding alcohol, spicy foods, fatty food, and coffee can also help. Some people find a glass of milk helpful; for others, milk can actually bring on an attack. Eat slowly, and avoid eating just before you go to bed. Try sipping warm (not hot) mint or ginger tea after a meal.

Hemorrhoids

These are varicose veins around the rectum and anus. They're made worse by straining (so constipation can cause or aggravate them), and they can make your life a misery with itching and pain. Avoiding constipation is vital if you're at risk for hemorrhoids; try putting your feet up on a stool while you're sitting on the toilet. Various creams are available to treat hemorrhoids, but make sure any pharmacist you consult knows that you are pregnant, or ask your doctor for advice.

Varicose veins

These can be the result of the extra strain on your legs. They usually appear as bulging, bluish veins under the skin. Support pantyhose can help, as well as plenty of walking, which helps the blood return to your heart. Sit with your legs higher than your head for at least half an hour a day, or lie on the floor with your bottom against a wall and your legs up on the wall.

conditions of concern

While the majority of women enjoy pregnancy without any serious problems, for a small percentage expecting a baby triggers cause for concern. Prenatal care is designed to identify women at risk of serious conditions before problems arise. The good news is that even if you are one of the few who may be at higher risk, it's more than likely that with medical help you and your baby will both be fine.

rare and serious conditions

This highlights the importance of never ignoring your prenatal appointments. Also, if you have an inkling that things may not be fine, don't wait: always act right away so if there is a problem, it can be dealt with as soon as possible.

There are a number of conditions that can cause potentially serious problems. These are the most common, although remember that even these are relatively rare. Always speak to your caregivers if you're worried you might be at risk.

Preeclampsia/toxemia

A lot of the prenatal care you receive is focused on watching out for the first signs of preeclampsia. It's most common in first-time mothers, although it's also a risk for women who had it in their previous pregnancy. Fortunately preeclampsia, also known as toxemia or pregnancy-induced hypertension (PIH), is uncommon. If you include its mildest forms it occurs in five to 10 percent of pregnancies – some women

when to call the doctor

If you develop any of the following symptoms, act quickly – call your doctor, midwife, or the labor floor at your hospital, or get yourself to a hospital:

♦ bleeding that is bright red and/or profuse

♦ severe abdominal pain

♦ nausea and/or vomiting combined with blurred vision or headaches

♦ a sudden drop in the number of times your baby moves over a period of several hours

♦ pain below the ribs

♦ you think your water may have broken or is leaking.

Managing preeclampsia
If you are diagnosed with early onset preeclampsia, you will need plenty of rest, but if your symptoms are mild you may be able to stay at home. Your blood pressure and urine will be monitored frequently.

who develop preeclampsia may have had high blood pressure before their pregnancies.

Preeclampsia isn't fully understood, but basically the mother's body systems become increasingly unable to cope with the pregnancy. It almost always develops after 30 weeks, and may be a sudden or gradual onset. It's characterized by a rise in blood pressure; protein in the urine; and edema, or swelling in the ankles, feet, and hands. Although you should have any troublesome signs checked, there are other reasons why you might have swollen ankles or protein in your urine; but occurring together, two or three of the above symptoms should be taken seriously.

You'll be monitored closely, and if the situation seems to be worsening, your baby may need to be delivered. This is done to prevent preeclampsia from progressing to eclampsia, in which the mother has seizures. Advances in the care of premature newborns mean that today many more babies survive preeclamptic pregnancies. The pregnancy can't be continued once preeclampsia becomes severe because it puts the mother and baby at risk. But mild preeclampsia may be managed for up to several weeks.

Diabetes

If you have preexisting diabetes you've been considered "high risk" since the start of your pregnancy; however about 1–2 percent of women develop glucose problems during pregnancy called gestational diabetes. This means your body isn't producing enough insulin to regulate your blood sugar. Women with diabetes have too much sugar in their blood. Insulin is a hormone that helps the body use sugar, the body's main source of food. Gestational diabetes usually resolves after delivery.

Symptoms include feeling thirsty and weak, although diabetes can occur without symptoms. Your doctor will check your urine sample for glucose, or your blood sugar, which can indicate diabetes. If you have gestational diabetes, your pregnancy will be closely monitored and you'll follow a special diet or take insulin.

Placenta previa

This means the placenta is attached to the lower uterine wall and partially or totally covers the cervix. When you go into labor, the placenta would be expelled before the baby, endangering his life. If you have placenta previa, you'll need a cesarean section. It is usually found during routine ultrasounds, but any bleeding during your pregnancy can be a sign of it.

Monitoring your pregnancy
If you are found to have a condition which is potentially serious, your pregnancy will be closely monitored, often with frequent ultrasounds.

"I had sudden-onset preeclampsia in my first pregnancy. Over the space of a couple of days my ankles became elephantine, my hands were swollen, and I was hardly passing any urine. I called my obstetrician and she sent me straight to the hospital. My blood pressure was high, and through that night it climbed even higher: at dawn the doctor said the baby had to be delivered. I was only 29 weeks pregnant, and my tiny daughter was born a couple of hours later. She was in the intensive-care unit for eight weeks, but she's fine now. My second pregnancy was problem-free, and I had a vaginal delivery, despite a cesarean with my first."

PHILIPPA CASEMAN, 33, MOTHER OF JADE AGE 3 YEARS AND MATTHEW AGE 8 MONTHS

coping with **miscarriage**

If you have bleeding, call your doctor right away. Sometimes, sadly, it is a sign that your pregnancy is in trouble. (This isn't always the case – if you have bleeding, but an ultrasound shows a fetal heartbeat, there's a good chance everything will be fine.)

If you have a miscarriage, it's a devastating blow for both you and your partner. Your caregiver will discuss with you whether to go home and wait for the baby to miscarry naturally, which may involve cramps and blood loss, or to have a D&C, which means surgically emptying the uterus under anesthesia. You may get over the physical pain very quickly, but the psychological scars take longer to heal. Miscarriage is above all a terrible shock, followed by weeks and maybe months

of wondering why it happened. You will need time to grieve.

Usually there are no answers as to why your baby has died, although some babies die because they were not developing normally. If this was your first attempt to have a child, you may have worries about whether the next pregnancy will end the same way. This is unlikely; having one miscarriage doesn't mean you'll have another next time. If you do have a series of miscarriages, you can be referred to a specialist for tests to evaluate the cause.

Although it's hard, don't blame yourself for what happened. Feelings of guilt and anger are common, but it is very unlikely that there is anything you could have done to prevent what happened.

your birth choices

Every birth is a unique event, a huge turning point, and a time to celebrate. The little person you know so well, and yet don't know at all, will be in your arms at last. If this is your first baby, the birth will also mark the end of your old way of life and the beginning of a new phase: there's no going back, and it won't always be easy, but it will be enormously enriching and lots of fun.

understanding the options

Talk to your caregiver about how you can best prepare for the sort of experience you'd like birth to be. Spend time focusing on the birth itself – thinking about how you'd like it to go.

Of course, what happens during your labor will, to some extent, be determined by events on the day: there's nothing set in stone about labor and childbirth, so it is important to keep an open mind. However, being as prepared as possible, and finding out about the options beforehand, can really help you make the most of the birth of your child.

You probably have your own ideas about the type of birth you want, but at the same time you know that labor isn't a process that's possible to predict, and you have to be open-minded about the need for medical intervention if it becomes necessary.

Plan for the best-case scenario: try to be optimistic about how things will go, while accepting that if you do need medical help and therefore don't get quite the experience you'd hoped for, you will, at the very least, all emerge safe and healthy. Discuss your hopes and ideas with your birth partner, and make sure you are both comfortable with the plans.

Write your thoughts down in a birth plan, and make sure you have it with you

when you go into labor (see page 67). Here are some of the options you might like to consider:

Active delivery

Active childbirth is the term used to describe a delivery in which the mother is upright, usually away from a bed, and in which she has freedom of movement throughout or through most of her labor. From a physical point of view, it's the most efficient way of giving birth because it enables you to use gravity to maximum effect. Active birth also allows a woman to remain more "in control" of events; she's less likely to feel like a "patient" if she's not on a bed and can move her body when she feels it is necessary.

Most maternity units are very sympathetic to women who want an active birth these days. Almost all home and birth-center deliveries are active births, and an increasing number of hospital deliveries are active as well.

Traditional delivery

The tradition in Western societies during the past 30 or so years has been to give birth lying on a hospital bed, possibly using footrests to help push the baby out, or lying on the left side with the right leg raised. This sort of birth is still favored by some midwives, and by obstetricians if the birth is assisted (see below), or if you've needed continuous fetal monitoring to chart the baby's heartbeat during contractions. There have, however, been some changes in traditional deliveries.

home **birth**

Home births make up less than three percent of the total number of births, although figures vary widely between areas.

A home birth isn't for everyone. It presents potential hazards to both mother and fetus before and after birth that require standards of safety that cannot be matched in the home. Many women choose a hospital setting for their deliveries, comforted by the knowledge that an obstetrician, pediatrician, and an anesthesiologist for pain control, are nearby.

Some women feel the need to be close to the technology that is at arm's reach in a hospital, just in case they need intervention – the risk of death to newborns delivered at home is nearly twice that of newborns delivered in hospitals. Newborns delivered at home were also at higher risk for having low Apgar scores.

The hospital is also the best place for your delivery if you have had a complicated or high-risk pregnancy such as a multiple birth, or if there are any indications that you might have a difficult birth or a postpartum hemorrhage.

Mothers-to-be are now offered choices previously not known, including drug-free deliveries, fathers-to-be in attendance, the availability of lactation consultants, and a choice of delivery positions such as squatting, which takes advantage of gravity.

Assisted delivery

If you need assistance you'll definitely be lying on a hospital bed when you deliver, probably with your feet in stirrups. This sort of birth becomes necessary due to the slowness of the pushing stage of the labor, or if your baby shows signs of distress.

Forceps or vacuum deliveries (in which a suction cup is attached to the baby's head and used to help ease it out of the birth canal) both fall into this category, and are carried out by obstetricians, usually after the pushing stage of labor has gone on for a long period of time (see page 75). These procedures have a good safety record for both you and your baby.

water **labor**

Being in water during labor has become increasingly popular over the past 25 years. Water may help reduce pain and your chances of tearing because it helps you relax. Although delivery in water is still unusual, many women use water to help them manage pain during the first stage of labor.

Most birth centers, and an increasing number of hospitals in Canada, now have water-birthing rooms. It can be difficult, though, to book these in advance. You may have to hope one is free on the day you need it.

Ideally, the water should be at body temperature (98.6˚F/37˚C). If the water is hotter, the mother may be at risk of dehydration and high blood pressure. A study of the use of water in labor indicated that labor is more efficient if the mother entered the water only once she had reached 5cm dilatation.

Though the Society of Obstetricians and Gynecologists of Canada has not yet endorsed water births nor issued guidelines, most doctors and midwives advise that you leave the pool for the third stage because the relaxing effects of water could theoretically increase bleeding after delivery or encourage retention of the placenta.

Cesarean section

This is a surgical delivery in which your baby is born through an incision in your uterine wall. A cesarean may be elective (planned) or it may be an emergency, in which case you'll have been in labor first and something will indicate the need for a surgical delivery. During the past few years the cesarean-section rate has increased dramatically, and approximately one in five deliveries in Canada is now surgical. It is a major operation, and, as with all abdominal surgery, you will need time to recover after the birth. This means that you will not be able to perform certain activities, including driving, for a few weeks.

Deciding where to give birth
Before making a decision, visit the delivery rooms with your partner and make sure you feel comfortable with the arrangements. The staff will be pleased to answer your questions, and you will find it reassuring to know what to expect when you actually go into labor.

who's who at **the birth**

The family doctor or obstetrician
He or she will attend a traditional delivery and take charge of an assisted delivery. Obstetricians usually perform cesarean sections if needed.

The midwife
A midwife will be present during labor and attend a low-risk delivery in a hospital or home setting.

The labor-room nurse
This nurse may be with you during labor.

The family doctor or pediatrician
He or she will check on your baby's health if there are any complications.

The anesthesiologist
He or she will administer an epidural or anesthesia for labor or a cesarean.

preparing for birth

It's worth thinking about what you'll need to have ready for the birth well in advance – although you've got an EDD (estimated date of delivery), there are about five weeks during which it would be completely normal for your baby to be born. That's because anything from 37 weeks' gestation is considered "term," and up to 42 weeks is quite common.

a unique event

Now is the time to make your detailed plans for the birth. Taking care of these arrangements will help you feel more calm when you go into labor.

There are several points you should consider when making your plans.

♦ How to contact your birth partner (and/or the baby's father, if they're not the same) when you go into labor.

♦ Keep the telephone number of your doctor, midwife and/or the labor floor of your maternity unit or birthing center close by so you can call if you have any problems, or to let them know you're on your way. Keep the number, along with your insurance card and registration papers, in a safe place that you can access easily.

♦ If you've been given your prenatal chart, make sure that it is in your bag or somewhere prominent because you will need to take it with you to the hospital or birthing center.

♦ Pack what you need to take to the hospital or birthing center.

♦ Make sure you know how you'll travel to the hospital, and how long the journey will take.

♦ Check if you will need to pay for the parking lot and what change you will need.

♦ You will need to make arrangements well in advance for your older child or children to be taken care of while you're both at the hospital. Make sure your child understands what will happen, who will be taking care of him, and when he will see you again.

Practical matters

It is wise to plan some practical matters before your delivery. You may need to tie up loose ends at work, for example, or reschedule impending appointments until after the birth of your baby. Make sure that any arrangements you make for the care of your children (or pets) are flexible – remember your due date is only an

what to pack

For you:
♦ two or three old nightgowns, a couple of baggy T-shirts, and a bathrobe
♦ two or three nursing bras
♦ breast pads
♦ slippers
♦ several pairs of underwear, either cotton or disposable
♦ toiletries: toothbrush and toothpaste, washcloth, towel, brush and comb, hair ties, face cream, shower gel, shampoo, makeup, small mirror, perfume
♦ plastic bags for dirty clothes
♦ clothes to wear home
♦ snacks for you and your partner
♦ magazines, books, or other diversions
♦ two copies of your birth plan
♦ health insurance and hospital preregistration information.

For your baby:
♦ diapers and wipes
♦ stretchies and suitable nightwear
♦ undershirt
♦ sweater or coat and a hat to come home in, depending on the weather
♦ blanket.
Do not forget that you must install a rear-facing infant seat into the car in which you are bringing the baby home.

estimate, and you don't want to be caught unprepared! You may also want to arrange for someone other than your partner to do the videotaping at your birth (if you chose to do so). That way he or she is able to focus on your needs alone.

A good time to make arrangements is when you pack your bags for the hospital or birthing center so that everything will be ready when the time comes.

Dealing with your concerns

Even for women having their third or fourth child, there are always moments when the journey ahead seems daunting. Everyone has concerns before their baby is born – what's important is that you are able to share them with someone: your partner, a friend, your midwife, or doctor.
♦ Talk about what's worrying you with your partner, and ask him about his concerns. It's a good idea for him to come with you to your childbirth classes (see page 49) so he is as well informed as possible about the birth process, and to at least one third-trimester prenatal visit so he can raise any issues with the doctor or midwife.
♦ You'll inevitably talk to friends and family members who've had babies recently. Their experiences can be helpful, but remember that every birth is different. Don't assume that what happens to other people will necessarily be similar to what happens to you, your partner, and baby.

birth plan

Writing a birth plan is a great way to consider your options and ideas before the big day. By stating your preferences now, you can let your caregivers and birth partner know what kind of birth you want for you and your baby.

A birth plan should not be a description of your ideal birth – everyone would like a natural, virtually pain-free labor – but a discussion of how you would like the birth to progress and your feelings about certain procedures. Be realistic. If you produce a birth plan that states that you do not wish to have any interventions at all, you will be disappointed if this cannot happen. It is better to consider all the possibilities, and look for the best outcomes in all cases.

Birth Plan

I am looking forward to the birth of my first child, and I have written down a few of my ideas on how I hope my labor will progress.

1. **Support person** – My partner, Dan, will be with me throughout the birth.
2. **Monitoring** – I understand that you routinely do a 20-minute electronic fetal monitoring session, which is fine. If all is well, I would like the baby to be monitored from then on with intermittent monitoring.
3. **Positions** – I don't think I will want to be restricted to the bed, and would welcome the use of other active birth aids.
4. **Pain relief** – If necessary, I may request pain medication. I hope not to need narcotics or an epidural, although in the event of a cesarean section, I would like to have epidural anesthesia so I can be awake for the birth.
5. **Amniotomy** – I would prefer not to have my membranes ruptured artificially.
6. **Episiotomy** – I would prefer to tear naturally than be cut.

Maria Peters

Your birth plan
Have two copies of your birth plan with you when you go into labor. Give one to your healthcare provider and keep one for your reference.

comfort aids **for labor**

In addition to the basic items you've brought to the hospital, you may like to have some other things for your comfort. Check with the doctor when you visit the maternity unit about whether you can bring extra items. These might include:
♦ soothing images for use in labor, such as photographs of loved ones, or relaxing places you've visited on vacation

♦ an extra pillow or pillows
♦ a CD player and CDs of relaxing music, plus spare batteries
♦ a cassette player and books on tape plus spare batteries
♦ a thick pair of socks
♦ a hot water bottle for pain relief
♦ a journal
♦ a big box of tissues
♦ lip balm
♦ a spray bottle, filled with cool water to spray your face.

what your **partner needs**

Your partner will need:
♦ a change of clothing
♦ drinks and snacks
♦ change for the public telephone or a phone card – you cannot use your cellular telephone inside the hospital because it can interfere with equipment
♦ telephone numbers for friends and family to let them know the good news
♦ camera and film, or video camera (check if video cameras are permitted)
♦ wipes to refresh hands and face
♦ a bag with basic toiletries.

labor

This is the culmination of the last precious months. Going into labor is exciting – once it's underway you know it can't be long before you hold your baby. On the following pages you will find suggestions for a variety of positions for labor that you might like to discuss with your caregiver.

going into labor

Many couples worry they won't recognize the early stages of labor, and will end up with a rush to the hospital or an unplanned home delivery. This does happen, but it is very rare.

It is far more common for couples to arrive on the labor floor thinking their birth is minutes away, only to find there are hours to go.

Knowing the signs

If you are tuned in to your body in the days and weeks leading up to the time your baby is due, you'll probably be able to spot some of the signs that your body is preparing for labor. However, be warned, this prelabor stage can last for two, three, or even more weeks, so don't be surprised if things don't happen quickly.
♦ A nesting instinct – the urge to rush around getting your house in order before the baby appears.
♦ Change in movement pattern. This is because there's now less space in your uterus, but also the baby seems to get a little quieter just before you go into labor. Talk to your obstetrician or midwife if you're concerned that your baby is moving a lot less than usual.
♦ In the days before the birth it is normal to lose 2–3lb (900g–1.4kg).
♦ You may experience slight diarrhea. This is your body's way of clearing out the bowel so it doesn't interfere with the birth.

♦ You might have a show. The plug of mucus and blood that has blocked the cervix throughout your pregnancy is expelled now that the cervix is opening to let the baby through. You may notice it on your underwear or when you go to the bathroom. If you are bleeding a lot, enough to need a pad, tell your doctor or midwife.
♦ When you see a fictional birth on television or in a movie it always seems to start with a woman's water breaking, but in real life this is a less common start to labor. If it happens, tell your doctor or midwife because most caregivers prefer the baby to be born within 24–48 hours of your membranes being ruptured since the baby can be at risk of infection without his protective amniotic sac.
♦ You may have weeks of prelabor or Braxton Hicks contractions. They tend to be quite variable, sometimes coming

Timing your contractions
When your contractions start, time them from the beginning of one contraction to the beginning of the next.

established **labor**

♦ Signs include at least two to four contractions every 10 minutes. These may feel like bad menstrual cramps.

♦ The amount of pain you may experience during the first stage of labor varies enormously between women.

♦ Most mothers agree it's easiest to cope with the pain if you continue with your normal life for as long as possible.

♦ Walking around doing ordinary activities keeps you moving, which seems to help the cervix to open.

every 20 to 30 minutes, or even at five to 10 minute intervals for a short time, then stopping abruptly. Contractions of actual labor often start like severe cramps, with pain radiating down your legs as well as in your back and abdomen. Real labor contractions get stronger, last longer, and become more frequent.

When to go to the hospital

Once you know you are in labor, you need to decide when to go to the hospital. However, it can be disappointing to arrive at the hospital thinking you're about to give birth only to discover that your cervix is only slightly dilated. A first labor can last up to 12 hours or more, and it is often better to spend several hours of this time at home. The following factors may help you decide when to go to the hospital:
♦ if your contractions are occurring five minutes apart or closer
♦ if you feel you need help to get through the pain of the contractions
♦ if your water breaks or you are bleeding.
  If you're in any doubt, call the doctor or midwife and explain your symptoms.

Arriving at the hospital

If you can, call your doctor or midwife before you leave home to let the hospital know that you are on your way. Once you arrive at the hospital, your doctor or midwife will discuss your symptoms and your birth plan (see page 67). Your temperature, blood pressure, and pulse will be taken, and your urine will be tested for blood, protein, and sugar.

  Hospitals sometimes monitor the baby's heart rate using a fetal monitor for about 20 minutes when you arrive. During this you will need to lie still on the bed. If all is well you should be able to be active, but monitored intermittently for the rest of the birth.

  Continuous monitoring may be needed if there are complications. Your doctor or midwife will then give you an internal examination to check how your cervix is progressing, and you can ask how far you are dilated. If you are concerned about anything or unsure about any procedures, let your caregivers know as soon as possible.

pain relief

Don't assume you'll necessarily need a lot of pain relief when you're in labor; some women do, some don't, and it's partly dependent on whether you've given birth before and on the position your baby is in for the delivery. But here are some options you'll want to consider:

♦ **Massage** This can be done by your partner and/or midwife. Massage of the lower back in particular can be a big help. Other tension points include your temples, scalp, shoulders, and soles of your feet. Make sure you're very specific about what you want and when.

♦ **Moving around and distraction techniques** Remaining active and moving around, both at home and once you reach the hospital or birth center, can take your mind off the pain of the contractions and also helps your body to use them to maximum effect. Movement also speeds

labor. Try walking, kneeling, swaying, or rocking. Distraction means using some device, such as visualization, or counting backward from 100 at each contraction, to try to blot out the pain.

♦ **Baths and showers** Warm water, in the form of a bath or shower, can soothe weary muscles, lessen tensions, and may ease contractions for many women in labor. Doctors and midwives usually recommend soaking during late active labor and transition. Make sure to have a stool in the shower; you might want to sit on it to save your strength and energy.

♦ **Narcotic medications** These kind of medications inhibit your brain's perception of pain. They shouldn't be given too close to the birth, though, because they can make the baby sleepy, which can sometimes interfere with his ability to breathe at delivery.

the first stage

During the first stage of labor, the cervix opens up to allow the baby's head to move into the birth canal. This stage is usually the longest. The contractions you feel are working to thin out (efface) and open up (dilate) the cervix.

If this is your first baby, this stage will probably take about 10 to 12 hours. Subsequent labors are often quicker, although every labor is different. Near the end of this stage, contractions become longer and stronger.

How you'll feel

No matter how confident you may feel in advance, don't be surprised if you feel a little scared at some point. The power of the uterus is awesome, and it can be daunting to feel you have been taken over by a process you can't control. Don't try to fight your labor. Allow your body to do its work, but don't be afraid to ask for support or pain relief if you need it.

Sitting forward
This is a good way to stay upright while resting. Rest on plenty of pillows so that you are comfortable. This is especially useful if you become very tired.

epidural **anesthesia**

This numbs the nerves in your spine to block out the pain of labor. This sort of pain relief can be restricting because it can stop you from moving around, and it may also increase your chance of needing an assisted delivery, but it is a very effective pain reliever. It can be used for a cesarean section as well as during a vaginal delivery.

Vertebra   Epidural space   Spinal cord

Syringe attachment   Hollow needle

"I went into labor in the evening. I was considering going to the hospital at 10 pm, but in fact we didn't actually go there until about 6 am the following morning – and the baby was eventually born at 3 pm! I was delighted to hear that I was already halfway to being fully dilated when I arrived, but then it all slowed down for a while. I think that was because I was adjusting to being in a new place."

JANET SIMPSON, 26,
MOTHER OF ALEX AGE 5 WEEKS

Your birth partner and the staff are there to help you and your baby. If you decide you need pain relief, try waiting 10–15 minutes before you actually request it. Things can change quickly in labor, and you may be more comfortable by then. You may be surprised by how much you rely on your birth partner for support during the birth, no matter how independent you usually are.

Your doctor or midwife will give you regular internal examinations. Ask how things are progressing. It can be reassuring to know that labor is moving forward.

dilatation of **the cervix**

The muscles of the uterus contract, pulling the cervix back and stretching it to allow the baby's head to pass through. Once no more cervical "lip" can be felt, the first stage of labor is complete; you have reached "full dilatation."

Hormone changes soften the cervix, which is still closed.

The cervix thins (effaces) and begins to stretch and open.

The cervix is fully dilated when it is 4in (10cm) open.

Positions for first-stage labor

During the first stage, try a variety of positions to see what feels comfortable.

♦ Try to stay upright because this presses the baby's head against the cervix, making your contractions more effective.
♦ Move around between contractions to ease the pain, but try to stay relaxed.
♦ Use the breathing techniques you learned in childbirth class.
♦ Do not feel inhibited about making noise if that helps you.
♦ Deal with each contraction one at a time, as it happens.

Back massage
You may find this helps alleviate backache, especially if your baby is facing toward your abdomen. Talcum powder or massage oil will help prevent friction if you are being massaged straight onto your skin. This position can also be comfortable for transition (see opposite).

Leaning
Your partner can support your body weight and massage your lower back if you wish. This position is ideal if you are walking around between contractions.

the second stage

Once the cervix is fully dilated, you move into what's known as the second stage of labor, when your body will push your baby out into the world.

Contractions in the second stage of labor feel different from the first stage because they're the feelings that compel you to bear down, or push, to help your baby out. This stage is longer for a first baby.

Transition

Moving from the first to the second stage of labor is known as "transition." It can last for a few minutes to an hour or more. For a lot of women it's a time of confusion. Suddenly having felt aware of what you were doing, you may feel unsure whether you can complete the task.

Kneeling
Squatting or kneeling positions allow the pelvis to open wide and use gravity to help you push the baby out. Kneeling on all fours can also be comfortable.

Sitting upright
Ask for extra pillows to prop you up if you wish. This position allows you to relax back onto the pillows between contractions.

labor support

Transition can be a tough time for you as the birth partner, especially if this is your first baby. This is the time when both you and the mother need the support of an experienced caregiver. Whether or not you've been helping the mother physically during the first stage of labor, your help may be required now to get her into a comfortable position for the second stage.

If you suffer from any kind of back problems, be careful not to injure yourself supporting her. She may want you to have cool washcloths or a face spray ready for her head between contractions. The second stage is hard, physical work. It's encouraging to be told when the head is visible, so keep an eye out for the first glimpse of your tiny daughter or son!

"Like a lot of first-time dads, I had little knowledge of what to expect. I was worried for my wife, and was afraid she was in too much pain, although when we talked about it afterward she said it was never more than she could cope with. I tried to focus on her and her needs and give her my attention."

MALCOLM STONE, 34,
FATHER OF EWAN AGE 6 MONTHS

Or it may be that your labor so far has been long and difficult, and you can't believe even more is expected of you. There may be slightly unpleasant physical symptoms during transition, too. Some mothers-to-be feel nauseous or even vomit, and others shiver. This is the stage when a lot of support is needed. You may want to be held by your partner, or you may want to be left alone, but it usually helps if there's someone there to remind you that you're doing well.

Supported leg
Prop yourself on cushions, then get your partner to support your leg while you push, this enables you to lie down without working against gravity.

Kneeling on all fours
Keep your hips below your shoulders and your legs wide apart. Rocking your hips from side to side may ease backache.

episiotomy

Episiotomies are no longer routine for first-time mothers, but they are not uncommon. A cut is made at the entrance to the vagina as your baby is being born so that you can push your baby out without tearing. There is a wide range of opinions on whether it's best to have an episiotomy or tear naturally: some experts claim that a tear heals more effectively. You should discuss the possibility of an episiotomy beforehand with your caregiver. One may be necessary if, for example, you need an assisted delivery. The best way to avoid either an episiotomy or a tear is to talk to your doctor or midwife about positions for delivery, and follow her instructions when the baby's head crowns.

your baby's descent **through the pelvis**

During the second stage, your baby is pushed through the bony structure of your pelvis and your birth canal.

♦ The baby's heartbeat may slow intermittently as you push during contractions, but this usually isn't a problem. Your nurse or caregiver will check on the heartbeat between contractions.

♦ As her head becomes level with your perineum, she'll be visible for the first time to your partner and the midwife or obstetrician, even if not to you. Ask for a mirror if you don't want to miss this moment yourself.

♦ She'll then disappear back into the birth canal between contractions for a while.

Eventually her head will remain at the edge of your vagina between contractions. This is "crowning." The nurse or midwife may tell you not to push to allow the tissues to stretch enough to avoid a tear.

The head is usually born facedown. Your midwife or doctor will check that the umbilical cord isn't looped around her neck. The baby turns her head to the side instinctively to take her first breath.

With the next two or three contractions her shoulders will be born and in another push her legs and bottom will be out, too. Ask if she can be put on your stomach immediately.

meeting **your baby**

Once your baby is born, the doctor or midwife will watch to make sure that she breathes quickly, and if she also cries or moves around, which is an extra sign that everything is fine. But if you've given birth in an upright or active position, you're the first person who'll be able to touch and hold her; often the feel of your hand on her back will stimulate her to take her first few breaths and fill her lungs with oxygen for the first time.

You may be a bit surprised by her appearance. She may still be covered in vernix, the greasy creamlike substance that coated her skin in the womb, or she may be bloody. Her face may be bright red or even blue, or it may look bruised from the delivery. A newborn baby doesn't look much like a baby who is a few weeks old, so be prepared.

You may be filled with love for this little person that you have waited to meet for so long, or you may simply feel overwhelmed by the whole experience. Lie back with your baby and congratulate yourself. You deserve it.

Your first family moments
For you and your partner, it's like taking part in a miracle: the baby you've given life to is here, and the adventure of parenthood has begun after all those months of waiting. At a distance of about 8–10in (20–25cm) she can see your face clearly and she will soon recognize your voice from the sounds she heard inside your uterus. Your baby will probably be weighed along with other routine procedures, but make sure both you and your partner have a chance to hold her and get to know your new baby. You can request that interruptions be kept to a minimum.

the third stage

The baby's arrival marks the end of the second stage of labor, but there's a third – the delivery of the placenta. Once the baby has been born, the doctor or midwife will place a hand on your abdomen and gently pull on the cord to ease the placenta out – they may ask you to push at the same time, but the hard work of delivery has now passed.

The placenta may slip effortlessly out of the vagina very soon after the baby arrives. This third stage of labor may be left to occur naturally since sometimes the placenta is expelled through conractions alone.

what to expect

It may take up to half an hour before the placenta arrives. You can help speed things up by breastfeeding your baby because the sucking action stimulates your uterus to contract, thereby helping to expel the placenta (if your baby isn't ready to suck, stimulating your nipples with your fingers will have the same effect).

The doctor or midwife may feel your abdomen to make sure the placenta has separated and may apply pressure or massage your belly to help the process along. You may be asked to push if necessary. The soft tissue that forms the placenta weighs about a pound and delivering it is painless. After you deliver the placenta, your doctor or midwife will examine it to make sure all of it has been expelled and will repair an episiotomy or perineal tear if necessary. You may also be given oxytocin, in your IV or by injection, to prevent bleeding after the placenta is expelled. Breastfeeding your baby may also prevent excessive bleeding.

birth procedures

During your labor you may require some medical help to bring your baby safely into the world. This ranges from routine procedures that give your caregivers the best possible insight into your baby's progress, to special treatments to give you both a little extra help if you need it. As part of your preparations for labor, make sure you understand what these procedures are and why they are performed.

types of medical help

Find out in advance what the routine is where you will be giving birth, and talk through all the possibilities with your caregivers.

No one can predict exactly what will happen when you go into labor, so learn as much about it as you can now.

Fetal monitoring

Fetal monitoring is routine for hospital deliveries, although how you are monitored, and for how long does vary. The baby can be monitored intermittently using a stethoscope or doppler, or continuously using electronic fetal monitoring. Some hospitals perform a 15–20 minute "admission strip" routinely.

You will be asked to sit or lie on the bed, and a belt will be placed around your abdomen. This records your baby's heartbeat via a printout, allowing your caregiver to monitor your baby's reaction to labor. Once your water has broken, the heartbeat can be monitored by attaching an electrode directly to the baby's scalp. This gives a very accurate reading, but it means that you will not be able to move around during labor. You may be offered continual monitoring if:
♦ your labor is induced
♦ you have an epidural
♦ you have had a high-risk pregnancy
♦ the baby is premature
♦ your baby appears to be stressed.
Ask why continual monitoring has been recommended. It could be because your caregivers have a reason to be concerned, or simply a matter of routine.

During the second stage of labor your midwife or doctor can use a handheld ultrasound to check the baby's heartbeat.

Episiotomy

An episiotomy (see page 72) is a surgical cut that is made to help the baby emerge from the vagina at the birth. You may need an episiotomy if:
♦ your baby is breech or has a large head
♦ your baby is in distress
♦ you have an assisted delivery (although it is not always necessary for a vacuum delivery)
♦ you cannot control your pushing, or the tissues have not stretched enough.

If you have strong feelings against this, talk to your caregivers beforehand.

breech **babies**

The majority of babies (about 97 percent) are head-down in the uterus by week 34 or 35. But a small proportion of babies are bottom-down, or breech, and remain that way. The obstetrician or midwife may try to turn the baby externally (see page 51). This technique is performed using ultrasound guidance. You may be advised to spend time in the knee-chest position, or on all-fours to encourage the baby to turn naturally. It is not painful, nor does it require anesthesia. If this hasn't happened by the time labor is imminent, your healthcare providers will probably suggest that you strongly consider opting for a cesarean section. A recent multinational study showed that a cesarean section in this case, is the safest option.

Complete breech
The legs are flexed against the body and the buttocks are the presenting part.

Frank breech
The baby's buttocks are presenting and the arms may be wrapped around the legs.

Footling breech
The feet are resting on the cervix. They will drop down once the membranes have ruptured.

An assisted delivery

This involves the assistance of medical instruments, such as forceps or a vacuum cup. Forceps are like tongs that fit around the baby's head and enable the obstetrician to ease the baby out of the birth canal. A vacuum cup fits onto the baby's head, a tube from the cup builds up a vacuum and the doctor can then pull as you push to help speed up the delivery. An assisted delivery is more likely if you have an epidural, or if this is a high-risk pregnancy.

Baby's head

Forceps

Forceps delivery
Forceps resemble large, separate tongs. They fit snugly over the baby's head and protect it as it progresses through the birth canal. Once the head has been delivered, the forceps are removed and the rest of the delivery can progress. Forceps delivery requires some form of local anesthetic (e.g., epidural or spinal).

induction

If you have not given birth by 41 weeks you may have special tests and induction may be suggested. This means your labor will be started artificially.

There shouldn't be any need for an immediate induction, unless your healthcare provider fears that your placenta isn't functioning properly; there are tests to check that your baby is thriving. Induction is usually urged more strongly at 42 weeks because there is evidence that some babies are at risk after this stage due to a gradual decrease in the efficiency of the placenta.

Membrane sweep

You may be offered this at your 41-week appointment. You'll be given an internal examination during which your caregiver will assess whether your cervix is softening in preparation for labor. The midwife or doctor will then gently push back the membranes adjacent to the cervix in the hope that this will stimulate the uterus to start contracting in the next few hours or days.

Amniotomy

This is also known as AROM (artificial rupture of membranes). A sterile, plastic, thin hook is brushed against the membranes just inside your cervix. Once the waters have been ruptured, the baby's head will move down against the cervix, which usually means contractions become stronger and more effective. Amniotomy is often used to speed up labor, in addition to starting it. Although it may shorten labor, it may also make it more painful.

Starting labor with drugs

Prostaglandin inserted directly into the vagina, using tablets, a gel, or a small "tampon" on a string, is usually tried first. Prostaglandin is found naturally in your body and it helps to stimulate contractions. Prostaglandin can be used to ripen the cervix for several hours or days. If this doesn't work, you'll probably be advised to have oxytocin, which is a synthethic version of the hormone that stimulates the uterus to contract. You will have an IV, and your movement may be limited as a result. Contractions can be very strong.

cesarean **section**

If you have a planned, or "elective," cesarean section you will have had time to adjust to the idea. However, if you need an emergency cesarean you may feel disappointed, or even cheated of the birth you had planned. Remember that the most important thing is the safety of you and your baby. Ask why you are being offered a surgical delivery because this can help minimize any negative feelings.

A cesarean section can be done under an epidural, spinal, or general anesthetic, although for some unplanned operations general anesthetic may be necessary. Ask if your partner can be with you throughout.

If you have an epidural or spinal, a screen is set up between you and the surgeon. The birth of your baby takes about five minutes and you can hold your baby while the placenta is delivered and you are stitched up.

The bikini incision
If you have a surgical delivery, the incision will be made just above the line of your pubic hair. When the incision heals, the scar is very discreet.

after the birth

The moment you and your partner have longed for is finally here, and your baby is in your arms at last. How do you feel? There's no right or wrong way to feel immediately after the birth. This is a time of transition, and your life has just changed in a huge way. It's going to take you and your partner awhile to work through the maze of emotions you may be feeling.

how you'll feel

You might feel exhilarated, excited, joyful, and delighted, and if so that's wonderful. However, not everyone has that response immediately, and you may find your feelings swing wildly in the next few days.

You may feel exhausted and want just to lie down and sleep, or you may feel a surge of energy and stay up all night, despite having had several hours of labor.

Becoming parents

The emotional response to having a baby is complicated in the hours and days after the birth. Many parents swing from feeling on top of the world one minute, to feeling low the next. You may feel a twinge of disappointment that you've had a boy when you wanted a girl, or vice versa, or you may feel a bit sad that the pregnancy is over and the real responsibility of parenting now weighs upon you.

You and your partner may feel closer than you've ever been, or you may both feel scared by the awesome change that this tiny new person has brought into your lives and your relationship. The important thing is to communicate with each other and to take each moment as it comes.

Your baby's first hours

♦ All your baby has ever known is the inside of your uterus, so birth certainly marks a huge change in life for him! What he'll need in the first minutes and

apgar **score**

One minute after he's born, and at five minutes after birth, five simple tests are done to ascertain how healthy your baby is. The tests measure:

♦ heart rate

♦ breathing

♦ muscle tone

♦ skin color

♦ reflex response.

For each test a score of 2, 1, or 0 is recorded, with 2 being entirely healthy and 0 an absence of response. Most babies score between 7 and 10 out of 10. If necessary, the tests are repeated at the 10-minute mark to see if the baby's responses have improved.

newborn tests

Shortly after the birth, your baby will have a number of routine tests in addition to the Apgar tests (see above). He will be weighed, the circumference of his head will be measured, and he will be checked for abnormalities. Although it can be upsetting to have your new baby taken away from you, this preliminary examination takes only a few minutes, and your baby will be in the hands of an experienced nurse or doctor.

Listening to the heart and lungs
It is not uncommon for newborn babies to have a heart murmur and this does not necessarily indicate that your baby will have a problem.

Feeling the abdomen
The doctor checks that all the internal organs are the correct size. He will also feel the pulses in your baby's groin.

neonatal **intensive care unit (NICU)**

About one in 10 newborn babies spends time in the neonatal intensive care unit (NICU). Many of these babies have been born prematurely, before 37 weeks of pregnancy, but NICUs aren't just for small or premature newborns. Sometimes babies born to diabetic mothers, for example, who may be quite large, are admitted to the unit for observation or because they need help. A stay in the NICU is always a concern for parents, but it's often not a long-term situation; a baby may be admitted for just a few hours.

If your baby is transferred to the NICU after the delivery, you'll be taken there to see him as soon as is practical. Your partner may be able to go to see the baby right away, and can return to you with information about what's going on and maybe a photograph. Information about your baby's health will be

extremely important to you both, and the hospital will do everything it can to keep you up to date on your baby's progress.

If your baby has a stay of a few days or even weeks in the NICU, you'll be encouraged to spend time there with him as soon as you're well enough yourself. You may be

discharged from the hospital's postpartum ward, so you'll be going home without your baby. This is a heartwrenching situation, but try to remember that your baby is in the best possible place.

You'll be shown how to do as much as possible for your baby. You should be able to help wash and dress him, hold his hands and, depending on how well he is and whether he's on a ventilator (breathing machine) or not, you may be able to take him out of his incubator to give him cuddles. You'll also be encouraged to express breast milk, probably using an electric breast pump, so he can be given your milk by tube or maybe a bottle. If he's not on a ventilator, you should also have opportunities to hold him close to you and your breast so he gets used to the idea of feeding directly from the breast.

hours of life is lots of close contact with you. Just as you will realize that you know this little person absolutely, so he will realize he knows you, too. Now he needs to get to know your scent, your face, your skin, your touch. He'll relish every moment he can spend close to you, so cuddle him and hold him close.
♦ Immediately after the birth is an important time for you to get to know your baby, so unless there are health concerns, you'll probably be given time

to spend together as a family.
♦ After the delivery of the placenta, your caregiver will examine your perineum to see if you need stitches. If you do need stitches, make sure you ask for pain relief.
♦ You'll be encouraged to put your baby to your breast in the first half hour or hour after the birth. Research shows that the earlier you breastfeed, the better the chances are of the baby latching on easily and breastfeeding going well.

♦ Don't worry if the baby doesn't show a lot of interest yet in the breast. If you had any drugs during labor these may make him drowsy, or the effort of being born may mean he is sleepy. Many babies who go on to breastfeed happily for many months take awhile to get started.
♦ The birthing room should be warm enough that you don't have to put clothes on either of you right away. Skin-to-skin contact is a great way to welcome your baby into the world.

Moving the hips and limbs
The legs and arms are moved to check alignment and length, and the doctor will also make sure the hips are not dislocated.

Checking the spine
The doctor or midwife will run a finger along the baby's back to see if the vertebrae are all in place.

losing your baby

The loss of a baby just before or at birth is one of the hardest things that a parent has to deal with. It's very rare, thankfully, but if it does happen to you, you'll need time and space to talk about how you feel with sympathetic people. It helps to get to know other people who have gone through the same experience. Many hospitals now have special bereavement counselors to offer support to both you and your partner. You'll be encouraged to both see and hold your baby, and to do as much as you can to help build up a store of memories. For example, you may want to keep a photgraph or a lock of hair as a keepsake.

the postpartum period

How you feel depends on a lot of things, but the most important is how the birth went. In the days after the birth you and your partner will get to know your baby, and you will need to begin to recover from the effort of pregnancy and birth.

starting family life

Women who've sailed through labor often feel elated, while for those whose experiences were not so straightforward can take longer to recover from the birth. But remember, in time you will be feeling good and enjoying your new life as a mother.

Recovery isn't just about getting over the birth physically (although that is obviously very important). It's also about working through often complex psychological issues brought up by labor and delivery. Your first step in dealing with both physical and psychological recovery is to have the support of a doctor or midwife you know and trust: this is a new mother's basic right, and hopefully you have it right now.

Communicating

Talk to your doctor or midwife about anything that's bothering you after the birth, and go through the details of your baby's birth with her. Talking things through with your birth partner is also important.

Adjusting to your new life

The hours and weeks after a baby is born are a time of big hormonal changes within a woman's body, and these can impact on how you're feeling physically and psychologically. But a lot more than "your hormones" are responsible for how you feel. Don't underestimate the huge upheaval your life is going through now, and not just your life but that of your partner as well. Changes in your life may seem exciting, or daunting, or horrifying: whichever way you view them, though, they're certainly significant.

Building a routine

Put a framework into your day as soon as possible. For many new mothers the first few weeks are eased by the presence of a partner on paternity leave, and perhaps a nearby mother, sister, or friend. Eventually, though, you'll be on your own with the baby, and you will need the support of friends whose situation is similar to yours. Contact women from your childbirth class, join a postpartum exercise or yoga class, or start a mother and baby group of your own.

postpartum **depression**

♦ A majority of new moms experience mild depressive symptoms, but only one in 10 develop postpartum depression.

♦ It can make you feel low, unsure of yourself, exhausted, vulnerable, extra-sensitive, and unable to make decisions.

♦ The warning signs of postpartum depression include persistent depression and thoughts of harming yourself or your baby.

♦ Depression can be difficult to recognize in yourself. Talk to your partner, your doctor, your midwife, a family member, or anyone else who's supporting you.

postpartum care

In the hours and days after the birth, your obstetrician or midwife will examine you on a regular basis. You can also help your body recover by doing some gentle exercise.

Your obstetrician or midwife will ask you questions about how your perineum feels; the amount of lochia, or vaginal bleeding, you're experiencing; whether you're urinating; and about your bowel movements. You'll be asked how your breasts feel and whether they're engorged; and whether your nipples are painful during or after feeding your baby.

If you experience heavy bleeding or pass a heavy blood clot; if you have any bleeding that smells unusual; if you have any difficulty urinating; or if you have chest pains, swollen legs, or a fever, don't hesitate to call your doctor or midwife, even if you have already seen her that day.

getting back into shape

If you practice your exercises every day, your figure will gradually return. It is very important to take things gently to begin with.

Do not attempt any vigorous exercise until your bleeding has stopped. Exercise a little and often, and always stop if you feel any pain. If you had a cesarean section, do not attempt any exercise (other than Kegel exercises and foot pedaling) until after you have had a checkup six weeks after the birth. Ask your doctor or midwife for advice if you have any questions about which exercises are suitable.

Kegel exercises

These exercises, which can be done from day one after the birth, will help strenghen your pelvic-floor muscles.

If you did Kegel exercises during pregnancy, it shouldn't be hard to start them again as soon as you are able. You can also do Kegel exercises if you had a cesarean section.

Pull in and tense your pelvic-floor muscles as if you were holding back urine. Hold for as long as you comfortably can then relax gradually. Repeat 10 times.

Gentle stomach toner
For the first week, just gently pull in your abdominal muscles as you breathe out, hold for a few seconds then relax.
After this, if you feel well enough, lie on the floor with your head and shoulders supported and your knees bent. Lift your head and shoulders as you breathe out. Hold for a few seconds, then relax. Repeat three times. Practice twice a day.

Foot pedaling
Pedal your feet up and down from the ankle to improve your circulation and prevent swelling. Practice hourly. Do this from day one.

Diagonal reach
Lift your head and shoulder and reach across to the opposite ankle. Lie back and rest, then repeat on the other side.

Side bend
Keep your hips facing forward and reach down as far as you comfortably can, moving slowly and smoothly. Rest your hand on the side of your leg.

Side leg lift
Keeping both legs in line with your hip and shoulder, raise the upper leg to shoulder height and then lower. This tones the hips and thighs.

Cat stretch
This will help to strengthen your back. Begin with your back straight, then arch your back slowly upward, like a cat. Stop if you feel any discomfort.

baby and child care

Caring for a baby or child is demanding, and routine tasks can be downright baffling to begin with. This section contains reassuring advice on how to handle and care for your new baby so that soon you will gain the confidence to care for her in a way that's safe and enjoyable for you both. There is also advice on how to handle your child's emerging independence, as well as a discussion of childcare choices if you will be returning to work.

caring for your newborn
birth to 6 weeks

You will spend many hours delighting in your newborn. Every baby is unique. Knowing what to expect – from her cry to the shape of her head to the touch of her skin – will help you feel confident about caring for her.

Meeting your baby

If you have an uneventful labor and delivery, you will be given your baby to hold as soon as she is born. One of your first questions will probably be "Is she all right?" and within the first few hours, medical staff will give her a thorough examination to reassure you that everything is fine. Before your baby leaves the delivery room, ID bands will be placed on both you and your baby.

What to expect

Healthy newborns come in all shapes and sizes but share certain characteristics:

♦ **Head** Your baby's head may look slightly misshapen – especially if her delivery was assisted by vacuum or forceps. This is because the soft bones that make up the skull are designed to give under pressure in order to pass through the birth canal. You may also notice a pulse beating under the fontanelles (soft spots in your baby's skull).

♦ **Skin** Your baby may be covered in a greasy substance called vernix, which acts as a protective barrier. She may also look slightly blue until her breathing becomes more regular and her circulation improves.

♦ **Hair** At birth, some babies are still covered in a fine layer of downy hair, known as lanugo. This falls off during the first week.

♦ **Body** Your baby's breasts and genitals may look swollen because of the hormones you have passed on to her via the placenta before birth. The swelling will go down in a few days.

checking **her reflexes**

From the time she is born, your newborn has an incredible range of skills and reflexes that will help her survive. Several of these reflexes will be tested by your healthcare professional to check that your baby's central nervous system is functioning well.

♦ **Sucking, rooting, and swallowing reflex** Your baby's most basic reflexes include sucking, which she will have practiced in the womb. She will also instinctively turn her head towards the touch of a breast or finger on her cheek near her mouth as she searches for food – this is known as rooting. Swallowing is also a reflex action.

♦ **Startle reflex** Also known as the Moro reflex, if your baby's head is not supported when she is held she will throw out her arms and legs with her fingers extended. This reflex usually disappears by about two months.

♦ **Stepping reflex** If your baby is held upright with her feet touching a firm surface, she will automatically make stepping movements. This reflex usually disappears at about one month.

♦ **Protective reflexes** Although your baby may appear to be utterly defenseless, she actually has several protective reflexes. For example, if a blanket or pillow falls over her eyes, nose, or mouth, she'll move her head from side to side and flail her arms to push it away so she can breathe and see. Or if an object comes straight toward her she'll turn her head and try to squirm out of its way.

♦ **Tonic neck reflex** You may notice that when your baby's head turns to one side, her arm on that side will straighten, with the opposite arm bent as if she is fencing. Do not be surprised if you don't see this response, however. It is subtle, and if your baby is disturbed or crying, she may not do it. This reflex disappears at five to seven months of age.

♦ **Grasping reflex (see left)** Place a finger in her palm and your baby will automatically grab hold of it.

getting to know your newborn

He looks tiny and fragile, but your baby is sturdier than you think. Learning to handle him safely and confidently will help you enjoy close physical contact – one of the most powerful ways you can get to know your newborn.

the first few days

After months of carrying your baby and wondering about him, he's finally here, cradled in your arms.

The first few days with him will be an emotional time for both you and your partner. Your feelings will be many and varied, and may include the following:

♦ an incredible sense of wonder and pride at what you've produced

♦ overwhelming exhaustion as a result of labor and sleepless nights

♦ a feeling of connection so close that when your baby cries, you feel like crying, too

♦ tearfulness and confusion because of the huge hormonal shift occurring in your body.

As you get to know your newborn, your emotions will start to settle down. And one of the most rewarding ways of feeling close to your baby and bonding with him is through physical contact – by touching your baby, holding him, cuddling him, stroking his skin, and feeling his skin against yours.

Holding and handling

Always approach your baby slowly and quietly. Before you even touch him, make your presence known through voice and/or eye contact. The gentle and caring way in which you handle your newborn will communicate your love to him – he adores being held in your arms.

He has barely any head control, and his head will flop uncomfortably if it's not held up. If it does flop back, your baby will feel as if he's going to fall and his whole body will jerk in fright. This is known as the startle or Moro reflex. Supporting your baby's head properly

when you hold him will help him feel safe and secure. Never jiggle or shake your baby's head.

♦ When picking up your baby, either slip one hand under his neck and head and the other under his bottom before lifting him gently toward you, or lift him under the arms, using your fingers at the back of his neck to cradle his head.

♦ When carrying him, either cradle him in the crook of one arm with your free arm supporting his back and bottom or hold him against your chest with his head on your shoulder and your free arm supporting his back and head. Once you feel confident, and while he is still small, you can carry him using one hand.

new dads

For dads, the experience of becoming a parent is different, but just as intense as it is for moms.

New fathers may feel overwhelming tenderness toward their baby as well as an enormous sense of responsibility and anxiety about keeping this tiny person safe and secure. They may also feel excluded and jealous of all the attention given to their baby.

Spending time with their new baby – whether it involves soothing, dressing, changing diapers, carrying, or just cuddling – is very important for new fathers, helping them increase the feelings of closeness and intimacy and calming their natural fears and worries.

Holding a newborn
This grandfather picks up his new grandchild, slipping one hand under her neck and head and the other under her lower back and bottom, then lifting the baby toward him. When laying the baby in her crib, he makes sure he is supporting the baby's head with one hand and the lower part of her body with the other.

Safe handling
Make sure your hands are clean before changing your baby and remember to wash them after changing her diaper.

using **a sling**

Your baby loves being close to you, when he can feel your warmth and hear your heart beat. Carrying your baby in a sling or baby carrier will help you comfort him, rock him to sleep, or keep him close, as well as leaving your hands free for shopping or doing the chores. Choose a sling that's easy to put on and take off, comfortable to wear, and suitable for your partner, too.

Dressing your baby

Dressing a tiny baby without pulling and tugging is an art, but one you will quickly master. Relax and take your time – if you are calm, your baby will feel calm, too.

♦ Place your baby on a soft towel on a flat surface. Never leave your baby unattended, especially if the changing surface is higher than the floor. Select clothes that are easy to put on and remove.

♦ Stretch open the neck of his undershirt before gently easing it over his head.

♦ Reach into the sleeves to find your baby's arm, then pull the sleeve back over it rather than tugging his arm through.

Out and about

As soon as you feel ready, take your new baby out in a sling or a stroller (if the seat reclines flat). If you are taking him out in a car, you are required by law to secure your baby in a correctly installed rear-facing infant seat. Don't use the front of a car that has a safety airbag on the passenger side – if the airbag inflates, it could seriously injure your baby. The safest place for all children is in the backseat.

Meeting friends
As soon as you feel up to it, get out to meet other moms with babies of a similar age; this can quickly develop into a useful support system.

breastfeeding your baby

Breastfeeding can create a deeply fulfilling bond between you and your baby. Learning how to breastfeed takes practice. The more you do it, the easier it gets, and the more milk you will produce.

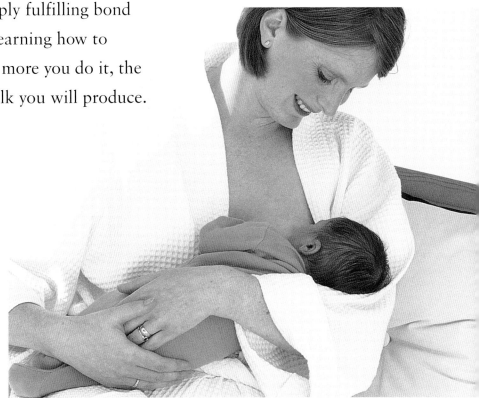

a good start

When she is breastfeeding, your baby loves the closeness and warmth of skin-to-skin contact, seeing your face and hearing your heart beat.

Breastfeeding is good for your baby because your milk gives her the best possible nourishment. Breast milk is the ideal food for your growing baby, with all the nutrients she needs in exactly the right amounts. It also contains antibodies that will help protect her against illness and infection, and it offers added protection against respiratory problems and allergy-related conditions, such as eczema and asthma.

Getting underway

To begin with, your breasts will produce colostrum – a golden-yellow fluid that starts your baby's digestive system and protects against infection. After a few days, your milk will come in.

♦ **Choose a comfortable position** You can feed your baby sitting or lying down. Use pillows and cushions to support your back

Preparing to nurse
Stroking your baby's cheek with your finger, close to her mouth, will encourage her to open her mouth wide to nurse.

latching **on**

Helping your baby latch on to your breast correctly is the key to successful breastfeeding. Stroke her cheek with your finger so that she opens her mouth wide. Move her toward your breast, aiming your nipple at the roof of her mouth. When she has a good mouthful she will close her mouth, forming a tight seal. She should have all of the nipple and as much of the areola (the pigmented ring around the nipple) as possible in her mouth – otherwise, she may tug on the nipple and make it sore. If you are unsure about her position, ease her off the breast (see opposite) and try again.

Feeding action
Your baby draws milk out of your breast by squeezing the nipple against the roof of her mouth and sucking.

Positioned for comfort
You will find the position that is most comfortable for you when breastfeeding. Some women find resting their baby on cushions helps bring her up to the breast, and leaning against a wall or chair can help support your back.

and arms, and to support your baby's head, back, and hips. If you are sitting, use a footstool to support your feet.

♦ **Hold your baby correctly** You and your baby should be tummy to tummy, with her nose opposite your nipple and her head and body in line – not crooked.

♦ **Help her latch on** Check her position – start again if you don't think she is latched on correctly (see opposite).

♦ **Watch for readiness** Your baby's sucking will stimulate your let-down reflex – the release of a hormone called oxytocin, which causes the milk glands in your breasts to release milk. When this happens, you will hear your baby swallowing. You may also feel a tingling sensation, contractions of your uterus, or you may leak milk from the opposite breast.

♦ **Ease her off the breast** Your baby may fall asleep once she's full and naturally come off your breast. Otherwise, don't pull her off the nipple. Instead, slide your pinky into the corner of her mouth to break the suction.

How many feedings?

For the first few weeks, your baby will want to be fed every few hours or so, spending between 10 and 20 minutes at each breast. She will let you know when she is hungry: feeding her on demand will keep her happy and help establish your milk supply. If possible, let her empty each breast before switching to the other (if you take her off too soon she'll nurse only on the watery foremilk and miss out on the rich hindmilk) and alternate which breast you start with to help keep up your milk supply.

Taking care of yourself

As you get the hang of breastfeeding you will realize you can do it anytime, anywhere – it's easy to be discreet if you wear loose tops or drape a scarf over your shoulder.

Don't forget to take care of yourself. Get plenty of rest – accept all offers of help and try to sleep whenever your baby sleeps. Eat well-balanced meals regularly during the day – it is essential to eat and drink enough.

after a **cesarean**

If you had a cesarean birth, your baby may feel drowsy as a result of the anesthesia and not be very interested in nursing right away. But encouraging her to breastfeed as she grows more alert will give her a good reason to wake up. Initially you may find it more comfortable to breastfeed lying down.

"Our first day at home Elsie nursed every hour. She sucked really hard, and my nipples became sore. A lactation consultant from our local hospital was wonderful: she showed me how to make sure Elsie was latching on properly, which made all the difference. Within a few days I could feed her comfortably and began to really enjoy the experience."

LINDA MORRELL, MOTHER OF ELSIE AGE 8 WEEKS

tips for success

When breastfeeding is going well, you will feel like the proudest mom on earth, but don't worry if it's challenging at first.

Remember that both you and your baby are learning a new skill – perfecting the art of breastfeeding can take time and patience.

Your emotions

In the first few weeks after birth you may be tired and emotional, making common tasks seem overwhelming. You may feel as if all you do is feed your baby because he demands food every couple of hours.

Try to persevere – as your baby learns how to suck more efficiently he'll go longer between feedings. By two months he'll need feeding only every four hours or so. Meanwhile, the hours spent nursing provide an ideal opportunity for you to get to know your baby and develop a deep connection.

Refusing the breast

There are many reasons why babies refuse the breast and most can be easily resolved.
♦ Your breasts may become so engorged (overfull, painful, and hard) that your baby has difficulty latching on. Relieve their fullness by putting a warm washcloth

on them or soaking them in a warm bath. You could also try expressing some milk.
♦ Your milk may be flowing so fast it causes him to gag. Express some milk to take the pressure off and reduce the flow.
♦ Your breast may be covering his nostrils, making breathing difficult – gently pull the breast back from his face.

♦ His nose may be stuffed up, making breathing difficult. Ask your healthcare professional for advice.

Sleeping through feedings

Some infants can get as much milk as they need during the first three to five minutes, and once full may fall asleep at the breast in

protecting **your breasts**

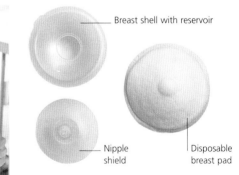

Breast shell with reservoir

Nipple shield

Disposable breast pad

If your breasts leak milk between feedings, you can protect your clothes and keep your nipples dry (which will help prevent soreness) by using absorbent breast pads, which fit neatly into your bra. Plastic breast shells can also be used – these have a reservoir to catch leaking milk. Nipple shields may be used temporarily while your baby is nursing to help protect sore or cracked nipples.

expressing **milk**

You may be breastfeeding, but that doesn't mean your partner or another caregiver can't feed your baby, too. After the first month or so you should be producing enough milk to express some into a bottle. You can store it in the refrigerator or freezer and use it when you need to have a break from nursing. There are two ways to express: by hand or with a breast pump. Expressing milk by hand can take longer than using a pump. If you choose to use a pump, there are a variety of products to buy or rent, ranging from hand- and battery-operated to electric pumps. Whichever method you opt for:

♦ wash your hands and nails before expressing

♦ help stimulate the flow by applying a warm washcloth to your breasts before you pump – looking at your baby or pictures of him may also help

♦ store the expressed milk for up to 24 hours in the refrigerator or, if you are away from home, in a cooler with ice packs.

Expressing by hand
Place a warm washcloth on your breast to help stimulate the let-down reflex. Then, with your fingers under your breast and your thumbs above, squeeze gently and rhythmically around the areola until the milk flows or squirts out. Repeat this action all around the breast.

a state of blissful contentment. If, however, he hasn't emptied your breast, you could gently wake him up after half an hour or so (changing his diaper will wake him) and offer him some more. If he's still hungry, he'll wake up and finish his feeding.

Unsettled feeding

If your baby seems fussy or unhappy during feeding and unable to settle into a gentle rhythm, he may be frustrated because he's not getting enough milk. This can happen if your baby isn't latched on properly. Take him off the breast, soothe him so he is calm, and then try latching him on again (see page 86).

Sore nipples

If your baby is not latching on to your breast properly or he pulls at your breast when he comes off, your nipples may become sore or cracked. There are several steps you can take to help prevent this from happening.

♦ Check your baby's position at every feeding – he should have the nipple and much of the areola in his mouth.

♦ Ease him off the breast gently when he's emptied each one.

♦ Make sure your nipples are dry before putting your bra back on, and keep them dry between feedings – use breast pads to soak up leaking milk or, if you leak a lot, use a plastic breast shell with a reservoir to collect the milk (see *protecting your breasts*, opposite). This milk can then be refrigerated or frozen, and given to your baby later in a bottle, if you wish.

If one of your nipples becomes sore or cracked, consult your doctor before using creams or lotions.

bottles and bottle-feeding

Once breastfeeding is well established, an occasional bottle will give mom
more freedom and allow dad, grandparents, sitters, and even older siblings
a chance to enjoy bonding with the baby during feedings.

happy feeding

Holding your baby close, gazing
into her eyes and talking soothingly
to her while she feeds from a bottle
will help you to feel close and bond
with her.

Keep bottle-feeding a loving occasion by:
♦ getting close – you can enjoy skin-to-
skin contact if you open or lift your shirt
and hold your baby close to your chest
♦ never leaving her with a bottle propped
up in her mouth – not only could your
baby choke, but she needs your affection
as much as she needs feeding
♦ stopping when she has had enough –
your baby knows when to stop, so you
shouldn't force her to finish a bottle.

Feeding techniques
♦ Warm up the milk before offering it
to your baby: run the bottle under warm
tap water or put it in a pan of warm
water. Do not use a microwave. Always
test several drops of the formula on the
back of your wrist to be sure it is warm,
but not too hot.

preparing formula

When you are preparing bottles of
formula, always follow the manufacturer's
instructions: the ratio of powder to water
is carefully calculated to give your baby
the optimum nutrition. You can prepare
one bottle or a batch of bottles at a time.
Keep the prepared milk in the back of the
refrigerator until needed (discard after
24 hours if it is not used).

♦ Gather together everything you need:
bottles, nipples and caps, plastic knife,
measuring scoop from formula container,
funnel, and pitcher.

♦ Use ordinary tap water or cooled, freshly
boiled water (refill the kettle each time you
prepare a new batch) and pour the correct
amount into a clean baby bottle.

♦ Measure the exact amount of formula
powder with the scoop provided, leveling
off with a knife.

♦ Add the powder to the water.

♦ Put the top on the bottle and shake
thoroughly until all the powder has dissolved.
Cool quickly by putting toward the back of
the refrigerator (not the door) while still hot.

♦ Keep the bottle tilted so that milk fills
the nipple and she doesn't draw in air.
♦ Tilt your baby slightly in your arms –
if she's lying flat, she'll find it difficult to
swallow and may gag on the milk.
♦ Burp her after an ounce or so (put
her on your shoulder or sit her on your
lap and pat her back gently to help her
release swallowed air).

How many feedings?
The best way to make sure your baby has
enough is to treat bottle-feeding just like
breastfeeding. Offer her the bottle whenever
she seems hungry and don't worry about
how much she takes. Your formula-fed baby
will be satisfied for longer than a baby fed
on breast milk – so she may be happy to
feed every three to four hours. Some babies,
however, will take less more often.

Your breast milk
Even just a few days of exclusive
breastfeeding after your baby
is born will give her a great
start: colostrum – the first
milk that your body produces –
is packed with important nutrients

that will help protect your baby against
infection during her first 72 hours of life.

Whether or not you are breastfeeding,
your breasts will become full of milk
between the second and fifth day after
giving birth. This can be uncomfortable, but
it is only temporary. If you don't breastfeed,
the milk will dry up within a few days.
Meanwhile, to help ease any discomfort:
♦ take hot showers or soak your breasts
in a hot bath
♦ ease the pressure by squeezing out a
few drops of milk
♦ put an ice pack on your breasts if you
are not breastfeeding
♦ wear a support bra that fits well.

Breast and bottle
It is possible to alternate breastfeeding and
bottle-feeding successfully once your milk
supply is established – some moms choose
to introduce formula at this point, while
others express their breast milk for their
baby to be fed from a bottle (see page 89).
There are a number of reasons why you may
want to combine breast- and bottle-feeding:
♦ giving a bottle means your partner can
share in the feeding

♦ you may be planning to return to work and need a caregiver to feed your baby while you are away.

The best time to introduce a bottle to your breastfed baby is after six weeks. By then your milk supply is well established and your baby is less likely to suffer from "nipple confusion" – breastfeeding and bottle-feeding require different sucking techniques. Introducing a bottle to an older baby can be difficult because by this age most babies prefer a soft, warm breast to a bottle nipple.

Some moms breastfeed first thing in the morning because it involves no preparation. And an evening breastfeed, after your baby's bath and before bedtime, can make you feel close. Bottle-feeding often works well during the day. Another option is to alternate between breast and bottle feedings.

When you first introduce a bottle, your breasts may feel uncomfortably full until they adjust to your new feeding routine. The process is gradual, but after a few days you will feel more comfortable.

cleaning bottles

To prevent your baby from getting sick, you need to clean her bottles carefully after each feeding. Always wash your hands before touching clean equipment.

If the local water supply is reliable, rinse the bottles and nipples separately and then wash them using hot, soapy water. Use a brush to make sure any deposits left in the bottles have been removed. Turn the nipples inside out and make sure the holes aren't blocked. Carefully rinse again in fresh water.

If the water supply is not reliable, wash the bottles and nipples, then put them in a large pot, cover with water, and boil for 10 minutes. All the items must be fully submerged during the boiling period. Use tongs to remove the hot bottles and allow them to cool before filling. Don't dry your clean bottles and nipples on a kitchen towel. Drain them on paper towels.

A dishwasher may be used to wash your bottles and nipples, especially if it has a hot cycle. However, rubber nipples will deteriorate quickly in the heat of a dishwasher.

Sharing the joy
Introducing your baby to bottles allows your partner to share in the joy and closeness of feeding.

taking care of your baby

Your newborn may seem so fragile that even a task such as changing a diaper can seem overwhelming at first. But don't worry, you will quickly become confident in taking care of your baby.

changing diapers

With up to 10 diaper changes a day, you'll quickly become an expert at keeping your baby comfortable and dry with a minimum of fuss.

Most mothers find disposable diapers easiest – they are convenient and super-absorbent. However, reusable cotton diapers also have advantages. You can buy them or use a diaper service that includes laundering. Some cotton diapers fasten with Velcro tabs or snaps, and don't require the use of a waterproof cover. In the long run, a diaper service may be cheaper, if less convenient, than using disposables.

What's in his diaper?
During the first day or so after birth your baby will pass greenish black sticky stools, known as meconium – a substance that lined his digestive sysem while he was in the womb. If you are breastfeeding, within a few days his stools will be yellow and soft. If you are formula feeding, his stools will be pale brown, more solid, and smellier.

Your newborn's urine may look slightly red at first – this is because of harmless substances called "urates," which look red on the diaper. Once the urine flow is established, he will urinate more frequently because his immature bladder is unable to hold fluids for any length of time.

If you have a newborn girl you may notice a tiny amount of vaginal bleeding. This is normal in the first week and is caused by hormones passed on to your baby from you before birth. A clear or whitish vaginal discharge is also normal and will stop after a few days.

YOU WILL NEED   CHANGING PAD • COTTON TOWEL • DIAPERS • DIAPER BAG • BABY WIPES

---

caring for the environment

Concern about the environment may make you think twice before buying disposable diapers for your baby. Disposables are not biodegradable and the 4,000 your baby will need in his lifetime will sit in a landfill for up to 200 years! In contrast, cloth diapers are manufactured from a renewable source and can be reused. Bear in mind, however, that the manufacture and cleaning – especially if you are using a diaper service – also has an impact on the environment.

1   *Use a wipe to clean between your baby's leg creases and around the genitals. With girls, wipe from front to back. Dry with a soft towel to avoid diaper rash (see page 218). Never leave your baby out of arm's reach.*

2   *Slide the clean diaper under your baby so the top is in line with his waist. Bring the front up between his legs, and hold it across his tummy. Fold the sides into the center and fasten the tabs. Always wash your hands after changing a diaper.*

sponge bathing

In the early days, when your baby comes home, you can keep him clean by simply washing the parts of his body that really need it.

Apart from dribbling milk and needing diaper changes, newborn babies don't get very dirty. Because many newborns don't like getting wet or being naked for too long, concentrating on the parts of your baby that really need washing will help keep crying to a minimum.

Be prepared

Get everything ready beforehand. If your baby is on a surface that is above the floor, use a safety strap or keep one hand on him at all times to make sure he does not fall. Put the bowl of warm water out of his arm or leg reach to avoid it being knocked over.

The key to keeping your baby happy is to work as quickly and calmly as possible. This will get easier as you become more practiced. Meanwhile:

♦ talk and sing to your baby – the sound of your voice will help soothe him

♦ a rattle or overhead mobile may also help keep a fussy baby calm.

taking care of **the cord**

About four or five days after the birth your baby's umbilical cord will probably fall off – although it can take as long as two weeks – leaving a small sore area that may take a few days to heal. To prevent infection and speed up healing, remember to:

♦ keep the area clean and dry

♦ turn the top of your baby's diaper down to keep the cord exposed to the air and clear of urine.

Never pull the cord – it will come off when it's ready. A few drops of blood may appear as the cord starts to separate. If the belly button becomes sticky, weepy, or looks red, speak to your healthcare professional.

YOU WILL NEED   BOWL OF TEPID BOILED WATER • COTTON BALLS • TWO SOFT TOWELS • CHANGING PAD • CLEAN CLOTHES

1   Moisten a cotton ball in cool, clean water and gently wipe your baby's face. Lift his chin and wipe underneath. Avoid poking inside his nose – nostrils are self-cleaning.

2   Clean his eyes by wiping from the inner corner outward, using a clean cotton ball for each stroke. Wipe over and behind his ears (never inside) using a clean cotton ball for each ear.

3   Uncurl his fingers and wipe his hands with a clean, moistened cotton ball. Clean his feet and underarms using fresh cotton balls for each new area and pat him dry after cleaning.

your baby's skin

Your newborn's skin feels soft and supple, but it's also very delicate and needs special attention. Taking care of her skin – whether as part of your normal cleansing routine or as part of a baby massage – will have benefits for you both.

caring for her skin

Your newborn's skin is very delicate, and unlike a child's or adult's it can be easily damaged. It is prone to dryness, chafing, and irritation.

In addition, your baby's pores are not yet working efficiently, which means she will possibly develop a few pimples. Although it may affect your baby's appearance, most are harmless and don't require treatment.

What to expect

Most newborns develop a few pimples or acne and minor rashes in their first few days and weeks.

♦ **Milia** These are small white pimples or spots that usually appear on the face, especially the nose and chin. They aren't itchy and won't bother your baby. They are just the result of immature sweat glands and will disappear without treatment.

♦ **Heat rash** If your baby's skin becomes too warm she may get small red pimples on her face and upper body. Check the room temperature and make sure she isn't sleeping under too many blankets.

♦ **Erythema toxicum** This is a rash of red pimples or spots with raised white centers appearing on different parts of a baby's body. They will disappear with time without treatment. However, erythema toxicum can be confused with more serious rashes, so check with your healthcare professional.

♦ **Peeling** You may notice during the first few days that your newborn's skin peels slightly – especially on the palms of her hands, soles of her feet, and her ankles. This is perfectly normal, especially if your baby was born past her due date. After a few days the peeling will go away.

Caring and bonding
Caring for your new baby's skin gives both of you the opportunity to experience the benefits of touch, helping you form a strong emotional bond with each other.

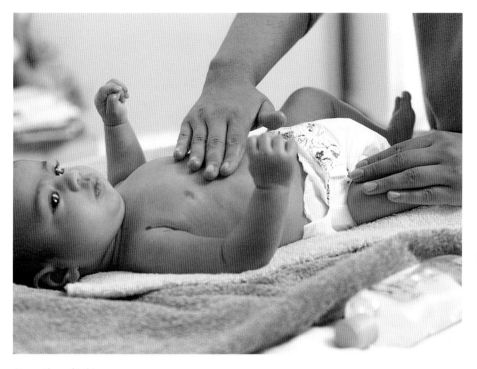

Smooth, soft skin
Lotion and oil can help keep your baby's skin smooth and soft. Use a moisturizer specially formulated for babies to help alleviate dry skin.

Different skin types
Your newborn's skin is soft and delicate. All babies have different skin types with a wide variety of textures and levels of dryness.

◆ **Cradle cap** Many babies between the ages of two weeks and one year develop crusty flakes of skin on their scalps that can spread to the eyebrows and behind the ears. Massaging a tiny amount of baby oil into your baby's skin at night will help soften the flakes. Wash her hair with a mild baby shampoo the following morning and most of the flakes should wash away.

◆ **Diaper rash** This can occur because ammonia and other chemicals in urine/feces irritate your baby's skin. Apply a protective emollient or thick barrier cream containing zinc oxide to her bottom at each diaper change (see page 218).

◆ **Dry skin** Make sure the temperature and humidity in your home aren't too extreme and try to keep your baby out of the wind when you are outside. If she has very dry skin, use a moisturizing baby bath product and apply a moisturizing cream to extra-dry areas.

Artificial heating in winter may make your baby's skin dry. Putting a humidifier in her room at night is recommended for stuffy noses as well as dry skin. Be careful when using a steam humidifier because of the risk of burns.

Best for baby
There is a large selection of infant skincare products available from which to choose. Only use ones that are gentle to both skin and eyes. This is especially important for newborns, who do not have fully developed blink reflexes or tear secretions. Adult products are best avoided because they may contain ingredients that could irritate your newborn baby's skin.

the importance **of touch**

Touch is important for healthy emotional development and communication between parents and babies. In addition, your loving touch does more than just comfort your newborn; it can actually help her grow.

The effect of touch on growth was first discovered in premature infants. These tiny babies are often separated from their parents and isolated in incubators, and are touched and cuddled much less than full-term babies. A study carried out at the Touch Research Institute in Miami, Florida, compared a group of premature babies who were massaged with a group who were not. It was found that the massaged infants gained weight faster and were ready to go home with their parents an average of six days earlier than other infants. When they were eight months old, massaged babies had gained more weight and were more fully developed than babies who were not massaged.

Your loving touch is vital to your baby's growth. Touching occurs during everyday activities such as feeding, bathing, rocking, and baby massage. See pages 96–97 to find out how to massage your baby.

© 1998 Johnson & Johnson Consumer Companies, Inc.

massaging your baby

Massage is a wonderful way to show your baby that you love him, as well as helping to soothe him when he's fussy. It has health benefits, too, including boosting the immune system, and improving circulation and muscle tone.

WHAT YOU NEED BABY OIL OR LOTION • SOFT TOWEL FOR YOUR BABY TO LIE ON • CALMING MUSIC

how to massage

You can massage your baby from about two weeks. Choose a time when he is not sleepy and do it in a warm room with warm hands.

A good time to massage is the last thing at night, after your baby's bath, when he is calm and relaxed. It's also best to do it between feedings: if he has just been fed he may be too full to be comfortable; similarly, if he is hungry he may quickly become fussy.

If your baby doesn't like being undressed, leave his undershirt on and just work on his legs and arms. Otherwise, work from the head down with light strokes, massaging both sides symmetrically. Be very gentle at first, increasing the pressure only when and if your baby is obviously happy. When you have massaged his front, turn your baby over and begin massaging his back, working from the head down.

If your baby becomes fussy, it's best to stop and try again another day.

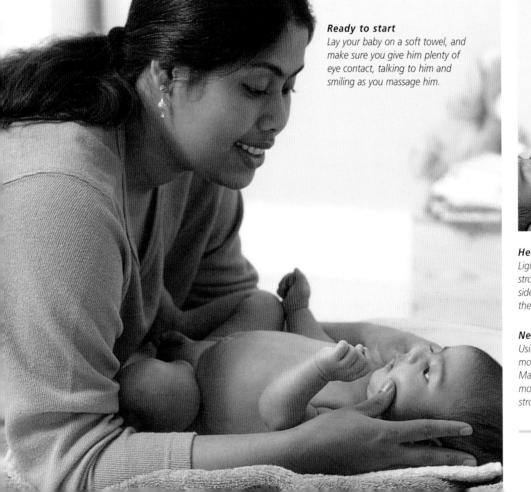

Ready to start
Lay your baby on a soft towel, and make sure you give him plenty of eye contact, talking to him and smiling as you massage him.

Head (top)
Lightly massage the crown of his head using circular strokes (avoiding his fontanelles), then work down the side of his cheeks. Massage his forehead working from the center out, moving across his eyebrows and ears.

Neck, shoulders, and arms
Using a downward motion, stroke his neck, then move on to his shoulders, working from the neck out. Massage his arms by gently squeezing them as you move along. Massage his wrists, hands, and fingers, stroking each finger with your fingertips and thumbs.

Smiles and kisses
Keep your baby interested by giving him lots of smiles and kisses – talking softly and singing will also help him enjoy the occasion.

Chest and tummy
Gently stroke your baby's chest using a downward motion. Rub his tummy using a circular motion, working clockwise and outward from his belly button with your fingertips.

Legs
Work from his thighs to his knees, stroking in a downward motion around the shins, gently squeezing them as you go.

Feet and toes
Rub ankles and feet, stroking from heel to toe and then gently massage each toe.

when your baby cries

Crying is normal for your baby. It is, after all, the only way she has of letting you know what her needs are. By learning what her different cries mean, you can respond and comfort her promptly, helping her feel safe and secure.

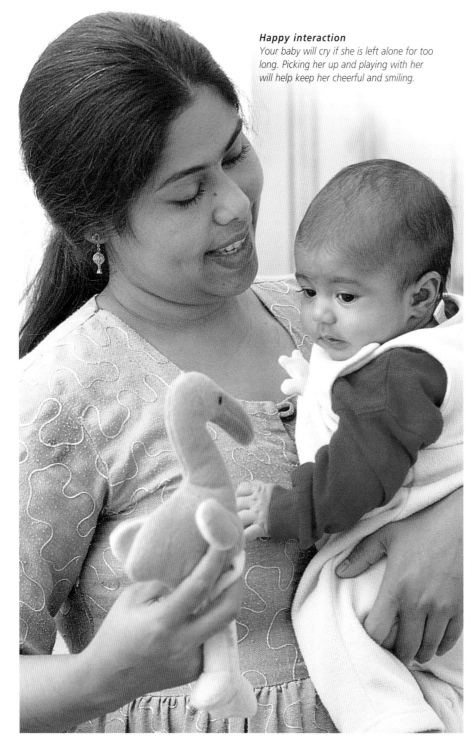

Happy interaction
Your baby will cry if she is left alone for too long. Picking her up and playing with her will help keep her cheerful and smiling.

why babies cry

Although your baby's cries may all sound the same at first, you will soon discover that she has a crying "language" and that different cries mean different things.

Learning how to interpret her cries will help you respond effectively: go to her promptly whenever she cries. During her first few months you cannot spoil a young baby by giving her attention, and if you answer her call for help, she will cry less in general.

Hunger

A cry that starts slowly and builds to a loud crescendo usually indicates that your baby is hungry. Because this is the most likely reason your baby is crying, offer to feed her first, unless you are certain she has had enough.

Pain

A baby in pain – because of an ear infection for example – will cry in a very distinct way, beginning as a shrill scream, followed by silence and short gasps. The cycle is then repeated. If you think your baby is sick take her to your healthcare professional.

Upset

Babies often cry in a fussy way when they are upset. The cry will increase in volume if you don't respond, and is distinct from a hunger cry. Your baby may need:
♦ **A cuddle** Newborns often just want physical comfort, and being held in your arms may be enough to calm her down.
♦ **Sleep** Babies sometimes have trouble falling asleep and cry to express their frustration. Laying her down somewhere

Safe and secure
Sometimes babies cry simply because they need a cuddle. Holding your baby close, talking to her, and comforting her will often quickly soothe away her tears.

warm and quiet may help her settle herself down to sleep.

♦ **Stimulation** Even newborns get bored lying in their cribs for long periods wide awake. Pick her up and talk to her.

♦ **Peace and quiet** Loud noises, bright lights, unexpected faces, a sneeze – all of these everyday occurrences can upset a newborn baby. Comfort her and keep her close.

♦ **A diaper change** Lots of babies hate being left in a dirty or wet diaper, especially if they have diaper rash, and a diaper change will not only relieve her discomfort but also distract her.

♦ **Cooling down or warming up** Your baby may be too hot or too cold. Newborns can't fully regulate their own temperatures so you need to monitor and adjust the temperature of her environment. Ideally, the room should be about 61–68°F (16–20°C) for a baby dressed in an undershirt and stretchie. You can check your baby's body temperature by feeling her tummy or the back of her neck – if her skin feels clammy, she's probably too warm.

♦ **A chance to cry!** Some babies have crying spells, often at the same time every day (although this is different from colic). Try to comfort her using one of the following soothing techniques.

Soothing your baby

If your baby is crying for no obvious reason, try these ways to soothe her:

♦ carry her in a baby carrier

♦ rock her in your arms, in her stroller, or sit and rock in a rocking chair

♦ swaddle her – some babies feel more secure when wrapped firmly (see page 100)

♦ sing to her or play soothing music; rhythmic noise or vibration can also help

♦ take her out for a walk either in the baby carrier or stroller, or for a ride in the car

♦ burp her to relieve any trapped gas bubbles

♦ give her a warm bath.

Coping with crying

On average, babies cry for one to four hours a day, and you'll quickly get used to coping when she's fussy. Sometimes, however, crying can be draining on your energy and emotions. When you need a break, put your baby in a safe place, such as her crib or stroller, and take some time out to calm yourself; or let your partner, a friend, or relative take over for a while. Babies are alert to their mothers' moods, and if you are tense or irritable your baby will feel it and cry more. No matter how tired or angry you feel, never shake your baby – this can cause blindness, brain damage, or even death.

Twins and more...

Crying newborn twins rarely set each other off – although they often have similar needs at similar times. Mothers of multiples discover ways of coping – putting the crying baby in a stroller or bouncy chair and rocking with a foot while feeding the other baby, for example. Pacifiers are also useful.

If you find you are struggling, don't forget that every new mother needs help – and you need it twice as much. Ideally, get help with chores as well as, or instead of, baby care.

intense **crying**

Intense, inconsolable crying is quite common in young babies. The crying often starts at the same time every day, usually in the early evening, and your baby may also pull up her legs and scrunch her face. These symptoms may be referred to as colic (see page 219). Ways to cope include:

♦ planning ahead – if the crying starts at the same time each night, try to have someone with you to take over when fatigue sets in

♦ experimenting with different carrying positions – try laying your baby across your forearm because a different position can help shift stomach or bowel contents (or gas)

♦ taking her out for some fresh air – this can work wonders.

Most babies learn to self-regulate and self-soothe by about four months.

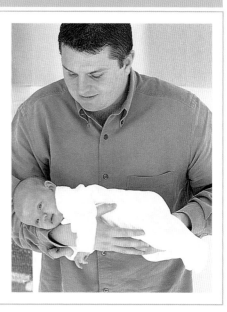

sleep and your newborn

New babies spend most of their time nursing and sleeping, and at first they don't distinguish between day and night. It's natural to worry about your baby while he's asleep, but if you follow your doctor's recommendations, such as putting him to sleep on his back, he will be safer.

helping your baby sleep

Your newborn will seek the amount of sleep his body needs: he will fall asleep when his body needs rest and wake up when he's recharged.

According to the National Sleep Foundation, newborns sleep an average of 14½ hours a day. How long your baby sleeps depends to a large extent on his weight and feeding patterns: the less your baby weighs, for example, the more often he will need feeding and the less he will sleep. However, all babies are individuals and tend to break the rules. Some new babies find it hard to settle down and may need extra comfort.

1 Lay your baby on a light, folded blanket, with his head placed on one of the corners and his arms by his side. Gently pull one side of the blanket across your baby's body.

♦ **Swaddling (above)** Wrapping your baby firmly in a soft, light, slightly stretchy blanket or shawl can give him the tactile comfort he needs and will prevent him from involuntarily jerking his legs and arms, which may be keeping him awake.
♦ **Comfort sucking** A fussy baby will almost always be soothed if he has something to suck on – such as his finger or a clean pacifier. The gentle rhythm of sucking can soothe him to sleep.

2 Pull the other side of the blanket across and tuck it in so that your baby is swaddled. Place him on his back in his crib to sleep.

baby **monitors**

A baby monitor is useful if you live in a large apartment or house and cannot hear your baby when she wakes up in another room. The most common type is a sound monitor. This works through radio waves and has two units – one to transmit your baby's sounds and the other to receive the sounds. Systems may be electric or battery operated. Check for good reception.

sleeping with your baby

During the first few weeks and months, you will want your baby close by at night, not least because of frequent feedings. Some parents move their baby's crib next to the bed while others prefer to have the baby in their own bed. Close contact not only feels wonderful, it may also decrease parents' concerns about their baby's well-being. However, bed sharing or cosleeping may be hazardous under certain conditions. The American Academy of Pediatrics (AAP) recommends that adults (other than the parents), children, or other siblings should avoid bed sharing with an infant. In addition, if a mother chooses to have her infant in her bed to breastfeed, she must carefully follow recognized safety guidelines (see *sleeping safely*, opposite).

sleeping **safely**

Sudden Infant Death Syndrome (SIDS)
Crib death (SIDS) is the most common cause of death in babies under one year of age (see page 225). It is therefore wise to take precautions known to reduce the risk.

Do....

♦ put your baby to sleep on his back with his feet at the foot of the crib to prevent him from wriggling under the covers

♦ make sure bedding such as blankets and sheets are not loose; tuck covers in securely; blankets should be tucked in around the crib mattress so the infant's face is less likely to become covered by bedding

♦ make sure the mattress is firm, in good condition, and a good fit for the crib

♦ keep the room temperature constant (about 61–68°F/16–20°C)

♦ learn infant CPR (see page 268).

Don't...

♦ place soft materials or objects such as pillows, quilts, comforters, sheepskins, or stuffed toys near or under a sleeping infant

♦ ever put a hot-water bottle or electric blanket in your baby's crib.

If you are sleeping with your baby...

♦ use light-weight blankets, not adult bedcovers for your baby

♦ make sure your duvet and pillows are not near his head and cannot cover his head

♦ do not smoke or use substances such as alcohol or drugs that may impair your ability to wake up and be alert if a problem arises.

Sweet dreams
The newest member of your family will spend most of his time sleeping.

how you'll feel

In the first few weeks after birth, you'll experience many emotional and physical changes and a wide range of feelings. However, as you and your baby slowly get to know and understand each other, life will start to settle into a routine you can both enjoy.

now that you're a parent

If this is your first baby, every baby-related task, from the first breastfeed or bath to the first outing, will be a new experience

Sometimes the challenges and the responsibilities can seem daunting, especially in the early days when you feel tired and uncertain. You may find yourself asking your healthcare professional lots of questions. You may also feel you are being given too much advice as friends and family try to help you, too. With each passing day, however, your confidence will grow as you learn what works for you and your baby.

Your body after birth

You may feel some pain and discomfort as your body starts to recover from birth:
♦ you may have after-pains as your uterus contracts and decreases in size – and you will bleed for two to three weeks as the uterus sheds its lining. Slight spotting may continue for up to six weeks
♦ if you have had stitches, are bruised, or have hemorrhoids, going to the bathroom will feel uncomfortable for several days
♦ when your milk comes in, between two and five days after giving birth (see pages 86–89), your breasts will become full and heavy, but any discomfort usually lasts only a day or so.

dealing with tiredness

The biggest adjustment you are likely to have to make is coping with lack of sleep at night. Try to make life easy for yourself:

♦ follow your baby's rhythms, and try to rest whenever your baby is napping

♦ don't be too concerned about sleeping. Just unwinding – soaking in a warm bath, listening to music – will conserve your energy

♦ prioritize chores and do only those that are really essential. Let others do the cleaning and fixing of meals

♦ take care of yourself by eating regular, nutritious meals

♦ accept all the help you can get, especially for household chores

♦ agree with your partner to take turns sleeping late on the weekend – knowing you can catch up on sleep at least once a week will help you get through the other six days.

Bonding with your baby

During the first few weeks you need time and space to bond with your baby. Sometimes bonding begins as soon as you see your new baby; sometimes it takes longer. Bonding has no time limit.

Many mothers feel overwhelmed by a flood of emotion as soon as they first see their baby. This is enhanced if they can hold their baby right away and let her nurse.

Some mothers, however, feel dazed after childbirth – especially if they have had a difficult labor or their baby needs special care. Others feel anxious about their baby. Or maybe their baby looks different from what they imagined, or isn't the sex they'd hoped for. In some cases mothers who have difficulty bonding are experiencing postpartum depression (see page 78). If you think you aren't bonding, or you feel depressed, talk to your doctor or therapist. They can give you advice and support.

Whatever your experience, be reassured that if bonding doesn't happen immediately, it can happen just as happily weeks or months later. Spend time with your baby: make eye contact, talk to her, and enjoy close physical contact as much as you can.

"The first few days at home after giving birth to Maddy were stressful – looking back I think I was trying to do too much. My pediatrician emphasized how important it was to rest. Now I take a rest whenever Maddy naps."

KATRIN HAMBLE, MOTHER OF MADELEINE AGE 5 WEEKS

take a break

Getting time to yourself when you have a new baby can be a challenge. There will be days when finding even half an hour for making phone calls, let alone soaking in the tub, seems impossible. But it's important to remember that your baby doesn't need to be with you every minute of the day – and if you are lucky enough to have a friend or relative nearby who'll care for her every now and then, you should jump at the chance! At this age your baby will happily be cuddled, carried, or pushed around the park by someone else – and as long as she is handed over warm and well-fed there should be no reason to worry.

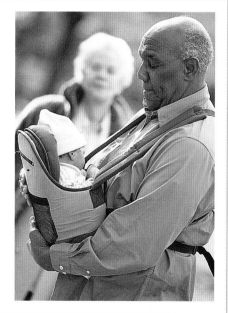

Grandparents are great
Grandparents are usually delighted to be given the opportunity to take their grandchild out for a walk by themselves – make the most of their help.

caring for your baby
6 weeks to 12 months

As your baby grows and develops, you will need to adapt the way you care for him – whether it's introducing him to solids, keeping up with his increasing mobility, or simply getting him into a good routine.

Rapid change

Almost every day with your new baby brings change. The first few months will be spent keeping him warm, clean, and well-fed. Then as he grows and develops and starts to gain more control over his body – entrancing you with smiles and playing with anything he can lay his hands on, from his toes to your nose – you'll need new ways of nurturing and caring for him.

New challenges

Between four and six months he will have doubled his birth weight and be ready for real food to fuel his growing energy needs.

"I have to look at photos to remind myself that Ben was once a tiny newborn. He's such a big boy now, and such a character – always on the go. We have a great routine – after breakfast we go shopping or to our local mother and toddler group. After lunch we might meet with friends for a play date or go to the park. Then it's dinnertime, bath, and bed."

KATIE JARRETT, MOTHER OF BEN AGE 12 MONTHS

He'll spend more of his day awake, playing, being with you as you go about your daily activities, and slowly you will start to develop a routine.

In his second six months, as he masters new and exciting skills – such as sitting up and crawling – he'll be off exploring his environment and taking his place as a vibrant member of the family.

Practical care – such as bath time and dressing – will become a new challenge, as will helping him learn how to pace himself and how to rest, sleep, and settle down when he's tired or unhappy.

Back to work

Many mothers return to work at some point during their baby's first year. This can be a particularly busy time for lots of families, but once you've found someone your baby feels loved by and secure with, you will discover that you can happily balance work and family life.

Outdoor activities
As your baby gets older, the practicalities of caring for her change, and outings, such as a trip to the park, can present a whole new set of adventures.

feeding and weaning

Feeding your baby real food for the first time is an exciting event. Between four and six months she might be ready for her first taste, and some time in the second half of the first year she'll be sitting in a high chair joining in with family meals.

starting on solids

If your baby can hold her head up well, seems hungrier than normal, wakes more often during the night, or is interested in the food you eat, she's probably ready for solids.

If you're unsure about introducing solids, talk to your healthcare professional. Your baby won't be able to digest foods properly before four months. In fact, the World Health Organization recommends breast milk and/or formula alone until six months. But by six months this will no longer provide all the necessary nutrients.

Four to seven months

Begin by offering your baby a teaspoon or two of "infant" precooked, dehydrated rice, barley, or oat cereal once a day. Wheat and mixed cereals should be introduced last because they may cause allergic reactions in very young babies. Baby cereals require no cooking; just add breast milk, water, or formula, and stir. Most babies seem to prefer bland tastes initially. You might also offer:

♦ purées of cooked apple or pear
♦ mashed banana
♦ purées of cooked vegetables such as sweet potato, carrot, cauliflower, and broccoli.

Offer one type of food at a time so if your baby has an allergic reaction, you'll know which food is the culprit. Stick to baby breakfast cereals and fruit and vegetable purées until she's seven months old, building up until you are offering her three solid meals a day. Unless instructed by your doctor, don't add baby rice or other solid food to your baby's bottle.

Eight to 12 months

At this age your baby needs between 750 and 900 calories each day, about 400 to 500 of which should come from breast milk or formula (about 24fl oz/680ml a day).

Your baby will be ready for a whole range of tastes and can share many family meals – provided there's no added salt or sugar. To help get her used to textures start mashing or chopping her food. If she spits the lumps out at first don't rush her. Instead, once she can hold them, help her discover new textures and give her lots of chewing practice with finger foods such as chunks of soft fruit, well-cooked pasta, toast, and small pieces of cooked vegetable. Always watch for choking in case she bites off a piece too big to swallow.

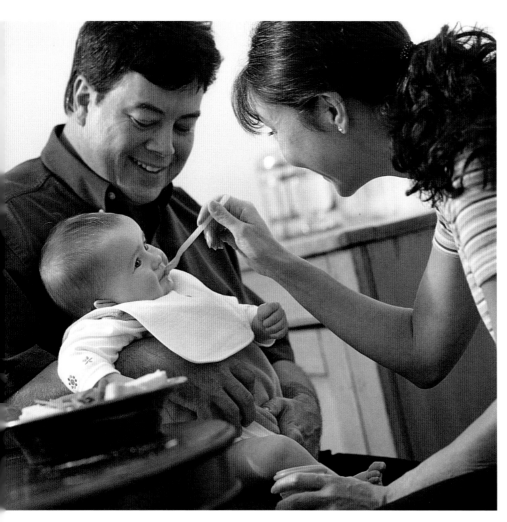

Ready for food
Starting your baby on solids is an exciting new stage. Take it slowly and as she starts to get the hang of it, you will find it an enjoyable and satisfying development.

Over the next few months you can introduce the following:
♦ bread, breadsticks, pasta, breakfast cereal, rice, potatoes, couscous
♦ meat, poultry, fish (check for bones and avoid shellfish), eggs (feed her only the yolks since their nutritional value is higher and they're less likely to cause allergies than the whites), lentils, beans (try to include at least one portion a day because these are good sources of protein and iron)
♦ more fruit and vegetables – try mango, melon, green beans, and peas
♦ cheese, full-fat yogurt, cottage cheese, cow's milk with cereal or in a cheese sauce.

Foods to avoid

Certain foods can pose health hazards and should be avoided in the early stages of your child's life. Others should be avoided to minimize the risk of allergies.
♦ **Up to six months** Milk products such as cheese, yogurt, and cottage cheese; fish, citrus fruits, eggs; wheat-, rye-, or barley-based foods such as bread, pasta, wheat flour, teething biscuits, and some cereals, because they contain a substance called gluten which babies are sensitive to.
♦ **Up to 12 months** Avoid cow's milk as a drink – although from six months you can start to add small quantities of it to breakfast cereals or as a cheese sauce; egg whites; honey in liquid or solid form because it can contain spores that cause infant botulism – babies' digestive systems are immature and spores can germinate and cause disease. (This is not the case for honey in commercially made baby foods because a different process is used.)

♦ **Up to four years** Don't give your child hard, smooth foods that need to be chewed because youngsters can't chew with a grinding motion until the age of four. Whole peanuts shouldn't be given until age seven or older because they present a choking hazard. Peanut and other nut products (however smooth) shouldn't be given until your child is two years old because of the risk of allergies.

From bottle to cup

As your baby progresses to three meals a day, you can start to introduce a two-handled cup so that she can take sips of water or diluted fruit juice during mealtimes. Those with soft spouts are easiest for first-timers. You'll need to hold and tip it for her to show her how it works.

Initially she may use it as a plaything, so choose a nondrip system because chances are the cup will often be waved and

Homemade purées
Use a blender to purée steamed or lightly boiled fruit and vegetables, then freeze teaspoons of the purées in ice-cube trays and defrost as required.

being **vegetarian**

If you are bringing your baby up as a nonmeat eater, make sure she's getting enough protein and iron from other foods. After six months, she can eat hard-boiled eggs, excluding the egg whites – but no more than three a week – beans, and lentils. Iron supplements may also be a good idea. If you are excluding eggs and dairy products from her diet she may need vitamin supplements and calcium. Ask your healthcare professional or the North American Vegetarian Society for further advice.

thrown. Try to persevere, however, because it's important that your baby is weaned off the bottle earlier rather than later: drinking from a cup is better for her speech development and teeth (the liquid spends less time in contact with the enamel coating), and if she drinks from a bottle too long it may become a security object.

Common challenges

♦ **Loss of appetite** Your older baby may eat less and demand more milk instead if she's teething. Once the new tooth comes in her appetite will pick up again.
♦ **Grabbing the spoon** Lots of babies prefer to feed themselves and from an early age will try to grab the spoon. Satisfy her need for independence by giving her a spoon of her own, but use one yourself as well – slipping in mouthfuls when you can.
♦ **Refusal to eat** If your baby rejects the food you give her, don't make it into a big issue. Simply try again later.

bathing your baby

Bath time can be an enjoyable experience for you and your baby. It's natural for parents to be cautious at first. However, there are lots of ways to help build confidence and make bath time a success.

starting a routine

You don't need to give your baby a bath every day: at first two or three times a week is fine.

As he gets older you may want to increase this. Lots of mothers find that once they feel confident, bath time is a relaxing and soothing experience, and they like to make it a part of their everyday routine.

If your baby doesn't enjoy being placed in a tub, you can give him a sponge bath – simply hold him on your lap with a bowl of warm water nearby and, removing the minimum amount of clothes at a time, gently wash him.

Bathing your older baby

Soon your baby will be ready for the big bath. Most babies make the transition easily, especially if they love playing in water and have some sponges, plastic cups, and bath toys to keep them amused. To keep your baby safe see page 264 and follow these guidelines:

♦ keep the water shallow (up to 5in/13cm)
♦ always check the temperature of the bath water to make sure it's comfortable for your baby, regardless of his age
♦ wrap the faucets with a washcloth
♦ baby-bath seats can help you support your baby, and help save your back
♦ don't allow your baby to pull himself up to standing unsupported in the bath
♦ never leave your baby alone in the bath, even for a second.

YOU WILL NEED BABY BATH OR NON-SLIP MAT IF USING ADULT BATH • COTTON BALLS OR WASHCLOTH • CLEAN, WARM WATER • TWO FLUFFY TOWELS • BABY BATH, LOTION AND/OR BABY SHAMPOO • CLEAN DIAPER

1 Keep the water shallow – up to 5in (13cm). Set the hot water heater no higher than 120°F (49°C). Check the temperature of the water with your elbow before putting your baby in – it should be just warm. If you use a thermometer, it should register about 85°F (29°C).

2 Undress your baby, remove his diaper, then wrap him up in one of the towels. First, clean his face using a soft washcloth or cotton balls (see sponge bathing, page 93).

3 Wash his hair by holding him firmly over the bath and cupping your hand to apply the water. Use a little baby soap or baby shampoo. Rinse well.

five steps to a
happy bath time

Step one
Your child is more likely to enjoy his bath if he's not tired, and is neither hungry nor has just eaten (if you give him a bath right after a meal he may spit up).

Step two
Babies become cold very quickly so make sure you bathe him in a warm room and be sure to have a towel on hand that you can wrap him in when you've finished.

Step three
Use a mild soap or shampoo.

Step four
Smile and chat soothingly to him – playing water games will help him associate water with having fun.

Step five
Dry him and dress him quickly to keep him as warm as possible.

4 *Remove the towel and gently put your baby into the bath. Support his head and shoulders with one arm and his legs and bottom with the other.*

5 *Using the hand that was under his bottom, gently splash water over your baby's body. Give him time to kick his arms and legs if he wants to. A young baby needs constant support in water so never take your hand off him or leave him alone in the bath.*

6 *Lift your baby out of the bath, wrap him in a warm towel, and dry him thoroughly. Put on a clean diaper and dress him.*

taking care of your older baby

During the coming year your baby will learn how to sit up and crawl. As she becomes more mobile, simple tasks such as dressing her and keeping her clean and warm may become more challenging.

dressing your baby

Dressing a wriggly baby can be a challenge, but if you are patient and gentle it will become easier with practice.

Choose clothes that are easy to put on and distract your baby with smiles and chatter to keep her happy and relaxed. Lots of babies don't enjoy being dressed or undressed, so try to make the procedure as quick and easy as possible by choosing clothes that are easy to put on and take off.

Remember to stretch neck openings wide before easing clothes over your baby's head, and pull sleeves back over your baby's arms rather then tugging her arms through them. Wrap up your baby against the cold – hats are especially important because a lot of body heat is lost through the head. Be sure to take off extra layers when you bring your baby inside again so she doesn't overheat.

Until your baby is walking well, all she needs on her feet are socks or similar coverings to keep them warm. Make sure they are soft and roomy – the bones in a baby's feet are very pliable, and even tight socks may misshape the toes if they are worn a lot.

Lots of mothers really enjoy choosing clothes for their baby. Check:
♦ style – look for snug clothes that will keep your baby warm and cozy. Snaps and wide necks are best because these make dressing and undressing your baby easier. All-in-one suits are ideal
♦ fabric – look for soft, stretchy fabrics that are machine washable and colorfast. Leaking diapers, dribbles, and spills all mean your baby's clothes will need frequent washing. Your crawling baby will need clothes made from sturdy fabrics that protect her knees, but that will not restrict her movement.

safety in **the sun**

If your baby is less than six months old she should be kept out of the sun.

♦ Keep her cool with lightweight clothing – in hot weather she needn't be dressed any more warmly than yourself.

♦ Older babies should be allowed in the sun only for a limited time and only if they are well protected. Dress them in light-colored clothes made from lightweight, tightly woven fabric and cover any exposed parts of their faces and bodies with sunscreen (minimum sun protection factor 30 – consult the instructions on the bottle). Keep your child out of the sun during the hottest part of the day.

♦ Use a sunshade or an umbrella to keep your baby in the shade. Make sure she wears a wide-brimmed hat to protect her face and eyes.

♦ See page 267 for more sun-safety tips.

Let's get you dressed
Encourage your little one to let you get him dressed by making it fun – sing songs or play peekaboo, for example – and let him do the simple things himself.

Ready to go?
It's important to make sure your baby is appropriately dressed in cold weather. Hats and coats are essential – no matter what your baby's opinion!

Hat's on, hat's off
If the minute you put a hat or coat on your mischievous baby he whips it off, wait until you're outside and he's distracted – then slip it back on again.

taking care of your baby's nails

Your baby may already have long fingernails when she is born – and they will continue to grow rapidly.

It's natural to feel nervous about cutting them, but knowing how and when it's best to cut will help you keep her free from scratches when she waves her arms around.

Fingernails

Scratch mittens are one way of preventing your baby from scratching herself – but she needs to discover her hands, so it's preferable not to use them. Instead, check her nails every couple of days and cut when necessary.
♦ **What to use** Use a soft emery board, baby nail clippers, or blunt-ended toenail scissors.

♦ **When to do it** You will find that your baby's nails are softer after a bath. If you can't get your baby to hold still while you cut her nails, try to cut them while she's asleep.
♦ **How to do it** Hold one finger at a time between your forefinger and thumb, safely

enclosing the rest of her hand with your remaining fingers. Try to press down on the finger pad, pulling it back out of the way while you cut.

Toenails

Your baby's toenails will grow much more slowly then her fingernails. Check them every couple of weeks. Toenails also need to be cut, with a similar technique to that used for fingernails (see above).

You will notice that they often curl around at the end. Unless the skin around the nail looks red and inflamed there's no reason to worry. As your baby gets older the nail will harden and become better defined.

sleep and your older baby

Sleep is essential for your baby – it helps him grow and develop properly. Understanding your baby's sleep patterns and following some simple guidelines will help develop sound sleep habits – and give you all a good night's rest!

establishing a sleep routine

Not getting enough sleep can cause your baby to be irritable. Encouraging good sleep habits now will help him avoid bad sleep habits later.

♦ **Distinguish between night and day** Help your baby learn that nighttime is sleep time and daytime is playtime with different rooms for nighttime and daytime sleep. During daytime naps, keep light and sound at a normal level. At night, turn off the light and keep the room quiet.

♦ **Start a bedtime routine** As your baby's memory skills improve, he'll begin to look forward to this ritual and understand that it's a time to sleep, not to play. Follow the same pattern every night – a warm bath, a cuddle/play/story, final feeding, and then into the crib, drowsy but awake.

♦ **Let him lull himself to sleep** Although it's tempting to let your baby fall asleep in your arms, this won't help him learn to fall asleep again on his own if he wakes up later in the night. Put him in his crib when he's well-fed and sleepy but still awake.

Teething troubles

Teething can keep babies awake at night. First teeth usually appear between six to nine months. Common signs of teething include one or all of the following: swollen, reddened gums; excessive drooling; an inflamed cheek; desire to bite down on anything he can get in his mouth. You could:

♦ give him a chilled teething ring to chew on, but it should be made of firm rubber
♦ gently rub a teething gel on his gums
♦ massage his gums with your finger tips.

"I give my baby something cold to chew on – teething rings are great, but a chunk of frozen bagel works just as well."

SOPHIE DEWAR, *MOTHER OF RORY*
AGE 8 MONTHS

wakeful babies

At night

Your older baby is likely to sleep as much as 12 hours a night without needing a middle-of-the-night feeding. Beware of the possible problems ahead: as his separation anxieties intensify in the next few months (see page 171), he may start to resist going to bed. He may also wake up more often in the night looking for you. However, if your baby is used to settling himself down, he should quickly fall back into a deep sleep. If he cries to be picked up, try the strategies on page 113 to help him sleep through the night.

During the day

Daytime naps are good for your baby – he probably still takes two: one in the morning and one in the afternoon. The more rested he is, the happier he'll be during the day and the easier to settle down at night. However, as he gets older and becomes more interested in the world around him he may find it harder to nap. If he resists a daytime nap yet obviously needs one, try to put him down before he gets overtired. If he still resists, take him out for a walk or a drive. Many babies nap easily in the stroller or car and even 20 minutes will refresh him.

nighttime **waking**

All babies wake several times during the night. Respond quickly to your baby's cries – he may need changing or feeding. After six months, he will feel secure enough to soothe himself back to sleep when he wakes up at night. If his crying becomes desperate, however, check on him (see box below). If he seems fine, kiss him, tell him he's OK, and leave again. You may have to do this several times over the next few nights, but stick with it – at this age most babies learn by the sixth or seventh night that they are OK without you and can get themselves back to sleep.

Why older babies cry

Your older baby may cry at night because he's been disturbed. If he's still sleeping in your room after six months, he's more likely to wake up when you come to bed or cough or turn over at night. Now may be a good time to move him into his own room.

He may also cry at night if he is frightened of being separated from you. For the first time he is beginning to realize that you and he are different people – and when you vanish he has no idea when, or if, you will return. If your baby has become very clingy, give him lots of reassurance. When you leave him during the day always give him a kiss and a hug as you say good-bye; looking happy and calm will help him feel reassured. The more secure he feels, the faster – and more smoothly – this phase will pass.

checklist: **is he OK?**

If your baby cries during the night and can't settle himself down, he may:

♦ be too hot or too cold

♦ need his diaper changed

♦ be in pain because of teething, diaper rash, or illness

♦ be anxious about something, such as a new caregiver or a change in his routine.

going back to work

Returning to work after you've had a baby can be an emotional time. Your main concern will be that your baby adjusts well and continues to feel loved and secure. The more time and preparation you give yourself, the easier the transition will be.

making it work for you

Finding the right person to care for your child when you return to work may take time, but it's important that you feel confident with your choice.

Introduce your baby to her caregiver early on and build up the time they spend together so she has the chance to adjust. Asking your caregiver to keep to your baby's routine will help your baby become used to being cared for by somebody else.

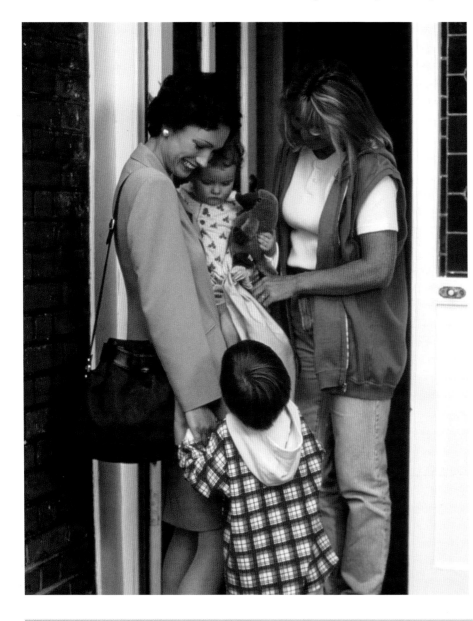

Childcare checklist

With the right person, your child will thrive. Whatever age your child, a good caregiver should:

♦ be warm and friendly – babies and toddlers need lots of physical affection and attention
♦ listen and watch carefully
♦ enjoy chatting to your child about what she is doing
♦ be fun and imaginative – older children especially need planned activities and creative playtime
♦ be patient and prepared to go at your child's pace
♦ join in with her play without taking over
♦ be one step ahead – looking out for difficult situations before they happen
♦ be consistent about what your child can and can't do.

You will also need someone who:

♦ can get along well with your child
♦ agrees with your ideas on how to take care of children
♦ knows how to keep your child safe, especially when learning to crawl and walk
♦ understands basic first aid.

You and your child's caregiver

Your child will benefit from seeing you getting along with her caregiver, and good communication will help maintain good relations and a good standard of care. Treat her as a partner, not a rival.

♦ Help get your child settled before you leave, join in with chores at the end of the

Going to family daycare
Family daycare providers take care of children in their own homes. They are often mothers themselves, and are especially sympathetic to the needs of your child.

day, help plan special events or activities.
♦ Find time each day to chat about what's happened – you need to know if your child is trying out a new skill or looks like she's coming down with a cold – and always thank your caregiver for her day's work.
♦ Meet regularly to discuss any problems or changes. There's rarely a right or wrong way of doing something, so be prepared to be open-minded.

Daycare
A good daycare center will have plenty of toys and activities designed for your baby's age – and she'll benefit from socializing with other babies.

Coping with tears

It's natural for babies to become more clingy as they grow older, and separation anxiety is an important emotional milestone. When you leave your baby she has no idea when, or if, you will return, so help her cope by:
♦ giving advance warning – 10 or 15 minutes before you leave tell her what's happening
♦ acting calmly – kiss your baby good-bye, give her a hug, and go without a fuss.

You may worry that by returning to work you are neglecting your baby or that she will become more attached to her new caregiver. Try not to worry – you will always be the most important person in your baby's life. And developing another warm and loving relationship will be good for her.

Stay-at-home dads

A growing number of fathers are staying at home to care for their children. If you plan to be a stay-at-home dad, you can get a lot of good advice from mother and baby groups. Ask your healthcare professional about other stay-at-home dads – building up a network of friends will help overcome isolation and provide playmates for your baby as she gets older.

childcare **choices**

If a close relative cannot look after your child, you have lots of other options to choose from. Whether you decide to have your child cared for in your own home or choose to take her to someone else's home or to a childcare center will depend on your finances and your personal preferences.

Baby-sitters, nannies, and au pairs
For your child, being taken care of by a baby-sitter, nanny, or au pair means staying in familiar surroundings and getting individual care and attention. Life will also be easier for you because you won't need to transport your child each morning and evening. However, nannies and baby-sitters do not need to be registered – so you must carefully check references and background. They can also be expensive. And if the nanny or baby-sitter is alone with your child, it will be difficult to check how well she is doing the job. Au pairs, although cheaper, are live-in and are not trained in childcare.

Family daycare
Usually mothers working in their own homes, family daycare can be the most affordable type of childcare. Licensing regulations vary in each province. Not all family daycare centers are licensed. Your child will be in a friendly family environment and will be able to join in lots of familiar household activities. She may also have other children to play with. As with nannies, baby-sitters, and au pairs, it's difficult to check what happens when you are not there, so it's important to get feedback from other parents who have used the same daycare.

Daycare or childcare centers
Often privately run or linked to community non-profits such as churches, YMCAs, or synagogues, these also need to be registered. Toddlers and preschoolers will find the structured programs stimulating and fun. There will be a number of staff, which means you won't be affected if one of them is sick. However, staff turnover can be high, which may be unsettling for your child. Good daycare centers fill up quickly, so start your search sooner rather than later. Most daycare centers are licensed, although regulations vary widely.

your new family

Becoming a family is exhilarating and challenging. Shared love for your new baby will bring a new dimension to your relationship. Making time for yourselves as a couple is also important for everyone.

the joys of parenthood

As your baby grows so does the reality of family life, and you will find there are increasingly few times when you and your partner are alone together.

If your baby is not with one of you, he is with the other. Life revolves around his needs – which can't be put aside until later. As a result, time that was once spent with each other as a couple is now spent on your baby.

Shared parenting

Adjusting to this new way of life can be challenging. Few couples sail through the first year as parents without conflict of some sort. There's less time to talk, to feel close, to spend time caring for each other. Issues such as who's doing most of the chores and getting the least sleep can be potential sources of conflict. Often neither partner feels they are getting the love and attention they need; and as resentment builds, the relationship can begin to deteriorate.

Shared parenting can hugely reduce the stress on a relationship – taking on equal responsibility for child care and household chores can benefit both parents and be good for your baby, too. Even if one of you is working full-time, finding a way to share the domestic workload on the weekend and in the evening can help create a happy household.

Family outing
Going out and spending time together as a family is as important for you as parents as it is for your new baby and his siblings. Don't forget sun hats and sunscreen.

Finding time for yourselves

Spending time together as a couple is vital. Make it a priority – when you and your partner are feeling close and supportive, any stress and strains will be easier to handle. Here are some suggestions:

♦ hire a weekly baby-sitter so you can go out regularly together as a couple

♦ ask grandparents to help out, perhaps for the occasional weekend away

♦ one night a week agree to switch off the television, order in, and have a quiet evening together at home

♦ when possible, get help with chores such as ironing and cleaning – and use your free time for each other

♦ book vacations with travel agencies that offer on-site child care so you can spend a couple of hours a day doing things together such as sightseeing or relaxing on the beach.

Additional children

If this is your second – or third – baby, you will probably find yourself feeling even more tired, and pulled in more directions emotionally and physically than ever before. From the moment baby number two comes on the scene it's all change – every moment of the day is spoken for and when they finally sink into their crib and bed, you'll probably collapse, too!

Caring for more than one child can be extra difficult if your older child is feeling resentful of the new baby's arrival. In step-families, an older child can feel particularly excluded if you and your new partner have a baby together.

Keep family life as happy and relaxed as possible by being extra sensitive to your older child's needs.

♦ Make sure he still sees his friends, and keeps up with any activities or playgroups he was already going to – keep life as normal as possible.

♦ Encourage him to help – recognize that he will probably enjoy bringing you a clean diaper and playing with the baby at bath time, as long as his help is encouraged and freely given.

♦ Give him special time on his own so that he still feels precious and important.

♦ Be positive – if he's acting boisterously around the baby or playing too loudly, suggest a different way of playing rather

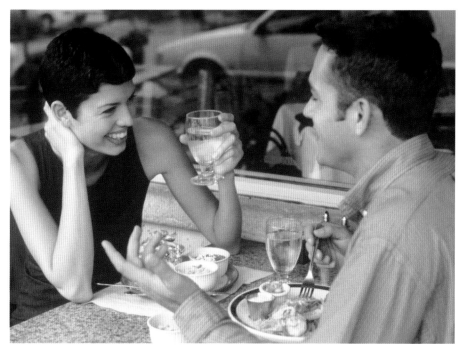

Time to talk
Making time just for you and your partner to be together may take some organization, but it is essential for maintaining a happy relationship. A meal out provides an ideal opportunity to enjoy each other's company uninterrupted.

than simply telling him not to do something, so he doesn't become resentful of the new baby.

♦ Help nurture a good relationship – tell your older child how much the baby likes him by saying things like "Look, he's smiling at you" or "You make him laugh when you do that."

Single parents

Being a single parent isn't easy – in addition to the financial strain, caring for a baby on your own can be relentless, exhausting, and lonely. Trying to stay in

control of your life is important for you both – the more confident and happy you feel, the more love and attention you will be able to give your baby.

♦ Take good care of yourself – eat well, exercise, and get plenty of rest.

♦ Try to make sure you have regular time away from your child so you can, for example, relax with friends, go to the gym, or see a movie.

♦ Develop a good support network – friends, relatives, community organizations, and health professionals can give you practical and emotional help.

"I love my son and have no regrets about being a single mother. Occasionally I think it would be nice to have someone to share Jacob's achievements with – I wonder if my mother gets fed up with me telling her how wonderful he is! But otherwise I enjoy being able to do things my way – and my family is always there to help when I'm tired or just need a break."

CATHY WILCOX, MOTHER OF JACOB AGE 9 MONTHS

caring for your toddler
12 to 24 months

As your baby becomes a toddler, caring for her also means helping her learn how to do lots of new things for herself. Whether it's washing her own face or starting to use a potty, she'll love learning how to be independent.

Stepping forward

Over the next few months your little one will become increasingly independent. She'll take her first steps, say her first words – and whether it's finding her favorite cup, sliding backward down the stairs, or learning how to put on her hat, you'll be thrilled by her achievements.

As the year progresses, there will be lots of new and exciting experiences for both you and your baby. She'll soon be ready, for example, for her first pair of real shoes, to make the move from her crib into a "big bed," to have her first haircut, and to take her first steps toward potty training.

Exploring the world

As your toddler becomes more physically adventurous, exploring her environment will be part of everyday life. Toddlers are into anything and everything. They love to feel, taste, touch, and empty things – it's how they learn about the world. Being prepared for messes – dressing your toddler in suitable clothing, using mess mats under the high chair, designating a particular corner of the room for activities such as painting and Playdough – will help a lot.

Similarly, as she becomes more active you'll need to become increasingly careful about her safety. She needs space and a sense of freedom to explore her environment

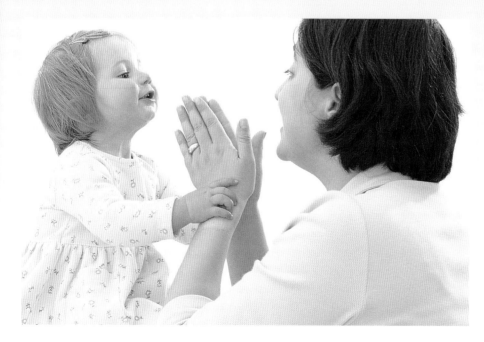

"Emily is really steady on her feet now – and she's so excited about being able to walk. She seems much happier now that she can do more for herself."

JACKIE FRENCH, MOTHER OF EMILY AGE 16 MONTHS

– so treating her with kid gloves isn't the answer. But you can make sure she has a safe environment to explore. Check your house for hidden dangers, such as unstable furniture and unlocked windows, and install any necessary toddler-safety devices, such as safety gates (these should be used as soon as your baby can roll over), safety covers for electrical outlets, locks for cupboards with household cleaners, door slam protectors, and corner guards on sharp cabinet and table corners (see pages 262–265).

Emotional outbursts

At some point during this year, your toddler may also have her first tantrums. Despite all her new physical skills, your child will often find she can't manage – or simply isn't allowed – to do what she wants. Tears, temper, and frustration are natural, but you'll quickly learn how to handle tricky behavior such as this. And it's reassuring to know that at this age, upsets are quickly forgotten. Your toddler may be sobbing now, but she'll soon be smiling again.

feeding your toddler

Your toddler can now feed himself and enjoy most foods – but that doesn't necessarily mean he'll eat everything you put in front of him. Picky eating is common at this age, but with the right approach you can avoid mealtime battles.

what he's eating

By now your toddler is eating mainly family meals, although they should be prepared with less salt and sugar than for an adult.

You will be offering him food that he can chew, although – apart from softer food such as banana – you will need to chop it up into bite-size pieces. Be aware of food he might choke on, such as raw carrots, grapes, uncooked peas, celery, hard candy, or other hard round foods. Choking can also happen with meat products, such as burgers, sausages, and hot dogs, so these should be cut lengthwise and into smaller pieces. Always supervise your child while he is eating. Using a five-point high-chair harness will prevent him from falling and choking on food.

Use as many fresh ingredients as possible – processed foods are high in salt, sugars, and artificial flavorings. Choose foods from the four basic food groups:
♦ meat, fish, eggs, and other proteins
♦ milk, cheese, yogurt, and other dairy products
♦ rice, cereals, potatoes, yams, bread, pasta, sweet potatoes, and other carbohydrates
♦ fruit and vegetables.

Remember that a low-fat, high-fiber diet isn't suitable for a child. Your toddler should have whole rather than skimmed milk, and full-fat dairy products.

Finger foods
Starting to feed herself will give your toddler a great sense of independence – but remember never to leave her alone with food because of the risk of choking.

Feeding himself
Your toddler will be able to feed himself, but he may be slow and tempted to play with his food. You may want to spoon in the occasional mouthful yourself. Giving him finger food he can easily manage himself – such as small sandwiches and pieces of fruit – may help.

For the sake of his teeth, your toddler should also be drinking from a sippy cup. Keep an eye on how much fluid he has. At this age a total of 16–20fl oz (450–560ml) of whole milk per day is more than enough. If he drinks more, he may not feel hungry at mealtimes.

Large quantities of fruit juice can have a similar effect because the sugar content is usually high. It may also cause diarrhea and increase the risk of tooth decay. Limit the amount of juice to 4fl oz (120ml) a day. Offer water as an alternative to juice and milk – at this age tap water is perfectly safe.

Fun with food
Make healthy food look inviting by letting loose your imagination: funny faces and food cut into interesting shapes will have great appeal for your child.

"It's not often we can all sit down for a meal together – Mark works long hours during the week. But we do try to have a family meal on the weekends. It means planning ahead and eating a bit earlier for Hannah's sake – she still has a nap in the afternoon, and if she's tired then she's not interested in food. I always cook something I know she enjoys too, such as pasta, so there are no tantrums."

SHARON HILL, MOTHER OF HANNAH AGE **21** MONTHS

food **fads**

Lots of toddlers become picky eaters. From around 18 months they have a surge of independence and want their own way whenever possible. Food inevitably becomes a battleground – and lots of mothers find their good-natured babies become picky toddlers. You should never force-feed your child. Instead, stay as calm and neutral as possible and remember that it's just a phase. As long as your toddler is gaining weight and growing, his health won't be at risk. Meanwhile, encourage healthy eating by:

♦ giving your toddler a choice of two of his favorite foods. Children at this age are overwhelmed by an open-ended choice. They respond well to :"Do you want to have X or Y?" For example, jelly (X) or cheese (Y) sandwiches

♦ keeping mealtimes fun – sit down with your toddler and eat together. If he sees daddy eating corn he might try it, too

♦ making the food look good – small piles of chopped food attractively arranged look tempting and not too overwhelming

♦ praising your toddler when he eats well or tries something new; and persevering – children's likes and dislikes change all the time.

healthy **snacks**

Toddlers are often on the move and using up lots of energy. Their small tummies digest meals quickly and they soon become hungry again. When this happens their blood-sugar levels dip, making them irritable and tired. A healthy snack between meals is ideal for boosting their energy and lifting their spirits. When choosing what kind of snack to give your toddler, think in terms of a nutritious mini-meal. Suitable snacks to offer include:

♦ thin vegetable sticks such as raw carrot and cucumber

♦ fresh, chopped fruit (dried fruit can stick to teeth)

♦ crackers, rice cakes, oat cakes with cream cheese

♦ banana slices

♦ yogurt

♦ cubes of cheese and sliced baby tomatoes.

Always stay close to your child when he's eating in case he chokes.

sleep and your one year old

Your toddler's sleep patterns will change a lot as she grows up. Although she may be ready to give up her morning nap at 18 months – or abandon napping altogether by the time she's four or five – she'll always need healthy sleep habits.

getting enough sleep

At a year old, your toddler will be sleeping for about 14 hours within a 24-hour period, although this may drop to about 12 hours by her second birthday.

Part of this will be taken as daytime naps. These are vital if your toddler is to get through the day without becoming cranky and also to prevent her from getting overtired, which can make nighttime sleep a problem. Even if your toddler wakes up early or is wakeful at night, don't be tempted to drop daytime naps. If your toddler needs waking from a nap, make sure she has plenty of time to adjust – rushing her to eat lunch or get dressed will only make her unhappy.

Good sleep habits

By now your toddler should be sleeping through the night on her own. Illness, a developmental milestone (such as learning to stand alone), or going on vacation may temporarily disrupt your toddler, but once she has recovered or is back in familiar surroundings, she should settle back into a good sleep pattern.

If, however, you are still coping with bedtime battles or wakeful nights, it's not too late to help your child learn how to sleep well. Start with a regular bedtime routine (see page 112). With practice your child will learn to settle down happily on her own, in her own bed. If she's still waking in the night, see *Nighttime waking* below for how to help her sleep through the night.

from crib to bed

When your toddler tries to climb out of her crib or she is too big to sleep in it comfortably, it's time to move her into a grown-up bed. To help your child feel secure about the change:

♦ choose a time when her life is settled – if there's a new baby or new caregiver to get used to, or she is getting over an illness, for example, put the move off for a while

♦ let her help you make the bed and choose some favorite toys to be in it, too

♦ entice her in by getting in yourself – children love imitating grown-ups!

♦ put some cushions on the floor next to the bed so if she falls out at night she won't hurt herself

♦ if she is hesitant, let her start off with daytime naps in the big bed before putting away the crib for good.

sleep solutions

Bedtime battles
Calm your toddler down with a relaxing bedtime routine (see page 112). Reading a story in bed can help get her ready for sleep. Offer her a special toy or blanket to cuddle, give her a kiss, say good night, lower the lights, and leave. Be calm but consistent. If she cries, wait a few minutes then go back and say "Good night sweetheart. I love you. You need to go to sleep. I am not going to pick you up. Good night." Then leave the room. You may have to do this every 15–20 minutes, and for the next few nights, too, but your toddler will eventually get the message.

Nighttime waking
Check that your toddler is OK, calm her down, then say good night and leave. If she cries again, wait a few minutes to

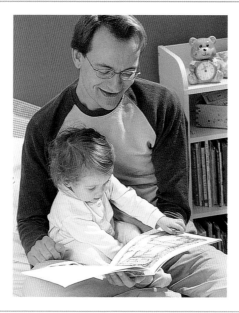

see if she settles down before repeating the procedure. You may have to do this through the night and for the next few nights, too, but eventually your toddler will realize that she can go back to sleep without your being with her.

Early waking
Postpone bedtime by 10 minutes each night for a few nights until your toddler is going to bed an hour later and hopefully waking later, too. Put heavy curtains or Venetian blinds on the windows to keep the morning light out and leave some toys out (not in her crib) to distract her when she wakes. If it's very early let her cry for a while – she may settle herself down again. Or follow the procedure above – check on her, say good night, and leave. Repeat until she gets the message.

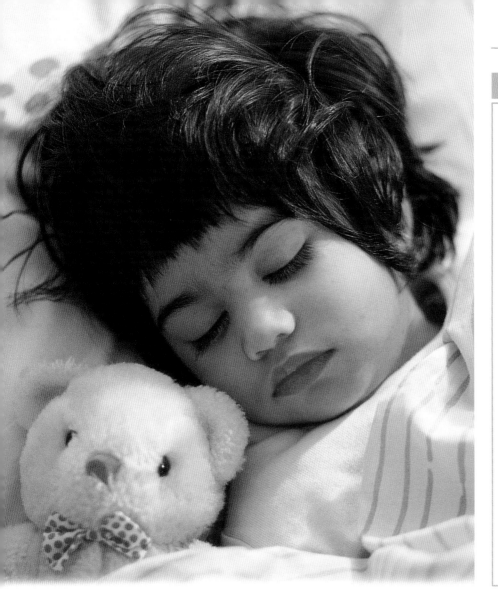

staying in **her own bed**

If your toddler comes into your bed at night and you want to discourage the habit, you need to be firm and put her right back into her own bed every time she leaves it. This can be exhausting, but your toddler will eventually get the message.

♦ Choose a couple of days when you can catch up with sleep during the day or decide to take turns – mom first night, dad second night.

♦ As soon as your toddler appears at your bedside, take her back to her room. Tuck her in and leave saying, "Mommy's going back to her own bed now. See you in the morning."

♦ Give her something to take comfort from – maybe one of your T-shirts to cuddle.

♦ Stay calm and patient so your toddler feels secure about settling down on her own.

♦ Be prepared to get up numerous times on the first night and maybe the second, too – however tempting it might be to give in one night, this will only confuse your toddler.

♦ Don't feel guilty – a good night's sleep is just as important for your toddler as it is for you.

Your toddler still needs a daytime nap to help her get through the day. Whether she is ready to go back to bed in the late morning, before lunch, or early afternoon, setting up a routine helps her know what to expect. Try to put her down before she's overtired.

Sleep tight tips

A well-rested toddler means a well-rested parent – who'll have more energy for the day ahead. Keep these points in mind when dealing with sleep problems, and you should both get a good night's sleep:

♦ keep bedtime the same every night
♦ keep the bedtime routine relatively short, winding down gently
♦ stick to the same order of events each night to help your toddler know what to expect
♦ leave a night-light on for reassurance
♦ don't use bedtime as a threat or a punishment.

Getting help

If your toddler continues to have sleeping problems that are making life difficult, speak to your healthcare professional. Often support from an expert can give you the extra confidence needed to foster good sleep habits. She may also refer you to a sleep clinic, or, more likely, to a psychiatrist or developmental specialist, depending on the nature of the sleep disorder.

Early risers

If your child wakes up early, leave a few toys out for her to play with – these may distract her long enough to allow you to get the extra sleep you need.

practical care of your toddler

Your curious toddler will need lots of care and attention when it comes to keeping clean. Some tasks – such as dressing and hair washing – may be more of a challenge than before. A few simple strategies will help you get the job done.

keeping your child clean

You can't expect your toddler not to get a little dirty during the day – but you can help him learn some basic rules of hygiene.

Work and play
Your toddler will enjoy playing with his toothbrush, but he should always be supervised, and will need your help to get the job done properly.

The more often your toddler is reminded about basic cleanliness, the quicker it will become a habit. Explain that we can't see germs, but that doesn't mean that they aren't there and that's why it's important to wash his hands after going to the toilet and before eating. Then make it fun: washing hands together, for example, and seeing who can make them the soapiest and rinse them fastest is a good game.

From around 18 months onward your toddler will love doing things for himself, especially if he thinks they are "grown-up." Give him a stool to stand on so he can reach the sink and check that he knows which is the hot and which is the cold faucet.

Tooth care

Your toddler will need his teeth brushed at least twice a day. After breakfast and after his evening meal is ideal because cavities form when the naturally occurring bacteria in the mouth combine with sugars in the food residues left on the teeth, producing an acid that attacks the tooth enamel.

Use a small, soft-bristled brush and a pea-size amount of toothpaste containing fluoride. Too much fluoride could cause permanent tooth stains. Sit your child on your lap, gently holding his forehead to keep his head still. What's important is to brush each tooth inside and out. Differently flavored toothpastes and fun toothbrushes can help encourage a reluctant child.

Now is a good time to get your toddler used to visiting the dentist every six months for a checkup. Do your best to make the occasion fun. If he's nervous, sit him on your lap in the "magic" chair so the dentist can have a quick look inside his mouth.

Like a grown-up
Keep a stool handy for your toddler to stand on in front of the sink, and she will be delighted to start washing herself.

The magic of soap
Teaching your child good cleaning habits at this age will help make sure that she maintains them for the rest of her life.

Nail care

Keeping your toddler's nails trimmed will help him avoid scratching himself or others, and prevent the spread of infection because nails can harbor dirt and germs. Use specially designed blunt-ended scissors or nail clippers for safety and always cut toenails straight across (see page 111). If your toddler is frightened, try:

♦ trimming in the bath underwater – water is soothing and makes the nails softer

♦ doing your own nails first – show him what fun it is

♦ distracting him with a song such as "This little piggy."

Bath-time fun

Your toddler will probably spend many happy hours playing in the bath – especially if your provide him with plenty of bath toys, such as empty and clean shampoo bottles, plastic boats, funnels, and cups. If your toddler refuses to get into the bath, try:

♦ focusing on his chance to have fun – "look at these bubbles" – rather than just getting clean

♦ giving him a bath at an unexpected time – when it's not part of the everyday routine – may have more appeal

♦ jumping in with him – bathing together may be more fun than doing it alone!

Hair care

By now your toddler will probably have lots of hair and, though reluctant, will need to have it washed and cut more frequently.

♦ **Hair wash** Prevent tears by using a baby shampoo. Ask your toddler if he wants to tip his head backward or forward – he may also like to hold a washcloth over his eyes or even wear a pair of swimming goggles. Encourage him to help lather up the shampoo before rinsing quickly but thoroughly. The promise of a special game or story afterward may help your toddler cooperate.

♦ **Haircut** Prepare your toddler for his first haircut with a game of "hairdressers" so he has an idea of what's going to happen. He may prefer to sit on your lap rather than in the hairdresser's chair to begin with. And it may be worth taking along some favorite snacks to distract him when necessary. Give him lots of praise for sitting still.

getting **dressed**

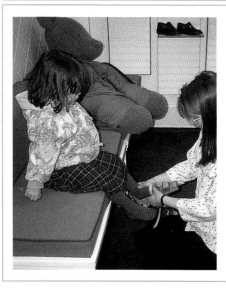

Your toddler's drive for independence may make dressing trickier than it used to be. She may no longer lie still and let you do all the work. The key to success is to make her feel involved in the process – give her a choice of what to wear, hold sleeves and pants open for her to put her arms and legs into herself, and let her do the simple parts, such as pulling up her skirt, herself. Singing and playing games such as peekaboo can help.

Once your child has been walking well for a few weeks, she can have her first pair of real shoes. Go to a reputable shoe store that will measure her feet – width and length – to find the correct size. Then check the fit of her shoes as often as once a month during this period (see page 185).

independence and tantrums

Your growing toddler is desperate to do things for herself. And although you'll need to stay calm and have plenty of patience, encouraging her will build her confidence and help avoid frustration.

asserting her independence

As your toddler realizes that she is a separate person from you, she'll want to start doing things on her own.

Although letting her try new things may slow you down sometimes, in the long run, the more your toddler can do for herself the happier she'll be. She may, for example, soon be going to daycare or you may be expecting another baby – and you won't always be available to do things for her.

Independence is also vital for her emotional development; gaining a strong sense of herself by being able to do things on her own will do wonders for her sense of self-esteem.

Giving your support

Despite her desire for independence, your toddler still needs you. In fact, your support is more important than ever – she may want to do things on her own, but she is still trying to master a lot of new skills and will often need your assistance. Give her plenty of encouragement and praise to motivate her. She will love sharing how clever she is with you, so expect to spend a lot of time watching and applauding her.

Ways to help

♦ Allowing your toddler to try something you know she can't do then stepping in and taking over will probably leave her upset and tearful. Instead, be helpful, but let her feel as if she's done it on her own.

What a clever girl!
Your enthusiasm and praise is the best reward when your toddler tries something new – even if she finds it difficult to master at first.

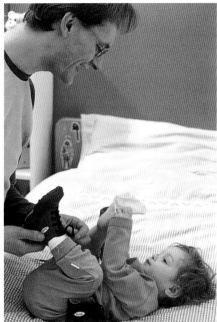

"I can dress myself!"
Your toddler loves being able to do things himself.

♦ Rather than prevent your toddler from trying something because it will slow you down – such as getting herself dressed in the morning – build in extra time to let her be successful.

♦ Make sure your expectations are realistic. All children develop at different rates, so resist comparing your toddler with others. Instead, watch for when she wants to try something new, and help her step by step.

♦ Provide a safe environment – playgrounds can give your toddler the chance to be adventurous and help develop her sense of independence without putting her in danger.

Gaining confidence
Providing a safe place to play and explore – sandboxes are ideal – will help build your toddler's self-esteem and his confidence. Don't forget the sunscreen!

Being consistent will help your toddler learn to accept certain limits – if the house rule is "no cookies before dinner" stick with it, however loudly she yells. At the same time, avoid too many limits. Setting as few as possible will help your child stay within the boundaries.

why your **toddler cries**

Your toddler may desperately want to be grown up, but she still needs lots of cuddles and comfort. Chances are she'll easily burst into tears during the day – and tears can sometimes turn into tantrums if not dealt with quickly. Common causes of tears at this age include:

♦ **Frustration** Either your toddler's desire to do something is beyond her capability or else she is prevented by you from doing what she wants. Try to help her when you can and find as few reasons as possible to say no to her. Use redirection instead.

♦ **Tiredness** This is especially true at bedtime – try not to let your toddler become overtired because she'll be even harder to put down. A happy bedtime routine (see page 112) will help her relax and feel calm and secure.

♦ **Insecurity** Fear of being separated from you can last for many months (see page 171). Having a comfort object such as a special toy or blanket can provide the extra security she needs when you are not around.

♦ **Boredom** Because your toddler is spending more time awake, there's more of a chance that she will get bored. And although she will love her toys, her attention span is still short, so they won't keep her amused for long. Although getting tasks done with a toddler in tow can slow you down, remember that being with you is her favorite activity.

♦ **Injury** Your toddler is more mobile than ever before and consequently will be much more prone to bumps and falls. Even a little scratch can bring on serious sobbing. Always be sympathetic – your child will forget about the injury much faster if you tell her you know how much it hurts.

♦ **Teething** Between 10 and 14 months your toddler is likely to start cutting her first molars. These are harder to cut than incisors and could make your toddler feel miserable. Try the same remedies you used when she was younger (see page 112).

♦ **Hunger or thirst** If your toddler becomes dehydrated or her blood-sugar level drops because she's hungry or thirsty, she's more likely to be irritable and difficult. Make sure she has regular healthy snacks throughout the day – once in the morning, once in the afternoon, and even if necessary, before brushing her teeth at bedtime. And encourage her to drink plenty of fluids – ideally plain water.

Temper, temper
When you first see your toddler throwing a tantrum it can he quite a shock as she screams, kicks, and even hurls herself to the ground, oblivious to everyone and everything around her.

coping with tantrums

Not all toddlers have tantrums – but around 18 months, when they experience a surge of independence, this behavior is more common.

Your toddler has many new physical skills, can understand a lot, and is determined to explore his capabilities. But he often finds he can't manage, or isn't allowed, to do what he wants. Tantrums – kicking and screaming, hitting other children, or refusing to cooperate over the simplest task – especially if he is overtired, are an expression of the overwhelming frustration he feels when this happens.

Understanding your child

Tantrums often happen when your child is feeling less secure than usual or your attention is less closely focused on him. You might, for example, be with friends when your toddler wants something from

you. It's hard enough for him to make himself understood when he can't talk well, and harder still if his parent is distracted or he is away from home and feels less secure than normal.

Thinking about the world from your toddler's point of view can sometimes help you see why he behaves the way he does. Knowing which situations your toddler finds hard to deal with can help avoid the frustrations that lead to tantrums.

Encouraging good behavior

At this age it's important to help your child understand what good behavior is. You can do this a number of ways:
♦ Give your toddler lots of praise and encouragement when he behaves well. Make your praise as specific as possible. Notice when he does something good, and tell him how pleased you are. He'll enjoy knowing that he's made you happy and this will encourage him to behave well

again. Don't expect too much – his learning will be slow because he has a very short attention span, but over time he'll understand how he can get positive attention from you.
♦ Ignore some of the bad behavior. If you get angry with him when he does something he shouldn't, he'll learn that one way to get your attention is to behave badly. Instead, if for example he throws a book, which may hit another child, call a time-out.
♦ Redirect him when you can. If you see a potentially explosive situation arising – he refuses to put on his coat when it's time to go out, for example – sing him a funny song and quickly slip his coat on while he's enjoying your antics.
♦ When you help him get dressed or put on his shoes or finish a puzzle, be subtle and diplomatic so he thinks he did it himself.
♦ Give him choices whenever you can. Letting him feel as if he has some control

over a situation can make all the difference. If, for example, he always refuses to wear the clothes you select, pull out a couple of reasonable choices and let him decide which he'd like to wear.

♦ Recognize your toddler's triggers – and preempt them when you can.

♦ Avoid shouting or aggression – with him and with others, such as your partner. Children learn by example.

♦ Reward systems are great. The best rewards aren't treats or candy, but attention from you.

♦ Don't take a firm stand if it's not important. Does it matter if he wears the red socks today, for instance? There is no point in inducing a tantrum by forcing him to wear the yellow ones that you chose.

♦ Use positive phrases to get him to do things. Toddlers are continually testing you and the boundaries you set, and if you listen to yourself you may realize you spend a large part of each day saying "No."

♦ Structure the day to avoid boredom and try to go out at least once a day. Think ahead for rainy days, and have a list of activities ready to amuse him.

Thinking ahead about which situations your child finds difficult – the supermarket when he's tired, or leaving a friend's house – can help you avoid them, or be ready with ways of dealing with them.

"Joe has already learned to scream to get his own way. I used to give in to him, but when it kept happening I realized I had to be firm. Now, when he throws himself on the floor, I just walk away. Then he usually gets up and runs after me. I've also learned to be more creative. He was banging on the TV the other day and the more I said 'no' the more he did it. So I got a tin cookie can and said: 'Come and bang on this, it sounds better.' He quickly forgot about the TV and really enjoyed banging on the can!"

ANNE MARSHALL, MOTHER OF JOE AGE 24 MONTHS

tantrums: what you can do

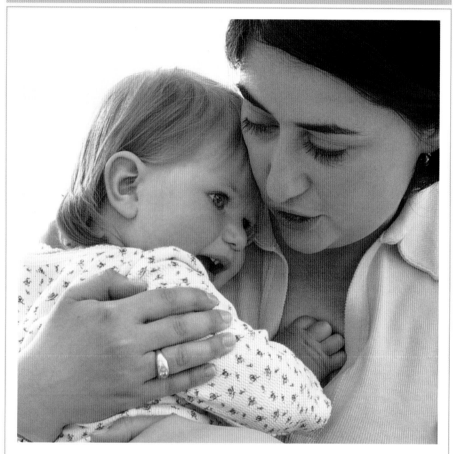

Even though it's natural for your toddler to want to assert himself, dealing with a tantrum – especially if it's in public – may test even the calmest parent. A full-blown tantrum is especially upsetting, for you and your toddler. Your child may fling himself onto the floor, kick, scream, make himself throw up and – most terrifying of all – hold his breath and turn blue in the face. Be reassured, however, that he won't harm himself – before he is in danger his own reflexes will force him to breathe again.

When your child has a tantrum:

♦ If possible, sit it out, as long as your child is not in danger. The sooner your child discovers that you are not responding, the sooner he'll stop.

♦ Stay calm – remind yourself that you are the adult, he is the child. Show him by example what is acceptable behavior.

♦ Improve your capacity to cope by not being embarrassed by your toddler's behavior – every toddler has tantrums and any mother who might witness the tantrum is probably just relieved it's not her child.

♦ Remain kind but firm – if you change your mind, or give in, your toddler will simply learn that tantrums work. If he knows you won't change your mind, he will eventually realize that it's not worth the battle.

♦ Remember that tantrums are a normal part of a toddler's development and it's important not to take them personally; they are not aimed at you.

starting toilet training

You know your toddler is growing up when she makes the big step out of diapers and into underwear. Although most children learn to use the toilet between two and four, there's no definite timetable. Your child will decide when she's ready.

is she ready to start?

Social pressure to toilet train your toddler can be intense – but until she is physically and emotionally ready there's nothing you can do to help speed up the process.

First, your child's nerve pathways from her bladder to her brain need to be fully mature. This can happen as early as 18 months and means she will begin to realize when she's peeing or pooping. But she still won't be able to predict when she needs to empty her bowels or bladder – it will be some time before she's familiar with the feelings of needing to go and has the physical control to hang on. Signs of readiness are easy to recognize; just follow her cues.

Signs to watch out for

The more ready your child is for toilet training, the faster and easier it will be. Signs that she is ready include:

♦ knowing when she is peeing or pooping – she may stop playing, stand still, look at you, go red in the face, and even try to tell you what's happening

♦ if she is naked, looking at the puddle she has made and clutching herself

♦ understanding what you are talking about when you show her a potty and explain what it is for

♦ willingness to try sitting on the toilet or the potty – even if she isn't actually using it

♦ wanting to copy you and use the toilet or wear real underwear.

introducing **the potty**

Even though at 18 months your toddler probably isn't ready to start using the potty successfully, you may like to have a potty around the house to give her the chance to get used to it.

♦ Choose a potty that won't tip over when it's sat on or when your child stands up. It should be curved inside for easy cleaning, with a molded back support, have a splash guard at the front, and a slot for carrying. Your toddler may like to help choose one.

♦ Put the potty in the bathroom next to the toilet and encourage her to sit on it before a bath, when you take off her diaper. If she does anything praise her, if she doesn't, don't worry. If she resists sitting on it, don't make a fuss – just try again a week or so later.

♦ Let your toddler see you using the toilet – most toddlers enjoy copying their parents.

♦ Remember, this is just about introducing the idea of the potty – not getting your child out of diapers. The more prepared your toddler is, the easier toilet training will be (see pages 138–139).

Make it fun

You should never force your child to sit on a potty or insist that she stays on it when she's obviously had enough. There's no harm, however, in a little extra encouragement. Sometimes this is all that's needed to spark an interest in potty training. You could, for example, try:

♦ getting a child's picture book about using a potty from a bookstore or library and reading it with your toddler

♦ surrounding her potty with things to look at – such as her favorite books and toys

♦ suggesting she can watch a video while she sits on the potty

♦ playing games together that involve her stuffed animals and dolls using the potty

♦ giving her lots of praise even if she sits on the potty and then gets up without having done anything.

Take your time

If you start trying to potty train your child, and she has repeated accidents, stop and go back to diapers for a few weeks.

Don't be angry with your toddler – it's not a reflection on her or on you. Making an issue out of it may delay progress even further. And after all, there's no hurry – your toddler will get there in her own time. Even if you are expecting another baby and would prefer not to have to deal with two sets of diapers, you won't want to deal with

Sitting position
Your toddler may be comfortable playing like this, but it is better for her legs to discourage her from sitting in this "W" position.

puddles and potties at the same time as coping with a newborn. Also, your toddler will be more responsive if she doesn't have to adjust to other changes in her life such as getting used to a new sibling.

"From very early on we had a potty in the bathroom, although it wasn't until Daniel was about 22 months that he tried sitting on it. Occasionally this coincided with a pee – and I'd praise him ecstatically! But I didn't push it – he obviously wasn't really interested. When he was about two years and two months he clearly knew if he was pooping. Because this generally happened around the same time each day – shortly after breakfast – I'd suggest he sit on the potty while I read him a book."

JOANNA HILL, MOTHER OF DANIEL AGE TWO AND A HALF

family life

One minute he's testing your patience, the next melting your heart – one thing is certain, with your toddler you will never be bored. Living with an emotional whirlwind can be tiring, so take a break occasionally and find time for yourself.

riding a roller coaster

Life with a toddler is full of extremes. One minute he's clinging to you refusing to let go, the next he's wriggling out of your arms and refusing to be cuddled.

He's bursting with energy, and moves fast, but usually in the opposite direction from you! He wants to be with you, copy you, and join in with everything you do, yet he also rages against you, and it seems as if nothing you do is right. He's like an emotional whirlwind, and living with him can be tiring. Providing him with a safe environment – in the home, or out – will give him the chance to explore without putting himself in danger or forcing you to rein him in all the time (see pages 262–266).

Going at his pace – allowing yourself extra time to get to the post office, being there for cuddles when he wants them, and not minding when he doesn't – will also help both of you avoid feeling frustrated.

Handling your feelings

There will be times when your toddler pushes you to your limit with his irrational behavior and your patience snaps. Losing your temper occasionally is understandable – talk to other mothers of toddlers and you'll discover that you are not alone. Feeling guilty won't help – forgiving yourself will. Apologize to your toddler, explain that it was what he did

Part of the family
Your toddler will love joining activities, although she may get frustrated if she can't keep up. Find a task she can manage and give her lots of praise.

having **another baby?**

You may find that you are starting to think about having another baby and wondering how to space your children. Some parents think that the closer in age children are the more likely they are to be friends, while others feel that the bigger the age gap the more time and energy there is for each child. There are no hard-and-fast rules – each family is different, and what works well for one may not work so well for another.

If you do decide to go ahead and expand your family, there will come a point in your pregnancy when you need to prepare your toddler for the arrival of his new sibling.

♦ Wait until the last few months of pregnancy before talking to your toddler about it – when he can see your growing belly he'll find it easier to understand what's happening.

♦ Explain to your toddler why your tummy is growing; let him touch and stroke your belly and say "hello" to the baby inside.

♦ Find a picture book in the library to help him identify with another little boy expecting a new baby in the family.

♦ Talk about friends and family who have younger brothers and sisters.

♦ Include him as much as possible in the preparations so he doesn't feel left out.

♦ Look at photos together of when your toddler was a baby, and give him lots of care and attention to help reassure him of your love.

– and not him – that you didn't like. Then give him a hug. He'll forget about it quickly, and it will help if you can, too.

Time for yourself

Spending quality time with your toddler, doing something you both enjoy, such as baking a cake or having a bath together, will help you feel close to him.

It's important also to spend some time on your own. Your toddler demands your constant attention, and sometimes the daily routine can feel pretty relentless. You can give him your best only when you are feeling happy and refreshed. Take a break whenever you can – whether it's a weekend away with your partner or an afternoon spent shopping on your own.

"When he's not tired, hungry, or coming down with a cold, Louis is angelic. He smothers me with affection, makes me laugh, and is a great companion. And as long as I'm one step ahead of him – ready with a snack when he needs one, avoiding tricky situations – the day goes smoothly. I try and make sure I get some adult contact during the day. Getting out of the house is really important – especially on days when Louis is fussy or clingy."

*PHILIPPA DESMOND, MOTHER OF LOUIS AGE **20** MONTHS*

caring for your toddler
24 to 36 months

Your toddler is growing up fast – she can run and jump, put on her own coat, and will soon be out of diapers and starting daycare or nursery school. She's full of life – and desperate to grow up – but she still needs lots of hugs and cuddles, too!

Growing up

This is an exciting year for you and your toddler. She is now a real companion – and you will have lots of fun together, whether it's walking in the park, looking at books, or making cookies. Family outings can be more ambitious – lunch at your local pizza restaurant, for example, can be an enjoyable occasion for everyone, even if you have to take a few distractions with you.

Your toddler will enjoy playing with other children, too – and you may decide later in the year that she's ready for nursery school or daycare. This is a big step for her, and you, too. Knowing what to expect – and how to handle her feelings as well as your own – will help make this a happy experience.

Sometime during this stage you may say good-bye to diapers – at least during the daytime. Recognizing when the time

is right and giving your toddler a lot of praise and encouragement will help make toilet training a success.

Facing fears

Although she's desperate to feel independent, your toddler will still sometimes feel anxious and come running back into your arms. She has a better understanding of the world around her, but she's not always mature enough to make sense of it. It's common for children of this age to develop fears – whether it's being scared of the dark or frightened of dogs. Lots of support will help these fears pass.

Your time

As your toddler becomes increasingly independent, she may be less demanding at home as she discovers ways to occupy herself. And once she starts daycare or nursery school, you may find yourself on your own for a few hours during the week.

Both you and your toddler will face a period of adjustment as you settle into your new routines. She may be extra tired when she comes home and test the boundaries more than usual. Meanwhile, unless there's a second baby to care for, you will be looking for ways to spend your newfound free time.

"Our favorite day is Tuesdays. We go to the park to feed the ducks together and then have hot chocolate and a bagel at the diner. It's a treat for both of us!"

LIZZIE WOODS,
MOTHER OF JACK AGE NEARLY THREE

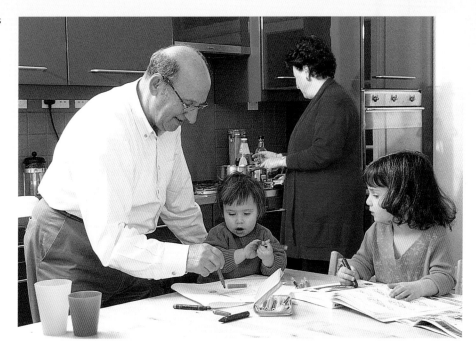

food and your child

Your toddler is eating a wide range of food and loves taking part in family meals – at home or in a restaurant. She's also mixing more with other toddlers, and you may find that candy and sugary drinks become harder to avoid.

a healthy, balanced diet

Your child still needs protein for growth, carbohydrates and fats for energy, and fruits and vegetables for vitamins and fiber.

So continue to offer your toddler foods from the four main food groups (see page 106). Try to serve four small portions of fruit and vegetables a day – for example, a tangerine as a snack, carrots with lunch, diluted orange juice as a drink, and banana and yogurt as a dessert. If you can't buy fresh fruit and vegetables, offer frozen, canned, or dried varieties.

After two years, your toddler can have low-fat milk, although if she is very active she may benefit from the additional energy provided by full-fat milk. She should have about 16fl oz (450ml) a day. If she won't drink milk, supplement her intake with full-fat cheese and yogurt. Avoid processed foods because toddlers need a full compliment of nutrients to stay healthy. Similarly, don't give too many high-fiber products because the extra fiber can prevent minerals from being absorbed properly.

Remember to include oily fish, such as tuna fish, salmon, and sardines, as well as white fish. Lentils and beans are a great meat alternative, but your toddler's digestive system won't be able to handle large portions every day.

five tips for
healthy eating

♦ Avoid foods that are high in saturated fats and additional salt and sugar.

♦ Steam, bake, grill, or boil foods rather than frying or roasting.

♦ Use as many fresh ingredients as possible.

♦ Give her water or diluted fruit juice when she is thirsty.

♦ Offer raw vegetables (carrot, celery, or cucumber sticks), fruit, or bread as snacks.

Family meals
Getting together as a family at mealtimes is an important aspect of family life – but don't expect too much from your toddler.

Eating with the family

Life is so busy for most families that sitting down together for a meal sometimes doesn't happen as much as we'd like. Eating together, however, is one of the best ways of encouraging your toddler to enjoy her food. She loves imitating and is more likely to try something new if she sees mommy or daddy enjoying it.

Chatting around the table will also give her a chance to develop her social skills and watching how you behave will help lay the foundations for good table manners. Try:

♦ eating together as often as possible – if you can't get everyone around the table at the same time, sit with your toddler so she's not eating alone

♦ getting your toddler involved – encouraging her to help you set the table, or take a dish out to the kitchen will help her enjoy the sense of occasion

♦ avoiding arguments – mealtimes should be a chance to relax and enjoy each other's company. Try not to get drawn into battles over food likes and dislikes

♦ not to expect too much – your toddler won't have the patience to sit unoccupied at the table for too long. Once she's finished, let her leave.

Dining out

Going out to eat can be fun for the whole family. Explain to your toddler beforehand what to expect and chances are she'll rise to the occasion.

♦ Time your outing – if your toddler is tired, or too hungry to endure a wait, she is unlikely to behave well.

♦ Choose a child-friendly place – lots of restaurants provide highchairs, crayons and paper, plus a special children's menu.

♦ Take your own distractions – a favorite book or selection of small toys will help keep your child amused while she's waiting for her food or when she's finished.

♦ Go for speed – select a restaurant that serves food without much of a wait and choose what you want as quickly as possible. When your toddler has obviously had enough, you and your partner may need to take turns taking her outside for a change of scenery.

♦ Avoid the danger of spills by bringing her own cup with a lid, even if she can usually manage without a lid.

♦ Order her favorites – she'll enjoy her meal more if she's served things she likes.

♦ Give her lots of praise – telling her how grown up she has been will encourage her to behave well next time, too.

Eating on the go
Children often get hungry when they're on the road, so take lots of healthy snacks such as bread sticks or fruit with you.

protecting **her teeth**

♦ Avoid using candy or desserts as a reward.

♦ Avoid offering fruit juice in excessive quantities because it can cause tooth decay. Dilute juice or offer water or milk instead.

♦ Tell relatives and caregivers about your candy policy so they can stick to it, too.

♦ Avoid sweetened or carbonated drinks.

♦ Remember that dried fruit contains a lot of sugar, which can also cause tooth decay. Keep it for mealtimes or outings.

♦ Check food labels: sugar can appear in many forms, including dextrose, glucose, honey, corn syrup, fructose syrup, and concentrated fruit juice.

♦ Brush teeth after breakfast, at bedtime, and after eating candy, if possible.

toilet training

Your toddler is ready to come out of diapers, and you've bought his first pair of underwear. Choose a quiet day to try toilet training: be prepared for the occasional accident, and remember to give plenty of encouragement and praise.

ready, set, go

Sometime this year your toddler will probably make the big step out of diapers and into underwear, if it hasn't happened already.

Between the ages of 18 and 36 months his bowel and bladder muscles will mature, helping him to predict when he needs to use the toilet. If you've already introduced the idea of the potty (see page 130) and he's watched you both using the toilet, your toddler will have a definite idea of what's expected. But how do you know when to take the plunge and start leaving his diaper off?

tips for easy training

♦ If you can, start toilet training in the summer, when your toddler can run around in the backyard without a diaper on.

♦ Dress your toddler in clothes he can easily manage himself – zippers on pants and buckles on overalls are hard for small fingers. Pull-up pants with elastic waistbands, skirts, and dresses are best.

♦ Suggest that your toddler use the potty after a meal – a story or video may provide an incentive.

♦ If you have a few successes, persevere – switching back to diapers occasionally because it's more convenient may confuse your toddler.

♦ When he has an accident, don't react negatively – just remind your toddler what the potty is for and change him without a fuss.

♦ Encourage your toddler with lots of praise and remind him how grown up he is now.

Ask yourself:
♦ is he interested in using a potty?
♦ can he indicate when he has the urge to go? Watch for the look on his face – is he clutching himself, aware that something is about to happen?
♦ can he pull his pants and underwear down without your help?

Leaving his diaper off

Buying some underwear together will help focus your toddler's attention. Make it a special occasion – tell him he's a big boy now and let him choose which design he'd like. Choose a morning or afternoon when you are both at home together, then take off his diaper and explain that without it on he will have to use the potty when he needs to pee or poop. After the first couple of mornings or afternoons, start to leave the diaper off for longer and more frequent periods. Meanwhile, give him plenty of reminders and encouragement.

Staying calm

Expect accidents and don't get angry or make a big deal out of them. For your toddler, using a potty instead of a diaper is all about learning a new skill. Put any pressure on him and he'll quickly decide it's not worth it.
♦ Never force your child to sit on the potty, even if you are sure he needs to use it – your toddler likes to think he's in charge and may prefer to assert himself by refusing to do what you want.
♦ Avoid words such as "good" or "bad" – if your toddler has an accident one day, just remind him that tomorrow he may not.
♦ If your toddler does have an accident, try to hide any feelings of disgust that you may have – it may not be pleasant, but your toddler may be upset or worried about pooping if he sees you reacting badly.
♦ If there are many accidents, it may be a sign that he's not quite ready yet. Wait a week or more before trying again.

Going out

Minimize the chance of accidents by always putting your toddler on the potty before you go out. You could also take the potty with you. Just in case, take a spare set of clothes, too. Many mothers use training

I'm so grown up
Teach your toddler how to flush the toilet and wash her hands each time she uses it so good hygiene quickly becomes a habit.

pants or pull-ups for outings because they absorb accidents, yet can be pulled up and down just like ordinary underwear.

Using a toilet

Once your toddler is happy using a potty he may want to try the toilet. He'll need a sturdy stool to step up on and a toddler toilet seat so he feels safe. Your toddler may want you to hold him while he's on the toilet. Even if he can get up and down easily and pull up his own underwear and pants, he will still need help wiping himself for a while yet. For a girl, that means teaching her to wipe from front to back, particularly after bowel movements, because contact between the feces and urethra or vagina can lead to urinary tract or vaginal infections.

Nighttime training

Even when your toddler is dry during the day, he may still need diapers for daytime naps and at bedtime. Encourage him to use the potty before going to sleep. Once you've noticed that he is regularly waking up early in the morning with a dry diaper, you can leave it off at night. Because there may still be the occasional accident, put a waterproof cover on his mattress.

why is he having accidents again?

Sometimes a toddler who has been out of diapers for a while will suddenly start refusing to use the potty and having accidents. If there's no medical cause (such as a urinary tract infection), it might be that your toddler is feeling anxious about something – such as a new baby in the family – or is reacting to the pressure to perform. Or maybe your toddler isn't getting to the potty or toilet in time because he wants you with him – it can be many months before children of this age are able to manage in the bathroom entirely on their own.

Show your toddler that accidents are not a problem – simply change him while reminding him gently about the potty. A little variety might help – a different-colored potty, new toilet seat, some more grown-up underwear, or fancy toilet paper. Encourage your toddler to feel grown-up in other areas of his life, and he may feel less of a need to assert himself when it comes to using the potty.

crying and sleep

Your toddler's ability to cope with his active life will depend a lot on how much sleep he has. Many seemingly trivial things will make him cry as he struggles to understand the world around him.

a need for sleep

Your toddler needs between 10 and 12 hours' sleep within each 24-hour period, although during a growth spurt you may find he needs more.

Depending on how early he goes to bed, when he wakes up, and how much stimulation he has during the day, your toddler may or may not still need an afternoon nap. Some go for a couple of days without a nap, then every third day or so make up for it with a long afternoon sleep.

Crying and comforting

Toddlers at this age can cry a lot. Being overtired is a common cause for tears. Low-grade whining is usual, too, especially

dealing with fears

Here are some common toddler fears and ideas on how to handle them.

♦ **The dark** Put a night-light in his bedroom or leave the door open wide and the hall light on.

♦ **Thunder and lightning** Hold him close and talk about the loud noise. Read a story that he enjoys.

♦ **Monsters under the bed** Cuddle up together and read some books about scary creatures – laughing about the "monsters" will help him feel more at ease.

♦ **Going somewhere new** Explain what will happen so he knows what to expect. Make it sound fun and exciting.

♦ **Animals and insects** Let him see you petting a friendly dog or acting enthusiastic about a spider you've found in the garden. He'll gain courage from your responses.

Nighttime comfort
Lots of toddlers like to take a special doll, teddy bear or blanket to bed to help them feel calm and relaxed as they fall asleep.

when your toddler wants something he can't have. Your child is also experiencing many new emotions – such as guilt, jealousy, and dislike – and sometimes these feelings will cause him to cry. Until he learns to manage these feelings, they may simply overwhelm him. One way to help is to tune into your toddler – and then change your own mood. If you are irritated when he gets angry, for example, try being gentle instead. Meeting his anger with yours will only make him more upset, whereas sympathy and understanding can make all the difference.

It's also common for children of this age to become easily frightened. Although you might not be able to banish fear from your child's life, you can make a huge difference in the way he handles it. Telling your child, for example, that he's silly will only make him more scared because he has to face his fears without your support. Instead, take his fears seriously and encourage him to talk to you about them. Your child trusts you, and if he sees that you are not worried, his own fears will become manageable.

Bed-wetting

It's not unusual for an otherwise dry toddler to wet the bed occasionally at night. Nighttime accidents often continue up to five or six years, especially in boys. Make sure that your toddler always uses the toilet before bedtime and use a waterproof cover to protect the mattress. Stay calm when accidents happen so your child doesn't become anxious. If accidents continue, you may want to go back to nighttime diapers for a while. If bed-wetting persists check with your healthcare professional.

"Our neighbor's dog always barked when we went to visit. Violet was terrified of the noise and became frightened of all dogs. When we went to the park, she'd run crying into my arms if one came anywhere near her. Then we went on vacation with friends, and they brought their dog, Rosie, too. Violet saw the other children playing with Rosie, and my husband and I made a point of petting and talking to her as well. During the week she became calmer when Rosie was around and even tentatively tried to pet her. She's now much less scared of all animals – and more confident in herself."

EMMA COLE, MOTHER OF VIOLET
AGE **36** MONTHS

coping with **nightmares**

Nightmares

Occasionally children have bad dreams. If your child seems happy during the day there's no reason to worry – although you might want to find out if he saw something scary or inappropriate on television or in a book. If your child wakes up at night, go to him right away and reassure him that it was just a dream and dreams can't hurt him. Tell him that everyone has dreams – and when he goes back to sleep it will be gone. Show him that he's safe in his bedroom, then stay with him until he falls back to sleep.

Night terrors

If your child appears to be awake – eyes open – but frightened and thrashing around in bed he may be having a night terror. Seeing your child like this is very upsetting, but you need to stay calm. Sit next to him to make sure he doesn't hurt himself, but don't try to wake him. Remember that he is not actually awake, even though he may look as if he is, and anything he can see or feel is only part of the night terror. After a while he will become calm and, without waking, settle back down. In the morning, he will remember none of it.

starting nursery or preschool

Your older toddler will enjoy making new friends and playing with new toys at nursery school or preschool – but how will she cope with leaving you? Choosing the right setting, and helping her to settle in, will make it easier for her to enjoy this new experience.

preparing **your child**

♦ The more secure your toddler feels, the more easily she'll be able to handle new situations. Long before she starts preschool remember to keep praising her and boosting her confidence.

♦ Going to play group together will help your child be comfortable with other children – once she starts wandering away from you to play, you know she'll soon be ready for preschool.

♦ Once you've chosen a preschool or nursery school for your toddler, go for a visit so she knows where everything is and can meet the staff.

♦ Find out how each session is run and, a few days before she starts, talk to your toddler about what to expect.

♦ Help her learn a few skills such as how to put on and take off her coat, drink from a cup, and go to the bathroom on her own.

♦ Don't overwhelm her with the newness of it all – too large a buildup may make her feel anxious.

♦ Be positive – acknowledge any worries she has and talk about them, but don't let your child pick up on any anxieties you may have. She will gain confidence from you, and your calmness will be reassuring.

what to expect

Preschool is good for your toddler – she'll learn how to play with other children, experience new ideas, and get used to being away from home.

But starting nursery school or preschool (they're virtually the same) can still be unsettling. Although your toddler wants to be independent, she also needs lots of reassurance. She has little concept of time, and although you tell her you'll be back in half an hour, she will learn only through experience what this actually means.

Getting her settled

The first day will probably be difficult for both of you. If you've prepared your toddler beforehand (see opposite), getting her settled may be a little easier.

Most nursery schools and preschools will encourage you to stay at least for the first session. Sitting quietly watching will allow your child to get involved without worrying that you're going to disappear suddenly. Once you can see your child happily involved in an activity, tell her you're going to go shopping and will be back soon (make sure to come back when you said you would).

Say good-bye and leave calmly and without hesitation: if your toddler sees you hovering around the door, she'll think you don't want to leave her there. But never slip away without telling your child you are going – tears may be upsetting for you, but if your child is feeling nervous, disappearing without warning will only make things worse.

If your child is clingy and cries, you may want to build up the time you are away gradually over the next few days until she is happy to see you go. If the crying continues every time you leave, it could be just for your benefit – the staff will probably tell you that once you have left she is fine, and you can always look through the window to check for yourself.

Choosing the right place

Some nursery and preschool programs are offered in the morning only, while others offer a full-day program. If your child has become accustomed to spending a lot of time with you (or other caregivers) at home, she may feel more comfortable with a morning preschool or nursery program. On the other hand, a child who is particularly independent, or whose mother has gone back to work, either full-or part-time, might feel perfectly comfortable with a full-day program.

Preschool and nursery schools offer similar activities, including art and music, sand and water play, fantasy play, outdoor games, story time, cooking, and other creative activities – and your child will have plenty of opportunity to play with other children, helping her develop social skills.

dressing **herself**

Teaching your child a few practical skills such as dressing herself can make settling into nursery school a little easier. Choose clothes with fastenings that are not too hard to work.

♦ Help her practice taking her coat on and off by herself – if it has a zipper, attach a ring to the tab to make it easier for her to pull up and down.

♦ Most toddlers can manage shoes with Velcro better than buckles and laces, although they won't necessarily get them on the right feet.

♦ Pants with elastic waists are much easier for your child to pull up and down than those with zippers. Show your child how to sit down to put her feet into the pant legs before standing up to pull them up.

♦ Dresses with fastenings on the front rather than the back will be easier for your daughter to button by herself.

Before you make any decisions about which preschool is best for your child, try to visit several. Points to look for include:
♦ are staff welcoming and friendly, and do they look as if they enjoy their work?
♦ how many children are there? Do they seem happy? How are they disciplined?
♦ is it a stimulating environment?

To get a feel for the school, ask if you can stay for a while. Think about the needs of your child. If she is energetic and outgoing, she may thrive best somewhere with lots of outdoor space. If your child is shy, you may want to look for a small and intimate preschool.

"In our neighborhood most of the children go to nursery school. Katrina loves going but she's mature for her age and we're hoping she'll be offered a place in our public school's pre-K program next year. A more structured environment would be better for her."

SALLY HUGHES, MOTHER OF KATRINA AGE NEARLY THREE

the next step

Starting your toddler in preschool will be a big step for you as well as him. You may be thrilled by your newfound freedom, or experience a sense of loss as he starts to develop a life of his own. Being prepared can help.

a new routine

When your toddler starts preschool or nursery school, you may have conflicting feelings.

On the one hand, you are proud of his step toward independence – and probably excited, too, about the freedom it gives you. On the other, you are anxious about his safety and well-being – suddenly he is out of your sight for part of the day, and you have no control over what he's doing.

You want him to be happy and feel special, but you may also feel jealous about the close relationship he has with his teachers.

It's natural to feel protective of your child – but it's important not to hold him back because of your own fears. Feeling confident about your choice of preschool will help calm a lot of worries. Talking to the staff about any concerns you may have and getting to know other parents and their children will also help. Try not

to let your toddler sense your worries: appearing relaxed and confident about this big step will help him take it in stride.

Time for yourself

Once your toddler starts preschool you will have a few free hours to yourself. Unless you have a new baby to care for or are occupied with part-time or freelance work, it may feel strange being without your toddler. Or you might feel overwhelmed by all the things you can do now that your hands are free!

Bear in mind that a few hours each day passes very quickly. Trying to cram a hundred and one tasks into that short amount of time will leave you feeling exhausted. Doing nothing, however, may leave you feeling lonely. Managing your time so there's a balance between doing something for yourself, working, and keeping up with the chores will be more satisfying. If you can't think of what to do, here are some ideas you might want to include in your weekly routine.

♦ **Exercising** You could join a gym, go swimming, or go jogging with friends. Exercise is great for boosting your energy and lifting your spirits, and if you are planning another baby now's a good time to get into shape for pregnancy.

Shaping up
Enjoy your newfound free time once your toddler starts preschool. Exercise at home or outside can give a great boost to your spirits.

♦ **Relaxing** Giving yourself a chance to recharge your batteries helps family life go more smoothly – relax on the sofa with a good book, soak in a hot tub, or sunbathe in the backyard.

♦ **Taking a class or doing part-time work from home** These can be both stimulating and satisfying.

♦ **Meeting friends for coffee** Talking with friends or colleagues who don't have children gives you a much-needed break from the concerns of parenthood.

At home

In the early days, your toddler is likely to be more tired after his sessions at preschool or nursery school and you may find him grumpy and difficult to deal with. This is an age when toddlers are typically testing the limits set by their parents – and tiredness can make children dig in their heels even more if they don't like what they are being told.

Tears and tantrums can be especially upsetting if you've missed your toddler while he was away. Try to remember, however, that it's because he feels secure and happy with you that he can behave the way he does. Also:

♦ don't expect too much from him when he's back at home – sitting down quietly reading stories together or watching a video might be more relaxing than a trip to the supermarket or dinner with friends

♦ avoid confrontations as much as possible. Although it's important to continue to set secure limits, try not to say "no" too often – instead use humor or a gentle challenge (can you finish your peas before I finish mine?) to get him to do what you want

♦ give him lots of support and reassurance – knowing that you can cope with his feelings, even if he can't, will eventually teach him how to manage them himself.

Sibling rivalry

Life at home with your toddler may be even harder if you have a new baby. Toddlers often display either overwhelming love or extreme dislike for a new arrival – sometimes both feelings almost simultaneously. Feeling threatened by a new brother or sister is entirely natural

Brothers and sisters
With time and patience your toddler will learn to love his baby brother or sister – and one day soon they will be great friends.

– although you can do a lot to help smooth the way by preparing your toddler in advance (see page 133). Once the baby has arrived and the novelty has worn off, try to minimize sibling rivalry by making sure your toddler has his own space and toys to play with well out of the baby's inquisitive reach.

Spending time together playing games both your baby and toddler will enjoy – such as hide-and-seek or singing songs

– will encourage your toddler to see the baby as a potential playmate. And don't forget to put aside some special time every day when you can be alone with your toddler so he still knows he is important.

"When the girls were just over two they dropped their afternoon nap. By dinnertime they were often very tired and emotional – and early evenings were a nightmare! I also felt very frustrated – I no longer had a couple of free hours when they were asleep to get things done. Now that they're in preschool, Martha and Josie love it – and having time for myself is wonderful."

CAROLINE WATTON, MOTHER OF TWINS MARTHA AND JOSIE AGE THREE YEARS

development

Watching your child grow and learn is one of the most satisfying aspects of being a parent. From reaching out to grasp your finger, to crawling or learning to draw, her physical growth and social, emotional, and intellectual development are inextricably linked. The following pages explain a young child's development at every stage, and will guide you on choosing the right toys and activities so that your child can make the most of learning through play. You will discover how to bring out the best in your child, and, equally important, how to let her enjoy just being a child.

your developing baby
birth to 6 months

From the moment she is born, your baby will develop at an amazing pace. At the same time, every achievement that she makes, every new milestone that she passes, is a result of all that you do to make sure she is happy, secure, and loved.

Your baby is unique

The most important point to remember as your newborn grows is that babies develop at different rates. Like all babies, yours will eventually smile, lift her head, babble, and grab things, all at her own pace. She won't do something just because a book says she will or because you want her to. The "right time" will be when she is ready.

Charts and books such as this one can offer only general guides to how babies develop. You cannot speed up the development timetable, but if you are giving your baby lots of love and attention, you are giving her exactly what she needs to develop at her own pace.

Your baby's development doesn't happen in isolation from the rest of the world; she can learn and progress only by being part of it. Having you, your partner, siblings, friends, and family members there is fundamental to her learning and developing.

Not only does she learn by example, she needs acknowledgment, love, and encouragement from the people around her in order to reach her full potential. So by doing what comes naturally – cuddling her, talking to her, going to her when she cries – you are giving her a sense of security and confidence that allows her to learn.

You are developing, too

As your baby learns to do more and more, your skills as a parent will adapt to meet her new needs. By your baby's four-month birthday, you will probably have established a daily routine for her, revolving around feeding, napping, going for walks, bathing, and going to sleep at night. A routine will help you both feel secure and confident, and will provide the foundation of your life together as a family.

The development process

Development is rarely a linear process: occasionally your baby's development may seem to take a step backward. For example, she may have slept through the night for several weeks and then suddenly start waking up every three hours again for no obvious reason. Such seemingly backward steps are perfectly normal –

in fact, they are often a sign that she is about to take a developmental leap forward. You may find that a week or two down the line, she is considerably more alert and responsive to people and events around her, or she is sleeping less during the day than before.

By playing games such as "This Little Piggy" on your two month old's toes, you are introducing her to the delights of anticipation (in this particular case, the tickle at the end) as well as the nature of counting rhythms. A game of "Hide the Teddy" with your five month old will help her understand that objects exist even when she cannot see them.

playing is learning

Playing with your baby provides the fabric of her learning experiences. Every time you play or interact with her, you are not just entertaining her – you're teaching her valuable lessons about herself, yourself, and the world.

For example, by shaking a rattle for your new baby, you are helping her learn to focus as well as introducing her to the concept of cause and effect – after a while she will begin to understand that shaking the rattle is what makes the noise.

While playing simple games, you'll find your baby is developing her own sense of humor, and she will soon start to let you know just how funny she finds your jokes!

the first 6 months

Each time you pick him up, play with him, talk or sing to him, smile at him, or soothe him, you are giving your baby information about his world and what it means to be a human being. Above all, you are teaching him that he is loved.

how your baby learns

The security you give your baby gives him the confidence to explore his environment. As the weeks and months pass, he will delight and impress you with a dazzling array of new skills.

He will start to control his own body and learn that he can influence his environment (by kicking at toys hanging from his baby gym to make them move, for example). He will respond to you with real excitement, communicate his needs and desires, and

know just how to make you laugh. He will also respond to the sounds, rhythms, and tones of language and will love to practice his own. He will be fascinated by his environment and become an active participant in everything going on around him. Best of all, your baby will become adept at expressing real pleasure in life – smiling, gurgling, cooing – and he will know just how to make you feel this pleasure, too.

Being your baby's "teacher" doesn't mean you have to give him constant stimulation or surround him with bits of colored plastic. "Playing" with your

baby during these early months is about providing for his basic needs: food, warmth, comfort, touch, and love.

Helping his development
Research shows that parents tend to do this naturally, but here are some pointers on how to help him get the most from his developing sense of awareness.
♦ **Stimulate his senses** Before he can move around independently, your baby explores the world with his five senses – sight, touch, taste, hearing, and smell.
♦ **Face him** Make eye contact with your baby. This will help him learn to communicate and feel secure.
♦ **Get him involved** Point out things, describe them, and talk to him constantly. By doing this, you are helping him pick up language as well as stimulating his curiosity.
♦ **Repeat yourself** Babies learn by repetition, and you'll help him by repeating words to promote recognition.
♦ **Take his lead** Don't push your baby to play if he's not in the mood; learn to read his cues.
♦ **Act it out** Describe and demonstrate whatever you are saying or doing. Babies really respond to exaggerated expressions.
♦ **Entertain him** Play new games, think of new songs, and give him new experiences

when you can, so he doesn't get bored.

♦ **Respond to him** If he cries, cuddle him. If he laughs, laugh with him. Acknowledge how he's feeling.

♦ **Tell him he's fantastic** Just like adults, babies love to be encouraged and told how clever they are.

Your baby's temperament

Many factors contribute to your baby's temperament. Genetics, gender, social environment, and number of siblings all play a large part. Of course, most of these factors are not within your control, and you will become very aware that you cannot choose your baby's personality.

But by far the most important of all influences on your baby during the first months – and years – of his life is his relationship with you. You may not be able to choose what "type" of baby you have, but the way you interact with him and respond to him now can have an incredible influence on his developing character.

Evolving personality

Whatever personality he has, he will benefit from your love and attention. By following his cues and being as nurturing as possible, tending to his needs and responding to his cries when he is tiny, you can help him establish a strong sense of confidence and self-worth. Feeling confident and secure is not only a major asset in life, it is also fundamental to healthy development.

Remember that your baby's personality is constantly evolving. Try not to stick any labels on him, such as "shy" or "cranky," because this can affect the way you respond to him. Nobody can predict what sort of person he will be. You will undoubtedly delight in discovering all aspects of your baby's emerging personality.

birth to 6 months: your baby's milestones

The following is a general guide to baby development. Remember, there is a wide range of what's "normal" for each month. If you have questions, ask your baby's pediatrician or family practitioner.

The first month
♦ recognizes your voice and smell
♦ may try to lift his head when on his tummy
♦ sticks out his tongue in response to you doing it
♦ starts to uncurl from fetal position

The second month
♦ lifts his head for a few seconds
♦ smiles for the first time
♦ coos in response to you
♦ loses some newborn reflexes
♦ makes smoother movements
♦ shows excitement when he knows you are near
♦ can see things farther away
♦ opens and closes his mouth in imitation of you when you talk to him

The third month
♦ becomes more interested in people around him
♦ starts to notice his hands
♦ can open and close his hands and play with his fingers
♦ may hold his head without support for a few seconds
♦ may briefly push himself up on his arms when lying on his tummy
♦ grasps a toy in his hand
♦ swipes at toys
♦ reaches out and grabs at things
♦ experiments with vowel sounds
♦ may gurgle

The fourth month
♦ head control becomes steady
♦ uses hands to explore his own face and objects of interest
♦ may make recognizable sounds
♦ can remember some things – for example, that a rattle makes a noise
♦ can recognize people closest to him as individuals, and will have a distinct reaction to different voices
♦ is naturally outgoing and not at all shy or self-conscious

The fifth month
♦ grabs his toes and puts them in his mouth
♦ may try to take his weight on his legs when held upright
♦ starts rolling over from front to back
♦ turns his head away when he doesn't want any more food
♦ reaches for toys he wants
♦ concentrates for short periods
♦ puts everything in his mouth
♦ raises his arms to be picked up
♦ wants to be included in everything
♦ becomes excited at the prospect of food

The sixth month
♦ holds his head steady
♦ keeps his head in line with his body when pulled to sitting position
♦ grasps objects
♦ enjoys sitting up with support
♦ starts to chuckle
♦ blows bubbles and makes a raspberry
♦ changes tone of voice to express himself
♦ initiates interaction: knows he can get your attention by making sounds and banging objects

birth to 2 months

It may seem that all your newborn does is eat, sleep, and cry – but from the moment she is born, she is developing new skills with incredible speed. By the end of her second month, her personality will really begin to shine through.

key **milestones**

♦ lifts her head for a few seconds
♦ stretches out and uncurls from the fetal position
♦ first smile at about six weeks
♦ starts to imitate your mouth movements when you talk to her

physical development

During the early weeks, your baby will still be curled up, with her legs drawn in and her hands clenched.

Even before she was born, your baby was exercising her muscles – and now she has a lot more space to do it in. When she is awake and alert, she will punch the air and kick her legs vigorously, especially in response to stimulation or when she is agitated or crying. These movements are jerky, random, and uncontrolled at the moment, but they strengthen her muscles and stimulate her nervous system, paving the way for more controlled attempts later on.

During her second month your baby will spend more time awake. You could try putting her under a baby gym on the floor, so that she has something to swipe at. She will miss most of the time to begin with because even though her arm movements are becoming more purposeful, her coordination and her ability to judge the distance between objects are still developing.

Remember that babies want and need to be with their parents when they are awake, so try to keep to a minimum the time your baby spends entertaining herself. She would much rather be interacting with you.

A nose for security
A newborn baby will recognize her mother's unique smell just hours after birth and quickly associates it with the comfort of being held in her arms.

Head control

Before your baby can control her body, she needs to master the art of holding her head up unsupported. Until she has full head control – which may not come until she is four months old – you must always make sure you support her head when you are holding her.

Over the next few weeks her neck muscles and the muscles at the top of her spine will gradually strengthen, allowing her to support her head herself. By eight weeks she may be able to raise her head to a 45-degree angle for a second or two when lying on her tummy.

Uncurling and stretching

During her first few weeks your baby will begin to stretch out and uncurl from her fetal position. Her knees and hips will be stronger, and they won't be as flexed as before. And the tightly clenched fingers of your newborn will unfold one by one into an open hand, ready for grasping objects.

By the end of this stage, if you put a rattle into the palm of your baby's hand she will probably try to grasp it automatically and hold on to it for a little while.

learning skills

Your baby is learning and developing all the time – and the main way she does this is through her relationship with you.

She is incredibly receptive to any kind of contact you have with her: notice how she becomes calm and concentrates when she hears your voice, or how she watches your moving lips with fascination as you talk to her. Watch her carefully and you may see her move her body in excitement when she knows you are near. She gets enormous pleasure from this relationship, and her brain is being stimulated, too, making it easier and more pleasurable for her to respond to loved ones in the future.

Vision

Your baby's senses are exquisitely attuned to help her take in all the information she needs for survival and development.

Her vision will go through many changes during the first month. At first, she'll see only the edges of things because the center of her visual field is still blurred. She'll like to look at objects held about 8–15in (20–35cm) in front of her – just the right distance for watching your face as you feed or hold her. Focusing on your face and the faces of other family members is important to your baby. By one month she'll be able to focus on things as far away as 3ft (90cm).

first **smile**

Your baby's first real or responsive smile will appear at about six weeks. You'll know it's a real smile because her eyes light up at the same time, and, as you respond by smiling back, it becomes stronger.

Although she may have made previous practice runs during the early weeks of her life, you'll recognize the real thing because she'll use her whole face, especially her eyes.

This is a real breakthrough in her development. The more she smiles at you, the more you will smile back and talk to her. Her happy face cannot help but engage you in interaction with her, and this is exactly what she needs to develop into a social human being.

Happy days

Once she has learned to smile, there will be no stopping her. She will smile at anyone she sees to begin with, especially if someone is looking at and talking to her. But within just a few weeks, you will notice that she is more choosy about who she smiles at; she will quickly learn to tell the difference between familiar and strange faces.

More than anything else, this is a very enjoyable stage in your baby's development. Her smile is telling you that she is happy to be with you. So smile back at her and let her know you're happy, too!

toy **box**

Mobiles

Newborns prefer a mobile with bold colors and contrasting patterns. Musical mobiles that move will also fascinate her and help her develop her "tracking" skills. Be sure to attach the mobile securely to the side rails of her crib. Hang it high enough so your baby cannot reach it or pull it down, and remove it when she is able to get up on her hands and knees, or when she reaches five months, whichever comes first.

Mirrors

Buy an unbreakable mirror that's specially made to attach to the inside of your baby's crib or playpen so she can entertain herself when you're not nearby.

Books

It's never too early to introduce your baby to books. Choose board books designed for young babies, which have clear, bold pictures of faces, babies, animals, or patterns. They will help your baby familiarize herself with everyday faces and objects. Sit her on your lap and talk about the pictures, pointing out things as you look at the different pages.

To begin with, she won't want long sessions with a book, but as her vision and mind develop, she will get more and more out of them.

Rattles

Your baby will love holding a rattle and enjoy the sound it makes when you shake it for her, even if she can't do much with it herself at the moment.

Baby gym

A baby gym or crib gym (one that you hang over a stroller or crib) has an array of interesting objects hanging from it to interest your baby. Choose a gym with toys that make a noise as well as those that are colorful. She'll love things that

squeak, rustle, or rattle. Move her position from time to time so that she can look at all the different toys.

Share what you've learned with others. Show siblings and other family members how to hold her so that she can respond more fully.

Talk to your baby

Even at this stage, your baby is tuning in to the tones and rhythms of language all the time. Talk to her as much as you can, and try to use exaggerated modulation in your speech. It's OK to use "baby talk" at this stage of her development. You are beginning to teach her the building blocks of conversation. It won't be long before her understanding of language becomes more sophisticated and she may start to respond to you by making little noises or moving her mouth when you talk to her.

Memory for detail

Although your baby's memory is very short-term in the early weeks, her ability to remember is improving and becoming more sophisticated all the time. To help stimulate her memory, let her experience things with more than one sense. For example, she is far more likely to remember a toy if she has been allowed to touch it as well as look at it, because her memory will include details such as shape and texture as well as outline and color.

emotional development

Your newborn is a little bundle of emotions. From the first few moments of life, she is very sensitive to the moods and feelings of the people to whom she is close.

You may notice, for example, that your baby becomes agitated if you are feeling upset or worried, and that she seems more calm and content when you are feeling relaxed. This emotional sensitivity is an important newborn characteristic.

In later stages of development, it will help her adjust her behavior and enable her to respond appropriately to the people around her. In other words, her awareness of the moods and feelings of others is fundamental to her development into a social human being.

You will probably find, particularly in the early days, that it is hard to understand exactly how your baby is feeling or what it is that she needs or wants. But over time, as your relationship develops, she will soon become easier to read, and both you and your baby will find the time you spend together increasingly emotionally rewarding.

By her second month, your baby is learning to recognize and respond to you. The most rewarding response at this stage is undoubtedly the appearance of her first social smile at about six weeks old (see page 153).

Calm contentment

You will be able to tell when your baby is feeling happy or content because she will lie peacefully, looking intently into your eyes or at her surroundings. These moments may be short-lived to begin with because most of her time will be spent eating or sleeping, but they will be very pleasurable for you both when they do occur.

Quiet, content times are very important for your baby for many reasons. They give her brain's higher centers the chance to take over. This means she can exercise her curiosity, practice focusing on things, and, most important of all, give you some undivided attention. And just being with you will make her feel secure and happy. These periods when your baby is quiet yet alert are some of the special moments when you and your baby can really get to know one another.

Knowing that your baby is content can be incredibly emotionally fulfilling – it is a sign that you are meeting her needs. This will increase your confidence as a parent and, at the same time, strengthen your bond with your baby.

A time to cry

For now, your baby's physical requirements take priority over everything else, and she will express herself accordingly. She will cry to let you know she is hungry, tired, or uncomfortable, or feeling vulnerable and in need of a cuddle (see page 98).

Respond to your baby's cries and make sure you give her all the reassurance she needs. Lots of attention and love now will teach her how to respond positively to you and help her develop into a secure and confident baby.

After a few weeks, although she will still cry as all babies do, she will also begin to discover other ways to get your attention and communicate with you. You will notice she starts to use her whole face and body to get the response she wants.

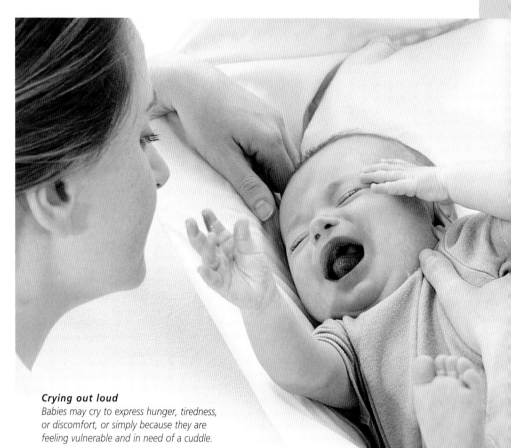

Crying out loud
Babies may cry to express hunger, tiredness, or discomfort, or simply because they are feeling vulnerable and in need of a cuddle.

learning through play

You are your baby's number-one favorite plaything. Talk to her, rock her, sing to her, or put on some music and dance around the room with her – all these activities will bring her pleasure and stimulate her, with positive results.

Copy cat!

Try sticking out your tongue at your baby every 20 seconds when she is looking into your eyes, and you may soon see a tiny tongue sticking back at you. Be patient – it may take her a minute or two to respond.

Light and shade

Your baby's attention will be caught by objects with bold patterns of light and shade: your face, a Venetian blind, or a black-and-white picture, for example. This is because strong contrasts are easily picked out even with poor vision.

♦ Draw black-and-white patterns and faces and stick them onto the wall by her crib.

♦ Place her crib near a window where there is a play of light and shade.

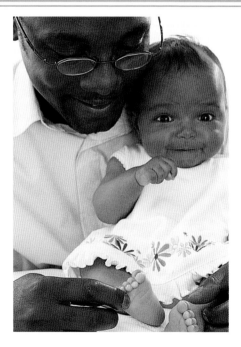

Playful interaction
Supporting her head with his body, this father plays "This Little Piggy" with his baby's toes.

Sensory stimulation

♦ Splash water in the bath with her feet while you hold her carefully supported in your arms. This will stimulate her sense of touch without making her feel insecure.

♦ Prop your baby up in a car seat or a bouncy chair so she gets a good view of what's going on around her. Talk to her from different places in the room and watch how she tries to locate the sound. Games like this help her to coordinate sight and sound.

♦ Play "Ring Around the Rosie" or "This Little Piggy" to encourage her fingers and toes to relax. Wiggle her fingers and toes as you say the rhymes. This also reinforces your baby's ideas about enjoyment and interaction.

♦ Repeat the same song a few times, and see how long it takes before she learns to anticipate the tickle at the end.

♦ Your baby may also like it if you stroke the palm of her hand and her fingertips with anything soft or furry in texture. Try it and see how she responds.

2 to 4 months

Your baby is now more in control of his movements, and will become more communicative toward you using gurgles and smiles. He will be able to hold his head steady, and he has discovered a source of great pleasure: his hands.

physical development

As your baby gains control over his body, he will begin to understand how he can use it to learn more about his world.

His neck muscles will now be so strong that when he lies on his back, he'll be able to lift his head and hold it up for several seconds. When you grasp his hands and pull him to a sitting position, his head may no longer flop back, but will lift up as his body is pulled upward. Sit him in a bouncy chair or prop him up with a few pillows, and he may be able to hold his head steady. Lay him on his stomach and he'll begin doing mini push-ups, lifting himself with his hands and arms, and turning his head.

He may not be able to hold these positions for long at first, but every time he does it his muscles are strengthening. This gives him much more opportunity to take in his surroundings, and he will become increasingly curious about them.

Get ready to roll

His developing neck control marks the beginning of a whole new adventure for your baby. His increased strength, confidence, and ability to maneuver himself up onto his hands means that sometime over the next few months, much to his surprise and yours, he will suddenly find himself rolling over. Active rolling can start any time from about three months onward, but it can occasionally take place earlier and unexpectedly.

increasing **hand control**

Your baby's hand control is becoming more refined, and by his fourth month he may be able to grab hold of a rattle or toy if you give it to him, although he may not be able to let go of it yet.

♦ He will be fascinated by what his hands can do. They, along with his mouth, are his tools for the exploration of his world. He will use them for searching and exploring parts of his own face, such as his nose and his mouth. He will also use one hand simply to play with the other.

♦ He will still enjoy swiping at toys within reach and will occasionally manage to grab hold of one. When this happens he won't quite know what to do with the toy – except, of course, to put it into his mouth to explore it with his tongue.

♦ He will be intrigued by the sensation of holding different-textured objects, such as a soft, squashy toy and a cool, smooth, plastic one.

Never leave your child unattended on a bed, changing table, or any surface raised above floor level because he might choose this moment to roll over for the first time, and fall off.

Fascinating fingers

They may have been there all along, but your baby has only just noticed his hands. These will now become an ever-present source of fascination to him, and he will spend a lot of time lying still and intently examining his newfound fingers, watching as they interact with one another.

He will quickly learn to bring his hands together and play with his fingers, jamming them into his mouth, where he will enjoy sucking them. He will love to watch his hands as they clasp and unclasp, and will press his palms together in a clapping motion.

toy **box**

Textured toys

Now that he is grabbing hold of things, it's worth giving your baby lots of different textures to experience.

♦ Let him have a range of toys to explore: smooth plastic toys; toys that are squashy; "bean bag" toys that change shape as you hold them; toys with bumpy surfaces. Make sure they are safe for a baby to play with before you buy them.

♦ Allow him to touch different materials, such as fur, silk, velvet, water, and warm skin.

♦ His crib gym and play mat may also become more fascinating now. Let

him lie on a play mat that has lots of different textures on it.

Noisy toys

Toys that make a noise, such as a squeaky duck, will now be very entertaining. You'll need to help him squeak these for a while because they may still be too hard for him to manipulate, but he will love the surprise sound they make.

Once he has learned how to make a toy squeak, he'll get even more pleasure from it – and, what is more, he'll be continuing to learn about cause and effect.

Ball play

Your baby will be fascinated by objects that move – especially if he can control them. Try laying him on his tummy and rolling a brightly colored ball in front of him across his line of vision, about 2ft (60cm) away from his body. At first he will watch the ball intently as it moves from one side to the other, but he will soon come to anticipate this action and try to reach out to grab it on subsequent rolls.

Rattles and baby gym

He will enjoy holding a rattle, and he will pull at toys hanging from his baby gym with more confidence.

learning through play

Now that your baby is responding to you and conversing with you more, you will have even more fun playing and interacting with him. He still needs lots of cuddles, words of encouragement, and reassurance, but you can expand your repertoire with more adventurous activities such as bouncing games and singing.

Singing games
♦ Gently bounce your baby on your knee to the beat of his favorite song.
♦ Sing splashing songs in the bath, counting songs when you play with his fingers, lullabies when it's time to go to sleep – he'll love them all!
♦ Try patting out the rhythm of the songs on his tummy or hands as you sing to him. This will give your baby even more enjoyment.

Playing with finger puppets
Your baby will be fascinated by the distinctive and friendly faces of finger puppets. Bring them to life by moving your fingers, perhaps integrating the movement with a song or story.

Make a noise
♦ Now that he has found his hands, your baby might enjoy having a wrist toy or bell bracelet Velcroed around his wrist. He'll learn that by shaking it he's making the noise.
♦ Your baby will enjoy holding a rattle and will like the noise he makes when he shakes it.

learning skills

Your baby is already a quick thinker. He is now fascinated by his own body and is beginning to understand that when he wants to he can make it move by himself.

This is an important first step in your baby's understanding of the concept of cause and effect. He is also beginning to connect seeing with doing, which is the first step in developing hand-eye coordination.

Memory advance
Your baby's memory will now have developed sufficiently for him to remember certain people and events. One study of babies of this age found that they quickly learn how to kick a mobile attached to their crib to make it move. When the mobile was taken away for a week and then put back in place, the babies could still remember what to do.

Clarity of vision
His eyesight will have greatly improved since those first hazy newborn days, and your baby can now use both eyes together to focus on something, whether it's close up or on the other side of the room. This means that he is more able to judge the distance between himself and the things he is looking at, so his hand-eye coordination will be much better now.

This clarity of vision also means he can clearly focus even on something as small as a button and follow a moving object held a few inches away. When the object disappears, you may notice him continuing to stare at the space where he last saw it.

Sound combinations
Your baby will begin to experiment more with vowel sounds, and his vocabulary will range from brief, one-syllable squeaks and squeals to long "eh" and "oh" vowel sounds. He is beginning to discover which sounds are made by which combinations of throat, tongue, and mouth actions.

At first, these cooing, throaty gurgles will seem completely random, but you will gradually notice that the sounds your baby is making are directed at you when you talk to him. He is enjoying socializing with you, as well as the sound of his own voice.

emotional development

Your baby is learning that being friendly is rewarding because of the way you respond to him with cuddles, love, and soothing sounds.

Now that he understands this, he will smile even more, knowing that you will smile back. He will also welcome you with definite waves and wriggles when he knows you are coming to him.

Response and recognition

One of the most significant developments that your baby's sharpened memory brings is that he now has a very detailed image of the people closest to him, so he can recognize them as individuals. This starts to influence the way he interacts with you, your partner, his siblings, and anyone else with whom he has a lot of contact.

For example, now that he knows you, he may have very distinct responses to your voice, which are quite different from his responses to your partner's voice: seeing or hearing you may calm him down, while hearing his father's voice may make him excited, for instance.

Skilled expression

Your baby's different little noises are beginning to be recognizable now. He is becoming more skilled at expressing himself. For example, he may show his feelings of pleasure by making attempts to "coo" to you. He may even shriek with pleasure and giggle to express his delight. He will also be learning that loud screeching will bring you running to his side – another lesson in cause and effect!

Although your baby cannot repeat any words, he is listening to you and storing them all for the future, so the more you talk with your baby, the better.

Feeling secure

At this stage, your baby will probably be naturally outgoing and not at all shy or self-conscious. He will charm everyone with his smile, and although he'll prefer

Love and laughter
Your baby will not only smile when you smile now, he may even laugh out loud in delight when you do something he enjoys.

you over others, he will love to "talk" to people – other babies, complete strangers, even his own reflection. He is learning to take the lead, which is important for his self-confidence, and as you follow his lead, you learn even more about his emerging character and sense of fun.

By his fourth month, you may have decided to start a routine of regular naptimes, walks outside, feeding, baths, and bedtime. This helps him learn to anticipate the events of the day, and teaches him that his life has a pattern to it. It helps him feel emotionally secure and increases his confidence. Establishing a routine also helps him to trust that you are near, even if he cannot see you.

Having a structure to your day and getting out and about will increase your pleasure, too. You may find that it boosts your confidence and helps you feel in control of your new job as a parent.

4 to 6 months

Your baby will now be making controlled movements and may be starting to use her limbs to maneuver herself by rolling from front to back. She's becoming more aware of new situations and can detect changes in her surroundings.

physical development

Improved muscle control and understanding of what her body can do means that your baby's movements are now quite deliberate.

You will notice that she is much more effective in reaching and grabbing hold of what she wants, or positioning herself on the floor to play, for example.

Keeping steady

Your baby will now be able to hold her head steady when held upright, and will keep her head in line with her body without it falling backward when pulled to a sitting position – a major developmental milestone.

Although she may not be able to support herself sitting up yet, she will definitely feel happiest propped up in a sitting position so that she can keep an eye on what's going on around her and join in with everything. You may find she takes great delight in kicking the sides of her bath when she's in the water, or kicking out at any surface within reach of her toes.

Mighty muscles

Your baby will enjoy any activity that gives her a chance to push with her legs and feet – and doing this will help strengthen her muscles for crawling. If you hold on to her hands, she may try to bounce up and down, although she won't be able to hold a standing position for very long. Don't let go of her, because she does not yet have the muscle strength or physical coordination skills to take her own weight on her feet.

Baby love
At six months your baby will really demonstrate her love for you: she will want to touch your face, grab your hair, and will hold out her arms to be picked up.

When she is lying down the improved control she has over her limbs means she can now begin to roll over onto her back from her front. This is an important milestone because she is gaining control over her whole body, and paving the way for learning to crawl.

Staying focused

Your baby's eyesight and hand-eye coordination have improved so much that it is almost as good as yours. She can now deliberately reach for an object and bring it straight to her mouth. Faces are still her favorite thing to look at, and she is able to distinguish facial expressions now. She can tell a happy face from a sad face.

coordination **skills**

Your baby's visual skills now mean that she is able to judge how far away a toy is and maneuver herself to reach out for it and grab it with one or both hands.

♦ She will be able to hold a toy firmly in her grasp, with her fingers securely curled around it. If she holds a rattle, she may now know what to do with it (thanks to her improved memory).

♦ Her own body still holds great fascination for her, and she will love to grab her foot and suck her toes when she feels like it.

learning skills

Your baby is increasing her non-verbal forms of communication, using her body to make her point.

She will push you away if she wants to do something else; reach for something she wants to play with; or turn her head away to let you know she doesn't want something.

Learning to speak

Your baby is eager to communicate with you, and will try to make different sounds with her mouth.

She will practice using her tongue, poking it out and making a raspberry sound with her lips. Listen to her carefully. As she realizes that people use different noises to communicate, your baby will also become more adept at changing her tone of voice in the hope that you will turn and look at her.

She is probably more vocal in letting you know what she wants by making specific babbling sounds that mean "Pick me up" or "I want to play with that."

Listening to you

Although she doesn't understand the meaning of many of your words yet, she will understand their tone. She will be very sensitive to changes in the tone of your voice. A firm tone will stop her, but is also likely to make her cry. If overused, it will discourage her natural curiosity and learning later on. Reserve using "No!" for situations of danger.

Through watching your facial expressions she will begin to learn what you are saying. By allowing her to watch you as you speak, you are continuing to lay important foundations that will later help her to form words through imitation.

By her sixth month your baby is beginning to understand a little more of what you say. She may start to turn her head toward you when she hears you use her name in conversation and will understand often-repeated words such as her own name, "mommy," or "bedtime."

Concentration skills

Your baby will really be able to concentrate now, and some toys, games, and activities will hold her interest for longer periods.

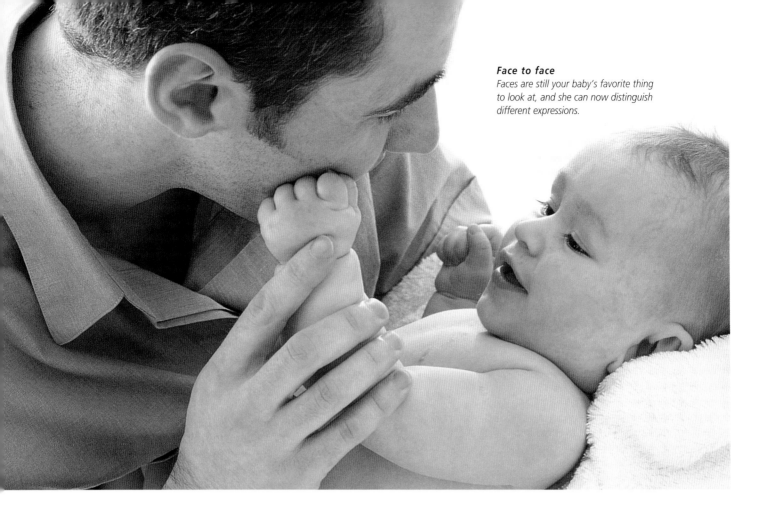

toy **box**

Surprise
Your baby will love games with an element of surprise. A jack-in-the-box, a pop-up clown, or a toy that makes a noise if you press it in a certain place will be great fun now. Encourage her to interact and use her hands and visual skills by helping her to push down on toys to make them pop up.

Music and movement
Your baby will enjoy toys that she can play with easily. A baby piano, xylophone, or a clear rattle with colorful beans inside will be lots of fun and will teach her about the power she has over things. Let her be the conductor of her own little orchestra.

Squeak?
Put a different toy into each of your baby's hands. Make sure they are pliable enough to make a squeaking noise with just one hand. Watch as she tries to work out which hand the noise is coming from when she presses.

Mat exploration
Her play mat will now be more useful. Although she is not crawling yet, your baby will be able to move herself around a little by rolling or using her arms. A brightly colored activity mat with attached toys will keep her amused as she explores the different areas on it.

Cuddly toys
Your baby will love playing with stuffed animals. Encouraging her to role-play with a favorite teddy teaches her sociability, gentleness, and kindness. It won't be long before she will start "looking after" her toys, too.

Make sure that all of your child's toys meet the required safety standards (see page 262).

Not only will she hold a toy, she will examine it, manipulate it, and feel and taste it by putting it into her mouth. This is her most sensitive area, so it's a natural place for her to put things to find out more about them. Always make sure that small objects are not within your baby's reach since she could easily choke on them.

Broader understanding
Your baby's greater comprehension of what is going on around her means that she will now concentrate on subjects for longer, whether it's looking at a toy in her hands or watching you.

She can now focus intently on one thing at a time – listening to music, watching you, examining a picture in a book, or scooping up a building block with her hands – before becoming distracted and moving on to a new activity. You can help increase her attention span by gradually minimizing distractions and gently redirecting her to a shared activity when her attention starts to wander.

emotional development

By now you will have a good idea of your baby's personality and her developing personal characteristics.

Although she may be happy to be held by strangers, she is now able to distinguish between people she knows and those she doesn't, and will show a definite preference for familiar faces – yours most of all.

She will get a lot of enjoyment from social situations such as watching other children play, sitting in her high chair at family mealtimes, and being taken to the park. These events also help her to interact with other people and feel comfortable in new situations.

Interactive family

Let her be a part of everything that is going on. Encourage her as she tries new things, and acknowledge her when she makes her own contributions – whether it's a gurgle or a hand lifted up with a toy in it to show you. Encourage everyone around her to respond to her in this way, too. Siblings, friends, your partner – they will all be sources of endless fascination for your baby, and the more attention she gets from them, the better.

This interaction also makes her feel part of the family, contributing to her emotional security and helping her develop social skills. These extremely important skills fall into two categories: learning how others think and feel, and learning how to care about others.

Getting emotional

As your baby becomes more mature emotionally, she will show a wider range of emotions in different situations. She can show you by bouncing up and down that she is excited, by gurgling with pleasure that she has seen something that gives her joy, by remaining quiet and watching warily that she is unsure of a situation, or by crying that her needs are not being met.

learning through play

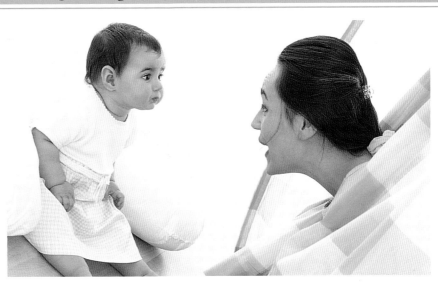

Your baby will still love singing, bouncing, and clapping games, and you will be able to be a little more physically playful with her now that she's stronger.

Hide and seek

To help your baby learn the concept of permanence, try hiding her teddy bear under a blanket. Pull away the blanket and watch your baby's face when the teddy bear suddenly reappears, or hide behind a curtain, then peep out. Your baby will slowly begin to realize you were there all along (see object permanence, page 182).

Physical fun

Because your baby's upper body is so strong and her head control is complete, she will probably now know how to roll over from front to back. Try playing floor games with her that allow her to show off her new skill and allow you to help her perfect it. She'll also enjoy being tickled on her tummy.

Cause and effect

Your baby will be delighted at her own skill at pressing buttons on simple toys to make sounds or a face pop up. She will also love knocking down a tower of plastic blocks, or swiping at a roly-poly doll that rights itself after it has been pushed over.

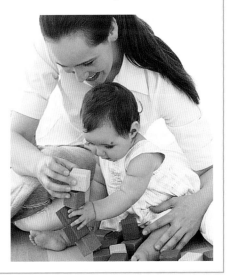

Change and growth

Although genes play a part in determining your baby's personality, she is already developing many of her own characteristics and preferences.

Many of the traits you see in your baby now will not necessarily stay with her for the rest of her life. For example, she may be impatient for solid foods at every meal or frustrated by not yet being able to move around freely and reach the things she wants, but this does not mean that she will grow into an impatient or frustrated child.

Remember that your baby has a long way to go before she can understand, reason, or use language to communicate effectively what she is thinking or wants. Your baby also still needs quiet time and may even sometimes want to be left alone. If a fun game suddenly ends in tears, try to anticipate her need for a break, and give her time to calm down and refocus.

your developing baby
6 to 12 months

During his second six months, your baby will develop new skills to help him explore his environment, assert his own will, and discover his independence. By encouraging him along the way, you will give him the confidence and self-esteem he needs.

The wider world

Reaching his natural milestones – such as discovering how to sit, crawl, and communicate – enables your baby to start really interacting with the wider world. He can see a favorite toy and move forward to grab it. His older brother may make a funny face to make him laugh, and he can make one back. If he meets another baby he can reach out with interest toward him.

Watching your baby acquire new skills is exciting and will give you a sense of his developing independence. The fact that he can sit on his own, crawl happily around the floor, amuse himself with a new toy, and feed himself at the table gives you a little taste of freedom – every now and then you may even have time to sit down with a cup of coffee! A daily outing in the stroller is another step in introducing your baby to the wider world and gives you both important "out and about" time together.

New relationships

Your baby will also become more involved and responsive to other people, especially close family members. With their instinctive sociability, babies at six months and older can start to develop a close bond with people other than their parents, such as grandparents and caregivers. This is a good time to help your baby establish separate relationships with people who will become important in his life – especially since, in a few months' time, "stranger anxiety" may make new friendships a lot harder.

Part of the family

During these next six months your baby will also really begin to enjoy his siblings or love to watch an older toddler or child bouncing around. And as he begins to move about himself and becomes capable of doing more things, many activities can be shared, such as singing songs together, playing clapping games, or a chasing game (on all fours) around the room.

Older children can also play the role of teacher for your baby. He'll love to imitate them and may try hard to look at a book or make the same sounds as his big brother or sister.

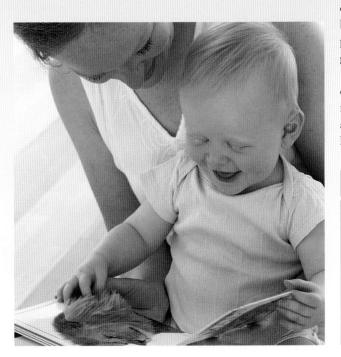

Shared reading
Your baby will start to take a greater interest in books as his concentration skills develop. Your baby will love looking at books with you, and he will benefit from the closeness.

making **friends**

If this is your first baby, his encounters with other babies will probably be a result of the friendships you have made during pregnancy and after birth. Over the next six months, your baby and your friends' babies may start to interact: gurgling, touching, imitating each other. But don't worry if your baby doesn't always want to participate.

the second 6 months

Your baby's mastery of physical and mental skills is staggering, especially when you think how she started life – as a tiny bundle with little sense of herself and the world around her. So how do these incredible changes take place?

how your baby learns

Genetics play a part in your baby's continuing development, but much of her progress depends on the kind of stimulation and attention she receives from you.

From the moment of her birth your baby is absorbing information, especially from the people closest to her. You are her first and most important teacher.

This isn't as overwhelming as it sounds, since your baby's natural way of learning is through play: if she shakes a rattle and discovers that it makes a loud noise, she's learning about cause and effect; when she tries to crawl over a mountain of cushions you've built for her, she's learning peristence and finding out how to balance and coordinate her limbs; and when she listens to you sing a nursery song, she's starting to understand emotions and language.

Encouraging your baby

How is your baby motivated? Again, partly through a built-in drive to discover and learn. But your encouragement and support are also incredibly important. When, for example, she eventually manages to wave good-bye as a friend leaves, it's your delight and praise

that boost her sense of achievement, and convince her that learning is fun.

Taking the lead from your baby is key to motivating her. When she's ready to try a new challenge, you'll see the signs. Understanding how and when your baby develops can help you prepare for each stage and be ready with the right kind of

Getting upright
During the next six months, your baby will learn to pull himself upright and stand on his own probably with the help of furniture or you for support.

games and activities to challenge her and fulfill her needs. In fact, making sure the family environment is fun and stimulating is one of the most valuable things you can do for her.

Playing with your baby brings you closer together and helps develop her self-esteem and sense of security, by showing that you love her unconditionally for who she is, not just what she can do.

A question of gender
Even though your baby may be showing clear character traits at a young age, her personality is still emerging. And in the same way that her character traits affect the way you respond to her, so your responses will have an impact on her personality.

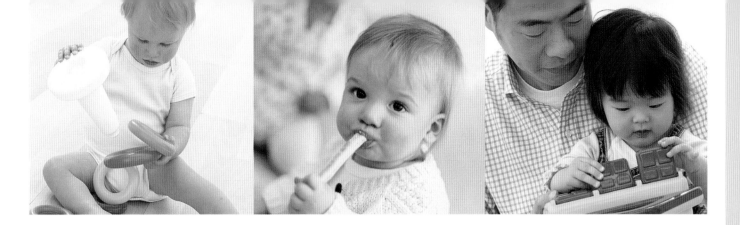

Although you may not consciously realize what you are doing, chances are that the way you care for and respond to your baby will also be affected by gender.

If you dressed a group of one-year-old boys and girls in the same outfits and put them in a room together, you would find it difficult to tell the boys from the girls. At this age, the differences in skill development are small. But, based on culture or tradition, some parents treat boys and girls differently, encouraging different toys and games for each sex. If left to their own devices, both are attracted to all of the toys, and they will benefit from being allowed to play with both "boy" and "girl" toys. What matters most is the love and respect the parent gives the child as a person, regardless of gender. This helps build self-esteem.

While boys and girls are naturally different – for example, girls tend to be more sociable and less adventurous, and boys are usually more physical and inquisitive – the way adults respond to them also tends to reinforce these gender differences. Adjusting your behavior toward them – encouraging your boy's gentler side, or stimulating your girl's sense of independence – will begin to help eliminate sexual stereotyping and allow your baby's own individuality to emerge.

by 12 months: **your baby's milestones**

Your baby will master a lot of new skills and reach many important milestones over the next few months. It's important to remember, however, that while each baby will reach all of the following milestones, the time it takes to reach them will vary from baby to baby. After all, every baby develops differently.

If you ever become concerned about your baby's development, speak to your doctor or healthcare professional.

Movement milestones
By 12 months she will probably:
♦ sit unsupported
♦ begin to crawl
♦ pull herself up to a standing position
♦ "cruise," holding on to furniture
♦ stand momentarily without any support
♦ be able to walk two or three steps on her own.

Hand and finger milestones
By 12 months she will probably:
♦ bang two blocks together
♦ use her hands rather than her mouth to investigate new objects
♦ feed herself finger foods

♦ try to hold more than one object in her hand at a time
♦ put objects in a container and take them out again
♦ let go of objects in her hand when she wants to
♦ point with her finger
♦ use the pincer grasp (hold a tiny object with her forefinger and thumb).

Social and emotional milestones
By 12 months she will probably:
♦ cry when you leave her
♦ become anxious and cling to you if strangers directly approach her
♦ enjoy imitating people.

Language milestones
By 12 months she will probably:
♦ babble; may even be able to say two or three recognizable words
♦ understand many words and start to imitate sounds
♦ listen carefully to you when you talk to her
♦ respond to simple commands
♦ recognize her name and other familiar words, such as "bye-bye"

♦ use gestures such as shaking her head for "no"
♦ try to imitate words.

Intellectual milestones
By 12 months she will probably:
♦ understand the meaning of "no"
♦ follow simple questions such as "where are your shoes?" and reply by pointing
♦ have an abundant curiosity
♦ find hidden objects easily
♦ explore objects in different ways (e.g., banging, throwing, dropping)
♦ understand cause and effect (when she shakes her rattle, it makes a noise)
♦ start to understand how objects are used (drink from a cup, brush her hair, listen to a voice on the telephone)
♦ know that something still exists even when she can no longer see it.

Some babies may also be able to stack blocks, for example, or say "mama" or "dada." These milestones aren't just about achievements. They are also indicators of your baby's healthy emotional and social development.

6 to 8 months

Now more than halfway through his first year of life, your baby is beginning to take a greater interest in the world around him. Being able to sit upright gives him a whole new perspective on his environment.

key **milestones**
◆ can sit upright unsupported
◆ starts feeding himself finger foods
◆ becomes anxious around strangers
◆ develops understanding of language
◆ recognizes his own name; may start to use some real words: "dada," "mama"

physical development

Constantly exercising his body over the last few months has helped your baby develop his muscles, balance, and control.

He may now be able to roll from side to side with ease, flipping himself onto his back and over again. He may also sit for long periods and lean forward without falling over. However, he still can't twist sideways or pivot at the waist, and may topple over when trying to reach for a toy.

On his own two feet

Your baby is growing stronger by the day and will be eager to flex his muscles and show off his skills. Pretty soon just sitting won't be exciting enough for him. Always looking for a new challenge, he may now try to stand, and make his first attempt by pulling himself up in his crib using the bars. In all likelihood he will collapse in a heap or remain stranded and yell for help – he hasn't yet developed the balance or coordination to lower himself down gently.

Reach for the toys
Once your baby can sit upright without using his arms for support, he will start stretching forward to grab anything nearby that looks interesting.

When you come to his rescue, support his weight and allow him to relax so that he can gently slide into a sitting position. All of this is great practice for the next important milestones: crawling, standing, and walking.

On the move

By his eighth month, your baby may be attempting to crawl. To crawl properly, your baby needs to be strong enough to push himself up on all fours and then discover that by pushing down with his knees he can move forward. First crawls are often backward, and it may be a week or so before he learns how to move forward.

Many babies don't learn how to crawl until they are between eight and 10 months; some don't begin to move until they are a few weeks older; and some never crawl at all, but go straight from scooting on their bottoms to walking.

Playing with toys

Once he learns how to sit upright and no longer needs his arms to keep himself supported, your baby will be working hard to grab anything nearby that excites him. Make sure there are always some toys, safe household objects, or baby books nearby to keep him interested – but don't expect too much. His concentration skills are still developing and even something he has never seen before will hold his attention for only a few minutes.

Hand-eye coordination

As his grip develops, your baby will be able to hold objects more firmly and steadily, turn them over to have a good look at them, put them in his mouth, pass them from one hand to the other, and even bang two objects together.

As his hand-eye coordination improves he'll be grabbing a spoon as soon as it's in sight, and probably overturning it before it reaches his mouth. You may like to offer him a two-handed cup to drink from. Before long, he may be drinking from it without your help. You may also want to start offering him finger foods, such as a piece of bread or rice cake. Never leave him alone with finger food in case he chokes.

learning **to sit**

Thanks to all the wriggling, twisting, kicking, and stretching he has been practicing in his first six months, your baby can now sit up on his own – at least for a few minutes, and probably longer. Sitting up enables him to look around more easily, watch family members coming and going, and reach out for toys to keep himself entertained – if only for a little while.

learning skills

Your baby's everyday routines are now very familiar to him. He can remember things that have happened before, and begins to recognize sounds and objects.

Your baby is starting to learn about object permanence. Up until now, when something disappears, your baby thinks it no longer exists. During this stage, he will begin to realize that just because he can't see something doesn't mean it isn't there. You can see this in action by partially hiding a toy under a towel. Chances are he'll try to lift the towel to find the toy – and by the end of his eighth month he'll look for it even when it's fully hidden.

Gestures and expressions

You'll notice your baby's understanding of language is developing faster than his ability to talk. He recognizes his own name and will turn his head when he hears you calling. He is also starting to respond to the names of familiar objects and people, glancing over at a favorite toy you've just mentioned, for example, or looking at his sister when you call her name.

First conversations

Real speech is still some way off, but your baby has lots of ways of letting you know what he's thinking. Gestures, for example, are now a regular part of his vocabulary – see him open and shut his hand if he wants something, shake his head or push you away if you're doing something he doesn't like, or try to wave when you say "bye-bye." Watch his face, too – his facial expressions will convey a variety of emotions.

At this stage your baby practices his babbling. You may start to notice that his singsong "conversations" sound increasingly like real words, such as "dada" or "mama." He will love to repeat strings of familiar sounds so give him lots of encouragement, and he will soon learn how to say the words correctly.

Comparing sounds

The covering of a nerve that connects the ear to the brain – allowing your baby to pinpoint where a sound is coming from – is complete by about his eighth month. Now he can compare his sounds with yours, and over the next few months he will increasingly attempt to imitate your sounds.

Discovery zone

Once he can propel himself in a chosen direction, your baby will be into everything: cabinets, drawers, and wastepaper baskets. He has an overwhelming sense of curiosity to discover more about each object's shape, size, and texture. Does it taste good? Does it do anything exciting? Although he can use his hands to great effect, your baby will still put things into his mouth, so take steps to childproof your home (see pages 262–265).

Your baby's understanding of objects is growing every day. He may now be beginning to see how things relate to each other – how a small box fits inside a big box, for example. More important, he is learning that something still exists even if he can no longer see it.

toy **box**

Cars and trucks
As your baby becomes more adept at sitting unaided, he'll begin to enjoy pushing cars and other wheeled toys along the ground. Get him a few in bright colors that are easy to handle and safe to put in his mouth.

Hand puppets
Use soft hand puppets with simply drawn faces that meet current safety standards. Because your baby won't be able to hold them himself yet, they should fit adult hands.

Nursery rhymes cassette player
If your baby enjoys listening to you sing familiar tunes to him, record a few songs on tape, or play a cassette of nursery rhymes while he has a quiet time. Encourage other family members to record stories and songs as well.

Bath-time toys
Toys to amuse your baby while he's in the bath can really come into their own now. Some stick to the side of the bath or to the tiles, others float or need filling with water. Even a simple floating ball or duck will give your baby lots of fun. Bath books are also a good idea. Wipe them dry after use to prevent growth of mold or fungus.

Squeaky, noisy, and musical toys
Babies love the sounds of squeaky toys. They will also enjoy the repetition of hearing a particular little tune over and over again. Buy toys that they can grasp easily and operate themselves.

Plastic stacking cups
Try to buy different-size cups in bright, contrasting colors that fit together well.

emotional development

Your baby is very loving – he'll kiss you when encouraged, hold his arms out to be lifted up, and pet his toys.

You'll notice that your baby is becoming more sociable, turning to listen to voices around him. He'll also want to join in conversations, responding to you, not just with baby babble, but also with a range of gestures and facial expressions. Watch him look at himself in a mirror, too. He doesn't realize that he is looking at himself, but he is interested in the baby he sees and will gurgle away in hopes of a response.

Loving you

You are still your child's favorite plaything. Has he dropped that toy again – and is he looking for you to come and help? Maybe it's not the toy he's after, but a chance to smile and laugh with you.

The pleasure your baby takes in your company is a sign that he is forming a deep and genuine bond with you, his main caregiver. You may find toward the end of this stage that if you vanish from sight for a moment, his bottom lip begins to wobble; he fears you've left forever. Return before the tears are in full flow, and he'll beam and bounce with happiness.

A separate person

Part of this deepening attachment comes from his realization that he is a separate person from you. This is a huge and important milestone. Over the next few months, he may become much more clingy and increasingly anxious when separated from you, even for a moment. Separation anxiety can be upsetting, but it is perfectly normal and often continues through toddlerhood. Reassure him with lots of love and attention, and in time he'll be more relaxed when you leave him for a while.

Meanwhile, he will also start to develop attachments to other important people in his life – his siblings, grandparents, or caregiver, for example. Encouraging these relationships helps him adapt to being without you when he needs to be cared for by someone else.

Fear of strangers

Your baby may be sociable and confident one minute, then fearful and shy the next. When he meets people he doesn't know well, he may bury his face in your shoulder, cling to you, and cry. Becoming anxious when unfamiliar people directly approach him is one of his first emotional milestones. Stranger anxiety is normal and can last for up to two years or more.

Try not to force your baby to be friendly and don't tell him he's being silly if he is shy because this will undermine his self-confidence – instead, praise him when he has the confidence to smile back at someone new. Give your baby enough time to warm to newcomers gradually.

learning through play

Your baby is quickly demonstrating that he has a growing curiosity to satisfy and an urge to explore everything. Give him a selection of activities to keep him busy for a short while, or help him discover how to crawl toward the toys he is showing interest in.

♦ By now your baby will love to play with pop-up toys that burst out when a button is pushed or a dial turned. Show him how to push them back down himself, and he'll develop strength and coordination in his hands and arms.

♦ Satisfy your baby's desire to discover new things by giving him a box that you have filled with harmless but interesting household objects for him to play with. This will give him a chance to explore them in his own time and will teach him more about the shape, size, and texture of different things. If he begins to tire of them, make a few small changes, such as putting a ball in the bowl to rekindle his curiosity in it.

♦ Help your baby learn more about the relationships between objects by giving him some plastic stacking cups in different colors, shapes, and sizes. It will be many months before he can fit them into each other the right way – or even stack them himself – but he'll enjoy trying. And when he needs a change you can build a tower and encourage him to try knocking it down – a game he'll love!

♦ There are lots of ways you can encourage your baby to crawl: make sure he has plenty of opportunities by putting him down on the floor whenever you can and placing a toy or something interesting just out of his reach to encourage him to try moving forward to grasp it. Keep his knees well covered so that crawling isn't painful or uncomfortable.

♦ It's never too early to start reading to your baby. Choose a few soft books that your baby can dribble and chew on. You can also have more special books that you get out to read, then put away safely.

8 to 10 months

Your baby's personality is really beginning to shine through, and as her physical skills continue to develop and she becomes more confident, she'll start to show you that she really has a mind of her own when she wants something.

physical development

Your baby may now be able to sit by herself for quite a while, as well as lean forward for a toy without falling over.

Don't expect her to play like this for too long, though: the physical effort of maintaining her balance is tiring, so after 10 minutes or so she'll be ready for a change.

Once your baby discovers how to move herself around – whether she's crawling or scooting – she'll move faster very quickly. It'll be a question of now you see her, now you don't, so you'll need to keep a constant eye on her to make sure she's safe.

If your baby is now crawling, she may attempt more challenging maneuvers such as crawling upstairs. Although stair climbing may help her learn how to judge height and depth and develop her sense of

balance, it is important to install safety gates so she can't attempt to climb the stairs without your assistance (see page 262). Going up is easier than coming down, and it will be awhile before she's ready to learn the skills needed to make a safe descent.

Cruising around

Very mobile babies may now be attempting to take a few steps while holding on to a piece of furniture. If your baby is becoming more confident, she'll soon discover how to move across a room using pieces of furniture as supports (see *safety*, page 262). Learning how to "cruise" like this is the last physical skill your baby needs to master before she begins walking without assistance.

Hand control

As she now begins to spend less time putting things in her mouth and more time exploring them with her hands, her hand movements are becoming agile and controlled. You may notice, for example, that she turns the pages of books by herself, even though it's usually several at a time. And she can accurately guide small pieces of food into her mouth with her fingers, making mealtimes slightly less messy than before. She can also bang two objects together by holding one in each hand.

Learning to point

If your baby is starting to point, this is an important milestone. Controlling the index finger is the first step to mastering a pincer grip – the ability to close the thumb and forefinger together to pick up tiny objects. It also helps her communicate

attention **span**

Your baby's sense of her environment is growing rapidly. She now notices and is interested in people and things up to 10 feet (three meters) away. At the same time, her attention span is increasing: she is becoming more absorbed in activities she enjoys, and you'll find it harder to distract her when, for example, you need to take something away from her.

with you by pointing out things she wants. Encourage her by looking at books together and pointing at things as you name them. And let her practice picking up tiny things such as raisins or cooked kernels of corn.

Roll play

Since her birth, your baby has been refining her visual skills and now she can judge the size of an object up to three feet (one meter) away. She'll know, for example, that a ball rolled from this distance will get larger as it comes towards her. Watch how she holds out her arms to catch it. Ask her to roll it back, and she may swing at it with no effect, but eventually she'll be able to return it in your direction.

toy **box**

Touch-and-feel books
A selection of different activity books will give your baby a new perspective on the world. Choose strong, brightly illustrated books with clear images and pictures and shapes made out of different textures.

Toy piano
If your baby has a toy with buttons to push, encourage her to practice pushing down and releasing the buttons. A toy piano or xylophone are toys your baby can grow into. For now, she will enjoy the random sounds she can make while also developing her listening skills.

Household objects
The simplest objects provide fun for a baby. When you are busy in the kitchen, your baby may love to play with some simple, safe kitchen utensils. Let her have fun with a few unused items such as a pot, plastic bowl, or wooden spoon. She may also like picking up an orange from a small cardboard box and popping it back in again, or taking dry clothes out of a plastic laundry basket and putting her toys or dolls into it.

learning skills

By now your baby is beginning to communicate more, letting you know that she is an important family member with something to say.

By the end of her ninth month, your baby may be able to recognize up to 20 familiar words, such as "cup" or "teddy." She'll also laugh in the right places when you sing her favorite songs, look for her sippy cup if you ask her where it is, and associate actions with certain words, such as saying "bye-bye" and waving her hand.

Making conversation

Your baby loves interacting with people, and will enjoy social get-togethers such as mealtimes. She will try to join in conversations. Her babbling is developing

173

all the time, and she may add new sounds to her vocabulary, such as "t" and "w." Her strings of babble will start to follow clearly the rise and fall of an adult conversation. And although it may still sound like nonsense, it is important for you to listen and respond, since this encourages her to keep trying.

Real words

Having discovered your delight when she says "dada" or "mama," your baby will probably now understand their meanings and use them to attract your attention.

If you make the sounds of specific words, such as "cat" or "bath," in time your baby may start to imitate you and repeat these sounds. Complete words won't emerge for another few months, but keep repeating the sounds and she may soon learn how to say the words back to you.

Understanding language

Your baby's understanding of language continues to increase faster than her ability to use it. She may also use gestures as well as sound to get your attention – perhaps waving at you or pulling your clothes – and will even repeat herself if you don't understand what she is trying to say.

learning through play

Around this age your baby can start to show off her problem-solving skills – as long as you can resist helping her when she faces a difficulty. Facing everyday challenges will help her learn to work things out for herself.

♦ Satisfy your baby's urge to explore, and her growing ability to problem-solve, with an activity board. Choose a board with cylinders that can whirl, dials that spin, and buttons that squeak. Show her how it works to begin with, then let her investigate at her own pace. At first she may only be able to do the simple activities, such as sticking her finger in a dial, but during the following months she'll soon figure out how to work the other activities.

♦ Playing peekaboo and hide-and-seek with your baby at this age helps teach her

about object permanence, and there are lots of variations: cover your head with a towel and let her pull it off, then let her try; hide behind the door with just a hand or toe showing before popping out and gently surprising her.

♦ Fill a basin with water and, using different spoons, cups, and containers, show your baby how she can fill and pour. Emptying and filling games are a good way to help your baby practice her hand movements and develop dexterity and hand-eye coordination. Water games are great for bath-time play, too.

♦ If your baby loves moving objects from one container to another, try making a surprise box full of interesting and harmless objects for her to handle, explore, put back in and take out again. To make the game more interesting, you could wrap some of

emotional development

Your baby is unique, with her own likes and dislikes. She may object if you take a toy away or want to play the same game again.

As her self-awareness develops, your baby will become more assertive and turn everyday activities into a battle of wills. You may find she is beginning to arch her back when she doesn't want to be put in her car seat or shake her head if you try to feed her something she doesn't like.

As frustrating as this behavior can be, don't forget how easily your little bundle of energy can be distracted! Her memory is short, and some fast thinking can refocus her attention: if she hates being dressed, sing her a funny song to help her forget why she made a fuss – or try redirecting your child's thoughts to what she can, rather than can't, do.

Her sense of humor

Your baby's first laughs were probably prompted by physical games such as being bounced on your knee or lifted high up in the air, and later by visual jokes such as shaking your hair around or putting her

bib on your head like a hat. Now that she is more mobile, she'll enjoy teasing you by doing things you don't like – heading toward a forbidden door and then looking back to see if you're watching, for example, or pushing the off button on the TV.

Developing fears

At the other extreme, this is the time when your baby may develop fears about things that haven't upset her before – the noise of the vacuum cleaner, perhaps. If she seems frightened of something, stay relaxed, comfort her, and reassure her that she's safe. This will help deepen her trust in herself and others.

Slowly familiarizing your baby with the object of her fear can help conquer this tendency. For example, let her examine the vacuum cleaner once it has been switched off and unplugged. Take things one step at a time, and she'll eventually get over her fears.

Laughing together
As your baby's sense of humor develops, she will love to tease you – and you will still get a lot of laughs from her when you bounce her on your knees or lift her high into the air.

the items in paper – she'll love ripping them open to see what's hidden inside. Never leave your baby alone with paper, however, because she may put it into her mouth and choke on it.

♦ Listening to different sounds will help develop your baby's emerging language skills. If you play a familiar tune that she recognizes on a xylophone or toy piano, it will spark her interest and may encourage her to start trying to create some wonderful sounds herself.

♦ Your baby may become more aware of the noises animals make, so now is the time to introduce some animal songs. Look at animal books together and let her hear you mimic all the different sounds they make. Once your baby learns to imitate lots of animal noises, her success will encourage her to copy other sounds, too.

♦ Babies at this age are intrigued by space – they love crawling behind sofas or around the backs of chairs. Your baby will probably also love to crawl through a play tunnel. Roll a ball toward her inside the tunnel so that she can see how it works. As she becomes confident, she'll love crawling through the tunnel or hiding inside from you.

♦ A daily trip to the park or local playground provides a good opportunity to spend time together. It also means you can encourage your baby's sense of spatial awareness, and improve her visual skills as you point things out to her.

♦ Satisfy your baby's need to explore with her hands – and encourage her sense of touch – with a "touch-and-feel" activity book that contains pictures and shapes made out of different textures.

10 to 12 months

As your precious baby approaches his first birthday, you will look back in amazement at the incredible changes that have taken place. He now has a unique personality, a wide range of emotions, and a strong sense of his place in the family.

key **milestones**

- ◆ may stand without support and even take some steps on his own
- ◆ can feed himself finger foods
- ◆ tries to imitate words
- ◆ can find hidden objects easily
- ◆ understands simple requests

physical development

At this age babies vary enormously in their physical achievements. Some have been crawling for a few weeks, while others are just getting started.

Your baby's balance has improved tremendously. He can lean sideways while sitting without falling over, and twist around to reach something behind him, enabling him to reach for things himself.

First steps

Toward the end of this stage your baby may take his first steps – a really exciting development. If he has perfected his balance while cruising around your furniture, he may start to let go occasionally, grabbing hold of something only if he totters. See page 262 to make sure you have taken adequate steps to ensure his safety if he should fall.

Initially, he may take a or two before falling; encourage him to try again, and he'll soon take more and more steps on his own. Moving the furniture slightly farther apart will also help him gain confidence. But be prepared for your baby to go at his own pace – lots of babies don't walk until they are 13 or 14 months old, and some not before 18 months. Don't worry if he is taking things slowly as long as his developmental patterns seem to be normal. If you have concerns, discuss them with his healthcare professional.

Feeding himself

Now that your baby has more control over his hand movements, he is more accurate in everything he does with them, including feeding himself with finger foods with no difficulty. Using a spoon isn't as easy to master, since it involves difficult hand-eye coordination in addition to good muscle control. But now that he can rotate his hand he is much better at getting food into his mouth, although it might still be very messy.

It is worth encouraging your baby to feed himself, since sometimes he may refuse someone else's feeding him, and he shouldn't rely on you entirely for all his food. On the other hand, it's still too early to leave it all up to him. Although he may start each meal enthusiastically, he'll quickly get tired and you may have to intervene to make sure that he is eating enough.

Throwing

Exploring different objects is still one of your baby's favorite activities, but now he will probably have stopped putting everything that he picks up into his mouth. How an object feels in his hands is more important to him, and he will experiment more and more with his hands.

For example, he will try to hold more than one item – such as two building blocks – in his hand at a time. This may be difficult at first as he drops one or both. Having discovered how to let go of something, he can now have great fun throwing things on purpose.

learning skills

You and your baby may be able to communicate together well, and his understanding of the world is developing quickly.

Your baby may still not be saying very much, but his understanding of language and communication is coming in leaps and bounds. He can now follow simple questions such as "Where is your cup?" and will probably reply by pointing or looking in the direction of the cup. If you ask a simple question such as "Do you want a drink?" he may respond with a smile and move toward the cup.

If your baby has older brothers or sisters, they will find this a rewarding time since they, too, can begin to interpret what he is trying to express.

Some babies may be able to say two or three words by their first birthday, although often only you and the rest of the family can understand them. It may be weeks before your baby uses more words, which is completely normal.

Understanding concepts

As your baby's intellectual skills develop, you'll be able to watch him making more sense of his immediate world. Now, when he sees a picture of a dog in his book, he might relate it to his grandfather's dog or the dog he saw in the park and begin to

realize that even though every dog he sees looks different, they are all dogs.

He can now also grasp the idea of opposites. With the help of your explanations, he will understand the difference between wet and dry, hot and cold, big and little, and in and out.

Linking objects to events

Your baby's understanding of cause and effect is now well developed – he knows exactly what will happen when he bangs his drum (it makes a noise) or drops his block (you will probably pick it up!).

He's also beginning to match objects to their intended purpose. For example, he'll put a toy telephone to his ear just as you do with a real telephone, or pick up the washcloth in the bathroom and wash his face with it. This is an important step forward since he will use this understanding to help him when he starts to match what he says with the objects he wants to talk about.

Concentration and memory

You may notice that your baby can listen to very short stories from beginning to end. This is partly because he can now understand you and can give you his attention for longer periods. His developing memory and past experiences affect his actions and behavior. You may notice this in the way he loves to disrupt his routine

Becoming a book lover
As your child's concentration improves, he will start to listen to stories all the way through. Learning to enjoy books now will help him enjoy them throughout his life.

– crawling away when you want to get him ready for a bath or put his coat on, for example. Knowing what's going to happen next gives him a great opportunity to play a joke – at your expense.

emotional development

Your baby is eager to get involved in household chores, loves being with other babies, and may now become more attached to a comfort object.

By now, your baby will enjoy seeing other babies his own age – and may get excited when you invite friends over who have babies of their own. He can learn a lot by watching other children – and feeling at ease in the company of others will help him take his first steps toward learning how to make friends.

Now is a good time to join a play group, particularly if your baby doesn't have brothers and sisters at home. He'll still want to stay close to you, but he will be fascinated to watch and imitate the other babies and toddlers around him.

At this age, however, don't expect him to actively mix, join in, or share with the others. Your baby still thinks the world revolves around him, and while he'll be very happy playing alongside other children, he'll naturally assume that every toy is there just for him. He won't be able to understand the concept of sharing for another year or more.

your growing **relationship**

Your baby is very loving toward you and will shower you with hugs and respond to kisses when he chooses to. He can also become very self-focused, believing that he should come first when it comes to getting attention from you. At the same time, his sense of independence is increasing and his desire to explore means he won't sit contentedly in your arms for long.

Hugs and kisses
Your baby will enjoy the attention you shower on him – but he could be off to his next activity any minute now!

Copying and helping
Your baby is understanding the world around him more clearly than ever before, and he wants to be involved in whatever is going on. If he sees you busy wiping his high chair after a meal or sweeping the floor, he'll want to join in and he may try to copy you brushing your hair or washing your face, too.

He may also try to help speed your progress when you dress him by slipping his arm into his sleeve, or getting his slippers for you to put on his feet. Make sure you always tell him what you're doing and why. Give him a chance to try, too, although don't expect him always to do

exactly what you anticipate: many babies have tried to brush their hair with their toothbrush, for example!

Comforting objects
Around this time, lots of babies become attached to a special object such as a blanket or stuffed animal that they insist on taking everywhere with them. Known as a "transitional" or "comfort" object, this item will have a special place in your baby's life, helping him sleep when he's tired and reassuring him if he's unhappy, especially if you are not around to comfort him. This is especially true for babies still dealing with separation anxiety.

Your baby will probably rely on his comfort object for some time to come. Only when he finds other ways to deal with obstacles will he gradually give it up. Meanwhile, if you are concerned about cleanliness, try to have two identical comfort objects on hand in case one needs to be washed. This will also come in handy if one is lost.

Social skills
Although at this age your baby doesn't understand how or why he needs to have good manners, he loves imitating you and his siblings. Learning the way you behave will help him get along with other people as he gets older. Even before he can talk, your baby can learn social rituals such as how to wave bye-bye. And if he hears you using polite words, he is more likely to use those words himself once he can talk.

toy **box**

Shape sorter
Boxes should be durable and incorporate a selection of simple, recognizable shapes. Make sure the shapes are not so small that they fit easily into your baby's mouth.

Nursery rhymes
Nursery rhyme books and songs will give your baby huge pleasure as he becomes more familiar with the words and tunes.

Pull toys
If your baby is becoming actively mobile, he might enjoy playing

with a pull toy on wheels that he can pull behind him. These are often available in the form of animals or trains. For safety reasons, make sure the string on this type of toy is no longer than 8in (20cm).

Stuffed animals
Stuffed animals can become treasured possessions. Choose toys that have expressive or appealing faces to attract your baby's attention.

Toy telephone
Your baby will enjoy pretend toys such as telephones – especially those that make noises. Buy a safe, well-made version – the chances are it could be in use for a very long time.

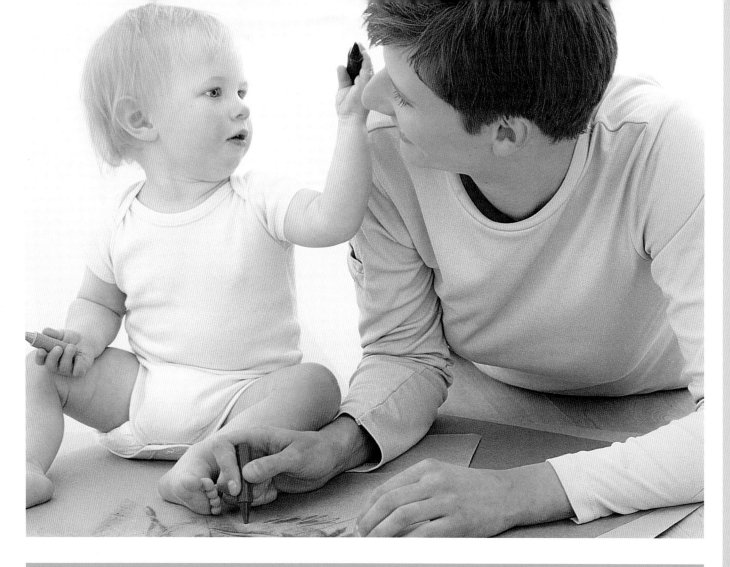

learning through play

Help your baby expand his understanding, and particularly his knowledge of the names of objects, with familiar songs and books. Try also to encourage him to share well-loved toys and develop his coordination and rhythm by playing clapping games with him.

♦ As your baby learns to turn the pages of a book, make sure he has plenty of them to look at, especially board books. Try to establish some regular quiet time together so that books become part of his everyday life.

♦ Your baby may now be able to hold his hands flat when he claps them together; if not, let him hold your hands as you clap them together. Let him sit on your lap, or on the floor facing you so he can watch and join in clapping games and songs. Putting words, gestures, and music together will help with first words as well as giving him the chance to play with and imitate you.

♦ Play "give and take" with your baby by offering him something new to look at. When he's finished exploring it, hold your hand out for him to return it. Most likely he will. If so, encourage his sharing by saying "Thank you!" If not, try again another time.

♦ Stuffed animals such as teddy bears and dolls will give him lots of play opportunities for many years to come. Use them now to help him learn social rituals – encourage him to kiss his favorites good night, or say good-bye when he goes out for the day.

♦ Your baby will love listening to song tapes and looking at books again and again. This repetition will help encourage his first words and improve his memory.

♦ If your baby is beginning to walk, he may be ready for his first pull toy. At first you may need to help him, but he'll soon enjoy pulling the toy himself.

your developing toddler
12 to 24 months

Having spent the first year learning about your baby's physical and emotional needs, the focus now changes. This second year is more about helping your toddler become a self-sufficient individual, branching out into the world, with you as a guide.

A whole new world

Your toddler continues to need your active encouragement to explore her capabilities and her surroundings. She will also need you to return to as a safe emotional base because, for all her apparent independence, she needs your love and reassurance.

Developmentally, the physical change is enormous. Once your child learns to walk, her horizons expand. And learning to talk opens up her world to you, and the whole world to her, in a new and exciting way. Your toddler will constantly attempt to move ahead of her immediate capabilities, which may lead to enormous frustration for her. Learning about limits, her own

and those set by you, is new for both of you. With patient teaching and encouragement, she can learn to follow basic safety rules and to cooperate with your expectations.

Recognizing limits

Toddlers cannot self-limit their activity. They tend to move straight from one activity to another without pause and to put every ounce of their energy into each. Your toddler will rely on you to help set the pace, so that she can manage to enjoy activities without overdoing them to the point of exhaustion, which is sometimes where the flashpoint of frustration ignites into a tantrum.

establishing a safe environment

Your toddler continues to explore things with her hands, but now this isn't limited to those toys given to her. She can move around her home, and everything is worth investigating, whether it's the dog's bowl or the CD player. How can she tell the difference between those buttons she can press and those she can't? It's not possible without your help, so remove items that can hurt her or be damaged (see *safety*, page 262), and direct her attention to activities that take advantage of her natural curiosity and pleasure in exploration.

Varying the pace

Toddlers still need lots of rest, and most will probably continue to need at least one daytime nap during this year. Well-rested toddlers will manage life better than those who are tired. And if your toddler is a poor sleeper at night, don't be tempted to keep her going all day in the hope that she will sleep continuously through the night. The more tired she is, the less easy she will find it to relax into a good sleep pattern.

Ultimately, this is a wonderfully exciting time for you and your toddler, full of new experiences. Understanding just what makes your toddler tick, and what her needs are, will help you create opportunities that bring out the best in her.

the second year

By the beginning of the second year, your baby will have developed a wealth of skills on which to build new ones. He has progressed from dependency on you to meet all of his needs to a very definite personality all of his own.

how your toddler learns

Initially your baby's skills were geared to basic survival, now they are enabling him to explore and expand his world with your help.

During your baby's second year, he is using all of his senses to gain experience and understanding of his world. Physical skills are greatly increased through mobility, and mobility is increased through the development and practice of physical skills. As a result, your toddler's cognitive, or learning, skills are influenced by his new view of the world. And emotional development moves ahead as your child utilizes these new skills to interact with others and learns to become more social.

By the age of 24 months, your toddler will have more in common with an adult than with his newborn self in terms of abilities.

Increased mobility

This period is one of increased mobility for your baby. It is about further exploring a newly developed ability to move from A to B. Initially this may be through crawling, but it also occurs through learning to walk upright, which enables greater movement and also frees up the hands. Once a skill such as walking has

been learned, progress comes through repeating it.

As your child becomes more proficient at moving around, he is able to see things in context and develop his spatial skills further. For example, it's hard to imagine a chair in context unless you can move around it. Also, if your toy rolls behind a chair, and you can get to it, you learn that when things disappear from view they don't actually disappear altogether. This is part of a learning process that the psychologists call "object permanence," meaning that something continues to exist even after you can no longer see it.

Communication skills

Long before first words appear, comprehension and a developing understanding of the meaning of what you are saying emerges. It is not until

the meaning of a word is understood that the spoken word follows, which is why repetition is so important. As you do something, constantly talk to your toddler, telling him what you are doing.

Potty at the ready
A major developmental milestone is reached when your child is ready to start using a potty, which can happen any time after about 18 months.

Eventually it becomes clear that your child understands simple words through his response to what you say. Long before he can say the word "shoes" he will help you look for his shoes when you ask him, for example.

Individuality

The rate of your baby's development depends partly on opportunities provided to develop different skills, but it also depends on the inclination and individuality of your child.

Some babies love to sit and focus on one thing at a time, absorbed in something stationary, while others are always on the move and eager to get up and around. Some will manage to get to where they want to go by crawling and show no inclination to walk, while others may spend a short time scooting on their bottoms before moving swiftly to walking, never having actually crawled at all.

Boisterous children

Some children need more activity than others. Boys tend to become more restless more often and concentrate for shorter periods on quieter activities (such as playing with blocks or toy animals) than girls.

If your toddler, girl or boy, becomes restless or frustrated, instigate a short period of physical activity such as a walk around the block with his pull toy or a game of hide-and-seek in the backyard or park. Once he has let off steam, he will be more willing to sit down with his crayons or toy cars again.

Calming activities, such as sitting together reading a book or listening to soft music while being cuddled can help your child enjoy some peaceful relaxing time.

1 to 2 years: your toddler's milestones

Your baby's milestones during the next 12 months are an important indicator of his developmental progress. Although all children develop at their own pace, there are a number of steps that you can expect your child to achieve during this year.

Movement milestones
♦ learns to walk unsupported

♦ walks, stops, and turns

♦ may be able to run, although may have difficulty slowing down to go around corners

♦ can squat to pick up something and return to a standing position

♦ carries something in his hand while walking; may carry two items, one in each hand

♦ climbs safely onto a chair

Hand and finger milestones
♦ self-feeds with a spoon

♦ graduates from a sippy cup or bottle to a regular cup

♦ learns to let go of objects

♦ throws an object, even if not in a straight line

♦ can use his finger to point at something he wants

♦ tends to use both hands equally

♦ may try to carry two items, one in each hand

♦ rotates wrist to unscrew an item

Social and emotional milestones
♦ learns to be happy apart from you for longer periods

♦ plays alongside another child

♦ likes to watch what other children are doing and imitate them, especially if the children are older

♦ shows loving behavior to a toy, pet, or other child

♦ picks up on your happiness or sadness, even if he is unable to understand it

♦ forms strong attachments to parents, caregivers, and other close family members

♦ begins to think about how he feels and how others feel

♦ understands what annoys and pleases you

♦ may help you with simple tasks

Language milestones
♦ talks about what he is seeing and learning

♦ progresses from single words to two-word phrases

♦ vocabulary expands to include up to 200 words

♦ responds verbally to questions you ask

♦ enjoys naming everyday objects when he sees them

Intellectual milestones
♦ remembers simple events that occur regularly

♦ makes connections between live objects and pictures

♦ learns the difference between what is real and what is not: can distinguish between the family car and a toy car, for example

♦ his imagination becomes more developed and he loves pretend play

♦ will enjoy looking at books both with you and on his own

♦ begins to understand the concept of possession

♦ may start to demonstrate an interest in toilet training toward the end of his second year

12 to 16 months

Your baby's increasing ability to interact with her world is becoming more and more evident now. She will take every opportunity to explore as she enjoys her newfound mobility and develops her cognitive skills.

physical development

Almost half of all babies learn to walk during this time, although many will still fall if they lose momentum.

Your baby may already have taken her first steps, either cruising from one object or person to another or setting off by herself. But if she has been walking since 10 months, or doesn't bother until 18 months, that is normal, too.

Provide lots of opportunities to use and strengthen the leg muscles in preparation for walking. Start by holding her hands as she practices putting her body weight on her feet while taking a few tentative steps. Babies' heads are big in comparison to their bodies, and heavy. Until their legs strengthen, balance is a little unsteady as a result.

When your baby begins to walk, she'll walk with her feet wide apart, toes pointing out, to give herself as broad a base as possible to improve her balance. And as she walks alone, her arms are held away from her body to help her balance. With time, instead of falling over, she will probably sit down deliberately if she feels she is losing her balance.

Fine motor skills

Your baby's fine motor skills – movements involving the fingers – are also improving through practice, along with hand-eye coordination. Learning to let go of something provides a quite dramatic shift in ability and brings together a number of skills.

When she was a baby, if you gave her an object, she would tend to grasp it and hold on to it until she dropped it accidentally or had it taken from her. This was because of the reflex to hold on that she was born with. Initially so strong, this reflex to cling diminishes over the first three months. Now she is reaching out, placing her hand over the object, deliberately picking it up, moving it to another place, and letting it go.

Hand movements are becoming more sophisticated. Your baby is beginning to turn her wrist in order to place an object more specifically into the place where she wants it to go. This movement is a bit haphazard at first because the physical development of the bones, which allows for greater manipulation, occurs over the first few years, just as the child is growing in maturity and dexterity. All this picking up and dropping of things – maddening though it can be at times – is part of the activity needed to practice these movements.

Point and pick

Your baby now begins to stretch her fingers into the right position to pick something up – she is anticipating what she intends to do. She will also stretch her arm toward something that she wants, to convey to you what it is.

At first, toddlers tend to point with their finger, hand, and whole arm when they want something, but over time they learn to use just the finger to communicate their wishes to you.

Left or right?

At this age, your toddler will probably use both hands equally. Some toddlers may begin to show a preference for using either the right or left hand when playing, feeding, or drinking from a cup, but most children do not consistently use one hand rather than the other until they reach about three years old.

The hand a child shows preference for is genetically determined. If both parents are right-handed, there is a 98 percent chance of their child being so, too. When one parent is left-handed, there is a 17 percent chance of a child being left-handed, and where both parents are left-handed, the probability increases to 50 percent. Don't try to deliberately influence which hand your toddler uses: she will use the one that feels most natural to her.

learning **to walk**

When babies are learning to walk, it is much more useful for them to learn with bare feet. A baby can tell a lot about the surface on which she is walking through what she can feel through the soles of her feet – whether the surface is smooth and soft, or hard and lumpy. Don't be tempted to encase your toddler's feet in anything but the softest-soled shoes and allow lots of opportunity for safe barefoot exploration. It is essential that you get your toddler's feet measured for length and width to ensure that the shoes you choose fit correctly. She will need properly soled shoes only when walking outside. You will probably notice that walking with feet encased in shoes demands a slight adjustment at first (see page 125).

learning skills

With the right balance of stimulation and time to assimilate new experiences, your baby's cognitive development is expanding in leaps and bounds now.

Your child's attention span is beginning to lengthen and, if she isn't distracted by feeling tired, thirsty, or hungry, she can focus on an activity for a little longer. This is because she is beginning to develop memory, through repeated activity, so she is beginning to anticipate the pleasure of a book when you suggest it, for example, or going for a walk, or having a bath. And during an activity, if she is distracted for a moment and discontinues it, she will return to what she was doing after the break.

Through the daily routine, your child develops an understanding of what might happen next. This understanding can then begin to be transferred to other events.

A sense of touch

We are all born with a need to be touched, but its development is dependent on having the experience of touching and feeling things as well.

Manual dexterity
This baby is enjoying her new-found ability to pick up toys and put them exactly where she wants them to be.

Our ability to distinguish among different textures comes from our experience of feeling them. Touching an object to see what it feels like also provides a baby or toddler with the opportunity to use her hands in a different way, that is, not to manipulate an object, but to use her sense of touch to find out something about it. She can learn to explore and experiment by touching different substances and textures, such as water or fabrics.

Verbal skills

Your baby's first words are evidence of her cognitive development and the beginning of an amazing new stage during which communication extends into verbal language. Toddlers learn language by hearing the spoken word, so talk to your toddler.

At this stage your child will probably be saying, or attempting to say, a few words. Children vary enormously: some will say nothing at all for months then suddenly come out with a three-word sentence, while others will continually attempt to say individual words, however inaccurately, until they make themselves understood. Often a child will begin by saying one word, such as "dog" or "daddy," but apply it to all animals or to all men.

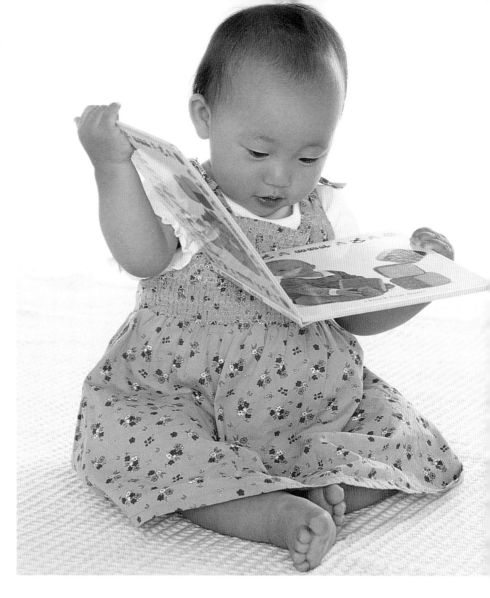

toy box

Stacking toys
These toys provide an opportunity to learn about sizes and how things fit together. Playing with stacking toys such as blocks also involves using the hand to pick up and put down. Show her how to stack two blocks, one on top of the other, and she will try to copy you. At first she will probably manage to stack only two blocks, but with playful practice she will soon progress to stacking three and four blocks at a time without any difficulty at all.

Push-down/pop-up toys
Although these toys rely on hand-eye co-ordination, they also help your child learn about cause and effect. When I do this – push down – then this happens – it pops up. It engages her attention because she is learning that one event leads to another, but doesn't yet know for sure that it will happen every time. Show her how it works, then let her make her own efforts. Is it easier to push down with the whole hand, or just one finger?

Pull toys
Pulling something along can be done for its own sake, or it can be incorporated into early, imaginative play – for example, putting a favorite toy into a toy stroller or wagon, and taking it "for a walk."

♦ A toy wheelbarrow in which things can be carried is also fun, as is a toy vacuum cleaner that can be used alongside an adult using the real thing.

♦ Some pull toys are designed to make a musical noise when used, while others may include a dog on wheels (which incorporates the pleasure of a toy animal into imaginative play).

♦ Some pull toys come with a set of building blocks that can be loaded and unloaded for extra fun.

Textured toys
Use a variety of textured items – egg cartons, building blocks, shiny paper, crinkly fabric, stuffed toys – and allow your child to explore their properties while you supervise.

learning through play

Water play really begins from birth, when your baby enjoys her first bath. Water is great fun to play with, and has lots of interesting properties that make it useful for exploration. Just pouring water from one plastic cup into another helps your child develop hand-eye coordination.

Water games
Provide a variety of different-size plastic containers. Much fun can be had with a plastic tea set with a small teapot, which challenges coordination further when trying to pour from the spout. Playing somewhere where spills don't matter or helping to clean up when they do helps your toddler gain confidence.

♦ Lots of bath toys provide opportunities for pouring, while others include possibilities such as turning on a faucet to allow water to flow through the toy.

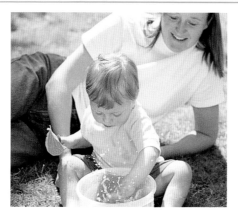

♦ Supervised water play introduces the idea of different weights – a cup of water feels heavier than an empty one – and provides opportunities to learn about other properties of water. For example, it always flows down, not up – and here are the beginnings of understanding why rain falls down and rivers don't run uphill. Your toddler can also learn about things that float, such as a leaf or a popsicle stick made of wood, and those that sink, such as a pebble – but remember never to leave your child alone with items that could be a choking hazard.

Wading pool play
Water play can be extended from baths to wading pools, where your toddler will learn to feel comfortable sharing space with other children, getting splashed, and participating in the rough and tumble of communal play. The confidence that this develops eases the way toward confidence in learning to swim.

♦ Never leave your toddler, even for a few seconds, in or near a body of water without supervision. This includes a tub, wading pool, swimming pool, fishpond, lake, the ocean, or even a bucket of water!

emotional development

Every baby has a unique personality. Making sure that all the physical needs of your baby are met really helps her emotional development at this stage.

It's hard to concentrate on learning to walk or to deal with new people in your life if you are tired, cranky, or hungry. Whenever possible, plan new activities or experiences for your baby when she is well rested so that both of you will have an enjoyable time.

By now, strong attachments have been made with a parent, a caregiver, and other close family members. Often there is an especially close attachment to one or two people if a parent and a babysitter share the daily care. It is within this secure emotional environment that babies optimize their development and learning.

Babies who are cherished, cuddled, and kissed learn, by example, how to pass on similar expressions of positive emotion to others, and you may also see this extended to their toys. Young children are often very

responsive to the emotional environment in which they live. They may not understand it, but they often pick up on your happiness or sadness – laughing with you, or stroking your face if you are sad.

The role of special toys
A favorite toy, to which a child can form an attachment, can help some children make the transition from your company to being happily alone. It can become a "transitional object." Many young children find the presence of a familiar stuffed animal or favorite toy reassuring at bedtime.

Toys can also help develop a child's imagination as they give their toy characteristics or act out happy or sad times with it. They can also use their toys to act out feelings. Talking to your toddler about feelings through a favorite toy can help her learn how to empathize. Does she look sad? Why does she look sad? How can we make her feel happy?

16 to 20 months

Toddlers are naturally curious and will learn to make important discoveries by themselves. Make sure you allow your child the time and space to develop his own ability to find out things for himself.

physical development

With his walking skills getting better and better, and with his arms free, it now becomes possible for your toddler to pick up and carry an object while walking.

This usually requires two hands, so balance has to have improved enough not to need the arms. Being able to walk, and stand securely, also opens up the possibility of reaching for objects that were previously out of reach. Don't underestimate how far a toddler can reach: make sure objects are placed far enough away to be out of danger. It's all too easy for a toddler to grab a cup of hot coffee left too close to the edge of a table.

Smaller movements

Because your child's fine motor skills are improving, he is more able to grasp a small object using his thumb and forefinger. This makes much smaller movements possible, such as zipping and unzipping a coat, although it may take some concentration and effort at first, and some children of this age will not yet be able to do it on their own.

Activities that encourage fine motor skills, such as pressing and turning knobs and twisting handles, now make your child more successful when playing games such as those that involve pushing a shape through a matching hole. Accuracy improves through play. Being able to achieve tasks independently – such as drinking from a cup – demonstrates his mastery of these skills.

Playing outdoors

Using their bodies in an energetic and expressive way helps children develop balance, coordination, and strength, and much of this sort of play needs to be done outdoors. Make sure that your child wears suitable clothing when playing outdoors – clothes that you won't mind getting muddy, and that won't get caught on anything when your child is trying to negotiate playground equipment.

Learning to be adventurous on swings and slides doesn't come naturally to every child, and yours might need some encouragement. But when he sees other children having fun, this will encourage him, too. Playing with other children also helps him to learn about taking turns.

Outdoor play can include games with balls. Choose a medium-size ball – a little smaller than a soccer ball and much lighter, so it won't knock your toddler over if thrown too hard, and so he can hold it in both hands. At first there will be very little hand-eye coordination, which is what makes actually catching a ball possible. This takes a lot of practice, but for now it is worth introducing the idea.

Learning to run

Your toddler may now be able to walk faster and even run a little without stumbling, although children at this age vary considerably in what they can and want to achieve. If he is chased or excited when playing, your toddler can speed up quite a bit. The large muscle groups in the legs have become much stronger through use, and give your child more control over stopping and starting when he is walking or running.

His movements are generally much more controlled now, and may include taking backward and sideways steps. What also becomes possible, with better balance and greater strength in the legs, is a kicking movement. At first, standing on one leg momentarily can be destabilizing and it takes practice to become proficient at it and then kicking out. Accuracy will be poor at first and, instead of actually kicking the ball, your child may stand on it, which won't achieve his objective – yet.

Throwing a ball

Once your toddler has learned how to let go, the next challenge is throwing. Although first attempts demonstrate that toddlers cannot throw with any degree of accuracy, this will improve with practice. Give your toddler scrunched-up paper balls or soft foam balls to throw. Make a game of throwing, rolling, and catching balls. Keep heavy objects out of reach.

learning skills

By this stage your toddler's understanding has increased to the point where he can easily carry out simple requests, such as "Give me the cup." But he may struggle with more complex requests.

If you ask him to put down his book, get his shoes, and close the door, this could be beyond his ability because it requires him to remember a sequence of events in order. He would probably be able to do all three things if you asked him to do them one at a time.

Language development

Your toddler's developing language may still be limited to one word at a time, but voiced in a different tone to convey different meaning. "Dadda!" might mean "Come here!" while "Dadda?", as he holds out a toy, might suggest "Help me." And "Dadda" said while pointing at a cup, might mean "I want a drink."

Soon two-word sentences begin, so you might hear "Dadda, here!" or "Dadda, please?" or "Dadda, drink." Reinforce what you hear by asking, "Would you like a drink?" This way, you let him know you've understood his request, and help him to understand how to say things correctly.

handy **work**

Little fingers and busy minds enjoy building materials such as those that fit together and come apart without too much effort. To begin with, your child may simply admire the shapes and spend time working out how one piece can fit with another – he may also chew the pieces when teething. But soon he will use the different pieces in more complex ways to turn them into a variety of increasingly sophisticated constructions. This kind of toy is a good buy because it lasts – and children of both sexes often have fun playing and learning with them well beyond their second birthday.

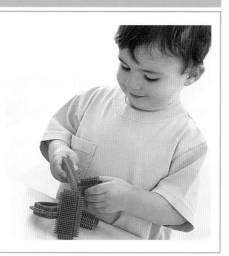

toy box

Building blocks
Blocks that fit together take the possibilities of ordinary building blocks a little further. They require a bit more in the way of deliberate coordination because the fit needs to be a little more accurate, and it takes more strength to push them together. But the rewards are greater because the blocks stay together.

Playing with building blocks that fit together is great for boys and girls. With a little prompting from you, they will soon learn to use their imaginations to build a house, or a garage, or just put the colors together in particular patterns.

Modelling clay
Making shapes out of soft, pliable, colored, non-toxic dough can give your toddler hours of creative play. Clear a space on the kitchen table and show him how to roll the dough with his fingers to make sausage shapes. He could also have fun making flat shapes, using a child's rolling pin and some plastic pastry or cookie cutters.

Sand play
Sand has all sorts of interesting properties that can be explored. It trickles through the fingers or a toy. It feels gritty and sticks to your hands. If you put a lot of sand into a large container, it gets heavy. If you make sand wet, it sticks together and will keep the shape of another object. If you have a backyard, it's worth having a sandbox. Sand must be fine and clean. You will need a selection of plastic containers, shovels, and other plastic toys to play with.

Improving vocabulary
Toward the end of this period your toddler will probably have a vocabulary of between 50 and 200 words. The development of memory and language are closely linked, so you may be aware of a big leap in his general understanding of the way the world works as his speech improves.

What he says is now becoming more sophisticated, too. Whereas before it was more a question of naming objects – dog, car, shoe – or linking an adjective with an object – a red bus – now he may be using abstract concepts. He may also show that he is beginning to understand that objects belong to people: "my car," for example.

Learning responsibility
At the end of a play session encourage your toddler to put the toys away. At this age, doing this is just as much of a game as anything else, and if it is presented as such it starts to pave the way toward taking care of belongings and putting them away after using them.

We call it cleaning up, and presume our child will find it boring – don't make that assumption and they won't either! Don't refer to it as "helping me"; it's a game and one he wants to play if you make it interesting by talking – "Here's the red one. Can you find the green one for me?", "And put it in the box! Now it's my turn." This will help him learn to value and take care of his possessions.

learning through play

Making a permanent mark, even if it's just a streak of purple on a white page, is quite a thrill the first time. It is very clear evidence that you can make something happen. And if this is joined by other colors, and eventually celebrated and tacked to the wall, it is a very rewarding process for a toddler.

Paper and crayons
First scribbles are very important – they are early expressions of creativity. Provide lots of paper – it doesn't have to be new, the back of junk mail is good – and half a dozen colorful, thick wax crayons that are easy to grip, in an easily accessible container for your child. You will need to make it clear that only paper should be drawn on, but if yours is a particularly expressive and experimental child then other surfaces may be considered fair game at first. You can see why a nice white wall might be thought suitable, so you will need to be very clear about what's OK and what's not.

♦ Don't worry about whether he chooses to use his right or left hand for drawing at this stage, because he may use both before he opts for one hand over the other. Children usually show their preference when they are about three years old.

♦ Your child's first experiences of drawing on paper gave him an idea of what he can achieve, and, over time, using crayons in this way helps him learn to control the movements of his hand. Using thicker crayons allows your toddler to experiment with his own way of holding the crayon when scribbling.

♦ Movements are large at first, covering wide areas of the paper. They become smaller over time as your child's fine motor control – the small movements he needs to make in order to write later on – improves.

♦ Scribbling with crayons (these should be non-toxic) allows your toddler to practice twisting and turning his hand. His hand-eye coordination as well as fine motor control need to come together to do this. Encourage your toddler to have fun and enjoy the patterns he makes so that he wants to continue to make more scribbles.

A time to read
By now your toddler will probably have a good selection of books, and visiting the local library to choose and borrow books is another activity that can be routinely enjoyed. Set up a special shelf or book box where you keep your child's books and where he can get them for himself. And always keep a favorite book in your bag when you are out because it will give your toddler something to look at and talk about if you are waiting somewhere.

Find time at least once a day to sit and read stories to your toddler. This quiet, absorbing activity will give you some peaceful, restorative time together. If you have more than one child, ask them each to choose a story, and read each story in turn. This will also help them to learn about taking turns and patience. Children need individual storytelling and reading time as often as possible.

Hearing stories read aloud encourages the imagination and helps your toddler learn to focus on your voice while having fun. Talk about the stories you read, asking questions about the pictures, as well as reading the words.

emotional development

You may notice that your child now knows what pleases you and may try out different behaviors to see what your reaction is.

This is an extension of his learning about how he can influence his world, and is a way that he learns to engage your attention. It is best simply to ignore any behaviors that displease you, so that he does not get attention for doing them. At this stage, he will want to please you, so it's worth giving positive feedback for desirable behavior: "Thank you for letting your friend play with your tractor" or "Good job – you've put all your toys back in their box," for example.

Becoming independent
You may also find that your toddler is willing to be independent of you in a group, just occasionally checking to see that you are available to him if he needs you. Sometimes, however, in new situations, the need for reassurance is temporarily increased. You may find a period of clinginess arises when a new adaptation is needed. This is normal behavior while getting used to a new situation. Give your toddler the reassurance he needs, but don't become overprotective: it will pass.

Playing with other children
Although your toddler might begin to understand about an object belonging to him, at this stage of his development he is unlikely to get too upset if it is taken away. Unless he has an emotional dependency on a favorite toy, he is more likely simply to reach for another toy and continue playing.

His interactions with other children are limited, and although he will enjoy being around other children of similar age, any playing he does is parallel rather than interactive.

By this stage he may smile at other children of all ages, and may like to watch what they are doing and imitate them, especially if they are slightly older.

20 to 24 months

Your toddler has become increasingly independent, but she still needs your unconditional love and understanding. She always will. Meeting her emotional needs means being aware of her fluctuating moods and adapting to support them.

physical development

The difference between the baby who couldn't walk just over a year ago, and the toddler who can now walk, run, and kick, demonstrates the amazing range of physical skills acquired over the second year.

Climbing on and off low furniture and steps is probably routinely attempted and achieved. If you watch your toddler you can see that she is usually very cautious, looking around to judge distances and stretching her leg to find the ground before stepping up or down. If you have stairs, teach your child to come down backward, on her hands and knees, which is much safer than trying to come down facing forward. If you are coming downstairs with her, she can walk down slowly, holding on to your hand.

Some toddlers try to jump up and down, but their feet may not leave the ground yet. All the time muscles are being strengthened and coordinated, and activities such as kicking a ball start to become possible.

Your toddler's ability to squat down and pick up something, then return easily to a standing position, is now proficient because of the increased strength and flexibility in her hip and knee joints. But her running may still be a little stiff, and she may have insufficient strength and coordination to run around corners without slowing down.

Using her hands
Carrying something in her hands as she walks is probably routine now if the object is not too large, and she may try to carry two objects, one in each hand. Her fine motor skills are now more developed, meaning that not only can your child use her hands to greater effect, she can also use tools more efficiently. This can range from digging in a sandbox with a plastic shovel, to scribbling on paper, to banging a drum.

Fun with sand
This child is enjoying playing in his sandbox with his mom, who shares the fun while supervising.

her knowledge with your questions or responses. This exchange causes a massive shift in understanding, as language and memory develop.

Language and memory

Memory and language are closely linked. It is much easier to remember something when it has a name than when it is just an abstract object. Talk to your toddler, because this will help develop her cognitive abilities. If you reinforce her efforts to communicate, it encourages her to continue trying. In addition, if you repeat what she says and build on it, this helps, too. For example, when she points and says, "Car", you say "Yes, that's your car. That's your blue car. Would you like to put your teddy bear in your blue car?" Not only are you responding to and reinforcing what she is saying, you are giving her a lot more relevant information.

You are also helping her develop the ability to think about what to do next, which helps develop her imagination. On another occasion when she is playing with her car and teddy bear, she will put the teddy in the car and move her language along, saying "Teddy in," for example. Then, over time, "Teddy in car" or "Teddy in blue car."

learning skills

By constantly building on what she already knows, your toddler continues to extend her understanding of the world.

Physical experiences help develop your toddler's cognitive skills. For example:
♦ She knows that toy cars go "brrrmmm, brrrmmm," but a plastic cow goes "moooo."
♦ Your child knows that a toy hammer

is for banging and uses it specifically for that purpose now.
♦ She can make connections between a toy car and the family car or a plastic cow and one in a book or in a field. She knows that each car has similar properties, but that they are different: one is real, the other is not.

And all the time your child is talking about what she is seeing and learning, which means that you are reinforcing

---

toy **box**

Puzzles
Finding the right place for puzzle pieces is a development of shape sorting and a precursor to simple jigsaw puzzles. It is all about identifying and matching shapes. You may have to show your child what is expected of her before encouraging her to try.

♦ Take the pieces out and choose one.

♦ Together, find the matching shape on the board.

♦ Place the piece next to the matching space so she can see how they match before putting the piece in place.

♦ Take your cue from your child – some children welcome help while others want to work things out for themselves.

Crayons and paper
Having been introduced to the idea of crayons and paper at an earlier stage, your child will want to scribble and draw regularly by now.

♦ Her hand movements are crude at first, but through experimentation with colors and shapes she will learn that she can exert greater control.

♦ Allow her to experiment with a variety of non-toxic crayons and felt pens. Talk to her about the colors and ask her what she is trying to express through her scribbles.

♦ Don't assume that you can interpret what your child is trying to draw – let her tell you about it.

fun with **finger paint**

Your child can use paints in a variety of ways without using a brush – she simply needs hands and feet. You need thick, non-toxic, water-based finger paint in a variety of colors.

You can experiment with one color at a time, or mix two to make a third, or mix them all together to make a dirty brown – which begins an exploration of color.

Finger painting
Finger painting is fun because it's messy and very tactile, and gives your child real hands-on experience with being creative. You will probably need several sheets of paper to experiment with different techniques.

Handprints
Handprints require a slightly different method, and possibly some adult help to paint one hand at a time, all over, and then to press it down carefully. First attempts may be a little smudged, but this activity provides a good opportunity to talk about fingerprints and individuality.

Footprints
Footprints require adult help if you don't want the paint to travel all over the house. Footprints make a unique record of your child's growth. You can compare different children's hand and foot sizes, and talk about whose are bigger or smaller.

Hands-on experience
This toddler's mother helps him paint thick dark blue paint onto the palm of his left hand. Once his hand is covered in paint, he spreads his fingers and presses his hand onto the paper. She is helping him develop his own handprint, and he loves doing it.

Pretend play
The development of imagination is helped enormously by encouraging pretend play. Pretend play usually begins through imitation. For example, when you played peekaboo, you pretended you had gone away by hiding your face and reappearing, and your baby copied you. This extends into other activities.

She will pretend to pour tea from a toy teapot into a cup, and milk from a toy milk carton. Then she will put in sugar and stir. She remembers a sequence of events and pretends to do it as part of her game. All the time your toddler is playing these games she is beginning to understand the distinction between what's real and what's not.

Learning about nature
Playing outdoors gives a child the opportunity to experience the natural world. It's not as easy to be aware of the weather, for example, when indoors – but you can feel the wind and see its effect on

learning through **play**

Toys, such as cars, trains, teddy bears, dolls, and toy figures, provide fun opportunities for imaginative play, whether your child is a boy or a girl. These toys also help your child develop her own stories and events, which she can act out with them.

Playing with dolls and toy figures
You will probably find that your child concentrates very hard while playing imaginatively with her toy figure or doll, and she may talk about what is happening in her game, chattering away to herself.

♦ Boys tend to talk less when they play with toy figures because their games are usually more active.

♦ Both boys and girls copy what they've seen in real life, and at this age will probably copy various parenting activities they have experienced.

♦ Your toddler may pretend to feed a doll, put it to bed, or give it a bath.

♦ Looking after a sick doll – giving it pretend medicine, putting bandages on its knees, or bandaging its arm is a great game.

the trees when you are outdoors. Walking in the countryside or a park provides an opportunity to look at leaves and other growing things, as well as older children riding bikes, scooters, or skateboards.

Talk about the leaves, the seasons of the year, how the temperature influences the way things grow. Keep it simple, but point things out and name them. All of this will help her observation skills and vocabulary. You can also point out things such as reflections in puddles and the shapes made by clouds in the sky.

Reading

By now, reading to your child is part of your regular routine. Although books are something that you can share with your child, also encourage her to use books on her own, perhaps suggesting that she look at a book in bed while waiting for you to come and settle her for sleep at night, or when she is having a quiet time during the day.

emotional development

Learning to think about others takes a long time, but as your toddler becomes more self-aware, physically and then emotionally, she will begin to extend her feelings about herself to others.

Empathy starts with those who are closest to her, which is why you may see some evidence of this in her relationship with you – on whom she is still so dependent – but not necessarily with others.

Loving family members create the emotional security that allows your toddler to consider the feelings of other people. For example, if you point out that an older child is upset, your toddler may express sympathy by giving the child a kiss and a hug.

As your child experiences more of the world, and develops the language to talk about her experiences, she begins to think more about both how she feels and how others feel. This may become apparent first of all through expressions of her own feelings – happiness, anger, sadness – which can sometimes feel overwhelming and may be expressed in a tantrum.

Managing feelings

Feelings can now be expressed in a variety of ways and learning how to manage them, especially in a group, is the beginning of your child's social development. Your child's inability to manage overwhelming feelings may result in negative behavior toward other children. You'll want to help your child deal with this, but she has to have experiences with a social group in order to practice managing her feelings. Remember that a hungry, tired, or bored toddler is much more likely to exhibit negative behavior.

♦ Toys don't need to be sophisticated: an old shoebox and a kitchen towel makes a very good bed and blanket for a teddy bear to sleep in.

♦ Toddlers sometimes act out their own experiences with their dolls in order to make sense of events in their daily lives.

Playing with cars

Both girls and boys enjoy playing with cars and trains.

♦ At this age, toddlers still tend to play alongside each other, although elements of social play are beginning to emerge. Sharing a bunch of cars may not work now, but if each child has his or her own car they may happily play together.

♦ Look for opportunities to acknowledge and praise sharing, and try to head off potential conflicts before they occur. Children need coaches, not judges.

Car in the making
This toddler makes a car with his building blocks. He can then play with it, moving it around an imaginary world.

your developing toddler
24 to 36 months

During the third year of life your child will continue to develop into a physically dexterous, verbally competent, and emotionally expressive individual. He will also begin to experience what a magical, if sometimes frustrating, place the wider world can be.

Emerging independence

This is a time when your child progresses from being almost completely self-centered and limited in his outlook to becoming more aware of other people and events around him. It is also a time spent juggling your child's growing desire for greater independence with the limits of his abilities, which can often be out of balance and require your help.

Growing closer

This can also be the best of times for you as a growing family. Spending time together provides all sorts of fun learning opportunities – whether you are visiting the park, reading a book, or even walking to the store. Your child may also delight you with spontaneous outbursts of affection, disarming you with his endearing hugs, irresistible smiles, or infectious laughter while you, in turn, can respond in an equally spontaneous way.

Accentuating the positive

Although at this stage it may sometimes seem as if your child's favorite pastime is saying "no," it may be because this is one of the words he hears most from the grown-ups around him.

♦ Think about reducing the times you say "no" to your child: rephrase some of your answers with humor, or simple choices: "Do you want to put on your hat or your coat?"

♦ Reinforce positive behavior with plenty of praise.

♦ Remember, too, that when your child says "no" it is a reflection of his growing sense of self, which is positive and important – this is his way of learning what it means to be an independent person.

Your child needs your guidance, reassurance, and unconditional love. It's not easy, and can sometimes bring out the two year old in the best of us. So remember which one of you is the adult and retain your sense of balance as you make this journey from toddler to preschooler together.

toddler **traits**

It is important not to confuse family characteristics or potential personality traits with challenging toddler attributes. A stubborn or argumentative streak in a two year old is typical behavior for a child at this age, and is not necessarily a key character trait for later life. Even so, it can sometimes be challenging to live with a two-year-old child who just doesn't want you to put on his shoes or who seems to say "no" to every request you make! Be patient – the likelihood is that this is a passing developmental stage.

the third year

The biggest change you will probably notice in your child's abilities as he enters his third year is his increased understanding of his own world and his relationship to it, including the people around him.

how your toddler learns

During this year, your child's language skills will develop tremendously, opening up a whole new world of communication.

You may also find that your child is becoming more interested in what you are doing. By letting him join in as much as possible with your everyday activities, he will learn new skills as well as enjoy just being with you.

Talk to your child as you do things together. Describing objects, colors, and shapes, for example, will help to increase his vocabulary and language development. Acquiring the ability to communicate verbally is the start of a whole new aspect of your child's life.

Taming tantrums

At this age, it can be hard for small children to know how to wind down if they are tired, or accept that something

Puzzle power
Advancing fine motor skills is a key factor in your child's development as his increased abilities allow him the independence to enjoy more activities on his own.

has to finish. Your child may resist or rebel against ending a game he is enjoying because you have to go out, for example. It takes better memory skills to understand that finishing something enjoyable doesn't mean that it can't be done again another day. Explain this to your child and give him time to digest the idea.

Acquiring social skills

Most of what children learn about respecting other people's feelings is acquired through example and by observing others. If your child is treated with fairness and consideration, and then sees this repeated in the extended family and wider community, he will, in time, begin to understand what it means to be considerate of others.

Likewise, despite his typical toddler attributes of self-focus and possessiveness, it is important to encourage your child to mix with other children to help his social development. For instance, if an older child, who has already learned to share, plays with your child, your child can learn from the example of the older child.

Fine motor development

Your child's hand movements are becoming more precise. Turning the pages of a book one at a time, holding a pencil correctly, and using a cup with one hand are all examples of the greater dexterity he is now developing.

Your child is learning to focus on a single activity for longer periods of time. This in turn gives him the ability and concentration he needs to develop more creative tendencies, such as beginning to draw or play with puzzles using his improved imagination and observation skills.

2 to 3 years: **your toddler's milestones**

In terms of overall physical growth, which slows down between the second and third birthday, the most noticeable change during this third year is your child's body proportions. As his limbs lengthen and his muscles strengthen from being used, his posture becomes more upright, and he will have a flatter tummy.

Movement milestones

Your child's expanding physical abilities in turn give him increased coordination and balance. Now he can walk quickly, for example, and carry toys in his hand as he walks.

By the end of this year you can expect your child to be able to:

♦ walk upstairs using alternate feet

♦ bend down to retrieve a toy without falling over

♦ hop and skip

♦ pedal a tricycle.

Hand and finger milestones

By the end of this year you can expect your child to be able to:

♦ use a crayon to copy a circle onto a piece of paper

♦ turn the pages of a book one at a time

♦ rotate his wrist and unscrew jar tops.

Social and emotional milestones

With the development of the idea of the self, and of possessions, comes difficulty in sharing – either sharing you or his things.

As your child becomes more social, he'll start to anticipate events and express pleasure at certain activities, or begin to recognize particular children and grown-ups. His emotional range is broad, including anything from sheer pleasure and delight to frustrated rage.

By the end of this year you can expect your child to be able to:

♦ happily spend time away from you

♦ express affection to you and to other close family members

♦ show interest in other children.

Intellectual and language milestones

Until this point, your child's physical development, and what he learned from it, gave him the impression that what happens in his world is the result of something he has done.

This self-orientated view of the world means that a child of this age often takes things literally. He finds it difficult to differentiate between fantasy and reality: if you say, for example, "If you eat any more, you'll burst!", it is just possible from his point of view that this could happen.

Imaginative play also becomes important as your child tries to make sense of and seek explanations for events by acting them out, and learns to distinguish fact from fantasy.

By the end of this year, you can expect your child to be able to:

♦ follow a two-part instruction

♦ speak in sentences of four or five words

♦ be understood by non-family members

♦ play imaginative games

♦ match an object to a picture in a book

♦ sort objects into groups by color

♦ understand the concept of "two".

Making sense of it all

The journey that you take with your child over this year happens in fits and starts, and the challenge for you is to help your child make sense of it all through opportunity and activity, with you as his guide.

24 to 28 months

Your two year old's growing independence and the pleasure she derives from her discoveries makes this an exciting time. You can still expect her to let you know just how she is feeling – she will express herself openly with tears and smiles.

key **milestones**

♦ can hop, skip, and jump, as balance and coordination improve

♦ understands concepts such as up and down, in and out

♦ becomes more sociable; starts to learn to consider others

physical development

Your two year old's physical ability has progressed in leaps and bounds over the last 12 months and now she can walk, run, and climb.

What she needs over this next period are lots of opportunities to use her body and explore her capabilities, building greater strength in her limbs and increasing her coordination.

Although your child may be unable to continually jump and hop at this stage, for example, it won't be long before she incorporates an occasional hop, skip, or jump as she runs or walks. These skills have their own momentum and will become easier with practice.

Fine motor control

While your child's gross motor skills – such as walking and running – are improving, so, too, are her fine motor skills, which enable her to use her hands in specific ways to accomplish tasks.

At birth, your child's wrist and palm consisted of only three bones, in comparison to the 28 bones in an adult's hand. It isn't until the relevant bones grow and can be manipulated that the brain's ability to influence the supporting muscles can be more fully exerted. Once this happens, using tools (in your child's case, these are usually toys) becomes easier, whether it is a stick to beat a drum, a crayon for drawing, or a spoon to feed herself.

Practice makes perfect

As a baby, your child began by swiping at an object. Then she was able to grasp it with her whole fist, and now she can delicately pick up something very small between her thumb and forefinger. Not only that, her ability to pick up something, twist her wrist, and place it carefully down again is a considerable physical achievement.

Initially, every effort was put into trying to place and balance just one block on top of another, for example. Practice has made this easy, and now she may try to balance as many blocks as possible before they fall over – or are deliberately knocked down. Thus her ability to pick up an object in her hand has matured immeasurably: she can now do this with greater accuracy and judge far more easily where to place the block so that it will balance.

At play in the park

Playing in the park can also help improve your child's fine motor skills, although she still needs careful supervision since her high energy levels and expectations of her abilities can sometimes get her into trouble.

love of **repetition**

Your child may want you to read the same storybook over and over again. Children at this age love repetition, and sometimes object if you deviate from exactly what is written. They feel comfortable hearing the same stories over and over, and this repetition helps them to learn. They may also remember or recognize a particular word, and then notice it again if they later see the word printed somewhere else. You will probably find they like playing the same rhyming and clapping games over and over, too.

learning skills

Your child will make great progress throughout this year as her language skills develop and she begins to gather and express information in ways other than physical exploration alone.

Physical advances continue, too, of course, but it is the bringing together of her language and physical skills – for example, "When I do this, this happens" – that really helps her cognitive development.

The continued development of her memory, together with improving language skills, means that your child is beginning to form mental images of how things happen, which leads to an understanding of concepts.

Concepts such as in and out, over and under, are abstract ideas to a toddler. Showing your child the meaning – up the stairs, down the stairs; in the door, out the door – will further her understanding. Talk to your child about going inside your house, or show her how you put one stacking cup inside another, for example.

You will be able to see your child's understanding evolve as you watch her play and as you talk and explain things to her. For example, if she sees you put her teddy bear inside a box and you then ask, "Where is the teddy bear?", she will soon comprehend what it means for something to be inside the box. Keep demonstrating and then explaining things to her, and she will gradually begin to understand more about how the world around her works.

Improving concentration

You can also see the effectiveness of your child's memory at this age if you interrupt her activity to ask her a question. She can focus on you and then return to whatever it was she was doing. This is because she can now not only remember what she was doing, but what stage she had reached doing it. Part of being able to develop this technique involves what psychologists call "selective (or focal) attention" – the ability to switch off outside stimuli and concentrate on one thing at a time.

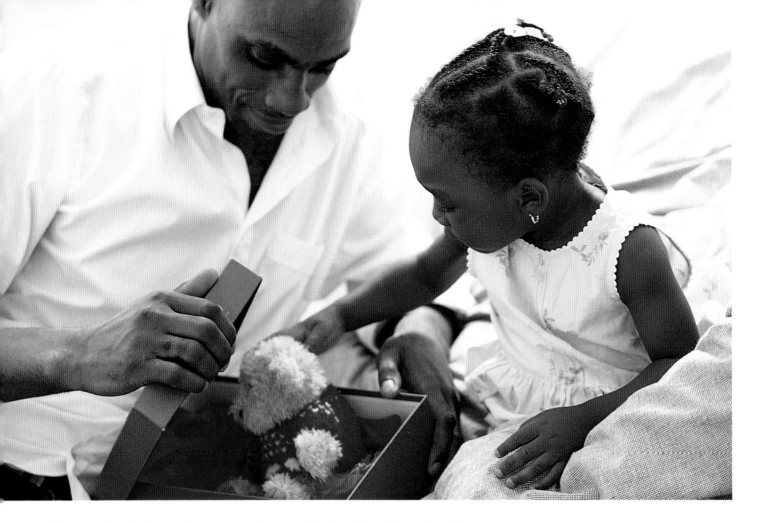

toy box

Matching picture cards
Choose matching picture cards that your child can grasp easily, and with simple images. Use only a few cards to begin with; as she gets older she can memorize more pictures.

Cassette player
Some children's cassette players enable children to record their own voices as they talk and sing, and are equipped with headphones for listening quietly to a favorite tape.

Books
Although your child will love reading the same stories over and over again, make sure you keep her stimulated by occasionally borrowing other books from your local library to vary the complexity of pictures and introduce new types of stories.

Scrapbook materials
Choose round-ended scissors that are easy for your child to open and shut with one hand, and a water-based glue that can be easily washed off her hands and clothes.

Painting equipment
Choose paint specially designed for young children and that will wash out of clothing. Thick finger paints in bright colors are the best choice. If you buy brushes, choose large brushes that are easy to hold.

Tricycle
Tricycles are good for outdoor play. Let your child get used to pushing herself along with her legs and learning how to steer before showing her how to use the pedals.

The benefits of books
If you say you are going to read a story to your child, her memory of what this involves and the pleasure she knows she will derive from it make her more willing to focus on the book for the time it takes to read a story.

She can then use this knowledge about what books involve and how to enjoy them to look at books by herself. This helps with developing her concentration and lengthening her attention span, while also gradually extending the range of her vocabulary.

Over the past two years you have probably collected numerous children's stories, from treasured first board books and favorite picture books to more sophisticated stories. All of these provide unique access to an imaginative world that helps your child learn about new ideas, cause and effect, feelings and facts.

This is the start of your child learning to read, so it is important to help her develop a natural curiosity about books and stories.

emotional development

Emotionally, your two year old will still appear to be selfish. This is our adult interpretation of her behavior. Her inclination is to put her needs first. Help her to think of the needs of others, too.

Encouraging your child to share teaches her to consider other people. It will also increase her socialization skills, which are learned primarily through imitation. If your child is treated with respect and affection, she will learn to treat others in the same way. However, if you are overly concerned with the feelings of others at the expense of those of your own child, you will diminish her self-esteem. Explain to her that other people are just as important as she is, but not more so.

At this age you may also have the advantage of your child wanting to please you, so through your relationship with her she can learn to extend her consideration to others around her. Focusing on this aspect will help her develop the idea that if something is nice for her, then it would be nice for someone else, too.

Expressing emotion

You can expect spontaneous and genuine shows of affection from your child by this stage, especially if similar attention has been lavished on her. It makes it much easier for her to accept and value other people's feelings if she feels accepted and valued, too.

Try to watch the language you use when managing your child's emotional behavior. She is not being naughty if she doesn't want to wait her turn to play with a toy, she merely needs a gentle reminder or explanation of how the process works or what her part in playing with other children is. If she can't grasp what you mean at first, wait with her, or suggest that she play alongside you until she learns that taking turns is a positive thing to do.

The emotional range of a two year old is broad, extending from sheer delight to frustrated rage. While the ability to express emotions freely is considered healthy, what your child needs to learn

is to manage her emotions and know which responses are appropriate. This takes practice and needs your help.

Managing emotion

Children may feel overwhelmed by the force of their emotions sometimes, hence the full-blown tantrum. These situations need specific management skills, but it also helps to keep in mind what might trigger such extremes of emotion. Some children cannot manage emotionally as well as others when they are tired or hungry, for example.

In the middle of emotional turmoil it is worth remembering that your child is also capable of expressing positive emotions. So finding an activity to share that she enjoys and allows her to express her happier side, will help her self-esteem, and increase your own pleasure.

learning through play

Giving your child lots of opportunities to explore what her body is capable of doing can help her physical development and her self-esteem. Help her develop her memory skills, too, by playing tapes and matching picture games.

♦ Outdoor playgrounds with swings and slides to enjoy are good because there are usually other children to share the experience, which also helps your child learn about taking turns.

♦ Soft modeling clay is a delight in itself, and your child may enjoy just squeezing it through her fingers before getting involved in more imaginative play. Creating flat shapes and making impressions in the

dough with cookie cutters or even just making handprints allows her to explore all sorts of interesting possibilities with modeling clay.

♦ Matching shapes or pictures is an important observational and premath skill. You may have given your child a shape-sorter, and then moved on to a puzzle where she has to select and place a flat shape into a matching place on the board. Now this skill can be developed into a simple game of similarities and dissimilarities. This in turn helps extend language skills to communicate ideas, observations, and feelings.

♦ A cassette player designed to be used by little fingers will give your child access to music and favorite stories on tape. You may also like to record yourself reading a favorite story for your child, and if there are stories with which she is familiar, she can look at the book while listening to the tape. This will increase the access your child has to the spoken word. Learning to listen attentively will be of great benefit to her, especially when she goes to nursery school or daycare. Make sure the volume can't be raised beyond a certain level, to avoid damaging your child's ears.

28 to 32 months

During these early years, you are your child's first teacher, and time spent together is invaluable. Even when life is very busy, find time to be together. Giving your child your undivided attention will give you both pleasure.

physical development

Your child needs plenty of physical activity to help expend some of the enormous amount of energy she exhibits at this age.

All forms of exercise help your child's spatial understanding, and, by extension, her balance and coordination skills. Getting plenty of exercise not only burns off excess energy, it establishes a positive body image and helps build a sense of self-esteem.

In addition, the connections built up between neurons in the brain, known as neural pathways, are formulated by regular physical, as well as cognitive, activity. This is why, once we have learned how to ride a bicycle, we never forget unless something interferes with the neural patterns imprinted in our brains. Therefore, a child needs practice in the larger physical skills – running, kicking, climbing, or pedaling a tricycle – to become competent, as well as build strength and use up energy.

With growing concerns about today's rising rates of childhood obesity, our

Getting physical
Outdoor play gives young children the opportunity to develop important physical skills such as coordination and balance, as well as improve stamina and strength.

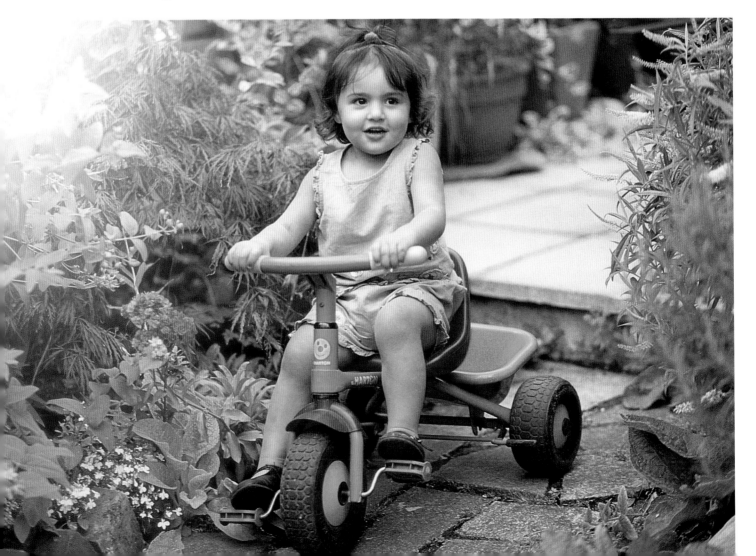

sedentary lifestyles, and children's lack of exercise, it is important to foster an enjoyment of exercise. Let your child walk rather than take the car, allowing her to sit in her stroller if she gets tired, or park farther away from the shopping mall than usual and walk there.

Hand proficiency

Given the opportunity, it's amazing what a difference practice can make to your child's ability to use her hands proficiently.

By this stage, you can expect your child to use her hands to do a variety of different things, from carefully turning the pages of a book to holding a pencil or unscrewing a jar. Practicing undoing buttons on clothes, for instance, can help her fine motor skills and develop her independence.

This maturing of fine motor skills helps in all sorts of ways, including encouraging your child to develop the confidence to try other things that were once difficult. Seeing her own progress, and enjoying the pleasure and satisfaction that it brings, encourages her to try other new activities.

awareness **of self**

Your child probably now knows that she is a girl – or he is a boy – and can distinguish between the sexes, although she may not always know why. She will also be able to refer to herself as "I" and may be able to describe herself in simple sentences: "I am hungry," for example. This growing awareness of self began months before, but its expression is now becoming clearer, and as your child's language skills improve she may be able to convey her thoughts more easily.

toy **box**

Jigsaw puzzles
Choose colorful puzzles that are not too difficult for your child. Some children will still be on six- or seven-piece puzzles, while others may have graduated to enjoying more complex ones. Well-made wooden jigsaw puzzles with clear, simple pictures are most suitable for small fingers and will hold a child's attention.

Ball play
Buy a medium-size, lightweight ball that your child can easily wrap her arms around to hold securely. Soft tennis balls are another option.

Toy dishes
A brightly colored, well-made plastic set of dishes, including cups and saucers, will give hours of pleasure. Make sure the pieces are sturdy enough for little hands. Toy pots and pans are great, too.

Dolls and dolls' clothes
You can buy dolls with appropriate clothes that are specially made to help young children learn about the process of dressing and undressing. Dolls stimulate imagination and also encourage role-playing games.

Picture dominoes
Make sure that the dominoes are large enough for young children to pick up and put down easily.

Plastic blocks
The chunkier the plastic pieces are, the more chance your two year old will have of being able to use her coordination skills and the strength in her hands to fit blocks together without becoming frustrated.

learning skills

Since memory is such an important part of what helps children develop intellectually, it is worth helping your child improve her memory skills.

At this stage it is still easier for children to remember language that is reinforced by physical activity, such as incorporating actions. In the same way, when you tell your child how to do something, show her at the same time – turn the page of a book carefully, or close a door gently, for example. This is especially important when your child struggles with abstract concepts.

Creating an impact

For all of us, remembering routines that happen every day is harder than remembering single events. You may notice that if you ask your child what she had for breakfast – even if it was only an hour ago – she may look at you blankly since the food she eats every day is not of much consequence to her. But if you ask her what she had for dinner on her last visit to her grandmother's house, she may easily remember.

Children are very much "of the moment," and remembering the mundane holds little interest for them. Something that may have been planned, discussed, and involved a change in the normal routine becomes an exciting event, and thus has a greater impact on a child.

Language skills

By now your child's vocabulary may include as many as 200–300 words. She may also be using connecting words between phrases, such as "and," while also adding details to her descriptions. Bilingual children may initially mix words from each language when they speak, but in general they should speak as fluently as their peers.

Asking questions

With this acquired vocabulary comes the question, "Why?" The process of questioning is valuable to your child because it helps her to understand, and it is likely to continue for many months. Answer the question simply, allowing for development of thought, rather than overwhelming your child with a complicated explanation.

Answering a two year old's incessant questioning is an art, and there cannot be many parents who haven't resorted occasionally to saying, "Because I say so!" However, be prepared for the comeback "Why?" You may even want to respond with your own question in a friendly tone, "What do you think?"

Speaking clearly

Children at this age may still speak unclearly or mispronounce words. This may be connected to the development of facial muscles. If your child still mispronounces most words, it is important to check with your healthcare professional to make sure she hasn't suffered any hearing loss, and then pursue a speech/language evaluation.

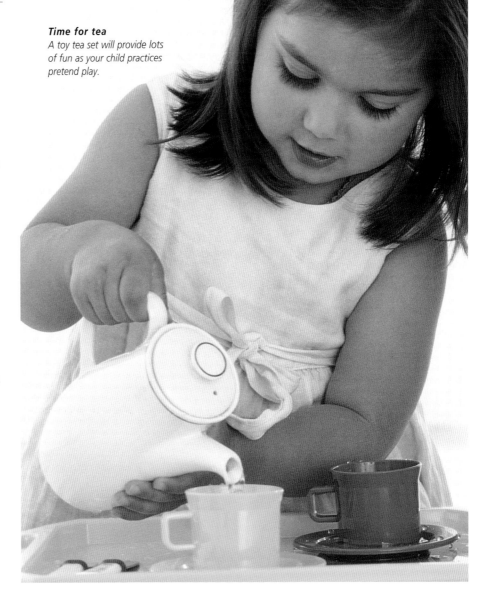

Time for tea
A toy tea set will provide lots of fun as your child practices pretend play.

emotional development

You may find that as your child becomes more social she starts to anticipate events and express pleasure at one activity over another.

She may also begin to express her excitement when she sees a friend she enjoys playing with. Forming attachments outside the immediate family circle is evidence of your child's widening emotional development. She is making relationships based on her own positive feelings about being a person, independent of you.

It is important to try and validate your child's emotions, even if doing so sometimes conflicts with your own feelings. With her improving language skills, articulating how she feels about someone, or something, becomes easier. She may not know what she feels at first, but you can help her explore her emotions. Don't disregard her feelings or tell her not to be silly if she appears hesitant about playing with another child, for example. Gently determine what it is that she doesn't feel comfortable about.

Expressing pleasure

In the same way, when a person or an event generates particular pleasure, ask your child what it is that feels good about the experience. Use this opportunity to talk to her about feelings, but keep it

learning through play

Simple jigsaw puzzles are an excellent way of training your child's eye to recognize matching shapes and to look at how things fit together. You can also help her manage a small task and improve her fine motor skills by giving her a doll to undress. Try playing singing games to improve her ability to listen to different sounds and follow rhythms.

♦ Introduce the idea of rhythm to your child by beating time. Pick out the rhythm of different words, or combinations of words, for example, the rhythm in your child's name: Martin becomes Mar-tin, Samantha becomes Sa-man-tha. In this way you introduce the idea of syllables with a game. Maybe an older sibling could play an instrument while you and your two year old beat time clapping your hands or tapping glasses filled with different levels of water.

♦ Getting dressed and undressed is a part of your child's routine and something she may be happy to attempt on her own. It can provide an opportunity to learn to undo buttons and zippers, which require small, precise finger movements. But these are skills of great value, and something your child needs to be competent at doing in due course. It also allows her to develop the sort of confidence needed to

manage small tasks alone, which will be to her advantage when she is away from home.

♦ You may also like to play dominoes with your child. This makes demands on her observation and memory skills and improves her ability to spot similarities. Although she is still too young to play this game on her own, she may enjoy playing with you.

♦ Simple jigsaw puzzles take the process of matching up shapes to a higher level, since they require good observation skills. Children find great satisfaction in trying to find the right piece and putting it in the right place. Learning to look at something in this very specific way is also good training for the identification of letter shapes later on. Puzzles can also be used to encourage the start of simple word recognition.

simple. By being attuned to your child's feelings and acknowledging them, and encouraging her to articulate them when she's ready, you are paving the way for her to learn how to explore and express her own feelings.

Other people's feelings

If your child learns at this early age that her feelings are valued, it will eventually enable her to consider other people's feelings in the same way and encourage her to treat people the way she'd like to be treated. Respecting your child's feelings teaches her that respecting another individual's emotions is equally important.

A child's viewpoint

Your child has probably developed a clear idea of what possessions are, but she still needs reminding that she can share what she has. Understanding what's "mine" at this age can result in a certain amount of possessiveness in children. However, all this is really just part of how they view the world around them from their own, very singular, point of view. Act as a guide to your child, by helping her open up her focus and incorporate a wider viewpoint.

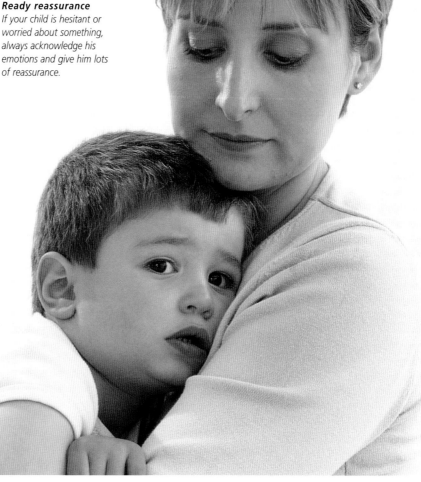

Ready reassurance
If your child is hesitant or worried about something, always acknowledge his emotions and give him lots of reassurance.

32 to 36 months

Your almost three year old is much more independent now, with his own developing interests and opinions. His personality is also becoming more clearly established, and he is learning to experiment and express his own ideas.

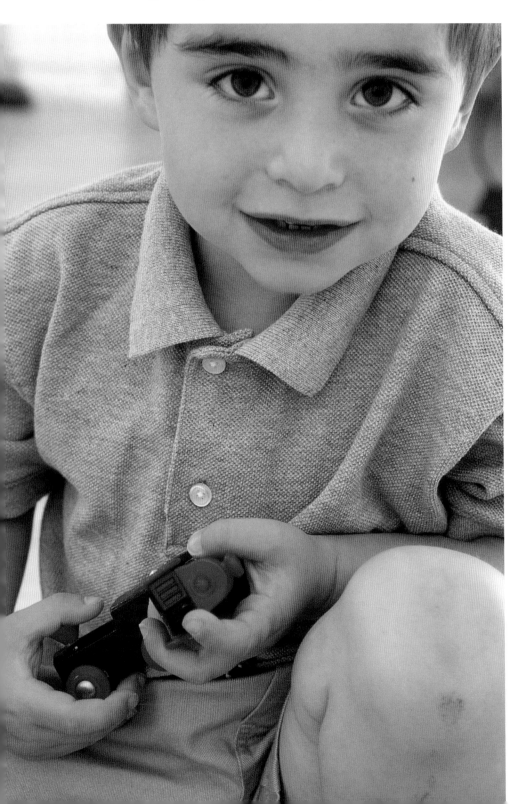

physical development

Your child now builds on the strength he has developed so far to climb up and down stairs, walk on tiptoe, and control his hand movements more accurately.

If you live in a house with a flight of stairs, your two year old may now be confident going up and down them safely on his own using alternate feet rather than taking just one step at a time. If you do not have stairs in your home, your child will inevitably have had less practice at this skill. However, he is probably beginning to climb stairs he encounters using alternate feet. Regardless of his ability, you should never leave your child completely unattended near stairs.

Improving motor skills
Jumping with two feet may now be possible for your child, although he may still be somewhat flat-footed. You might try suggesting games that encourage him to walk on tiptoe in bare feet. This activity strengthens his feet and enhances flexibility and balance.

Imagination and inventiveness
Allow your child to spend some time playing with his toys by himself. Inventing his own games starts when he is given opportunities to develop his imagination.

the concept **of time**

The concept of time is difficult for young children to grasp, but your child may be mature enough to know what you mean by "before and after." For example, he may understand if you say he can get down and play "after you've finished your lunch." This understanding is possible because of his developing experience and memory. Repeated activities such as mealtimes help define the course of his day.

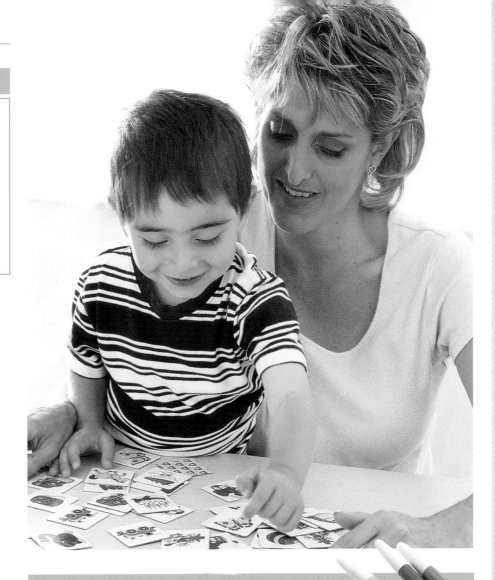

Your child may also be getting better at washing and drying his hands. Some fine motor skills, such as eating with a spoon or fork, are also improving, but may still be difficult.

Individual development
Some children may seem physically less able than others because they are so impatient to get from one place to another, or achieve a specific task; they might benefit from slowing down and taking things more easily. Other children can be very impulsive and don't allow themselves time to assess physical risk, so again, they may need some encouragement to slow down a little. If they show little natural fear or reservation, they may need guidance to take a some extra caution.

Structured activities
You may feel naturally inclined to reduce the level of physical activity undertaken by your child if he appears less physically able. However, guard against this tendency because it won't help him. In fact, increasing the amount of structured activities to help him learn to master physical skills more easily will be to your child's advantage.

As long as it helps him in an uncompetitive and fun way, think about whether he may benefit from joining a gymnastics or dance class for young children at your local sports center. Remember to keep giving him lots of encouragement to raise his self-esteem.

toy **box**

Simple board games
Focus on simple games with your child, such as age-appropriate board games. Go slowly and patiently as you play, and you may find he soon begins to pick up the rules of the game.

Dress-up box
It is worth keeping a large box full of old clothes and costumes for children to play with. Encourage them to think imaginatively about how they can adapt the clothes to suit who they want to pretend to be.

Picture cards
If you have already begun playing a simple version of this memory game with your child, you may want to buy a slightly more sophisticated version of the game if he is becoming proficient at it. Or you can make your own version by using pictures from old magazines and gluing them onto square pieces of cardboard.

Pens and paper
Buy large, non-toxic crayons, washable markers, and brightly colored paper to give your child many hours of fun. Use this time to teach your child to draw shapes and identify colors.

Foam letters
Many toy stores sell foam letters and numbers that stick to the side of the bathtub when they get wet. Choose large pieces that help your child recognize letters and numbers.

learning skills

Your child is now beginning to grasp the concept of simple number sequences and different categories.

Your child's knowledge of numbers began when you first sang number rhymes to him, although it wouldn't have been clear then what these words represented. Through frequent repetition, your child may have learned to "count" to five, or even 10, although in reality he has just been repeating a sequence of sounds.

Now, he will begin to use these familiar words to represent the more tangible concept of counting. The development of this understanding begins with forming groups, or sequences, of objects. Just counting three cars or two spoons is a start. Your child may also grasp the idea of different categories soon: 10 plastic animals in total, but three cows, five pigs, and two horses. You may even find him repeating numbers and number sequences in his games.

Nursery rhymes

Have you ever wondered why parents pass down favorite nursery rhymes through the generations? Perhaps it's from an intuitive knowledge that talking to your child helps him develop speech, but the repetition of nursery rhymes is also a useful preparation for reading. The constant repetition of the rhymes in early life means that your child becomes familiar with different word sounds. They also engage his attention, helping him pick up information about language and how it works.

Personal references

Your child should now be able to converse with you in short sentences rather than just in phrases, and he may now be able to continue talking about a topic for a short period.

Your child will probably now refer to himself as "I" rather than by his name, say "you" rather than use the third person, and refer to friends and family by name. This demonstrates how his cognitive skills have advanced over the year in identifying himself as an individual within his family, and referring to himself as such.

Visual memories

As his language skills improve, you will notice how good your child's memory and observation skills are becoming. Children have strong visual memories, so if your child has a broad range of vocabulary you may be surprised by how much detail he can give you about something. Encourage this skill by asking him to describe events or experiences in more detail.

emotional development

Attention-seeking behavior in two-year-old children can take different forms and having a tantrum is often one of them.

At this age, tantrums in children can be due to changes or events, or a learned response. If they surface in a previously well-behaved child, consider why his behavior may have changed. After the tantrum is over, calmly communicate that his behavior is not appropriate.

Emotional frustration

It's important to try and understand why a child responds to situations in an antisocial way. This can be difficult if a tantrum gets him what he wants in the short term. Tantrums are usually linked to a child's frustration and inability to communicate effectively. A two year old does not fully understand that there are things he cannot have (see pages 126–129).

Children need quiet time to imagine and be creative. This helps develop self-reliance, stimulates new ideas, and builds self-esteem. Children also have an emotional need for lots of attention, and while positive attention is better than negative, they tend not to make that distinction – any attention will do if a child feels he isn't getting enough.

The challenge of parenting is being attuned to your child so that you can accommodate his needs as they change. The basic principle is to ignore negative behavior and to be generous in your reward and praise of good behavior.

Coping with separation

By this age, your child should be reasonably happy when separated from you for an extended period of time, although some children are more anxious than others about separation. In order to feel comfortable about spending time away from you, your child needs to be able to hold on to the thought of you, and know that you will return to him, something which is learned partly through experience.

How you handle separation will also convey to your child what is expected of him. If you appear confident, you will convey to him your confidence in his ability to cope. If you are anxious or hesitant, he may pick up on this emotion, which might make it more difficult for him to feel confident without you.

learning through play

Imaginative play is very important for young children. Through it they learn to work out certain abstract concepts, act out scenarios, "try on" different ideas, explore feelings and ways of behaving – all within their own imaginations.

♦ Playing with other children is a learned skill, and is all about socializing, taking turns, and thinking about others. Help your child learn these skills by playing simple board games that are appropriate to his age group and encourage him to take turns. In addition, playing a counting game enables you to help him learn about numbers, plus their names and sequences. Focus on the pleasure and excitement of playing the game, regardless of who wins, so that winning is not your child's only goal when playing. By playing a game

repeatedly, the experience of winning or losing will become less important. It is more important at this age to have fun than to focus on winning.

♦ All young children should be encouraged to play games that rely on their inner resources. Playing house allows children to rehearse social roles; dress-up games stimulate this ability, and help develop the skills your child needs in order to dress himself. A big square of material, for example, can be a princess's cloak, a magician's cape, a magic carpet, or a baby blanket. Adults' clothes and accessories such as old hats or high-heeled shoes are another great attraction. Store-bought costumes, perhaps based on popular fictional characters, are also an option, as are doctors' and nurses' uniforms.

health

All parents want their children to be healthy, to enjoy life to the full, and to develop normally. As the immune system matures, minor illnesses are common in young children. It's always distressing for parents when their baby or child is ill, and it can be hard to know what to do. Always check with your healthcare professional if you have questions about your child's health. In this section, you'll find information to help you keep your child healthy and on what to do when your child is not feeling well. There is also advice on injury prevention and first aid to help you deal with emergencies, should they arise.

keeping healthy

Babies and young children develop minor illnesses, and babies, in particular, can become sick very quickly. Many common childhood illnesses are due to viruses and will resolve on their own. Luckily, there is a lot you can do to help keep your child healthy.

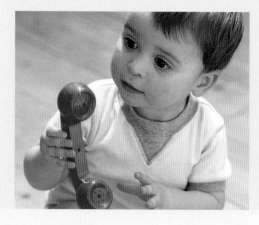

home life

People in a household may harbor the same germs, so normally you don't have to worry about kissing your baby. However, if you have cold sores or shingles, or are ill yourself, ask your doctor for advice.

At first, even minor illnesses can be a challenge for you and your child, but as a parent, you soon become adept at thinking on your feet, interpreting symptoms, and knowing how to make your child feel better – and get better – as quickly as possible.

There is a lot you can do to keep your child well. A warm, loving bond with you provides the right environment for children to thrive. There has even been evidence that this can help your child fight minor illness.

Infections tend to spread in the winter when there is more indoor play. Unless your child is sick, there's no reason to keep him from social contact with other children when the only option for play is indoors.

Exercise

A daily outing is a good idea from a young age. Take your child for a walk, visit a friend or relative, or explore the local park. Your toddler will enjoy lots of time outdoors, and you'll soon discover that parks and playgrounds are a great place for both of you to enjoy social interactions, too. When you go out, bring a stroller, even if your toddler is a good walker, because he may get tired and appreciate a ride home. Be sure your child is dressed appropriately for the weather before you leave the house.

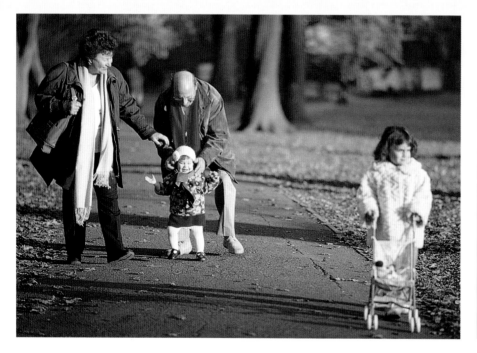

Out and around
Regular exercise, even just a short trip to the park, will help to keep your child healthy and is fun for the whole family.

key **points**

♦ Good personal and health habits can prevent a lot of childhood illnesses.

♦ As a parent, you play the most important role in keeping your child healthy.

♦ Think ahead about safety as your baby grows.

♦ Learn the basics about common illnesses before they occur.

hygiene

Cleanliness in the home, especially around your baby, is vital. Babies and their surroundings and toys all need to be kept clean to minimize the risk of infection, particularly when they start putting things into their mouths. Good hygiene practices such as hand washing after diaper changes are essential.

Always try to stay a step ahead of your child. Before long, a baby grows into a toddler, who needs to learn how to wash his hands, handle food properly, and acquire good hygiene habits.

Hygiene in the kitchen

The whole family should be scrupulous about kitchen hygiene.

♦ Take extra care when preparing your baby's meals or feeding supplies.

♦ Don't keep food that's already been served in his bowl; there are always bacteria on hands and silverware, and these thrive on leftovers.

♦ Change your dishtowel often and keep towels clean.

♦ Use different implements for handling raw and cooked foods, and for raw meat and vegetables.

♦ Bacteria thrive in warmth, so check the temperature of your refrigerator (32–41°F/ 0–5°C) for optimum efficiency.

♦ Keep cooked food near the top of the refrigerator, and raw food below. Germs from raw foods can contaminate cooked meals.

♦ Follow food use-by dates.

♦ For more kitchen safety advice see pages 262–263.

Household pets

Animals are part of many homes and they often give a family a lot of pleasure. Young children who grow up with a pet have the chance to learn about being gentle and responsible, and may even get a lesson in reproductive biology. Walking the pet can help promote a healthier lifestyle.

Safe meal times
Your baby relies on you, as a parent, to keep her surroundings as clean and germ-free as possible, both at home and out and about.

However, pets do harbor germs, so it's important for your child to wash his hands after playing with an animal, especially before a meal. If you have a dog, make sure that he is regularly wormed. Keep pets off the beds and preferably out of your child's bedroom. If you have a cat, keep the litter box clean and teach your child not to touch it. If you have a sandbox in your backyard, make sure that there's a cover for it and that it goes on when the sandbox is not being used; even if you don't have a cat, other pets in your neighborhood may use it as a litter box.

Research suggests that having mild infections in early life can protect against some illnesses later, but experts believe that animals may trigger asthma and other symptoms in families who have a lot of allergies. So if allergies are common in your family, you may need to think twice about getting a furry pet for your child.

the effects of **smoking**

The air that your child breathes has a profound effect on his health. Smoking reduces the ability of the air passages to fight off infection, and also reduces the amount of oxygen carried in the blood. Ideally, you and your partner should not smoke at all. If you do smoke, don't do so anywhere near babies and children, or in the house.

♦ Passive smoking is thought to be linked to a quarter of all sudden infant deaths (see page 225).

♦ Young children of smokers are more likely to suffer allergies, asthma, chest infections, and ear infections.

♦ Children whose parents smoke are often shorter than children from non-smoking families.

♦ Cigarette smoke contains carbon monoxide, ammonia, cyanide, and chemicals that are known to cause cancer.

♦ Many fatal house fires are started by cigarettes and matches.

immunizations

Immunization is an important means of protecting your child from certain life-threatening illnesses. Thanks to immunization programs, many serious illnesses have been more or less eradicated.

understanding immunization

All of the diseases your child is immunized against are serious and unpleasant infections. The more children that are vaccinated, the better the protection for the population.

A vaccine stimulates the immune system into making antibodies (proteins that can fight infection). A vaccine is a virus or bacterium, altered so that it can't cause illness, but can trigger antibodies that protect your child if she comes into contact with the disease.

When to delay immunization

♦ If you have any concerns about immunization, consult your healthcare provider or doctor for advice.
♦ A mild cold should not deter you from immunizing your baby.
♦ If your baby has a high fever, delay the immunization until she is better.
♦ Speak to your doctor if your baby has had a serious reaction to any previous injection, has an allergy to eggs or anything else, has had a seizure, is having treatment for cancer, or has any disease that weakens the immune system. It may still be safe for her to have the vaccine, but it might be necessary to take additional precautions.

immunization **timetable**

This schedule is recommended by the Canadian Pediatric Society. However, there may be provincial differences. Consult your doctor or public health nurse for more information. Keep a record of all immunizations and the dates to make sure none are missed (see page 281).

Birth ♦Hep B#1 (Hepatitis – may be administered in infancy or preadolescence)
1 month ♦Hep B#2
2 months ♦DaPTP-Hib#1 (Diptheria, Pertussis, Tetanus, Polio – given orally as IPV in some provinces – Hemophilus influenzae)
♦Pneumococcal* vaccine#1
♦Meningitis C* vaccine#1
4 months ♦DaPTP-Hib#2
♦Pneumococcal* vaccine#2
♦Meningitis C* vaccine#2
6 months ♦DaPTP-Hib#3
♦Pneumococcal* vaccine#3
♦Hep B#3
♦Meningitis C* vaccine#3
12–15 months ♦MMR#1 (measles, mumps, rubella)
♦Varicella* (chicken pox)
♦Pneumococcal* vaccine#4
18 months ♦DaPTP-Hib#4
4–6 years ♦DaPTP
♦MMR#2

* The cost of these vaccines are not covered by some provincial/territorial health plans. You may have to pay for them yourself.

Routine immunizations

The aim of immunization is to put an end to disease, a goal that has been achieved for example, in the case of smallpox, a deadly disease that was eradicated in 1980 through successful global vaccination. Routine immunization against infectious disease is just as important, however, for individuals. Vaccines provide one of the safest, most reliable, and most effective ways modern medicine has of controlling death and illness caused by infectious disease. Make sure your child is immunized against the following infections and viruses:

♦ **Polio** (*poliomyelitis*) A virus that causes damage to the nervous system and can result in permanent paralysis or even death.

♦ **Diphtheria** A bacterial disease that starts in the throat and can spread to the heart and the nervous system.

♦ **Tetanus** This is a potentially fatal bacterial infection that can cause paralysis of the muscles.

♦ **Whooping cough** (*pertussis*) A bacterial illness with fever that causes coughing

measles, mumps, and rubella (MMR)

There has been a lot of debate – and some parental anxiety – about the MMR vaccine. Concerns center around whether MMR can be linked with Crohn's disease (an inflammatory disease of the bowel) and/or autism (a disorder of development that affects a child's social skills). Both of these have become more common. MMR has been given for over 25 years and approximately 200 million doses have been used. No studies have demonstrated a link between MMR and autism or Crohn's disease. Like all vaccines, MMR can have

some short-term side effects: mainly fever (which can be high) and a mild measleslike rash about 10 days after the injection is given. If you are concerned about how your child will react to the vaccine, talk to your doctor.

Most doctors believe that the risks of measles, mumps, and rubella are far greater than any risks from MMR. Parents should remember that the effectiveness of any immunization program such as MMR relies on the immunization of as many children as possible.

spasms. These spasms and fever can result in vomiting, seizures, and lung damage.

♦ **Hib** (*hemophilus influenzae B*) A bacterial infection that can cause a range of illnesses, including meningitis and pneumonia.

♦ **Measles** A virus that can cause chest infections, seizures, meningitis, and permanent brain damage.

♦ **Mumps** A virus that causes painful swelling of the salivary glands. It can also cause meningitis and deafness.

♦ **Rubella** This is a virus that can cause serious birth defects in unborn babies. Although for the majority of children rubella is not serious, it can also result in joint pains and encephalitis (inflammation of the brain).

questions & answers

q **What side effects do vaccines have?**

a The needle itself causes brief pain, so it's typical for a young baby to cry. Often this occurs several seconds after the injection. You can breastfeed your baby or use a pacifier to comfort her. Soreness and slight redness are common at the injection site. A small lump can form, but this is harmless and usually painless, and resolves on its own. It's normal for a baby to be a little unhappy for a few hours or even a day or so after her immunization, and she may have a slight fever. Tender loving care will make a big difference in the way your baby feels afterward. You can give a small dose of Tylenol® for pain or fever. Follow your doctor's instructions for dosing.

q **My baby missed an immunization. Should she start all over again?**

a No. It's best to stick to the timetable if possible, but if your baby misses a dose, then she should have it late. She doesn't need to start the whole course of vaccines all over again.

Protecting your child
Although taking your baby for her immunizations can be upsetting for you as a parent, there is a lot you can do to comfort her afterward, and you should be reassured that you are doing your best to protect her health for years to come.

q **When do I need to call the doctor about side effects?**

a It's unusual to need the doctor after an immunization. However, you should call your doctor if your baby or child has a siezure (convulsion) after her immunization, or if she develops a fever over 102.2°F (39°C). You should tell your doctor if your baby has a lot of pain or redness at the site of the shot or has a more widespread rash. If your baby or child has any other symptoms that you don't understand, or you have any concerns, ask your healthcare professional.

q **If these diseases are so rare, why do we still need the vaccinations?**

a The vaccinations are the reason that many diseases are so uncommon today. However, the bacteria and viruses that cause them have not disappeared altogether. Some diseases are still common in other parts of the world, and travelers can bring them into this country. Without immunizations, certain infections could quickly spread here.

your baby's health

It's natural to worry about your baby's health. If you're a new parent, you may also be uncertain about what's normal. Taking care of a sick child can be a challenge. You'll want to do all you can to make him better, and to reassure yourself that you're doing the right thing.

illness in newborn babies

Infants under one year of age can have some of the same ailments as older children, but they can't tell you how they feel.

Their immune systems are also less developed, so illnesses that an older baby might shrug off can occasionally develop into something more serious. On the other hand, for about the first six months of his life a young baby has the benefit of antibodies he has acquired from his mother. This is why babies under one year old tend not to get common childhood infections such as chicken pox and measles.

Often parents just know when their baby isn't feeling well. This instinct develops over time, and as you get to know your baby, you will understand what is normal for him.

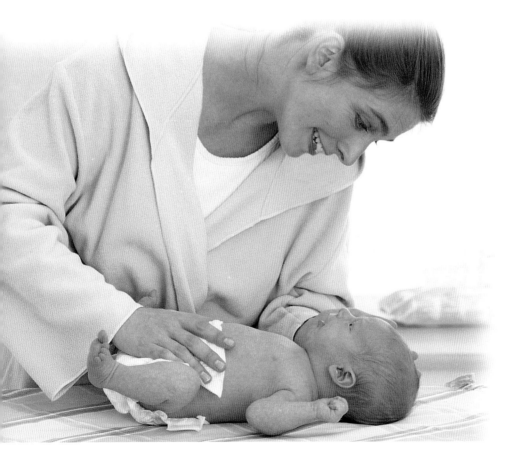

Common conditions

There are a number of ailments that are particularly prevalent in very young babies.

♦ **Dry skin** This is very common in babies, especially those born past their due date. Dry, flaky skin is usually found over the ankles and feet, or in the diaper area. This has nothing to do with eczema. Use a moisturizing baby bath product and apply baby lotion or oil after a bath (see pages 94–95) to soothe and relieve dry skin.

♦ **Diaper rash** Ammonia and other chemicals in urine can irritate a baby's sensitive skin. It is more likely to happen if a diaper is left on too long – that's why it is important to change your baby regularly, especially if he has loose stools. Cloth diapers are not better than disposables for avoiding diaper rash. Disposable diapers probably keep a baby's bottom much drier. At the first sign of redness, apply a thick layer of barrier cream containing zinc oxide.

If your baby develops a rash, when you've cleaned him dry him thoroughly and let him lie on a mat or towel without a diaper for 10–20 minutes and stay with him. You may need to do this three or more times a day until the rash clears. Smooth on a thick layer of barrier cream before putting on a clean diaper.

Diaper rash can also be due to thrush, an infection caused by a yeast called candida or monilia. If the rash doesn't improve, see your doctor.

♦ **Excessive crying** Long bouts of loud, inconsolable crying, usually starting at about two weeks of age, are often referred

spots and rashes

Babies can have many spots and rashes (see page 94). Most are harmless, but it is a good idea to be aware of some common conditions and to check with your healthcare professional.

Harlequin color change
Some areas of your baby's skin may be

Milia
These are small white dots, usually on the nose. They need no treatment, but see your doctor if any become very red.

paler than others. If you change his position, the pale part becomes brighter pink while the pinker part fades. This is a harmless sign of immature blood-vessel control.

Small facial blemishes
These may develop in the first few days and weeks. They come and go quickly. If they look red and infected, ask your doctor.

Stork bites (flat angiomata)
These are red or purplish V-shaped marks on the back of the neck or eyelids. They are usually harmless, and most will fade over the first few months of life.

Mongolian blue spots
Fairly large grayish-blue patches on your baby's buttocks or limbs; these are harmless.

Strawberry marks (hemangiomas)
Your baby may develop marks with a surface that resembles a strawberry. These stop growing at about six months, and then slowly recede. Ask your doctor for advice.

Cradle cap
These greasy scales on the scalp are caused by dead skin. It is not infected, nor does your baby have dandruff or eczema.

to as colic. These bouts of intense crying are common in the first three months, particularly in the evening, and may last for two to three hours. A baby may pull up his knees, go red in the face, and clench his fists. The cause is unknown, but recent research suggests that colic may simply be a more extreme form of normal crying.

For a small number of babies, physical problems (particularly digestive disorders) may be the cause of unexplained crying. Consult your doctor to rule out any possibility that your baby is ill and for advice on coping with colic. Try different ways of soothing your baby (see page 99), but avoid overstimulating him.

Take comfort from the fact that colic usually passes by three to four months of age. In the meantime, call on your family and friends for help during this period.
♦ **Trapped gas** Most babies suffer from trapped gas after feeding at one time or another, although some are more susceptible than others. Frequent burping during and after feedings is important. If your baby seems prone to gassiness, talk to your healthcare professional, who may

recommend an over-the-counter remedy containing simethicone. Simethicone breaks down gas bubbles in minutes and is safe because it is not absorbed into your baby's system.
♦ **Reflux** Caused by stomach acid and food traveling up the esophagus (food tube) during and after feedings, reflux can lead to abdominal pain. The "valve" at the lower end of the esophagus is immature and may not close properly. Symptoms are similar to colic, but tend to occur with, or after, every feeding. Keeping your baby in a more upright position, especially while feeding, can help. If symptoms persist, speak to your doctor.
♦ **Dehydration** Babies can lose fluid very easily when they have vomiting or diarrhea; even more so when they have both at the same time, as in gastroenteritis. This is why babies with diarrhea and vomiting need to see the doctor. It's important to recognize the warning signs of dehydration. You may find that your baby has less wet diapers than usual. As dehydration progresses, his skin will become less elastic than normal. Over his tummy, for

instance, it can look dry and wrinkled. His fontanelle may be sunken, his eyes may seem more deeply set, and he may become floppy and lethargic. These are signs of serious dehydration. Contact your doctor without delay if your baby shows any of them.
♦ **Navel bulge** If your baby's umbilical cord seems to push outward when he cries, he may have an umbilical hernia. Your healthcare professional will confirm the diagnosis. These hernias, unlike those in the groin, usually resolve on their own, although they can take months or sometimes even years to do so.
♦ **Sticky eye** Wipe each eye with a fresh cotton ball and cooled, boiled water – wipe gently outward away from the nose, and avoid touching the eyeball. Consult your doctor if symptoms persist. Babies under a year old are prone to conjunctivitis (see page 249). If the eyeball looks red or the eyelid swells, see the doctor.

four-week checkup

Four weeks after birth, your doctor will give your baby a complete checkup. The aim is to assess your baby's physical growth, behavioral development, and overall state of health.

what your doctor looks for

Your doctor will check your baby's body control and social responses, paying special attention to vision and hearing.

Not all babies do the same thing at the same time, so your own observations are very important, too. This is a good time to mention any concerns you may have.

♦ **Hearing** The doctor will check that a sudden noise startles her.
♦ **Muscle tone** The doctor will move your baby's arms and legs to assess muscle tone.
♦ **Reflexes** Certain reflexes that were present at birth will be disappearing by now (see page 83). Your doctor may look for the grasp reflex: when a newborn baby's palm is stroked, her hand closes on the finger, but this reflex may have disappeared by six weeks. The stepping reflex is a walkinglike action most new babies make when the sole of a foot is pressed onto the couch. This, too, disappears by six weeks of age.

Head circumference (right)
This provides vital information about how your baby is growing and developing.

Weight
Babies are weighed frequently to help assess their growth and development. By week four she should have already had at least a couple of "weigh-in" visits with your healthcare provider.

your developing **baby**

At *six weeks*, your baby will start to:
♦ watch faces intently
♦ follow a light or a dangling toy
♦ lie still to concentrate on your voice
♦ smile, especially when hearing your voice
♦ control her head more
♦ make some noises back at you
– when she's in the right mood.

Reflexes
The birth reflexes will begin disappearing soon. At birth, a newborn can tightly grasp a finger placed in her palm, but by six to eight weeks this reflex normally goes. The stepping reflex also disappears by six weeks of age.

premature **babies**

Your bond with your baby is as important as all the technology in the Neonatal Intensive Care Unit (NICU), so try to be as close to her as circumstances allow. Many parents feel intimidated by all the equipment, but you can still help care for your baby. She already knows your voice, so talk to her and touch her through the portholes of the incubator. This gentle stimulation is good for her. Skin-to-skin hugging may not be possible right away, but even diaper changes will help to form a bond. And there's evidence that a parent's loving touch can help premature or vulnerable babies thrive.

Sometimes it is hard for parents to feel confident in handling such a small baby. If you don't feel quite ready to hold your premature baby, ask the hospital nurses to show you what to do. With a little practice, your baby will reap the rewards of your tender care.

It can be a challenge to be optimistic, but try to stay positive. Your baby can feel this. Remember that every baby is different, so don't compare your baby's progress to that of other babies in the NICU.

It's reassuring to know that premature babies usually develop at the same rate as any other babies, but because they were born earlier they will take longer to reach the same level of development. So, at six months, a baby born three months' premature can be expected to have the social skills of a three-month-old baby. In time, any discrepancies become less obvious, and by the time your child is two years old there will be little or no difference between your baby and one who was born at term.

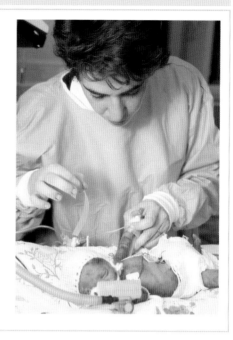

The doctor will also check for:
♦ eye abnormalities
♦ congenital dysplasia of the hip
♦ signs of congenital heart disease
♦ undescended testes in a boy
♦ small abnormalities such as birthmarks.

Measuring weight, length, and head circumference enables your baby's growth to be plotted on a chart. This will give a good indication of development. Don't worry too much about her exact length. This measurement tends to be approximate because babies still hold themselves curled up at this age.

Remember to take a spare diaper, and a bottle if you're bottle-feeding. A pacifier can also be a good idea if she uses one. The best time to schedule a checkup is when your baby is awake but not hungry: an hour after a feeding, for instance. This isn't always possible. Moreover, young babies are unpredictable and don't necessarily stick to a routine. There's no need to worry if your doctor asks you to come back at a later date to complete the behavioral parts of the examination.

Checking the heartbeat
Until your baby is about one year old, her heartbeat will be about 120 beats per minute, much faster than a child or adult heart. The doctor will use a stethoscope to listen to your baby's heart.

Checking the hips
Your baby will have been checked for hip dysplasia after birth, but it is still a possibility, so the doctor will manipulate her legs again at the four-week checkup.

Head control
The doctor will hold up your baby on her front in the air. She may also pull her up to a sitting position to see how strong her back is.

caring for a sick baby

If you think your baby may be ill, call your pediatric healthcare provider.
Together you can decide what's best – whether your baby needs to be seen
by the doctor or can be cared for at home.

what to expect

As you get to know your baby, you will
become more adept at interpreting
his symptoms. Your healthcare
professional will also advise you
on managing minor illnesses.

When your baby is feeling ill, he is likely
to be clingy and unwilling to be put down.
He may also be less playful than usual,
smile less, or seem miserable.

He's likely to need more time with his
feedings, especially if he has a cough or
cold. Give him all the cuddles he needs
and keep him close. Tender loving care is
very important to a sick baby's recovery.

Understanding symptoms

Babies under a year old have trouble
communicating their symptoms. All you
may notice is that your baby is not feeding
well, cries more than usual, or is just not
quite himself. The chart opposite lists
some of the most common ailments and
their symptoms. See pages 238–256 for
more information on diagnosis.

If you are concerned

If you are ever in any doubt about what is
bothering your child, see your healthcare
professional, especially when your baby
is very young. Parents often worry about
troubling the doctor unnecessarily, but it
is better to be cautious and go to see him
or her, if only to put your mind at rest.
Remember that parents do not acquire
the ability to interpret every symptom
immediately; learning to understand when
your baby is ill is a gradual process.

sleep

When your baby is ill, he may sleep more than usual. Sleep is restorative, so this is natural. However, you should be able to wake him when necessary. If you can't wake him, call the doctor immediately.

If he usually sleeps in his own room, move his crib into your room temporarily so that you can keep an eye on him. Don't worry that this will deprive everyone of rest; sleeping in the same room will benefit all of you because you will actually sleep more easily knowing you can go to him if he cries or vomits, and he will be reassured by your presence.

What you can do

Some babies sleep less when they're not feeling well, if for instance, coughs or stuffy noses keep them awake. This can make your baby tired and irritable, and he may be more clingy than usual. Try to comfort him and let him doze off in your arms if that's what he wants.

Chores and other household tasks will have to wait until he is feeling better. Right now, taking care of your baby is the highest priority so don't hesitate to ask for help around the house. When your baby sleeps, take the opportunity to put your feet up and rest. It's important to conserve your energy in order to give your baby the care he needs.

dealing with **illness**

ILLNESS	SYMPTOMS	WHAT YOU CAN DO
Common cold Caused by any one of many viruses. Very common in all ages.	Sneezing, stuffy or runny nose, trouble feeding, cranky, possibly mild fever.	Wipe baby's nose with a cotton ball or soft tissue. Call your doctor if your baby doesn't improve or is wheezing.
Ear infection (*otitis media*) Can be due to viruses or bacteria. More common in babies and children because of the shape of the Eustachian tube linking throat and middle ear.	Screaming baby. May refuse feeding and be inconsolable. Irritability, especially at night. May vomit or have diarrhea. An older baby may pull his ear.	See doctor for diagnosis. A course of antibiotics may be prescribed.
Croup Usually caused by a viral infection in the upper airways. Most common from three months to three years. Can recur.	Harsh, barking cough, especially at night, with wheezing and hoarseness. In severe cases, blueness from lack of oxygen.	Call your doctor. Inhaling steam can help ease breathing (see page 247).
Bronchiolitis An inflammation of the small breathing tubes (bronchioles). Occurs most often in infants. Possible link with asthma later in life. (Bronchiolitis is not to be confused with bronchitis.)	Runny nose, cough, and sometimes fever, followed by wheezing and rapid, labored breathing. Baby may fight for breath and chest may look sucked in between the ribs. In severe cases, baby is blue.	See doctor without delay. Bronchiolitis is usually due to a virus so antibiotics don't help. Home treatment includes use of a humidifier and nasal aspirator.
Chest infection Infection somewhere in the respiratory system (sometimes called pneumonia or bronchitis).	Breathless, rapid breathing and/or feverish baby. May have a cough. May wheeze, especially at night.	See doctor without delay. If pneumonia is caused by a virus, there is no specific treatment except rest and fever management.
Pyloric stenosis Overdevelopment of the duodenum muscle that controls passage of food from stomach to bowels. Occurs more commonly in boys under three months old.	Frequent forceful vomiting – called "projectile." If untreated, results in severe dehydration.	See doctor for diagnosis. Surgery is usually required to open the narrowed area.
Gastroenteritis (infectious diarrhea) May be caught from someone or from bacteria in food (see page 255).	Frequent loose bowel movements. May vomit and refuse feedings. Baby may be feverish and dehydrated.	If your baby has more than a couple of runny stools, vomits more than once, or seems ill, call your doctor without delay.
Meningitis (see page 244) Serious, but rare.	High-pitched cry; lethargy; blotchy skin; rash.	Seek medical help immediately.

understanding fever

Fever is not an illness: a rise in temperature is the body's reaction to infection. However, fever may be an indicator of illness.

Babies lose more heat from their heads, so they can easily get too cool, but they can also become unpredictably hot.

Fever may make your baby uncomfortable, can lead to dehydration, and may lead to seizures. It is important to check with your doctor to determine the cause of your baby's fever. Febrile seizures are especially common between the ages of five months and five years. They are distressing, and after one there is the risk of another (see page 272).

Normal body temperature

For a baby this is about 97.7–98.6°F (36.5–37°C). Taken from the armpit, anything over 98.6°F (37°C) is a fever. You may suspect your baby has a fever if he is irritable. Or he may be flushed or sweaty, especially on the back of the neck. These are good guides to skin temperature, but you can only be sure he has a fever (a high inner temperature) by using a thermometer (see page 226). Consult your doctor if you are worried: the younger your baby, the sooner you need medical advice.

Reducing a fever

♦ Check your baby's temperature, consult your doctor, and give acetaminophen (found in Tylenol®, Tempra®, Panadol®, and other medications) if your baby's temperature is over 100.4°F (38°C).
♦ Keep his room comfortably cool and dress him in lightweight clothing.
♦ Give him plenty of fluids to drink, and retake his temperature in half an hour.
♦ During your baby's illness, take his temperature every two to three hours until you're sure it is dropping without fever medications. If you're worried, call the doctor.
♦ NEVER GIVE YOUR CHILD ASPIRIN. Aspirin has been linked to Reye's syndrome, a serious liver disorder.

Sleeping safely
Make sure you follow the SIDS safety guidelines when putting your baby to sleep (see page 101).

sudden **infant death**

Although rare, Sudden Infant Death Syndrome (SIDS) – also known as crib death – is still the biggest cause of death in babies under a year old. Campaigns to educate parents and caregivers have led to a significant decline in the number of cases, however.

Nobody knows the exact cause, but SIDS is probably due to a combination of factors, such as overheating and infection. Although SIDS can affect any baby, it's more common in babies who are small, underweight, or who were born premature. Some babies had been sick beforehand. Perhaps their immune systems were too weak to cope with a minor illness.

Try not to spend a lot of time worrying about SIDS, but take precautions (see page 101) and if your baby is ill, get medical advice promptly. If you ever find your baby motionless or you cannot wake him, call an ambulance and start resuscitation (see page 268).

giving medicine

As a parent, it is useful to develop a good technique for administering medicine. Choose whichever method is most comfortable for you.

Your doctor may prescribe treatment, or you may need to give your baby over-the-counter medicine. Consult your doctor, pediatric healthcare professional, or pharmacist before giving your baby

any medicine. Medicines formulated for adults and older children can be dangerous for babies. Follow dosages carefully and use only the dispenser supplied.

Giving medicine from a syringe
A sterilized medicine syringe is useful for very young babies, and for doses under 2.5ml. Fill the syringe from the bottle before picking up your baby. Place the mouthpiece on his lower lip and gently press the plunger so the medicine goes slowly into his mouth.

Giving medicine using a dropper
Fill the dropper from the measured dose before you pick up your baby. Lean him back slightly to help the medicine go down. Place the tip of the dropper inside his lower lip or the corner of his mouth. Squeeze to release the medicine, making sure it is all released.

Giving medicine using a spoon
Babies from about six weeks old can take medicine from a spoon. Use the correct, clean measuring spoon, sterilized for a very young baby. Measure the dose before you pick up your baby. Touch the spoon to his bottom lip, then gently tip the spoon.

your child's health

Now that your child is growing up and is no longer a baby, you'll be able to tell more easily when she is ill because she may say that something hurts, point to a painful area such as her ear or her tummy, or tell you that she feels sick.

general symptoms

Even if she doesn't tell you how she feels, your child might be pale, or her cheeks may be flushed and her eyes glassy.

She may not be eating well or may be drinking either less than usual, or perhaps more than usual because a fever is making her thirsty. Sometimes a sick child vomits dramatically and without warning.

Your child may be less playful or less smiley than usual, she may cry more readily, or she may just be more clingy for your attention.

What you can do

Without a doctor's diagnosis it's difficult to know what to do when your child isn't feeling well, but you can better understand her symptoms if you refer to pages 238–261, where childhood illnesses are discussed. Never hesitate to call the doctor if you are uneasy or concerned about your child's health. If her condition appears to be serious, call 911 for emergency medical help. In these circumstances, it is natural for a parent to be worried, but try to act swiftly without panicking; if you react calmly, your child will feel less frightened.

checking **temperature**

Check if your child's cheeks are flushed (the area around the mouth may appear to be pale by comparison), or feel her forehead. A child's normal body temperature taken from the mouth is about 97.7–98.6°F (36.5–37°C). Armpit temperature is about 1°F (0.5°C) lower. Rectal temperature (which is rarely used now) is approximately 2°F (1°C) higher than armpit temperature. To be certain of your child's temperature, use a thermometer. Choose from:

♦ A digital thermometer (see right), which provides a clear digital readout of your child's temperature. Put her comfortably on your lap while taking the reading.

♦ An ear sensor (see far right) is easier to use if your child is restless; measurements need to be taken three times to ensure an accurate reading.

♦ A liquid-crystal strip, which is heat-sensitive and records the skin temperature when held to your child's forehead for 30 seconds. This method is popular because it's quick and easy, but it is not generally recommended by doctors.

Digital thermometer
This is battery operated, accurate, and almost unbreakable, so it's ideal for babies. For a baby, take the temperature from the armpit. A child's temperature can be taken from the mouth.

Ear sensor
This measures infra-red (heat) radiation in the ear canal and takes a second, so it disturbs your child very little. Pull gently up and back on the ear to take the temperature. The measurements vary, so use the same ear during an illness, and take three readings.

caring for a feverish child

When your child is ill, it's important to give her plenty of fluids. Reduce the fever if she is uncomfortable or if her temperature is over 100.4°F (38°C).

A fever is not an illness. It's a sign that the body is trying to fight off illness, so fever doesn't always need treatment. However, high fever can, occasionally, cause febrile seizures (see page 272), especially before the age of five. Bringing your child's temperature under control can prevent this. Fever can contribute to dehydration, which may cause fever, so it is important to break this cycle by giving fluids.

How your child will feel

A feverish child is hot and may be in discomfort, especially if dehydrated. She may be listless and seem to be very sick. Once the fever decreases, she'll often begin to perk up. When your child has a fever, she may shiver. This is because the surrounding air feels relatively cool to her hot skin. Despite this, avoid overdressing a feverish child or keeping the room too hot, because this prevents heat loss. Her temperature may rise even higher and she will feel worse.

home **medicine cabinet**

Useful items to have at home are:

♦ calamine lotion for itches and stings

♦ antiseptic spray or cream

♦ a thermometer

♦ assorted bandages for minor injuries

♦ acetaminophen to reduce fever and ease pain.

(Aspirin should not be used in children under 16 years old because of the small but possible risk of Reye syndrome, a serious liver disorder.)

Keep the medicine cabinet out of your child's reach, and lock it.

What you can do

Remove layers of clothing when your child has a fever. She may need only her underwear, pajamas, or other lightweight clothes when she's indoors. Giving her plenty of fluids helps control her temperature and counteract dehydration, so make sure she has drinks available in her favorite cup. If she's reluctant to drink, try offering her drinks she doesn't usually have. Sugary drinks are not good for teeth, but they provide energy and can tempt the tastebuds.

If her temperature is over 100.4°F (38°C), give a dose of acetaminophen. Sponging her skin with lukewarm water can be soothing if she's feverish. Don't use cold water because this makes blood

vessels constrict and slows down heat loss. Check her temperature again in about 20 minutes. Continue to monitor her temperature while she is ill, and call the doctor if it remains at 103°F (39°C) or more, if it lasts more than 24 hours, or if her appearance worries you.

Avoiding dehydration
Encourage your child to drink by letting her choose her drinks and take them from a favorite cup.

caring for a sick child

Like a baby, a child who is ill tends to be more clingy, and she may want to be hugged a lot. Give her the reassurance of staying close by.

what to expect

You'll want to be with your child as much as possible. Let her climb onto your lap as often as she wants to get the comfort she needs. She may also want to use a favorite old toy, or a discarded blanket or comforter.

Even an older child can become clingy when she's unwell, so don't be surprised if your child becomes less independent. She may want to follow if you leave the room.

Feeding your child
Allow your child plenty of time to eat. A little of her favorite food may tempt her, but don't worry if she doesn't seem very hungry.

If she has recently been potty trained, she may also be reluctant to use the toilet and lose bladder or bowel control temporarily. She could be as upset by this as you are, so don't be annoyed. Clean up the mess without making a fuss. Things will improve when she recovers. Meanwhile, use rubber sheets on the bed, and wear old clothes yourself.

Many children vomit when they are unwell, some more readily than others, and they don't usually make it to the bathroom in time. A bucket may not look attractive, but if your child has been vomiting it can be reassuring for both of you to have it close at hand.

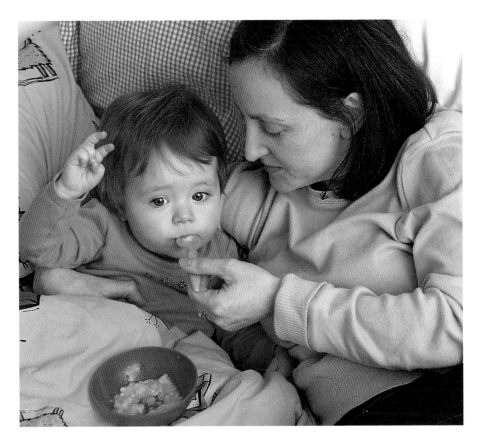

comfort **checklist**

♦ Give your child as many fluids as possible (unless she is vomiting).

♦ Read to your child.

♦ Let her doze off when she wants to.

♦ Allow her to nap or play (in her crib or bed) if she wants to.

♦ Make the bed often – if she's in and out of it a lot – so that it looks inviting.

♦ Keep a supply of paper towels and old bath towels ready for cleanups.

practical care

A sick child doesn't usually need to be confined to her bedroom. Unless your doctor has said otherwise, let your child be up and about.

If your child is very ill, she may prefer to be in her crib or bed so she can sleep, but most children are happy to be up and about, and this should do them no harm.

Clothing
To keep fever under control, it's important not to overdress your child (see page 227). Pajamas or a nightgown are usually sufficient around the house. A bathrobe, sweater, sweatshirt, and/or slippers may be needed as well depending on room temperature. If your child is hot and sweaty, or has been vomiting, a bath and a change of clothes will help keep her feeling fresh. For practical reasons, you may want to dress her in old clothes. However, newer, nice-looking clothes often wash just as easily as less attractive ones, and it's worth letting her wear whatever makes her most comfortable.

Drinking
Your child may not be hungry when she's ill, but she will need plenty to drink. Fluids speed up recovery and help replace the body fluid lost through sweating. This

is particularly important if your child has diarrhea or has been vomiting. If very severe, dehydration can cause kidney damage and can even be fatal.

Some children are especially thirsty when they're ill or feverish, but not all. Thirst can be a poor indicator of fluid need, so you may have to remind your child to drink. To entice her, you can let her have more or less anything she wants as long as it's not caffeinated or too salty. A straw can be fun and may make her drink more. Give her small amounts often; this is particularly important if she has vomited, because her stomach won't tolerate large quantities.

Eating

Don't worry if your child seems to have lost her appetite and isn't enthusiastic about eating. Unless your doctor has advised otherwise, your child doesn't need to eat while she's ill. For now, fluids are more important than food. Her appetite will come back as she gets better. Sometimes this happens gradually, other times it's very quick.

If she has a sore throat, she may feel like having food, but be unable to eat it. Offering soft foods such as mashed potato and ice cream can help. Ice cream is especially soothing for sore throats, and is often a favorite with young children.

Reassuring your child

Your child may be feeling ill and missing her friends and the routine at her play group or nursery school. Try not to worry, because your anxiety can affect her, and try to be with her as much as you can.

Ignore non-essential chores around the house for now. Save your time and energy for your child. You may not be very active physically, but looking after a sick child can be tiring, so you should accept any offers of help you can get.

See whether you or your partner can negotiate for time off work, or take work home with you. If you can't get time off and have to leave your child with someone else while you are at work, give clear instructions for her care and leave a telephone number where you can be reached at all times.

Being together
Most people in a household harbor the same germs, so unless your doctor has said otherwise, you can still cuddle up as a family.

entertaining **your child**

A sick child may have less energy than usual, but she still needs you to be with her. She may particularly appreciate having an old, favorite book read to her over and over again. Listening to stories on audio tape, putting puzzles together, and playing games will also please and entertain her.

If you need something new to do together, you could cut up old magazines and catalogs and paste the pictures onto construction paper to make a collage. You can make easy puzzles out of old greeting or birthday cards. Your child may also enjoy quiet time with a favorite doll or may want to watch a special video, but be sure to stay with her and watch it together.

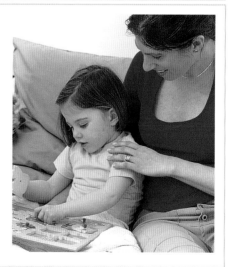

when to seek medical help

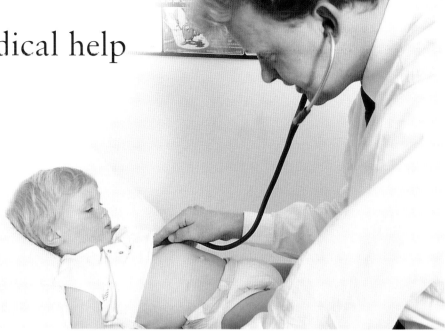

Call pediatric health professionals whenever you have a concern. It's important to distinguish minor ailments from more serious illnesses. The younger your child, the sooner you should seek medical help.

Young children can have a fever and a headache together, but a headache is rare in young children and can be an important symptom. Although it may be due to fever, a headache may be a sign of serious illness so consult your doctor.

Coughs and colds don't always need medical advice. Contact the doctor if your child appears short of breath, wheezes, or if his breathing seems labored. If your child has abdominal pain, his symptoms need assessment by a doctor.

Your child will generally be seen at the doctor's office. Feverish children don't get worse when you take them out for a short period of time, and most doctors will try to fit in a sick youngster. Call before you

go. If your child might be infectious, the staff may arrange for you to sit apart from the other patients. If you're not sure whether you need to see a doctor, telephone the office first or speak to your doctor.

Call your doctor if your child:
♦ is breathing very noisily or rapidly
♦ has trouble swallowing
♦ is unusually drowsy or irritable
♦ has abdominal pain
♦ has severe or persistent pain anywhere
♦ has a swelling in the groin or testis
♦ has a rash or a high or persistent fever.

understanding symptoms

SYMPTOM	WHAT IT MIGHT BE	WHAT YOU CAN DO
Fever	Common causes include upper respiratory infections, strep throat, ear infection, pneumonia, urine infection.	See the doctor if the cause isn't obvious, and if the doctor suggests it give one dose of acetaminophen.
Sore throat	This can be the start of a cold, virus, or strep throat.	See if the throat looks red or there are white spots. If your child is unwell or symptoms persist, see the doctor.
Cough	A common symptom, often due to a cold, upper-respiratory infection, pneumonia, or asthma.	See the doctor if your child is vomiting, short of breath, or has a persistent cough, especially without a cold.
Headache	A worrying symptom for parents, headache may be caused by fever. Other causes include meningitis or head injury.	See the doctor if headache persists after fever is reduced. If your child is vomiting, consult the doctor immediately.
Swelling in the neck	Usually caused by enlarged lymph nodes in response to viral illness, tonsillitis, or bacterial throat infection.	Feel along the underside of your child's jaw and on the side of his neck for swellings or tenderness. If the swelling is large or he seems ill, see the doctor.
Abdominal pain	Many possible causes including tonsillitis, urine infection, gastroenteritis, appendicitis, and anxiety.	Always see the doctor the same day.
Rash	Many causes, including eczema, allergies, and infectious illnesses such as measles, scarlet fever, roseola infantum, and bacterial diseases.	A mild itchy rash in a healthy child is unlikely to be serious – use calamine lotion and see how the rash develops. If the rash doesn't itch, check with the doctor. If your child is sick at the same time, don't delay.

giving medicines

Many medicines have flavors and colors that appeal to young children so they're less reluctant to take them. But this also means you need to take special care to keep them out of your child's reach.

When he's ill, your child may need to take over-the-counter medicines, medicines from your doctor, or sometimes both. Tastes differ dramatically. What one child loves, another may hate. It's not unknown for a child to spit out his medicine. If so, wait for him to calm and try again.

It can help to use a favorite spoon, to mix the medicine with jam, or to reward him with a favorite beverage afterward.

However, do not add your child's medicine to a drink since it may cling to the side of the glass or sippy cup, and you won't know how much of the medicine he has actually swallowed.

Drops

It's helpful to give drops quickly and confidently to minimize any fussing. Some children do not mind drops and will cooperate happily, but others are resistant, so be prepared.

♦ **Eyedrops** Settle your child comfortably on your lap, or on a bed or sofa. Hold his head steady with one arm. Gently pull down his lower eyelid and apply the drop or drops to the space between the eyeball and the lower lid. Wipe, or let him wipe, his cheek afterward. If your child resists, hold him more firmly, or ask another adult to help.

♦ **Ear drops** Put your child's head on your lap with his head to the side, so that he is comfortable. He will have to stay in this position for a minute or so. Hold his ear firmly but gently, then let the drops fall into the ear canal. Keep your child still for a few seconds. If he gets up too soon, most of the drops will come out.

in an emergency!

Go to the nearest emergency room, or call an ambulance, if your child:

♦ has difficulty breathing or is so short of breath he can't talk

♦ has a seizure (convulsion)

♦ loses consciousness

♦ has a serious burn (see page 271)

♦ has an accident and can't move a limb

♦ is bleeding severely

♦ has a headache, dislike of bright lights, or a rash that doesn't go away when pressed with the side of a glass (see page 244).

♦ **Nose drops** Position your child on his back or on your lap, and tilt his head back. Support his head with one hand and drop the nose drops into the nostril. Repeat for the other nostril if required. Try to get your child to sniff afterward; this will help get the drops up into the nose.

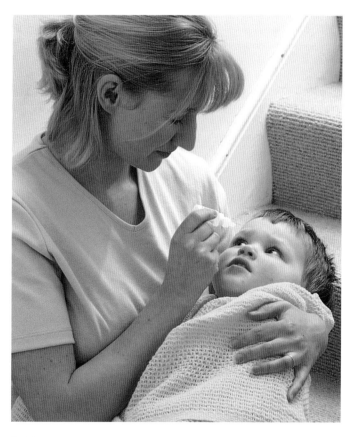

Eyedrops
These often need to be given three or four times a day so it is important to develop a good technique.

Ear drops
Have your child lay his head on its side on your lap. To allow the drops to go in easily, gently pull his ear up and back.

checkups and hospitals

Every child is different. Your child may feel perfectly at ease going to see the doctor, or she may feel frightened, insecure, or even apprehensive. Fortunately, there is a lot you can do to help reassure your child.

visiting the doctor

A healthcare professional who has an easy, welcoming manner with youngsters and their parents can make a big difference as to how your child feels during an examination.

It is also important to trust your healthcare professional's judgment. This will make the whole process easier for you, and your confidence will rub off on and comfort your child.

Examining your child

At first the healthcare professional will merely observe your child as you describe the symptoms. This is an important part of the consultation, and allows him to get an idea of how ill your child is and what's wrong. At the same time as the healthcare professional is assessing your child, your child is sizing up the healthcare professional, and assessing the working relationship you have with him!

He will examine your child's neck for enlarged lymph glands and check her ears with an otoscope. This may be uncomfortable, but is not usually painful. It helps if you hold your child on your lap or on the examination table, steadying her with your hands.

The healthcare professional will listen to your child's chest with a stethoscope and feel her abdomen with his hand.

Preparing your child
Treat healthcare visits as fun and try not to let your child see that you are concerned. A good healthcare professional will be experienced at putting young children at ease.

Again, this can be ticklish, and many children laugh. If your youngster is still in diapers, the healthcare professional might want to look at the diaper area. If your child is particularly ill with diarrhea or has blood in her stool, he may find it useful to look at a stool sample.

Your healthcare professional may also need to look at your child's throat. Babies and younger children tend to resist this, so he may leave this part of the examination until last. Don't worry if your child cries while her throat is being examined. You can rest assured that she will soon stop and, incidentally, a lusty cry generally gives the healthcare professional a good view.

questions to ask

♦ Is my child sick? Is it serious?

♦ What does the treatment involve?

♦ What else can I do to help?

♦ For how long will my child feel ill?

♦ Is it infectious?

♦ When should I bring her back? What should I do if she doesn't get better?

♦ When can my child return to her play group or nursery school?

♦ Are there usually other symptoms?

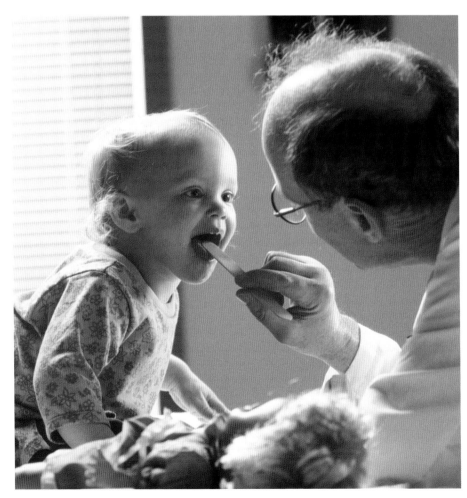

having an **operation**

It's natural to be concerned about an operation and to want to minimize any discomfort. Most operations are short and routine, and children recover quickly. You may be able to take your child home the same day, although she will need extra care from you for a while.

It is important to prepare your child. She needs to know what to expect. An anesthesiologist usually visits you and your child in the hospital beforehand, and you can ask how your child will be put to sleep. This may be by using a gas given by mask (which children don't usually mind), or by injection into an area made numb with anaesthetic cream (this is painless).

Tell your child that she'll wake up in a special recovery room so that she's not alarmed at finding herself somewhere unfamiliar. Try to be calm, whatever your own emotions may be. Reassuring smiles and lots of hugs and affection from you will boost her spirits. While you're waiting to go to the operating room, you can read a book or play a quiet game. Depending on the operation, your child may have to take medicine by mouth, about an hour and a half before, to make her drowsy. Even if she's very sleepy, she'll know you're there if you hold her hand.

You can usually accompany your child on the way to the operating room (or even carry her if she's a baby). In general, you'll be able to stay with her until she is asleep, and you can be in the recovery room as she wakes up. Depending on the operation, your child may be in pain. If so, ask for pain relief.

Checklist for operations

♦ Be calm and stay with your child as much as possible.

♦ Get the details you need from the surgeon, anesthesiologist, and nurses.

♦ Tell your child about the operation and give a simple explanation of why it will make her better.

♦ Explain that she can't eat or drink before the operation.

♦ Reassure your child that you'll be there when she goes to sleep and wakes up.

♦ Tell her she'll be in a special recovery room after the operation.

♦ Read a favorite book out loud to entertain your child and help pass the time.

♦ Talk about the things you'll do when she's back at home, but avoid excessive promises.

♦ Don't forget to smile.

a hospital stay

Tell your child well beforehand about her hospital stay.

You can help prepare your child by:
♦ answering any of her questions honestly and simply, without excess detail
♦ sharing books, toys, and videotapes that are related to doctors and hospitals
♦ encouraging her to practice her stethoscope skills on her dolls or teddy bears
♦ reassuring her that you and/or your partner will be with her at the hospital.

What you can do

If you stay with your child at the hospital, you may be given a bed, or you may have to spend the night dozing in an armchair. Your presence will help your child overcome her anxieties and recover more quickly. In most children's hospitals and pediatric units, parents take over routine non-medical care such as feeding and washing, which can be a real comfort for your child and also saves nursing time.

If you can't stay with your child, be there as often as possible and make sure that you're with her for any tests, operations, removal of stitches, or other procedures.

Packing a bag for the hospital

Hospital stays for children are usually very short, but you'll still need a number of essential items if your child has to go into the hospital for more than a day. Pack a small bag containing:
♦ bib and your child's favorite eating utensils
♦ pajamas or nightgowns
♦ slippers
♦ towel and washcloth
♦ soap
♦ toothbrush and toothpaste
♦ hairbrush or comb
♦ favorite stuffed animal, books, games, puzzles, and a cassette player for listening to music and books on tape
♦ diapers and diaper-changing equipment, if needed.

In addition, don't forget to pack a bag of overnight things for yourself if you are going to be staying in the hospital with your child.

special needs

The term "special needs" applies to children whose development, behavior, or ability to communicate and learn are such that they need extra special care to realize their potential and lead happy lives.

what are special needs?

Some babies and children have a long-term health condition that can affect their development. It is important to focus on what your child can achieve rather than on what he cannot do.

A child with special needs may have any one of a broad range of conditions, some of which arise before birth, while others develop later. Cystic fibrosis, for example, is inherited (see page 260). Down syndrome (see page 260) is not usually inherited, but it is congenital, meaning that a baby is born with it. Sometimes a child develops special needs because he is severely affected by a common condition such as asthma (see page 259), or because he has had a serious infection, such as bacterial meningitis (see page 244).

Getting help
A child with special needs is usually referred by his pediatrician for an evaluation to determine what services the child needs. In some states this is done through a government-sponsored program called Early Intervention. A social worker or caseworker usually coordinates a team of professionals to give your child the extra support he needs. This team may include a speech therapist, physical therapist, child psychiatrist, social workers, educational psychologists, teachers, and support groups. If you need extra help or want to discuss other avenues, you can access further medical, practical, and financial help for your family through your healthcare professional.

Other support
Although a team of professionals will support you and your child, parents of a child with special needs can sometimes feel isolated socially. Most families benefit greatly from contact with others who are in a similar situation. Talking to someone who has already faced and overcome the same challenges can inspire you to feel more positive and make it easier to handle day-to-day practicalities. This can be anything from getting more information about financial assistance to finding someone to care for your child while

where to find help

♦ Ask your healthcare professional about support groups.

♦ For rare conditions, get in touch with your local Early Intervention program. Check the Yellow Pages for the telephone number.

♦ Search the Internet, but bear in mind that many websites may not be authoritative or accurate.

Encouraging your child
As a parent, there is often a lot you can do to help your child lead a fulfilling life.

you enjoy an occasional evening out. You can make good contacts through self-help and support groups. Many have a network of local groups. A network such as this can lend invaluable practical and emotional support to you and your family. These organizations may also run helplines as well as publish useful information about the condition and the latest news on any ongoing research. See pages 280–281 for more information.

Playing and learning

Your child may be able to attend an ordinary toddler group, play group, or nursery school. This will help you be a part of the community, and will enable your child to socialize. Very young children will accept and play with a child who may look or behave differently from them.

Sometimes a child with special needs is offered specialized play and learning

facilities. Many children will gain more advantages from this than from attending a regular group where they may feel out of their depth or miss out on the kind of therapy they need. It all depends on the child and her particular needs, and you will want to give her the best chance of growing up and leading a fulfilling life. A child's needs can change over time, so it's worth periodically evaluating your child's services and attending follow up appointments with therapists, doctors, and other members of the team.

Unusual conditions

Occasionally, a child with special needs has a condition so rare that there are very few other children who have it, and very little information about it. Sometimes, there may not even be a firm diagnosis. Talk to your child's doctor or specialist about educating yourself.

coping with **your feelings**

You may feel you have missed out on the chance to have a healthy child and lead a "normal" family life. This is understandable, and you may experience some of the emotions that often accompany bereavement.

♦ At first, you may feel shock and find the news difficult to believe. An element of denial is common in the early days.

♦ When things don't go as planned, it's natural to try to find a cause or look for someone to blame. You might be angry with healthcare professionals, or resent your partner or even yourself.

♦ Feeling negative or depressed may follow. Some parents worry about being able to care adequately for their child.

♦ As you become more adept at coping with the challenges, you can learn to enjoy family life.

parenting a special-needs child

Patience and understanding will help you get the best from your child. It takes special skills to be a parent, and usually more so if your child has special needs.

There will be unique rewards for you and your family. You are likely to develop a particularly deep bond with your child. Children with special needs can be very happy and affectionate, making them especially loving and a delight to care for.

There may be times when you are feeling tired and are therefore feeling less upbeat. It's worth remembering that not every so-called normal child is easy all the time. Try not to be hard on yourself or your partner since you are probably already doing an excellent parenting job.

Staying healthy is a high priority, as well as making time for your partner and for any other children in the family. It is normal for parents of children with special needs to wonder what might have happened if they had done things differently.

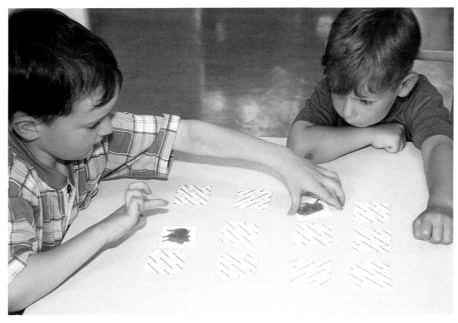

Sometimes they blame themselves. It's important to talk about these feelings and come to terms with them. Other parents in similar circumstances are often the best qualified to help, but don't hesitate to seek professional advice it you need it. Various organizations also provide valuable support.

Joining in
Depending on your child's needs, he may be able to interact well with other children. This sort of relationship can be beneficial to all involved.

complementary therapies

Parents often turn to simple self-help remedies to treat minor childhood ailments. Complementary and alternative therapies, such as massage and mild aromatherapy are good examples.

a different approach

Complementary and alternative therapies are growing in popularity. Practitioners aim to treat the whole person and usually spend a lot of time talking with parents, which can be very comforting.

Complementary therapies are generally used *alongside* conventional medicine, while alternative therapies are used *in place of* conventional medicine. Many of the therapies claim to promote a feeling of wellbeing and represent an appealing opportunity for parents to have more involvement in their child's health care. However, it's important to bear in mind that there's little or no scientific proof that many complementary and alternative remedies work, although there are a few areas where there is some evidence of their efficacy – a good example is massage, for helping babies to relax.

Get medical advice

If you're considering trying an alternative or complementary remedy on your child, you should always discuss it with your healthcare professional first. If you don't, you may risk missing or delaying a diagnosis of your child's condition. Your healthcare professional will talk to you about the safety and effectiveness of the therapy and will advise against it if there's a risk it will interfere with any medical treatment your child is receiving.

points to **consider**

If you're considering any alternative treatment for your child:

♦ don't give up any medical treatment or try a complementary therapy without discussing it with your healthcare professional first

♦ choose a reputable practitioner approved by the appropriate professional body

♦ consult someone who has experience treating the same age group as your child – ask to see qualifications

♦ beware of practitioners who claim to treat conditions nobody else can

♦ try to get a personal recommendation, or ask your healthcare professional if she knows a reputable practitioner

♦ tell your healthcare professional about any alternative remedies you are using for your child, especially herbal medicines.

Love and reassurance
The simplest and most pleasurable self-help remedy is to give your child plenty of love and reassurance when he's feeling ill.

types of treatment

There are many complementary and alternative treatments based on different theories, but they all differ from orthodox (allopathic) medicine prescribed by conventional doctors.

A single treatment may be enough to help symptoms or, depending on your child's condition, you may be recommended an ongoing program of treatment. Treatment can be costly, so be realistic about how much you can afford.

Osteopathy

This is a system of manipulation. The method most suitable for babies and children is the cranio-sacral approach, which is very gentle. Cranial osteopathy focuses on the skull. Some parents find it relieves sleeping problems and colic.

Massage

Massage is a centuries-old art of nurturing and healing. It's widely used to relax babies, improve their sleep patterns, and calm them when they are irritable. It's also been shown to help the development of premature babies in special care units. See page 96 to learn how to massage your baby, and ask your healthcare professional for advice.

Homeopathy

Homeopathy is a treatment based on the theory that a substance that in large doses causes specific symptoms can, in minute doses, relieve the same symptoms. Always consult a qualified practitioner for advice because these remedies should be taken under supervision. Homeopathic treatments are available from pharmacies and health-food stores. A common remedy for children is arnica for cuts and bruises. Treatments often need only a single dose.

Aromatherapy

Aromatherapy is based on herbal oils (essential oils), which can be inhaled as a vapor using a special burner or mixed with a neutral oil, called a carrier, then used as a massage oil. Essential oils must never be used undiluted. Many are toxic, so your child shouldn't taste or swallow even diluted oils. Make sure that any essential oil or carrier oil is suitable for young children – nut oils in particular should be avoided because of the risk of an allergic reaction.

♦ Tea-tree oil is mildly antiseptic. Used as a rinse when washing cloth diapers, it may help prevent or treat diaper rash.
♦ Lavender and tea-tree oils may help relieve the itch of chicken pox.
♦ A blend of tea-tree, rose, eucalyptus, lemon, lavender, and geranium oils is sometimes recommended for headlice.

Herbal medicine

Chinese herbal medicine may be useful for severe ezcema, while Western herbal treatments may be used for recurrent infections. Herbs can be very potent. In fact, some conventional medicines originate from plants. Herbal treatments can have serious side effects and can also interact adversely with other medicines. Consult a medically qualified herbalist and always talk to your healthcare professional first.

home remedies

Apart from complementary medicines, there are a number of home treatments and simple over-the-counter remedies that may ease your child's symptoms.

♦ **Ointments and vapors** These may help decongest the nose and throat. Some can be rubbed onto clothing or bedding, while others can be applied directly to the chest of older children. Follow instructions carefully, and ask your pharmacist if you are worried about any aspect of a remedy.
♦ **Fluids** These prevent dehydration and can also ease a sore throat. Lemon and honey drinks are especially good for throats. Only use honey for a child over one year old.
♦ **Soup** This is nourishing, and is a traditional home remedy for febrile illnesses. It can also soothe the throat.

Steam inhalation
Sit with your child while hot water runs into the bathtub and let him inhale the steam. This can help alleviate phlegm and coughs.

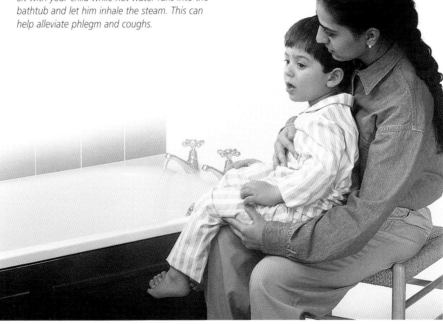

childhood illnesses

As she grows up, your child is likely to suffer acute (short-term) illnesses lasting a few days or a week. These are usually minor and often need no treatment other than lots of fluids and loving care from you. Some conditions will need help from your healthcare professional, and perhaps even a stay at the hospital.

This section is a guide for parents on a variety of common and not-so-common childhood illnesses.

You will find an explanation of each condition, a description of the typical symptoms, and advice on what you can do to care for your child after she has been diagnosed by your healthcare professional. This includes guidance on how to recognize complications and when to call your healthcare professional.

The information in this section is designed to provide you with insight to understand better what might be affecting your child.

The early part of the section covers acute illnesses, divided into related topics, such as skin and hair, for easy reference.

The latter part of the section covers chronic conditions, in other words, long-term diseases and disorders. These chronic conditions can rarely be completely cured, although the symptoms may come and go and there are often long periods of time when your child is completely well and free of any symptoms.

calling the **doctor**

It's only natural to be concerned when your child is not feeling well. For parents of very small children it can be particularly frightening. Remember that your doctor is there for you, too – to offer you reassurance and advice – as well as for prescribing treatment.

Call the doctor if:

♦ you suspect that your child may be ill

♦ you're not sure that you're caring for her in the right way

♦ your child isn't improving

♦ your child's symptoms do not fit the description of the disease

♦ your child's symptoms change, or she develops a new one.

infectious illnesses

Thanks to immunization, the pattern of many infectious illnesses is changing. Some, such as measles, are less common than they were, while others, such as parvovirus (fifth disease), seem more common. Growing awareness may be the reason for this, but it's also possible that young children having more contact with each other in play groups, daycare, or nursery school could increase the spread.

viruses and bacteria

The main difference between viruses and bacteria is that antibiotics don't work against viruses, only bacteria. An antibiotic may combat a range of bacteria, which is useful when your healthcare professional isn't sure which your child has. However, these broad-spectrum antibiotics interfere with harmless bacteria, too, which is why they should be taken only when needed.

Many bacteria and viruses spread in invisible water droplets in the air when someone coughs, sneezes, or speaks. Another method of spread is direct contact, especially from hands. Objects such as toys can also carry germs. Some infections spread from the gut of one person to the mouth of another via dirty hands.

IN AN EMERGENCY!

Call 911 for an ambulance if:

♦ your child has a seizure (convulsion)

♦ she is unusually drowsy

♦ she has a headache or stiff neck

♦ she develops dark red or purplish spots that don't fade when pressed with the side of a glass (see *The tumbler test*, page 244).

roseola infantum

This is a surprisingly common infection that affects babies over six months and children under two years old. Occasionally you may hear doctors mention it by its other names: *exanthem subitum*, and even baby measles, although it actually has nothing at all to do with measles.

SYMPTOMS

♦ sudden onset of fever 102˚F (38.9˚C) to 105˚F (40.5˚C) lasting three to five days

♦ runny nose, slightly puffy eyes

♦ mild diarrhea

♦ tiredness or irritability, and reduced appetite

♦ after the fever subsides, a rash of spots covering the body and often the face and limbs

Making the diagnosis

Before the rash appears, the diagnosis is difficult to make. Consult your doctor.

What to do for your child

There's a risk of febrile seizures (see page 272), so bring down her temperature with fluids and acetaminophen.

CALL THE DOCTOR if your child's fever persists once the rash has appeared.

IN AN EMERGENCY!

Call 911 for an ambulance if your child has a seizure (convulsion).

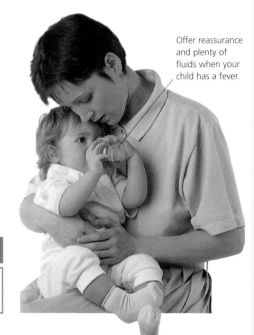

Offer reassurance and plenty of fluids when your child has a fever.

chicken pox

A single dose of chicken pox vaccine is recommended for all children between 12 and 18 months who have not had chicken pox. Older children should be immunized with a single dose at the earliest opportunity.

SYMPTOMS

- not feeling well before the rash appears
- spots that start as small red dots and turn into itchy, oval blisters that crust over
- sometimes, sores in the mouth that make it hard to eat

Making the diagnosis

This is usually easy since the rash is distinctive. It's most infectious in the early stages, a day before the rash appears, and it's catching until every blister has turned into a firm, dry crust. The incubation period is 14 to 21 days. One attack usually gives lifelong immunity.

What to do for your child

Keep your child cool and lightly clothed to make him more comfortable. Soothe itching with an anti-itch lotion. He may also appreciate an oatmeal bath. Keep

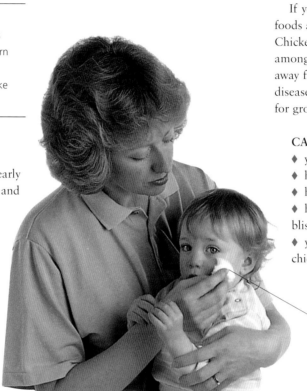

Gently dab on calamine lotion to soothe itching.

his fingernails short to minimize damage from scratching – scratched blisters tend to become infected and are more likely to scar, too. If itching is severe, try an antihistamine syrup, especially at night.

If your child's mouth is sore, give soft foods and plenty of soothing fluids. Chicken pox, a common viral disease among children, is catching, so keep him away from anyone who hasn't had the disease – chicken pox can be worse for grown-ups.

CALL THE DOCTOR if:

- your child is not acting like himself
- he has a high fever
- he refuses to drink anything
- he has a very large number of blisters, particularly near his eyes
- you or your partner have never had chicken pox.

parvovirus (fifth disease)

Parvovirus is a mild illness in children that is also known as fifth disease and *erythema infectiosum*. It's caused by a virus called parvovirus B19, which you can catch only from another person, by direct contact, and through infected droplets in the air.

SYMPTOMS

- a facial rash with a well-defined edge
- a fine, lacy red rash on the arms or trunk
- sometimes, a mild fever or cold symptoms before the rash appears

Making the diagnosis

This is often obvious, but blood tests can be done if there is a question about the diagnosis. Children with sickle-cell disease (see page 259) tend to become more seriously ill with parvovirus and can

develop severe anemia. The disease is also more serious in adults, who may not develop the rash and instead develop joint pain, with or without swelling. These symptoms can last a week or two, but occasionally the disease persists for months.

About half of all pregnant women are immune to parvovirus. However, those who aren't can sometimes miscarry as a result of infection in the early stages of pregnancy. There is probably less than a one in 20 chance of this happening, but it is wise to tell your obstetrician/gynecologist or midwife if you're pregnant and suspect you may have come into contact with parvovirus. The incubation period is from five to 20 days.

What to do for your child

There is no special treatment other than keeping your child comfortable and well hydrated. Since the disease is no longer catching once the rash appears, your child can usually continue going to his play group or nursery school.

CALL THE DOCTOR if:

- your child has a high fever or is not acting like himself
- your child is known to have sickle-cell disease
- you are pregnant.

hand, foot, and mouth disease

Hand, foot, and mouth disease is caused by a virus of the coxsackie group, and has no connection with the serious condition that afflicts farm animals called foot and mouth disease. The disease is spread in moisture droplets through the air, but is not very contagious, so not everyone who comes into contact with it develops symptoms.

SYMPTOMS

- spots and blisters on the hands and feet (mostly the palms and soles)
- spots in the mouth that make it hard to eat
- spots that don't appear all at the same time
- a mild fever a day or two before the rash

Making the diagnosis

It is usually easy for your healthcare professional to recognize hand, foot, and mouth, especially if there have been cases of it at your child's nursery school or toddler group. Unlike chicken pox, the spots aren't itchy, and don't usually occur much on the trunk. The incubation period is about 10 days.

Because several different strains of coxsackie virus can cause the illness, it's possible to get it more than once.

What to do for your child

Most children with hand, foot, and mouth disease are well. If your child has a fever, treat it in the usual way with fluids and acetaminophen (see pages 226–227).

Monitor his temperature. You don't need to put anything on the spots. However, if your child's mouth is sore, he'll appreciate soft foods so that he doesn't have to chew. Ice cream is a perennial favorite. You can also try yogurt, milk shakes, mashed potato, puréed vegetables or fruit (but avoid citrus fruits and drinks because they can make the mouth feel worse). A straw will make it easier for him to drink.

Most youngsters with hand, foot, and mouth disease don't need to stay home from nursery school or their play group, unless they're feverish or feeling unwell.

CALL THE DOCTOR if:

- your child has a high temperature that you can't bring down
- you're unsure of the diagnosis
- he refuses to eat or drink.

measles

Measles is an uncommon infection, but it is unpleasant and can be very serious, occasionally fatal. It's caused by a virus of the paramyxovirus group and spreads by infected moisture droplets in the air. Measles is very catching. More than nine out of 10 children who are exposed to it can expect to get it. Measles vaccine (the "M" in MMR) prevents most cases.

SYMPTOMS

- feeling sick, a high fever for up to four days, a cough, and a runny nose; during this stage, small spots inside the mouth
- a rash appearing on about the fifth day on the face and neck, then the trunk
- puffy, red eyes

Making the diagnosis

You should always consult your healthcare professional if you think your child has measles. The incubation period is 10 to 14 days. Measles vaccine, as MMR, offers good protection, especially if two doses are used (see page 217). One attack of the disease usually gives permanent immunity.

What to do for your child

Treat any fever (see pages 226–227), give your child plenty to drink, and soft foods if his mouth is sore. He will probably feel miserable and won't be well enough to go out. Keep him away from other children.

CALL THE DOCTOR if:

- you suspect measles
- call him a second time if your child seems to be getting worse, especially if he won't drink, is drowsy, short of breath, or has an earache.

Regularly check his temperature. If he can't hold the thermometer in his mouth, place it under his armpit.

mumps

Mumps is caused by a virus of the myxovirus group and spreads by moisture droplets in the air and direct contact. Thanks to the MMR vaccine, outbreaks in Canada are rare, but it is fairly common in those who haven't had the vaccine.

SYMPTOMS
- feeling unwell with a mild fever lasting no more than four days; headache; appetite loss
- pain and swelling of one or both parotid glands (saliva glands on each side of the face)

Making the diagnosis
When both sides of the jaw swell up and your child has pain when she eats, it's usually easy to diagnose. The incubation period is 17 to 19 days. Mumps is catching from a few days before the glands enlarge until they are back to normal. One attack gives permanent protection.

Children can occasionally develop pancreatitis, or mumps meningitis (which can cause permanent deafness). Older boys may get inflammation of the testes.

What to do for your child
Treat a fever and keep an eye on her temperature to ensure it stays under control (see pages 226–227). Chewing makes pain worse, so give your child soothing drinks and soft foods. Drinks are easier to swallow with a straw. Avoid citrus fruit, which tend to make the saliva flow and can increase discomfort. If possible, keep your child away from other children until the swelling has resolved.

CALL THE DOCTOR if:
- you think your child has mumps
- she has a persistent high fever
- she won't take any fluids
- she becomes unusually drowsy.

If your child has a fever, she might find it soothing to have her face gently sponged with lukewarm water.

rubella

Rubella (German measles), now rare in Canada, is a mild infectious disease, but can cause serious birth defects if a pregnant woman catches it. The cause is a virus of the togavirus group. It's contagious and can be spread by those who have symptoms and by those without them, which is why it's important to eradicate rubella by immunization (see pages 216–217).

SYMPTOMS
- a rash, often starting as small pink patches, on the neck, face, trunk, and limbs
- enlarged glands high in the back of the neck
- feeling sick

Making the diagnosis
Rubella is difficult to diagnose because the rash can look like many other conditions, including other viral infections. If it's vital to have a precise diagnosis, your doctor can arrange for a blood test, but children rarely need one.

Rubella spreads by moisture droplets in the air and is contagious for about two to three weeks, starting from one week before symptoms start. The incubation period is 14 to 21 days.

What to do for your child
Keep your child comfortable. Because of the risk of birth defects, warn any women your child has been in recent contact with, and keep her away from anyone who may be in the early stages of pregnancy.

CALL THE DOCTOR if:
- you think your child has rubella because you're unlikely to be able to diagnose it yourself, and also it's a reportable disease (which means it must be reported to the local health authorities)
- your child isn't better in four days
- you are pregnant.

whooping cough

Whooping cough (pertussis) is a serious, but uncommon, infection that inflames the whole respiratory system from nose to lungs. Although it can occur at any age, it tends to be worse in the under-twos and very severe in premature babies. There is a vaccine now to prevent whooping cough.

SYMPTOMS

♦ runny nose, cough, fever, and sore eyes
♦ worsening cough with uncontrollable bouts, sometimes followed by the typical "whoop"
♦ during a coughing spell, vomiting or even turning blue through lack of oxygen
♦ occasionally, seizures can occur

Making the diagnosis

A typical case of whooping cough is easy to spot once bouts of coughing and whooping begin. However, it's harder to diagnose in the early stages, when symptoms resemble a bad cold.

The cause is a bacterium called *Bordetella pertussis*. It spreads from one infected person to another via droplets in the air when coughing or sneezing. The incubation period is one to three weeks. There is a vaccine for whooping cough (see *Immunizations*, page 216).

What to do for your child

Give her plenty of fluids in between coughing spells. She also needs small meals to reduce the risk of vomiting.

IN AN EMERGENCY!

Call 911 for an ambulance if your child's breathing is labored, she turns blue, or she has a seizure.

Lean your child forward during a coughing bout.

Keep a bowl nearby in case she vomits. Avoid smoky atmospheres and overexcitement since these can trigger coughing. Antibiotics may shorten the illness, but have to be started early, which is rarely possible.

A child with whooping cough can be scared as well as distressed, so it's a good idea to sleep in the same room while she's ill. This may not give you much sleep, but you'll both gain reassurance from being close.

CALL THE DOCTOR if you think your child has whooping cough since she may need hospital treatment.

kawasaki disease

This is a fairly common illness in children under two that was almost unheard of 40 years ago and now seems to be getting more common. Its exact cause is unknown, but it's probably an infection. It affects many parts of the body and, although full recovery is usual, it can have long-term effects on the heart.

SYMPTOMS

♦ high fever that persists for five days or more
♦ red rash on the trunk, similar to measles
♦ enlarged lymph nodes in the neck
♦ sore, red eyes
♦ sore, cracked mouth
♦ swollen or peeling hands and feet

Making the diagnosis

Kawasaki disease is not difficult to diagnose when the symptoms are typical. Your child is likely to have it if she has many of the symptoms listed left.

What to do for your child

Keep your child comfortable and contact your healthcare professional. Aspirin is sometimes used for Kawasaki disease but it also has risks (see page 227) so don't ever give it to your child except under your doctor's supervision.

CALL THE DOCTOR if you suspect your child has Kawasaki disease.

meningitis

Meningitis means inflammation of the meninges, the membranes that protect the brain. It can be caused by many viruses and bacteria. A lot of the germs that cause meningitis live in the throat or nose of healthy people and cause no harm at all. It's not clear what triggers disease in some people, but it's more common where there's overcrowding and in households where people smoke.

SYMPTOMS

Baby

- a high-pitched or moaning cry
- refusing feedings and irritability when picked up
- drowsiness with limp limbs, or else limbs that are stiffer than usual
- pale, blotchy, sometimes clammy skin
- a tense, bulging fontanelle (soft spot)

Child

- severe headache and a dislike of bright lights
- stiff neck
- fever
- drowsiness and confusion, with flulike aches and pains

At any age

- a rash of red or brown pinpoint spots, or large bruises and purplish marks that don't fade when pressed with the side of a glass

Making the diagnosis

In the advanced stages, meningitis is easy to diagnose. However, the ideal is to spot it early, when a complete cure is most likely. The disease can develop very quickly. A child may seem well one moment, then within a few hours be extremely sick. In other cases, it may take one or two days to develop. Another problem is that the symptoms can be difficult to distinguish from other, less serious infections. If you suspect meningitis, always tell your doctor what you're thinking of.

Symptoms vary according to the age of the child. A baby or child with meningitis may not have all the symptoms listed, but he may not be acting like himself and may get rapidly worse.

The incubation period for bacterial meningitis is between two and 10 days, and for viral meningitis it can be up to three weeks.

What to do for your child

Call your doctor immediately or go straight to the hospital (the emergency room) if you think your child has meningitis. Tell the hospital you suspect meningitis as soon as you arrive. Never wait for a rash to develop since this is a late symptom and it's better to diagnose the disease earlier.

Tests must be done to confirm the diagnosis. If your child has meningitis, antibiotics are the usual treatment, often given in an intensive-care unit along with any other help he may need.

IN AN EMERGENCY!

Seek medical help immediately if you think your child may have meningitis. If he already has a rash that does not fade using the tumbler test (see below), go straight to the emergency room.

The tumbler test
Press the side of a glass against the rash. If it doesn't fade under pressure your child may have developed septicemia and needs emergency hospital treatment – now!

types of **meningitis**

Most meningitis is caused by either bacteria or viruses. But the disease can also result from a fungal infection, a blow to the head, some types of cancer, inflammatory disease such as lupus, or a sensitivity reaction to certain medications.

Viral meningitis is milder and complete recovery is usual. Bacterial meningitis is more serious and always needs emergency treatment in the hospital.

Meningococcal meningitis One of the most serious forms of bacterial meningitis, this can also cause septicemia (blood infection). Although treatment can still cure the disease, a child who reaches this stage is very sick and every second counts. There are several different types of meningococcal meningitis. Type B infection is more common in Western countries, while type C occurs in outbreaks. Type A is more common in parts of Africa and Asia. A vaccine is available to protect against meningitis C.

Pneumococcal meningitis Another very serious bacterial form of meningitis. It especially affects children under two years old and is linked with septicemia and other infections such as chest and ear infections. Long-term complications are common. There are several different strains of pneumococcal bacteria, so one attack doesn't protect against any future infection. A vaccine is routinely given at ages two, four, and six months, plus a booster at 12 to 18 months.

Hemophilus influenzae B (Hib)
Once a common cause of bacterial meningitis in children, but thankfully it has become much rarer now that babies are given the Hib vaccine (see pages 216–217).

respiratory infections

Respiratory infections are common in babies and children because there are many different viruses and bacteria and babies' immune systems have yet to mature. It's sometimes hard to tell which part is infected. Doctors often use the terms upper respiratory tract infection (URTI) for infections of the nose, throat, and larynx, and lower respiratory tract infection (LRTI) for infections in the trachea, bronchi, or lungs.

colds

The common cold is exactly that – very common. It's caused by a virus, but this can be any one of several hundred viruses, mostly of the rhinovirus group. Because babies and young children need to build up immunity to each virus one at a time, they get a huge number of colds as they grow up – more than six a year is not at all unusual while they are young, especially once they start nursery school or daycare.

Gently wipe his nose for him.

SYMPTOMS

♦ sneezing, and a stuffy or runny nose
♦ a sore throat and watery, sticky eyes
♦ a mild cough, especially at night when secretions run down the back of the throat
♦ a mild fever

Making the diagnosis

It's usually easy to tell if your child has a cold from the typical symptoms. Colds spread on moisture droplets in the air when coughing, sneezing, or talking. Your child will usually suffer more colds in the winter since more time is spent indoors with other people. The incubation period is about two days, and a cold can last up to three weeks. Complications include middle-ear infection (see page 248) and chest infection (see page 247).

What to do for your child

There's no cure, but there's a lot you can do as a parent when your child has a cold.

Children can't blow their noses, so wipe your child's nose gently for him. Use cotton balls rather than tissues because they are softer on a baby's tender skin.

Give your child lots of fluids to drink. Babies with a cold often seem to have little appetite because they find it hard to breathe and suck at the same time. So be patient with feedings; give your baby plenty of time to suck.

Over-the-counter preparations can be useful to decongest your child's nose. Check with your pharmacist or doctor about whether the preparation you buy is appropriate for your child's age. Saline

nose drops can help unblock a baby's nose, using a bulb syringe.

CALL THE DOCTOR if:

♦ your infant's temperature is higher than 100.4°F (38°C) for more than 24 hours
♦ your child seems to be ill
♦ you notice any new symptoms developing, such as wheezing, shortness of breath, or earache.

flu

Flu, or influenza, is always caused by a virus. There are many different strains of flu virus, the two main groups being influenza A and influenza B. Influenza A changes over time, and can therefore cause major outbreaks or pandemics (worldwide epidemics). Incidentally, flu is not caused by the bacterium *Haemophilus influenzae* B (see *Hib*, pages 216–217).

SYMPTOMS

♦ a fever, often very high
♦ aches and pains
♦ a slightly runny nose or sore throat
♦ vomiting, diarrhea, or abdominal pain
♦ listlessness and generally feeling ill

Making the diagnosis

The flu spreads in moisture droplets in the air. Adults are more likely to get the flu, but young children can develop it, especially between December and March. The incubation period is one to three days.

Because the flu is uncommon in the very young, it's important not to assume that it is the flu – he may be sick with something else, such as an infection of the ear, throat, chest, or urine, or even early meningitis. Even your doctor may be unable to tell at first, and may need to see your child again.

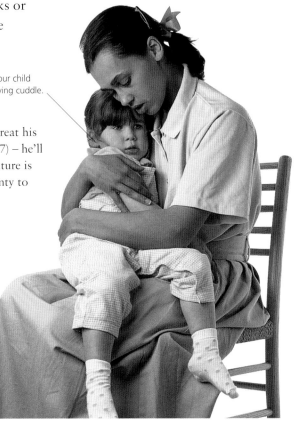

Soothe your child with a loving cuddle.

What to do for your child

Keep your child comfortable and treat his fever if necessary (see pages 226–227) – he'll feel much better when his temperature is under control. Give your child plenty to drink, and tender loving care.

CALL THE DOCTOR if:

♦ you're not sure if it's the flu
♦ his fever lasts for more than 24 hours
♦ he's increasingly listless
♦ he develops new symptoms, such as earache or breathlessness.

bronchiolitis

Bronchiolitis, an infection of tiny air passages in the lungs, usually affects babies under 12 months, although toddlers can get it, too. Bronchiolitis differs from bronchitis, which is not considered a pediatric condition.

SYMPTOMS

♦ cold and fever, progressing quickly to coughing, rapid breathing, and wheezing
♦ crackly or bubbling breathing sounds
♦ in severe cases, an indrawing of the chest between and below the ribs, shortness of breath, and turning blue from lack of oxygen

Making the diagnosis

Consult your doctor if your child has any of the above symptoms. Diagnosis is easy for your doctor to make, especially during outbreaks, but symptoms can resemble asthma (see page 259) and chest infection

(see opposite). Bronchiolitis tends to occur in early winter and is caused by a virus, usually respiratory syncytial virus (RSV). It has an incubation period of just a few days and spreads by droplets in the air. Some cases are milder than others but, on the whole, the younger your baby, the more serious it tends to be. Some children need to be hospitalized. Bronchiolitis can recur.

What to do for your child

Follow your doctor's instructions. If your child is mildly ill, give plenty of fluids and treat any fever, if necessary. You can also sit with your child in a steamy room, such as in

IN AN EMERGENCY!

Bronchiolitis can be an emergency, so don't delay. If in doubt, call 911 for an ambulance.

the bathroom, with the hot water running to decongest her air passages and ease her breathing. Doing this several times a day for 10 minutes can help. You may want to sleep in the same room as your child to keep an eye on her and to comfort her.

CALL THE DOCTOR if:

♦ your child is distressed
♦ she is unable to take fluids
♦ her chest is sucked in with each breath
♦ her breathing becomes more rapid
♦ she turns blue.

croup

Croup is a form of laryngitis that occurs from three months to three years. It's usually due to a virus, often RSV, the same virus that causes bronchiolitis. However, croup can be caused by other viruses, too. The larynx (voice box) of a young child is different from an adult's, which is why children get croup. The symptoms occur because the airways are narrowed, making breathing difficult.

SYMPTOMS
♦ a harsh, barking cough and noisy breathing, especially on breathing in
♦ hoarseness – may be worse in the morning
♦ in severe cases, rapid breathing and turning blue from lack of oxygen

Making the diagnosis
Although the cough can sound typical, croup isn't always easy to diagnose because it can be similar to epiglottitis and an inhaled foreign body. Epiglottitis (preventable by vaccine) is inflammation of the epiglottis, the flap of tissue just above the voice box that covers the airways during swallowing.

Epiglottitis is rare, but often due to infection with *Hemophilus influenzae* B (Hib). Because it's bacterial, it responds to antibiotics. With epiglottitis, the child often sits forward to relieve the narrowed airway, and he may drool because he can't swallow saliva. NEVER put anything into your child's throat, or look down it, when he is hoarse or wheezing. If it's epiglottitis, this can cause the epiglottis to block the airway, with possibly fatal results.

An inhaled foreign body like a nut can also block the airway if it lodges in the windpipe (see page 270). The incubation period of croup, on the other hand, is a matter of days, and it is possible to have it several times. Some children are prone to croup.

What to do for your child
A child with croup is often distressed. Keep calm and reassure him. For a mild attack, treat any fever and give plenty of fluids. Help decongest your child's airways by sitting him in a steamy room (see *bronchiolitis*, page 246). Going outside into cooler air can sometimes help.

CALL THE DOCTOR if:
♦ you're not sure it's croup
♦ your child's breathing gets worse
♦ he turns blue.

chest infection

Chest infection means any infection in the chest, from bronchitis to pneumonia. The term "lower respiratory tract infection" (LRTI) is the same as "chest infection." Some pneumococcal infections can be prevented by immunization with the pneumococcal vaccine.

SYMPTOMS
♦ cough, shortness of breath, and a fever
♦ harsh breathing sounds, or breathing that's faster than usual
♦ sometimes, vomiting

Making the diagnosis
You may suspect a chest infection from your child's symptoms, but your doctor needs to listen to his chest with a stethoscope to be sure.

Viruses and bacteria can both cause chest infections. Pneumococcus is one of the most serious bacteria, and it also causes meningitis and septicemia (see page 244). Most chest infections spread via phlegm and saliva droplets. The incubation period is short for all of these germs.

What to do for your child
Reassure your child. Regularly check her temperature and give her plenty of fluids. Keep meals small and frequent if she's coughing a lot or short of breath. A baby needs plenty of time for feedings.

Young children's chest infections can change rapidly, usually for the better, but not always, so watch your child carefully. Few children bring up phlegm when they are ill, but if yours does, encourage her to spit it out on a tissue rather than swallow it. Give prescribed medicines as directed.

CALL THE DOCTOR if:
♦ your child becomes short of breath
♦ her breathing is labored
♦ she fails to improve with treatment.

TUBERCULOSIS (TB)
TB is a chronic infection that's caused by a bacterium called *Mycobacterium tuberculosis*. It's common in many parts of the world, including Canada's inner cities and aboriginal communities.

Infection often begins in the lungs, then spreads to the lymph nodes inside the chest. From there, it can spread elsewhere. The incubation period is several weeks. There may be a cough, poor appetite, weight loss, fever, tiredness, and enlarged glands in the neck.

Doctors may suspect TB if you have any relatives with it or you have been in contact with anyone else who has it. The treatment is prescribed drugs. Always see your doctor if you think your child has been exposed to TB.

eye, ear, nose, and throat

Eye, ear, nose, and throat infections are among the most common childhood ailments. A child's immune system has yet to mature, and he's exposed to new viruses and bacteria almost daily. Lymph tissue in the nose (adenoids) and the throat (tonsils) mops up infection and mounts an immune response.

ear infections

These can affect the outer ear, which channels sound toward the ear drum, or the middle ear, which transmits sound vibrations to the inner-ear mechanism with the help of three tiny bones. The inner ear, which sends coded sound signals to the brain, does not usually become infected.

Check for a discharge if you suspect ear infection.

OUTER-EAR INFECTION (otitis externa)

In an outer ear infection, the ear canal itself is inflamed, often due to bacteria. This can happen if your child has eczema, or if he goes swimming a lot. Children also poke their fingers into their ears, which is another possible source of infection. Although it's called an outer-ear infection, you may not be able to see anything from the outside.

SYMPTOMS

♦ earache or itching
♦ discharge from the ear
♦ repeated pulling or rubbing the ear

Making the diagnosis

Your doctor will examine your child's ears with an otoscope to see into the canals.

What to do for your child

Give your child acetaminophen or ibuprofen for pain relief, and use ear drops as directed. Avoid getting his ear wet.

Keep him away from other children for a day or so since the discharge is usually infected. Gently wipe away any discharge from the ear, but avoid putting cotton balls or anything else inside the canal.

MIDDLE-EAR INFECTION (acute otitis media)

This means infection or inflammation in the space behind the ear drum. Sometimes only one ear is affected, but occasionally it's both. Viruses cause as many as half of all middle-ear infections, but it's not always possible for your doctor to know whether viruses or bacteria are the cause.

Infection reaches the middle ear from the throat via the Eustachian tube, which is narrower and shorter than an adult's. Some children are prone to repeated ear infections while they are growing up.

SYMPTOMS

♦ earache and fever
♦ inconsolable crying
♦ discharge from the ear

Making the diagnosis

Your doctor should examine your child's ears with an otoscope to see the drums.

What to do for your child

Relieve your child's pain with a warm compress over the ear. Give him pain relief in the form of acetaminophen or ibuprofen. If the cause is a mild virus, he may begin to improve on his own. Treat fever, if necessary, and offer plenty of fluids. Give antibiotics if prescribed.

CALL THE DOCTOR if:

♦ you suspect an ear infection
♦ you can't control his earache, he has a high fever, or he seems unusually ill.

GLUE EAR

Chronic middle-ear effusion (glue ear) is a build up of sticky fluid in the middle ear. Initially, your doctor may prescribe a decongestant, but a simple operation may be needed if the fluid persists and causes hearing loss. Under anesthesia, a tiny tube is inserted into the ear drum. The tube equalizes the air pressure on either side of the ear drum and allows the ear to dry out. After several months, the tube will fall out, the hole will heal, and hearing will be back to normal.

tonsillitis

Tonsillitis means inflammation or infection of the tonsils. Tonsils are usually large in children. They're also the doorway through which many germs pass, so are often infected with any of a wide range of airborne viruses and bacteria. Your child may recover from tonsillitis on his own, but antibiotics may be given if the cause is thought to be bacteria, such as streptococcus (strep).

SYMPTOMS
- fever, sore throat, and difficulty swallowing
- tender, swollen lymph nodes in the neck
- abdominal pain from enlarged lymph nodes in the abdomen
- sometimes, a rash that starts with spots on the trunk, spreading to the rest of the body

Making the diagnosis
Tonsillitis is difficult to diagnose if your child is suffering from mainly abdominal pain. However, you will probably suspect it if he complains of a sore throat, has difficulty swallowing, and is running a fever.

You may also notice that he has bad breath and a raw-looking throat, possibly with creamy spots in the tonsils. NEVER attempt to look down your child's throat if he is hoarse or wheezy, and never force open his mouth, because this may do more harm than good.

What to do for your child
Give your child tender loving care. Offer him plenty of soothing drinks, preferably warm, unless he prefers cold drinks and ice cream. Give pain and fever relief in the form of acetaminophen or ibuprofen (see pages 226–227).

CALL THE DOCTOR if:
- your child has a fever for more than 24 hours
- he has stomach pain, or can't swallow
- he doesn't improve within 48 hours.

IN AN EMERGENCY!

Call 911 for an ambulance if your child has trouble breathing.

conjunctivitis

This is an inflammation or infection of the lining of the eyeball or eyelids, and can be bacterial, viral, or allergic. It affects one or both eyes. The stickier the eyes are in the morning, the more likely it is to be bacterial. Babies get bacterial conjunctivitis because their tear ducts aren't completely formed until six months.

SYMPTOMS
- eyes that are sticky or crusty with pus first thing in the morning or after a nap
- a blob of pus in the corner of the eye
- rubbing the eyes in discomfort
- bloodshot eyes and/or swollen eyelids

Making the diagnosis
Conjunctivitis is usually obvious from the symptoms. However, your child may also have sticky eyes when he has a cold, and this often needs no special treatment.

Both viral and bacterial forms of conjunctivitis are contagious, spreading in the air and by direct contact. The incubation period is usually short.

Allergic conjunctivitis is uncommon in children under three, but can be linked to hay fever and other allergies. It tends to make eyes itchy or watery as well as sore.

What to do for your child
If your child has only mild conjunctivitis, with slightly sticky eyes when she wakes up, you may not need to see the doctor at all. Wash your hands, then gently wipe off the pus from his eyelids with a cotton ball that has been dipped in tepid water. Always wipe from the nose toward the outside of the eye. Use a clean cotton ball for each eye, and be careful not to touch the eyeball itself. Wash your hands again.

If you have been prescribed eye drops by your doctor, use them as directed (see page 231) and make sure that you complete the course, which is usually five days. While your child's eyes are inflamed, keep him away from nursery school or play group because conjunctivitis is catching until your child has had treatment for at least the first 24 hours.

Use a clean cotton ball for each eye.

CALL THE DOCTOR if:
- your child's eyes need wiping more than twice a day
- his eye is bloodshot or very sore
- his eyelids look swollen.

styes

A stye is a localized infection at the base of one of the eyelashes. It forms a small boil on the upper or lower lid. This is sore and painful, and the whole lid looks red in the early stages. Bacteria usually cause styes. Toddlers and older children get them because they often rub their eyes with less-than-clean fingers.

SYMPTOMS

♦ a red swelling on one of the eyelids
♦ a pus-filled lump in the swelling a day or two later
♦ a discharge before the stye dries up

Making the diagnosis

The typical appearance will probably tell you that your child has a stye. However, in the early stages a stye can look like conjunctivitis or an eye injury, so it helps if your child is old enough to be able to tell what, if anything, happened.

What to do for your child

Although styes are painful, they aren't usually serious and you can treat most of them yourself. To relieve your child's symptoms and ease swelling, wash your hands and make a warm compress for the eye. Dip a cotton ball into hot water, squeeze it out, then press it gently onto your child's closed eye for a few minutes. A few drops of water may trickle down her face, so give her a tissue to wipe her cheek if she wants to. Using compresses several times a day will help bring the stye to a head. When it bursts or discharges, just wipe away the pus with a cotton ball dipped in tepid water.

Press gently, taking care not to touch the eyeball.

CALL THE DOCTOR if:
♦ the stye doesn't improve within a week
♦ the redness spreads
♦ the whole eyelid is swollen and her eye looks bloodshot.

cold sores

Cold sores are a localized infection on the lip, or less often the nostril. They're caused by the herpes simplex virus and are very contagious. They often appear during a cold, hence the name cold sore. Once your child has a cold sore, the virus then lies dormant. Your child may get future attacks triggered by minor illness, strong sunlight, or nose picking. Babies or young children with herpes simplex can get a more widespread sore mouth with painful blisters.

SYMPTOMS

♦ tingling or pain on the lip or in the nostril
♦ a blister or a cluster of small blisters that appear a few hours later
♦ weepy blisters a day or two later that crust over and form a scab

Making the diagnosis

Cold sores can look typical, but sometimes may be hard to distinguish from impetigo (see page 252), which needs different treatment.

What to do for your child

If your child only has tingling, try wrapping an ice cube in a clean cloth and applying it to the tingling area for five to 10 minutes. This may stop the cold sore from developing.

If you notice cold-sore symptoms early, they often respond to acyclovir cream. This is an antiviral cream that needs to be applied regularly, several times a day – ask your doctor or pharmacist.

Stop your child from touching her cold sore, and keep her away from other children until the sore is completely dry and scabbed. Also, prevent her from sharing toys that she's likely to have put into her mouth because they may be carrying the virus.

CALL THE DOCTOR if:
♦ this is your child's first cold-sore attack
♦ she has more than one area affected
♦ the cold sore is near the eye
♦ your child looks sick
♦ she is not eating or drinking
♦ the cold sore looks infected.

skin and hair

Babies and children have beautiful healthy skin most of the time. However, it's easy for them to pick up infections and their delicate skin can look inflamed or irritated. Your child may scratch, causing more damage and scabbing. Once a scab forms, she may pick at it, which delays healing. You can't always stop her from doing this, but it's important to teach her good hygiene from an early age to help avoid infections.

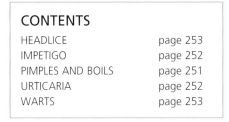

pimples and boils

A pimple is a small, infected red swelling anywhere on the skin. A boil is bigger and more painful. It contains pus, which eventually comes to a head and bursts, discharging creamy-yellow material. Both pimples and boils are caused by bacterial infections and can occur at any age. Most pimples and the occasional small boil are nothing to worry about. However, if your child gets frequent boils it may indicate that she has an underlying illness.

SYMPTOMS

Pimples

♦ a small, red, painless lump, usually with a white or yellow center

Boils

♦ a painful, angry-looking, red lump, perhaps with a white or yellow head in the center
♦ sometimes, tender enlarged lymph nodes

Making the diagnosis

This is usually obvious from the appearance of your child's skin, but splinters, foreign bodies, and infected cuts or abrasions can look similar. Sometimes lymph nodes near the site of the boil can become swollen and tender, for example a boil on the arm will cause swollen glands in the armpit, while a boil on the scalp will make nodes behind the ears enlarge.

What to do for your child

Pimples usually clear up in a few days without any treatment. Just keep your child's skin clean in the usual way. Don't be tempted to squeeze pimples or boils since you can spread infection and may cause scarring. After a boil bursts, simply clean the discharged pus with a cotton ball dipped in antiseptic, or in cooled, boiled water. If the area looks raw, use a clean dressing.

If your child has a boil in a painful place, such as her bottom, she may be more comfortable if you pad it with plenty of cotton balls or gauze held on with adhesive tape.

A large or deep boil may need to be drained by a doctor to let the pus out. Some are so inflamed and red that antibiotics are needed, but most resolve without medication. Your doctor will advise you on the best course of treatment.

CALL THE DOCTOR if:

♦ your child has a large or painful boil
♦ she has frequent boils
♦ she has many pimples.

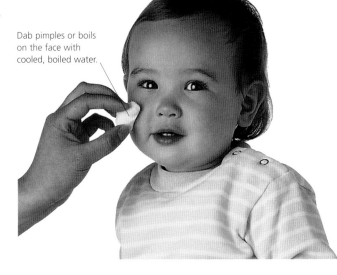

Dab pimples or boils on the face with cooled, boiled water.

urticaria

Urticaria, also known as hives, is an allergic skin reaction to any of a number of triggers, ranging from food and drugs to viral infections. It can also be caused by sunlight. Urticaria can occur at any age, but it's most common in young children.

SYMPTOMS

♦ raised areas of intensely itchy, red skin that spread and merge together
♦ rash lasting a few days or fading within hours

Making the diagnosis

Diagnosing urticaria isn't hard if your child has the typical rash, but determining what caused it is more of a challenge. In nearly nine out of 10 cases, the trigger remains a mystery.

What to do for your child

Keep your child comfortable by applying an even layer of calamine lotion onto the affected area. If the rash covers most of his body, a lukewarm bath, to which you've added about two tablespoons of baking soda, can be helpful first. You may also need to give your child an antihistamine to ease severe itching – ask your healthcare professional.

Your healthcare professional will help work out the cause of your child's urticaria. Think about any unusual foods he has eaten in the last day or so, new medicines, or any new garden plants he may have touched.

CALL THE DOCTOR if:

♦ your child is very distressed
♦ your child has frequent attacks of urticaria.

IN AN EMERGENCY!

Call your doctor immediately, or call 911 for an ambulance, if your child's face, mouth, or tongue is swollen, or if he has trouble breathing. He could be developing anaphylactic shock (see page 272).

Urticaria
With urticaria, or hives, the typical red, raised, itchy patches spread and merge together. They may last a few hours or a few days.

impetigo

Impetigo is a skin infection most commonly caused by the streptococcus or the staphylococcus bacterium. It's common in children over one year old, and gets into the skin when it's cracked, irritated, or has been picked. Impetigo usually starts near the mouth or nose, but can be almost anywhere on the skin, and spreads rapidly from the area where it first began.

SYMPTOMS

♦ a small cluster of red spots and blisters, often near the corner of the mouth
♦ enlarging spots that become yellow, burst, and form honey-colored crusts

Making the diagnosis

In the early stages, it's not always easy even for a doctor to tell the difference between impetigo and cold sores (see page 250). Both are contagious, but need different treatments.

Impetigo spreads by direct contact from person to person, and is very catching. Serious complications are rare, though kidney damage is a remote possibility. In children, impetigo is not usually serious, but young babies who get it can become very ill.

What to do for your child

There's a lot you can do to keep your child comfortable and stop impetigo from spreading. Discourage him from touching or picking at the area since this can spread the infection and cause scarring. Keep his washcloth and towels separate from the rest of the family's. Wash the affected area daily by dabbing it with a cotton ball dipped in warm water, then pat dry with tissues or paper towels and throw this away immediately to reduce the risk of infecting others. Don't take the crusts off unless they're already sliding away as you clean your child's skin.

Your child will need a prescription for antibiotic cream or ointment, and your doctor may also prescribe antibiotics by mouth. Make sure he takes the whole course of treatment. Meanwhile, keep him away from other children, especially babies.

CALL THE DOCTOR if:

♦ you think your child has impetigo
♦ it's widespread despite treatment
♦ your child develops a fever or looks ill.

warts

Warts are small irregular growths in the skin caused by a virus. The lump itself is made up of several layers of dead skin. A wart on the sole of the foot (often called a plantar wart) looks a little different because constant pressure prevents it from rising above the rest of the skin.

SYMPTOMS

♦ small, hard lumps of dry-looking skin that may occur singly or in clusters anywhere on the body, but especially the hands and feet
♦ tiny black spots in the center of each lump

Making the diagnosis

In the early stages, you might think your child has a splinter or some minor injury, but soon the appearance becomes more typical of a wart. Check your child's body for warts elsewhere, too.

Warts are catching and spread by direct contact. They sometimes also spread from one part of the body to another. They are very common and no treatment is needed

because the body's immune system makes warts go away within two to five years.

What to do for your child

Some children are bothered by their warts, but they're painless and harmless, so it's best to try to ignore them. They go away without treatment. Just cover them up if your child goes swimming, and keep his towels and washcloths separate.

If your child wants to get rid of his warts, you can try over-the-counter wart preparations – ask your pharmacist. They work by dissolving the wart, and treatment can be uncomfortable. Don't use any wart preparations on your child's face or genitals as these areas are too delicate.

CALL THE DOCTOR if:

♦ you're not sure it's warts
♦ your child's warts multiply rapidly
♦ a wart appears on your child's face or genitals.

MOLLUSCUM

Molluscum contagiosum is a collection of skin lesions with a characteristic pearly appearance and a pit in the center. It occurs in clusters and is common in children. It starts as small fleshy bumps, then takes on a shell-like look. It is contagious and should be treated by the doctor to avoid further spreading.

headlice

Headlice are a common infestation in children, especially at daycare or nursery school. Lice are small wingless insects that crawl on human heads, cling to the hair shaft, and suck tiny amounts of blood from the scalp to survive. Since lice can't jump or fly, they spread by direct head-to-head contact. Each louse lives for up to three weeks. Lice are said to prefer clean hair, but in truth they're probably not fussy.

SYMPTOMS

♦ brownish lice moving in your child's hair
♦ pinhead-size louse eggs, close to the scalp
♦ gritty brown powder on your child's bed, or empty white egg cases (nits) clinging to hair
♦ possibly itching, but this is a late symptom

Making the diagnosis

The best way to detect lice is to comb your child's damp hair with a special fine-tooth lice comb. Do this over a white surface such as a paper towel or sink to see what comes out. If you're not sure whether they are lice, you can put the pieces on tape and take them to your doctor.

What to do for your child

Relax. Headlice are not serious, nor are they a disgrace, and they're definitely not an emergency. The treatment is special insecticide lotion or shampoo applied to the scalp. Ask your healthcare professional which one to buy.

The comb-and-conditioner technique is a non-drug way of treating lice: saturate your child's hair with ordinary hair conditioner and comb it until the lice come out. Repeat the process every four days for at least two weeks. This is a popular method, but its effectiveness has not been completely proven. Check the rest of the family's hair for lice.

There's no need to keep your child home from nursery school or his play group, but tell his teachers, baby-sitter, or any other caregivers that treatment has begun.

CALL THE DOCTOR if you aren't sure that it's headlice.

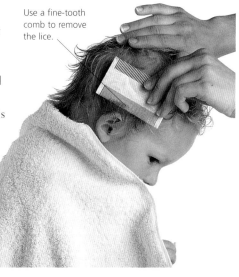

Use a fine-tooth comb to remove the lice.

bowels and bladder

Children occasionally have trouble with their bowels or bladder, and probably can't tell you how they feel. However, there are several signs to look for that may suggest your child has a problem, in particular, frequent, runny stools, vomiting, or foul or bloody urine.

stomachache

A stomachache can be a symptom of gastroenteritis (see right), especially when it occurs just before a bowel movement. Sometimes it's caused by overeating. But a stomachache doesn't always mean a problem with the stomach. The belly can also be painful if your child has an infection such as strep throat.

Appendicitis is another possible cause. The pain is likely to start in the middle before moving to the right side. It's rare in young children, but can be serious, so get help immediately. Children can also get a stomachache when they're worried about something. A stomachache and headache at the same time could be a form of migraine.

IN AN EMERGENCY!

Seek medical help immediately if:

♦ your child is in severe pain with a stomachache

♦ she also has a fever

♦ she passes blood in her stool

♦ she has stools like red currant jelly

♦ she shows signs of dehydration (see page 219).

urinary tract infection (UTI)

Bacteria get into the urinary system through the urethra, the channel that leads from the bladder to the outside. Many physicians will place a catheter into the urethra to the bladder to get a urine sample for culture. This is the most accurate way to determine if you child has a UTI.

SYMPTOMS

Baby or young child

♦ a fever, listlessness, or drowsiness

♦ refusing to feed or crying more than usual

Older child

♦ urinating more than usual

♦ burning or stinging when urinating

♦ stomachache and fever

♦ cloudy, foul-smelling urine, possibly with traces of blood in it

Making the diagnosis

Your doctor will test your child's urine. The ideal is to catch a sample in a sterile container to send to the lab – easiest with toilet-trained boys; with baby girls, stick-on bags may be used to collect urine.

Some young children have minor abnormalities in their urinary systems, which means that when bacteria enter the bladder they multiply and take hold.

What to do for your child

Make sure your child has plenty to drink, to help flush out bacteria. Keep an eye on her temperature and report this to your doctor, who will prescribe an antibiotic to clear up the infection. Your doctor will want to see her to rule out any abnormalities.

During toilet training, encourage good habits in your child by teaching her to wipe from front to back to help prevent bacteria from entering the urethra.

CALL THE DOCTOR if you suspect that your child has a urine infection.

Give her plenty to drink when she has a UTI.

diarrhea and vomiting

Gastroenteritis (infectious diarrhea) is the most common reason for diarrhea and vomiting. It can be serious in babies because they quickly become dehydrated. Breastfeeding protects against gastroenteritis so breastfed babies, when they get it at all, don't become as ill as bottle-fed babies.

SYMPTOMS

- ◆ diarrhea and vomiting, and refusing food
- ◆ a stomachache before a bowel movement
- ◆ a fever, particularly with dehydration

Making the diagnosis

It's usually enough to know that a child has gastroenteritis, and in most cases there's no need to identify the germ responsible. If your child fails to improve, your doctor may take a stool sample to test. A variety of bacteria and viruses cause gastroenteritis. They spread in contaminated food, or from the stools of someone else with the germs, which is why hand hygiene and thorough cooking are so important.

What to do for your child

To prevent dehydration, give her plenty to drink. Water is fine in most cases, or your healthcare professional may recommend an electrolyte drink. Alternatively, she can have dilute apple juice. Your doctor may

Keep a bowl close in case she needs to vomit.

recommend an oral rehydration solution available over the counter. Give it to your child in small sips at a time, or it will soon find its way back up again.

Make sure there's a potty close by at all times, or if your child has recently grown out of diapers, consider putting her back in them while she's ill. A bowl nearby in case she vomits will also help. Frequent sponge baths will help your child feel fresh.

Control your child's fever if necessary (see pages 226–227). Wash your hands often, especially when handling food, changing diapers, or cleaning the potty.

CALL THE DOCTOR if:

- ◆ your baby is under a year old, is vomiting, or has diarrhea
- ◆ your baby or child is becoming dehydrated
- ◆ she is not improving
- ◆ she passes blood in her stools
- ◆ she has a persistent stomachache.

pinworms

Pinworms are thin worms that resemble a piece of white cotton or thread about ½in (1cm) long. Although anyone can get pinworms, young children are most likely to have them.

SYMPTOMS

- ◆ an itchy bottom, particularly at night
- ◆ worms wriggling on the stool in the potty
- ◆ sometimes, no symptoms at all

Making the diagnosis

Pinworms live in the intestines. Their eggs spread from the stools of an infected person via dirty hands, as well as on toys and other objects. If your child has pinworms, she can reinfect herself with her own hands.

If you see the worms, you can be confident of the diagnosis. Otherwise, see your doctor. Alternatively, position a small strip of double-sided tape near your child's anus and leave it overnight. Take

anything that collects there to your doctor for an opinion.

What to do for your child

Medicine is available by prescription or over the counter from drugstores. The whole household needs treatment.

Bathe your child the morning after her pinworm treatment to get rid of any shed worms and eggs. To make sure that the worms are killed, wash all of her clothing, bedding, and towels in very hot water, ideally 140°F (60°C). Iron her sheets and nightwear.

Keep your child's fingernails short and make sure she washes her hands well after using the toilet, and before eating.

CALL THE DOCTOR if:

- ◆ your child is under two and has pinworms
- ◆ you're not sure if your child has pinworms
- ◆ you are or might be pregnant.

TOXOCARA CANIS

Toxocara canis is a worm found in the gut of dogs. It can cause serious illness in children, with stomachache, fever, and even blindness. That's why it's important to worm puppies and dogs, and to keep your child away from dog feces.

intussusception

This is rare condition in which part of a child's small bowel telescopes into the part ahead of it, as if it were swallowing itself. This makes the gut swell and creates a blockage. It is acutely painful and requires immediate hospital treatment. Intussusception most often affects babies under 12 months.

SYMPTOMS

- intense crying and pulling up legs with pain
- pallor, feverishness, and vomiting
- stools containing mucus and blood, resembling chicken fat and red currant jelly

Making the diagnosis

The cause isn't known for sure. It's not an infection, but it's thought that enlarged lymph tissue in the gut is linked with some of the cases. Intussusception usually needs a barium enema test in the hospital to diagnose it. This means putting a small amount of liquid barium into your baby's rectum to show his bowels on an X ray. Sometimes this test actually relieves the condition, but if it doesn't then your baby will need an operation. Although it's natural for a parent to be concerned when this happens, you can rest assured that the vast majority of babies recover very quickly – much faster than would most adults.

What to do for your child

Comfort your child and check his diaper, looking for any blood or mucus, and get medical advice without delay.

CALL THE DOCTOR if:

- you think your baby might have intussusception
- your baby has blood in her stools
- your baby has had intussusception before and now has a tummyache again.

balanitis

This means inflammation of the tip of the penis. It's usually caused by a bacterial infection, although yeasts such as candida can also be responsible. It's fairly common in uncircumcised boys, but balanitis may also be part of a more general diaper rash.

SYMPTOMS

- pain when urinating
- frequent rubbing or clutching of genitals
- pus in diapers or on underpants
- red, sore-looking penis tip, perhaps with swollen foreskin

Making the diagnosis

Balanitis is painful and often needs antibiotics. Your doctor will be able to diagnose it just by looking at your son, but may need to take a culture to find out exactly which germs are causing it. This involves gently dabbing the tip of the penis with a sterile cotton swab then sending it to the lab to see if it grows any bacteria or yeasts (see *thrush*, page 218).

Usually the infection affects only the penis and foreskin. However, your doctor may also want to test your little boy's urine to make sure it's not infected, too.

What to do for your child

Give your child frequent warm or lukewarm baths to ease the pain, and acetaminophen syrup if he needs it. Don't try to pull back the foreskin since this can do more harm than good (it's best not to pull back a young boy's foreskin anyway).

Give him the antibiotics prescribed by your doctor, which may be in cream or medicine form, or sometimes both.

After an attack of balanitis, your son's penis should return to normal. Recurrent attacks can occasionally cause scarring, which could mean you'll be advised to have him circumcised for medical reasons. However, this is fairly rare. Even if you have to see a specialist, surgery isn't always necessary as things often settle down by the time a boy is four or five.

CALL THE DOCTOR if:

- your child's penis looks sore
- he seems to be in pain
- he finds it difficult to urinate
- he doesn't seem to urinate properly after an attack of balanitis.

Give him antibiotics as directed.

chronic conditions

Most diseases are short-term conditions from which a child recovers completely. However, some disorders can have long-term effects. There is a range of these more chronic (long-term) conditions. Some, such as mild hearing difficulties, are noticeable only in certain situations, while others are more serious, posing greater challenges for the child and his family. Whatever your child's condition, there's a lot you can do to help him get the most out of life and to help others around him understand his condition.

CONTENTS

how to help

It can be distressing for parents to learn that their child has a chronic condition, but children themselves often cope well with all kinds of restrictions and take their treatments in stride.

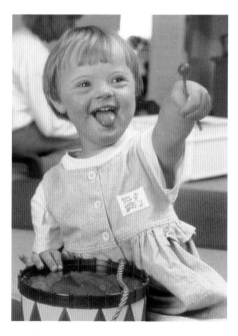

Positive parenting
By making the most of each achievement and adopting an upbeat approach to her treatment and care, you'll help your child meet every challenge.

Adopting an upbeat approach yourself is one of the best ways to help your child. It will also encourage others, such as caregivers and grandparents, to be positive, too.

Some disorders, such as cerebral palsy or cystic fibrosis, may mean that your child isn't able to do the things other children of his age take for granted. Sometimes the condition fluctuates, so your child may be well most of the time, but have limitations when the condition flares up. Asthma often falls into this category, so even children with severe asthma can have very good days.

Try not to label your child or over-medicalize his condition. These days, healthcare professionals prefer to talk about "a child who has seizures," for instance, rather than labeling him "an epileptic." The distinction is subtle, but not trivial.

Individual needs

Whatever your child's diagnosis, remember that he's an individual, and that each family is different, too. Therefore, not every generalization about a particular condition will apply to your child. There are many sources of information (see *further information*, above), including self-help groups. These usually involve getting together with other parents who have children with a similar condition and can offer support and practical advice.

It's important to focus on what your child can do and make the most of these abilities. As he grows up, encourage him and give him opportunities to do more of the activities he can manage. Try not to be overprotective. In time, he needs to grow up, meet others, and gain as much independence as he can.

further **information**

Always bear in mind that your child is an individual, so if you're not sure whether a particular treatment or course of action might benefit him, seek further advice.

Good sources of information include:
♦ your healthcare professional or specialist
♦ your hospital
♦ self-help and support groups
♦ libraries
♦ the Internet.

Remember that not all publications and Internet sites contain information you can trust, so be selective.

hearing loss

Hearing impairment in children is usually partial, but can be total. In some cases the middle ear doesn't conduct sound well (conduction hearing loss), often during or after an infection. In others, nerves in the inner ear don't send accurate signals to the brain (sensorineural or nerve hearing loss).

Symptoms

The signs depend on the degree of impairment, and which sounds are affected. Your baby may not respond to your voice, or may not hear you approaching and will look surprised as you come into view. Your child may fail to do what you ask. This can be normal toddler behavior, but hearing loss can genuinely make a child less cooperative. Look out for slow or immature speech – your child may speak less than expected or may repeat words less accurately than other children her age.

Sign language
If your child's hearing is severely impaired, sign language will help you communicate. This is good for her progress and doesn't stop speech from developing.

What to do for your child

Routine development evaluations can pick up hearing loss, but if you're worried at any time, consult your doctor. Look directly at your child when talking, speak clearly, and give her time to express herself. Minimize background noise. Your child may need specialist treatment for the treatment of middle-ear effusion (see *glue ear*, page 248).

strabismus

Cross-eye in an infant after about eight weeks of age may mean there's an imbalance of the eye muscles, leading to poor vision. It's important to treat a misalignment of the eyes promptly, otherwise vision will suffer.

Symptoms

Your child's eyes may face different ways, especially if she tries to follow your finger or a rattle. Her eyes may face away from each other or toward each other.

What to do for your child

Consult your doctor if you suspect a problem with your child's vision. Encourage your child if she needs to wear glasses, or a patch over the stronger eye.

Most young children accept the wearing of glasses and eye patches if their parents and friends take it in stride, too.

Occasionally surgery or injections into the muscles at or after the age of two is recommended to correct muscle imbalance. Older children may be given exercises to strengthen the eye muscles. Make sure your child does these as directed by incorporating them into her daily routine.

diabetes

Diabetes is due to a lack of insulin or unresponsiveness to insulin. Insulin is the hormone that allows glucose (sugar) into the body cells. Children with diabetes often develop symptoms suddenly and almost always need long-term insulin treatment to control their disease.

IN AN EMERGENCY!

Give her a sweet drink if she has stomach pain, is dizzy, and/or confused.

Symptoms

Your child may be very thirsty, or pass large amounts of urine. She may lose weight, or have a tummyache, vomiting, and become dehydrated. You may smell ketones on her breath – an odor like nail-polish remover. Some children suffer frequent chest and urine infections (see pages 247 and 254).

What to do for your child

Initially, once the diagnosis has been made, your child will need hospital treatment, initially as an in-patient.

There's a lot you can do to help your child to keep the condition under control, however. Give her her insulin injections regularly. Be confident – this is a lifelong illness and your attitude will influence your child's acceptance. Learn all you can about diabetes, and make sure that relatives and any other caretakers are well informed, too. Your child will need a carefully regulated diet and her blood-sugar levels will need regular monitoring for the rest of her life.

asthma

With asthma, the airways in the lungs are inflamed and become narrow during attacks. This can be triggered by infection, exercise, cold air, air pollution, and allergies. Asthma is more common in children over two. Severe asthma is easier to diagnose than mild cases. Your doctor may prescribe medicine to prevent constriction or to dilate the airways – if this helps, it's more likely to be asthma.

Symptoms

Your child may cough or wheeze, especially at night, and she may be short of breath following exertion. The symptoms often first start just after she's had a bad cold. Acute attacks can be frightening for a child and for those around her. She could start to turn blue from a lack of oxygen.

Encourage her to use an inhaler as prescribed.

What to do for your child

Keep calm and help your child breathe slowly, without panicking. Encourage her to use her inhalers regularly, and to accept this as normal. If she has a steroid inhaler, make sure that she rinses her mouth after using it. Avoid possible triggers, such as cigarette smoke, furry pets, and house dust.

sickle-cell anemia

This is an inherited condition in which the red blood cells are sickle-shaped because they contain an unusual form of hemoglobin. A child can only have sickle-cell anemia if both parents carry the trait. It's most common in those of African origin, and is diagnosed by a blood test.

Symptoms

Symptoms are wide ranging since sickle-cell disease can be mild or severe. Anemia can set in after a baby is four to six months old, with tiredness as the main symptom. Frequent infections also occur.

Attacks can be triggered by dehydration, infection, cold weather, or lack of oxygen.

What to do for your child

Make sure your child has all her immunizations. Vaccination for pneumonia is routine in the US. Make sure she doesn't become dehydrated, and protect her in cold weather. Learn all you can about the condition, and make sure that other caregivers are well informed about it, too.

eczema

Eczema is a skin condition that's common from four months. It may clear up as a child gets older, but not always. Eczema can run in families with asthma, hay fever, or other allergies. It often appears when a baby is weaned, but is less often due to food allergy than most parents think. In some cases, however, elimination tests under medical supervision can help diagnose the allergy.

Symptoms

Eczema is itchy, so you may notice your child scratching, especially at night. There can be dry or raw-looking areas on the face, or in the creases of the knees or elbows. Because eczema makes skin dry and cracked, it can become infected with bacteria, particularly in the diaper area, which can blister and weep.

What to do for your child

Clothe her in cotton fabrics that have been washed in a mild, non-biological detergent, and rinsed well. Keep your child's nails short to deter scratching. Avoid using soap on her skin – emollients in the bath and creams afterward will help. Your doctor may prescribe a mild steroid ointment.

Eczema
Itchy, red, cracked, and raw-looking skin is a typical sign of eczema. If the area becomes infected with bacteria, it can start to blister and weep.

cystic fibrosis

Cystic fibrosis (CF) affects glands that make mucus and certain enzymes. Sticky mucus collects in the lungs, which become infected, while lack of enzymes in the gut makes it hard to absorb fats. Treatment helps, but there's no cure. CF is inherited – it can be passed on if both parents are carriers.

Symptoms

A baby may not pass meconium stools (see page 92) at birth. Later, he may have constipation, diarrhea, or alternate between the two. His tummy may look swollen. Recurrent chest infections or a chronic, rattly cough are common. Children with CF have a higher than normal salt level in the sweat, and this is how the condition is diagnosed.

What to do for your child

Your child will need to be treated by a specialist, but there's a lot you can do as a parent. Your child needs a special high-calorie, low-fat diet to help with digestion. He will be prescribed extra vitamins, as well as enzyme capsules to take before each meal.

To keep his lungs clear, breathing exercises and daily physical therapy to bring up the sticky mucus from the lungs are a must. This helps to reduce infection and prevent lung damage. Once a physical therapist has shown you how to do these, you can do them yourself for your child. Always get prompt treatment for any chest infections.

Make sure that your child gets regular exercise, such as running or swimming, and any activities that involve stretching the trunk and arms. Your physical therapist will be able to advise you what's best for your child.

Newer treatments for cystic fibrosis include lung transplantation, and soon gene therapy may be possible, too.

down syndrome

Down syndrome is a chromosomal condition with multiple symptoms. The usual number of chromosomes is 23 pairs, but in Down syndrome there's an extra chromosome number 21, or a rearrangement of chromosome 21. It can be diagnosed before birth by amniocentesis or CVS (see page 21).

Symptoms

Children with Down syndrome have a round face, slanting eyes, and a wide nose. The mouth is usually small and the tongue relatively large, and the fingers and toes are often short. They usually have learning difficulties, which can be mild or severe. About half of all children with Down syndrome have either intestine or heart problems, and they can also suffer recurrent infections or anemia.

What to do for your child

Patience, love, and following your doctor's advice are the key to getting the best out of your child. Many children with Down syndrome are very affectionate, and can learn a lot with encouragement. You will need to work hard at this and concentrate on the things that your child can do and enjoys. Some children with Down syndrome go to mainstream schools and achieve a degree of independence.

Encourage your child
Many children with Down syndrome can learn with patience and encouragement from a loving parent.

autism

Autism is a disorder of development that affects a child's communication, social skills, and behavior. It can be mild or severe, and the cause is unknown.

Symptoms

More boys than girls have autism, and it's usually diagnosed between eight months and three years of age. It can be hard to diagnose and needs to be assessed by a specialist. Babies may dislike cuddles and make little eye contact. Children with autism favor complicated rituals for even minor activities, and throw tantrums if their routine alters. They may show repetitive behavior, such as rocking back and forth. Their speech is immature and they remain aloof. Some have learning difficulties, although others have normal or even superior intelligence.

What to do for your child

Although there's no cure for autism, there are many therapies that you can carry out with your doctor's guidance. Massage and physical therapy, for instance, can help, depending on your child's particular needs. He'll benefit from a structured and supportive environment and plenty of individual attention. With help, many children with autism can learn social skills and take part in society.

cerebral palsy

Cerebral palsy is a brain condition that causes muscle weakness. It's fairly common and can be mild or severe. The cause isn't known, but it's likely that many cases develop before birth. Although the condition doesn't go away, it doesn't deteriorate either.

Symptoms

These vary according to the severity of the condition, and the child's age. Children with cerebral palsy often have normal intelligence, but weakness makes it hard to show this, especially if speech is impaired.

What to do for your child

Make the most of his abilities. Remember that he is capable of loving, thinking, and learning, but his physical limitations make this hard to convey. Stretching and physical therapy techniques to do at home will keep his limbs mobile. Speech therapy is often needed, too. With help, your child may be able to attend a mainstream school.

Living with cerebral palsy
Cerebral palsy causes mild or severe muscle weakness, but a child's intelligence often remains unimpaired.

epilepsy

Epilepsy is a condition that causes recurrent seizures (or convulsions) during which electrical signals in the brain are disturbed. There are two main types – grand mal and petit mal – and, although children with epilepsy have no mental disability, both can interfere with learning if seizures are frequent.

Symptoms

In grand mal seizures, the child's eyes may roll backward or he may cry out before losing consciousness. Then he'll clench his teeth, and his limbs may become stiff or jerk. He may froth at the mouth or lose control of his bladder. Afterward, he'll feel dazed or tired.

In petit mal seizures, there's a short absence or trancelike moment lasting only a couple of seconds, during which the child won't be aware of anything.

What to do for your child

During a seizure, lay your child on his side, loosen tight clothing, and move any objects on which he could hurt himself. Otherwise, don't restrain him, and stay with him until it ends. When it's over, lay him in the recovery position (see page 269) and get medical help. Let him rest until he feels like getting up.

There's no cure for epilepsy, but regular medication can help prevent seizures. This is why it's important to give your child his medication as prescribed by your doctor. Be aware of situations in which he might get injured if he has a seizure (such as swimming), but try not to be overprotective.

attention deficit disorder

Attention deficit disorder (ADD) covers a range of behavior difficulties, including hyperactivity and attention deficit hyperactivity disorder (ADHD). It's most common in boys, and the exact cause isn't known, but both genetic and environmental factors are believed to play a role.

Symptoms

Your child will have an unusually short attention span and will often be very restless. He may be clumsy, impulsive, and disruptive. Although young children are all like this to some degree, in a child with ADD these characteristics are more pronounced.

What to do for your child

Your doctor will make the initial diagnosis. Sometimes ADD runs in families and, although there's no cure for it, there's a lot you can do to help your child.

Medication can increase your child's attention span, but it is not the only treatment. Consistent handling and a calm, loving atmosphere will help to bring out the best in your child. Be as positive as you can to build his self-esteem, and remember to always praise him when he's playing well. Be specific in your instructions to him and set clear boundaries so that he knows what is acceptable behavior.

A predictable daily routine will help to prevent his restlessness and improve his behavior, which in turn will benefit the whole family.

safety

The best way to keep your baby or child safe as she grows up is to see the world from her point of view. There are many tempting things to explore, which she'll do without any awareness of danger. To avoid potential hazards, you'll have to stay one step ahead of her as she enters each new stage of development.

When your baby is small, you need to supervise her constantly, even taking her from room to room with you to keep her safe. As she grows into an inquisitive toddler, you'll have to be just as watchful, although you can keep a greater distance in some situations so she learns some independence.

Pressing dangers
Never attempt to do the ironing with your young child around. Sit her securely in her highchair or playpen, or, better yet, wait until she's sleeping.

Toys and playthings

There are many ways to ensure that your child's toys and playthings are safe.
♦ Follow recommended age ranges on toy packages. The ages listed are there for safety reasons, not to indicate whether a toy is developmentally approporiate for the child. Children under the age of three can choke on small parts contained in toys or games and balls that are 1¾in (4cm) in diameter or less.
♦ Check the size of the toy and make sure there are no parts that could be swallowed.
♦ Before allowing a child to play with a toy, read the instructions carefully. If the toy is appropriate for your child, show her how to use it properly.
♦ Children under the age of eight can choke or suffocate on deflated or broken balloons.
♦ Watch for strings that are more than 12in (30cm) in length. They could be a strangulation hazard for babies.

Babies on the move

Once your baby starts to roll, and then crawl, she faces many more potential risks.
♦ Put covers on electrical sockets.
♦ Consider corner covers for tables and other sharp areas, and remove heavy, glass, or fragile objects until she's older.
♦ Never iron near her. Put her in a playpen, or leave your ironing until she's asleep.
♦ Keep hot drinks out of her reach.
♦ As your baby starts pulling herself up on the furniture, be aware of flimsy side tables, or shelves that may fall onto her.

Beware of stairs

Many injuries in the home happen on or around the stairs.
♦ Install gates at the top and bottom of stairs.
♦ When your baby learns to crawl, show her how to come down stairs backward.
♦ Make sure your banisters are safe, with gaps of no more than 4in (10cm) between the spindles. Horizontal bars could become a ladder, so change them or board them up.
♦ Never leave things on or near the stairs.
♦ Make sure that the latch on your front door is out of reach, or put a bolt high up on the inside to stop her from toddling into the street.

safe as **houses**

A general safety check around your home is always a good idea, but never more so than when there's a baby or young child in the house.

♦ Install window guards and locks, as well as cupboard locks where needed.

♦ Always keep matches and lighters well out of reach and locked away.

♦ Lock away chemicals and medicines.

♦ Install a smoke alarm, test it regularly, and replace batteries as required.

♦ Consider a carbon-monoxide alarm.

♦ Secure loose carpets and rugs.

♦ Make sure that furniture is made of flame-retardant materials.

♦ Install fire guards over open fires.

in the kitchen

The kitchen is the hub of the home and where many dangers lurk. It's also where you are most likely to be distracted, making it harder to keep an eye on your child. If it's practical, keep her out of the kitchen when you're cooking. If not, make sure safety measures are in place.

♦ **Lock it away** Keep household cleaners and chemicals locked away. Knives and other sharp objects should be out of reach in a locked drawer or cupboard. Make sure your child can't get into any plastic bags or wrap, which could be a suffocation hazard. Keep your garbage can where your child can't reach it. Install child-resistant locks on cupboards and drawers, and perhaps on the refrigerator and freezer, too.

♦ **Prevent burns** Install a guard around the stove, and always turn pot handles toward the back when in use. Keep your child away from the oven since even the outside of the door can be very hot. Avoid stray electrical cords – coiled or very short cords are better because your child is less likely to grab them.

♦ **Guard against fire** Keep matches out of reach. Keep a small fire extinguisher and a fire blanket handy. Learn how to put out small fires safely – for example, the correct way to put out a frying pan fire is to cover it with a wet towel.

♦ **Out of harm's way** Always use a safety harness in your baby's high chair. As well as eating in it, she can sit and play in it for a short time while you cook. You can put

a playpen in the kitchen if there's space. Older children can sit at the table and draw or play with modelling clay if you're busy, but you need to supervise them. An alternative is a gate across the doorway of the kitchen so that your child can play just outside it, where you can keep an eye on her while you cook.

♦ **Food and mealtimes** As you prepare food, wipe up spills right away to prevent slips and falls. Keep hot dishes in the middle of the table, so your child is less likely to reach them. Avoid using a tablecloth for now – a baby or child can tug it, bringing down anything that's on the table.

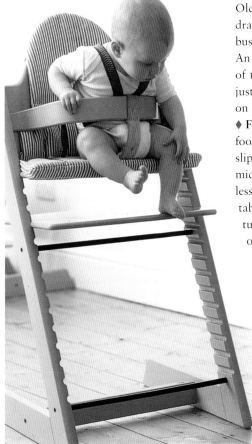

Safe seat
Always use a safety harness when your child is sitting in her high chair. Never leave her to eat unsupervised in case she chokes.

Around the oven
It's a good idea to install a guard along the front of the stove and turn pot handles to the back to prevent your child from reaching up and burning herself.

Cupboards and drawers
Locks on cupboards and drawers will deter little fingers from investigating their contents, but they're not completely childproof so be alert.

Dangerous substances
Household cleaners and chemicals should be locked away. Seek immediate medical help if you suspect your child has swallowed something (see page 270).

in the bathroom

Many babies and children are fascinated by water, and bath time is an enjoyable, and necessary, part of their daily routine. As a parent, you will delight in your youngster's fun, but bathrooms can be dangerous places and drowning in particular is an obvious risk. So it's important to be aware of any potential accidents at bath time, and take steps to prevent them.

♦ **A watchful eye** A child can drown in less than 5cm (2in) of water, so never leave him unsupervised or even take your eyes off him while he's in the bath. Make sure you have everything you need before putting him in the bath – it's unsafe to leave him for even a moment. Ignore temptations to answer the door or the phone. Put on the answering machine at bath time, if you have one.

♦ **Get a grip** If your baby can't sit up yet, always support him behind his neck while he's in the water. Once he can sit up, a steadying hand on his arm is a good idea. Always use a non-slip mat on the bottom of the bathtub.

♦ **Hot tips** Run all the bath water before he gets in – cold first, then the hot. If the faucet is still hot, wrap a towel or washcloth

Splash happy
A non-slip rubber mat in the bath will help your child feel secure and prevent nasty bumps. Be particularly watchful when siblings are around.

around it. Also cover or turn down any heated towel rails or radiators since children tend to grab at these. Turn down the thermostat on the hot water heater to 120°F (49°C) if you can, to reduce the risk

of your child burning himself if he plays with a faucet and succeeds in turning it on.

♦ **Other hazards** Keep the toilet-seat cover down until your child is ready for toilet training. All medicines, cleaners, razors, and even shampoos and mouthwashes need to be locked away safely. Remove keys and catches from the bathroom door to prevent a toddler from accidentally locking himself in. Instead, place a bolt high up on the inside of the door, where your child can't reach it.

in the bedroom

Your baby or child will spend a lot of time on his own in his bedroom, so you need to be confident that it's as safe as you can make it. To avoid the risks of overheating and suffocation, follow the advice on the prevention of crib death (see page 101).

♦ **Bedding** Duvets, crib bumpers, and sheepskins are not recommended for young babies because of the risk of overheating or suffocation. Make up your baby's crib so that his feet are at the foot of the crib and tuck in sheets and blankets securely. Don't give him a pillow before he's a year old.

♦ **Sleep tight** His crib should conform to current safety standards. Position it away from the radiator and out of direct sunlight. Keep the crib rail up until your

toddler tries to climb out, then leave it down.

♦ **Crib toys** Don't put toys in your baby's crib because they might suffocate him. Ideally, don't tie toys to the rails, but if you do, make sure the string is secure and less than 10in (25cm) long.

♦ **Changing stations** If you change him on a bed or changing table, keep your eye on him at all times. A mat on the floor is safest.

♦ **Secure windows** Install locks and window guards.

Safe and warm
Cover radiators in the most efficient way you can in order to protect your baby from burns.

other people's homes

You and your family may have done everything possible to make your own home safe, but there will be times when you're visiting other people, who may not have the same approach to safety as you do. If they don't have children, it's unlikely they've given much thought to child safety, or if their children are grown up, they may no longer have measures in place.

♦ **A close watch** In other people's houses, you need to be even more vigilant than in your own home. All the same, try to relax – you don't want anxiety to spoil your visit. Your child is bound to find things to explore safely. Just keep an eye on him.

♦ **Other children** If there are other children, be aware that they may not want to share everything, and that some of their toys may be unsuitable for your child.

♦ **Baby-sitting** If you plan to leave your child with someone else at their home for a couple of hours, talk about safety with them first. Fill them in on what your child can, and does, get into, and bring equipment, such as gates for the top and bottom of the stairs, if necessary. Anyone who takes care of your child should be only too willing to discuss any safety issues around her home and resolve them before your child arrives. But ultimately, if you're not convinced that a caretaker is safety-conscious enough, don't entrust your child to her.

home **visits**

Don't be embarrassed to talk about safety when you visit other people's homes – if you plan to leave your child there, it's vital.

♦ Check the room for potential hazards, and be extra watchful since you may be distracted while talking.

♦ Make sure others keep their mugs of hot tea or coffee out of reach.

♦ Be cautious of pets.

♦ Bring with you any equipment you may need and toys to keep your child out of mischief.

♦ Ask to close doors to rooms that may be particularly unsafe.

in the backyard

It's great for children to have a chance to play outside in the fresh air. If you have access to a backyard, there's a whole world for your child to explore and play in. But backyards also have their hazards. To help your child spend his time outdoors safely, spend awhile planning how to reduce the risks.

♦ **Secure your yard** Make sure that your child can't get out into the street by locking gates securely and keeping fences maintained. Remember that a child can drown in as little as 2in (5cm) of water. So if you have a pond, for the time being drain it, cover it with strong wire mesh or a trellis, or securely fence it off. Never leave your child unsupervised in a wading pool and always empty it after use.

♦ **Poisonous plants** Many plants are poisonous, among them yew, foxgloves, lupins, lobelia, and lily of the valley. Dig them up if possible, or make sure your child doesn't play in them. Teach him from an early age not to eat berries or plants from the garden. Get rid of all toadstools and fungi as soon as they appear.

♦ **Perfect pets** If you have a dog, make sure he doesn't relieve himself in the garden, or clean up immediately if he does. You can't prevent cats from doing so, but teach your child not to put things in his mouth, especially soil.

♦ **Check equipment** Regularly check jungle gyms and other backyard toys for safety, and make sure that little fingers can't get trapped in folding garden furniture. Use lawnmowers and other garden tools only when your child is not around. Keep equipment and chemicals locked away.

in the **park**

A trip to the park can be a fun outing that's good exercise for you and your child. Here's how to avoid accidents.

♦ Remember, there's no substitute for supervising your child.

♦ Use a play area that's properly fenced in to prevent your child from wandering off and to keep dogs out (see *Toxocara canis*, page 255).

♦ Swings should be right for your child's age. Children under one need the box type. Don't let him run near swings.

♦ Jungle gyms should be over a soft surface, not concrete.

♦ Be careful on slides, especially if your child tries to slow down with his feet.

♦ Playground equipment should not have any exposed screws or bolts.

Pond risks
While your child is still young, cover your pond with a grid or strong netting, or put a secure fence around it. Alternatively, consider draining it and filling it in until he's older.

out and about

Whatever your child's age, you need to consider his safety when you're on the road. It can be a nuisance to take precautions when you're going on a short car trip, but accidents can happen anywhere and in a split second, so it's just as important to protect your child when you go around the corner as when you're heading farther away.

Carriages and strollers

♦ **Strap in** Always make sure your child's harness and lap belt are buckled on every trip. If you do this from the very start, your child will have no trouble accepting it as part of the normal routine.

♦ **Well balanced** Keep the stroller well maintained and never hang heavy shopping bags from the handles or it may tip over.

On foot

♦ **Street drill** As soon as your child is old enough to walk alongside you, start training him on how to cross the street safely. Even though at this stage you'll be holding his hand, you can provide a running commentary. Tell him that you're finding

Streetwise
When you're out, talk to your child about street safety from an early age. Always cross streets safely yourself to set a good example.

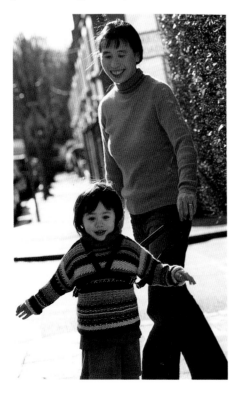

a safe place to cross, that you're looking and listening before you cross and while you cross. Explain traffic lights to him. To establish good habits on pedestrian crossings, always wait for the sign saying that it's safe to cross even if the road is clear, and never run across the street.

In the car

♦ **Safe journey** Holding a baby or child in your arms in the car isn't safe because in the event of an accident or sudden stop, your weight could injure him. You must provide a special car seat for him. Always choose a car seat that meets published safety standards, and buy it new to avoid possible hazards such as worn fittings and straps, or the possibility that it may have been in a car accident.

♦ **A good fit** Not all car seats suit every car, so before buying one, check that the seat you choose fits your particular model. The seat-belt buckle must never rest on the car-seat frame because it could snap in a crash. When fitting the car seat, pull the seat belt tight – the car seat should sit firmly and not move from side to side. If you're not sure, get professional help. NEVER put your child in a car seat on a passenger seat that has an airbag immediately in front of it – an inflated airbag can seriously harm or even kill a child. Check the car seat every time you go out in the car.

♦ **Correct choice** Make sure you have the right type of car seat for your child's size – his weight is a better guide than his age. Rear-facing seats are for babies from newborn up to about 22–28lb (10–13kg) weight. Depending on your baby's rate of growth, this will probably last 12 months or so. Forward-facing car seats are for children weighing from 22lb (10kg) up to 40lb (18kg). Your child could be in this for

Adjust his safety harness to fit on every journey.

Car seat
You can install your own car seat, but follow instructions carefully. Seek professional advice, if needed.

several years, so choose a model that you can use day in and day out. The ideal buckle is one that you can open easily, but that's too hard for your child to undo.

♦ **No distractions** Having purchased the seat, always use it. The harness must be adjusted and fastened securely on every trip, however short it may be. Babies often enjoy the car, but sometimes they cry from frustration, tiredness, or boredom. If this happens, stop the car as soon as you can. It's dangerous to drive with the distraction of a screaming baby or child. Toddlers sometimes try to undo their buckles. If your child succeeds, stop the car as soon as it's safe to do so. Secure the buckle again and tell him not to undo it. If he persists, stop the car again. It's a safety issue, so you mustn't give in, however willful your child may be. Be firm, but try not to get angry. If you need to attend to your child for any reason during the journey, stop the car. It's dangerous to take your eyes off the road for even a fraction of a second.

on vacation

Travel has many benefits for your child. With a little advance planning, you can have a great time on vacation with your baby or young child. Try to choose a destination that will be relaxing for you as well as safe for your child. You may not go far afield the first couple of years, but as time goes by you can be more adventurous.

Protective headgear
Babies and young children should always wear a sun hat. Choose one that has a wide brim and a flap to protect the back of the neck.

Going abroad

♦ **Immunizations** Your child's basic immunizations (see page 216) must be up to date. Depending on your destination, he may need other vaccinations or anti-malaria medicine. Ask your doctor since you can't always rely on the information provided by travel agents.

♦ **Proper paperwork** Don't forget that your baby needs a ticket, his own passport, and other travel documents, according to current regulations. Check that your travel insurance provides for all your medical needs abroad.

Travel by air

♦ **Flying high** Reserve your seats well in advance. If your child is under two, ask for a seat where you can install a car-safety seat. Pack plenty of diapers in your hand luggage, along with any milk or other food. Airlines can't always provide meals for youngsters, but are usually happy to heat up milk or food that parents have brought with them.

♦ **Air pressure** If you have a baby, give him a breast- or bottle-feeding (or a pacifier)

travel sickness

Any time from 18 months or so, your child may develop motion sickness. Most children grow out of it by adolescence.

♦ Make sure that your child can see out of the window when you are traveling in a car, plane, or ship.

♦ Adjust ventilation to get some fresh air and offer small but frequent meals rather than no meals.

♦ Don't give him books to distract him – play games such as "I-Spy" instead.

♦ Keep available a supply of bags, paper towels, and a change of clothes for your child, just in case.

during ascent and descent to avoid earache from pressure changes in the aircraft. A child can chew or suck on a candy, but supervise him in case he chokes. To prevent dehydration, give your child plenty to drink during the flight.

♦ **In-flight entertainment** Keep your child entertained with a selection of toys and books. Airlines often provide goody bags for youngsters, but he'll probably want the comfort of his favorite stuffed animal, too.

♦ **Jet lag** If you're traveling across several time zones, your child may be jet-lagged and unsettled for a day or two. Arrange mealtimes and bedtime around the local time as soon as possible. There's no harm in using a dose of your child's usual travel sickness medicine to make him drowsy before bed. See a doctor if he doesn't settle down within a couple of days, in case he's ill.

Sun protection

♦ **Skin care** Because young skin is so much more sensitive than an adult's, your child needs careful protection from the sun to avoid getting burned or overheated. For a baby under six months old, it's best to keep him out of direct sunlight. Use a parasol or sunshade on the carriage or stroller, and put him in a wide-brimmed hat. Keep his arms and legs covered with clothes made of cool but closely woven fabric, such as cotton.

♦ **Block it out** Keep your child out of direct sun at the hottest time of day, usually 10am to 4pm, depending on latitude. The sun is more likely to burn if you're near water, or at a high altitude. Always use a sunscreen to block the damaging ultraviolet rays. All children should use a sunscreen with a sun protection factor (SPF) of at least 30. Apply half an hour before going outside. Many sunscreens are waterproof, but even these need to be

reapplied every three or four hours if your child spends a lot of time in the water. Check the label on the bottle.

♦ **Cooler climates** Even in cooler northern countries a child can be seriously sunburned, making him uncomfortable and increasing his risk of developing skin cancer later in life. So it's smart to carry sunscreen with you when you go outside with your child, at home or on vacation. A cool, cloudy start to the day can give way to sunshine later.

♦ **Drink plenty** To protect against the dehydrating effect of sun and warm weather, make sure your child always has plenty to drink. If you're breastfeeding, offer feedings more often. Bottle-fed babies can have extra drinks of plain water, or fruit juice diluted with water.

Insect protection

♦ **Avoiding stings** Mosquitoes and other insects often love a child's tender skin, so cover up your baby's or child's arms and legs and smooth on some insect repellent (made for children) in the early evenings, when stinging insects are at their most active. In a malaria area, protection against mosquito bites with repellents and mosquito nets is as important as taking antimalaria medicine.

first aid

Children are inquisitive and often unaware of dangers, so unintentional injuries are common. Thankfully, most are minor, but it's vital to know what to do in an emergency. Learn first aid before you need it so you're prepared if the worst happens.

The first-aid procedures outlined in this section are for guidance only and are not a substitute for an in-depth knowledge of first aid. The best way to protect your family is for you and other caregivers to attend a recognized first-aid and CPR course given by such organizations as the Canadian Red Cross and St John Ambulance Canada. You are more likely to be able to save a child's life if you receive proper first-aid training and keep up-to-date with refresher courses every few years.

CONTENTS

ABC of resuscitation

IF YOUR CHILD IS UNCONSCIOUS, FOLLOW THE ABC OF RESUSCITATION:

A is for Airway **B** is for Breathing **C** is for Circulation.

For a baby (under one year old)

1 Gently stimulate the baby: tap her foot gently. If there's no response **CALL 911 OR ASK SOMEONE TO MAKE THE CALL FOR YOU**, then continue with the ABC of resuscitation. Never shake a baby.

2 Open her airway: on a flat surface, place your hand on her forehead and tilt her head back very gently. Pick out any *obvious* obstruction with your fingertips.

Check for breathing with your ear close to her mouth.

3 Check breathing: put your ear close to her mouth and feel for breaths. Also, look for any chest and tummy movement. Check for 10 seconds.

4 If your baby is breathing: cradle her on her side, supporting her head lower than her body (the recovery position for a baby). Keep her with you and wait for an ambulance. Keep checking her breathing. **If your baby isn't breathing:** begin Rescue Breathing. Put your baby on her back, breathe in, and seal your lips over her mouth and nose. Breathe out until you see her chest rise, then remove your mouth. Give two effective breaths. If her chest doesn't rise, tilt her head and try again to give two effective breaths.

5 Check circulation: look for movement, coughing, or breathing for no more than 10 seconds. If there are signs of circulation, give 20 rescue breaths, one every three seconds, then recheck circulation. Continue this cycle until help comes.

Press down on the chest to a third of its depth.

6 If there are no signs of circulation: start chest compressions combined with rescue breathing (known as CPR). Put her on a firm surface. Place two fingers in the middle of your baby's breastbone, just below the nipple line, and press down to one-third of the depth of her chest five times within a space of three seconds. Give one rescue breath. Continue for one minute, alternating five chest compressions with one rescue breath.

For a child (over one year old):

1 **Check for a response**: call your child's name and gently tap her shoulder to see if she reacts. If there's no response, **CALL 911 OR ASK SOMEONE TO MAKE THE CALL FOR YOU**, then continue with the ABC of resuscitation.

2 **Open her airway**: place one hand on her forehead and gently tilt her head back. Pick out any *obvious* obstruction from her mouth. Gently lift her chin.

Listen for breathing and check if you can feel a breath on your face.

3 **Check breathing**: put your ear close to her mouth and feel for breaths. Also look at her chest and tummy for any movement. Check for 10 seconds.

As you breathe out the chest will rise.

If your child isn't breathing: begin rescue breathing. Place her on her back, pinch her nostrils together, then take a fairly deep breath, and seal your lips around her mouth. Breathe out until you see her chest rise, then remove your mouth and watch it fall. Give two effective breaths, one breath every three seconds. If the chest doesn't rise, tilt her head farther back and try again to give two effective breaths.

5 **Check for signs of circulation**: look for movement, coughing, or breathing for no more than 10 seconds. If there are signs of circulation, give 20 rescue breaths, one every three seconds, then recheck circulation. Continue this cycle until help arrives.

The recovery position

Tilt the head back to ensure the airway is open.

Bend the top leg up to prevent her rolling forward.

4 **If your child is breathing**: put her in the recovery position. Place her on her side on a firm surface, with the uppermost arm and leg up. Tilt her head back to keep the airway open. Wait for the ambulance. Keep checking her breathing until help arrives.

CHOKING

If your baby or child is unconscious and you know he has choked, remove any obstructions (see page 270), then give CPR.

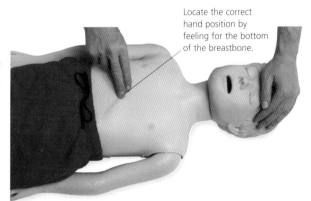

Locate the correct hand position by feeling for the bottom of the breastbone.

6 **If there's no sign of circulation**: start chest compressions combined with rescue breathing (CPR). Maintaining the head tilt with one hand, place a finger of the other hand on the lower tip of your child's breastbone. Replace the finger with the heel of the same hand and press down on the lower part of the breastbone to a third of the depth of her chest five times within a space of three seconds. Give one rescue breath. Continue for one minute, alternating five chest compressions with one rescue breath. Continue CPR until help arrives.

choking

Babies and young children put whatever they find into their mouths, so choking is a common emergency in the very young. It's caused by a piece of food, a toy, or other object becoming lodged in the windpipe. You must dislodge the object quickly to allow your child to breathe properly.

What can I do?

For a child (over one year old):

♦ Ask the child "Are you choking?"

♦ If the child can speak or cough, do not interfere.

♦ Do not feel blindly down the throat to remove an obstruction.

♦ If the child cannot speak or cough, stand or kneel behind him. Wrap your arms around his abdomen just above the line of the hips. Make a fist with one hand and place the thumb side of your fist against the middle of his abdomen, just above his navel.

♦ Grasp your fist with your other hand and press into his abdomen with a quick upward thrust.

♦ Repeat the last two steps as necessary. If he becomes unconscious, **CALL 911 FOR AN AMBULANCE**. Follow your ABC resuscitation protocol (see page 269), looking in his mouth after each cycle until the obstruction is cleared or help arrives.

IN AN EMERGENCY!

CALL 911 FOR AN AMBULANCE if:

♦ your child stops breathing

♦ you cannot free the blockage

♦ your child continues to choke after the blockage has been freed

♦ your child becomes unconscious.

Place a fist just below the rib cage.

FOR A BABY (UNDER ONE YEAR OLD)

♦ Lay your baby face-down along your forearm; give up to five sharp blows on his mid-upper back.

♦ Turn your baby face-up on your arm or lap, keeping the head lower than the chest.

♦ If back blows have failed, give five quick downward chest thrusts (one per second) in the same location as the chest compressions (see page 268).

♦ Repeat until the obstruction has cleared. If the baby becomes unconscious **CALL 911 FOR AN AMBULANCE**, then follow your ABC resuscitation protocol (see page 268), checking the mouth after each set of compressions.

poisoning

Keep all poisons locked away because babies and children are curious by nature. Be aware of poisonous plants as well as alcohol, household chemicals, and medicines. Poisons can also be breathed in or absorbed through the skin.

SYMPTOMS

Symptoms vary depending on the type of poison, but you may notice any of the following:

♦ vomiting

♦ diarrhea or stomach pain

♦ seizures

♦ drowsiness

♦ unconsciousness

♦ burns or discoloration around the mouth

♦ poisonous substance or container nearby.

What can I do?

♦ Try to identify the poison and how much was taken. If possible, ask your child what happened, and do not be angry with him. Remember that young children often put things into their mouths.

♦ Call the Poison Center, and if going to the hospital, bring a sample of the poison or the container to show the doctor.

♦ If you think your child has swallowed a chemical product, wash his skin and lips with water. Don't give your child anything to drink unless it's on your doctor's advice.

♦ If your child vomits, keep a sample to show the doctor, but you should never make your child vomit because this can make his condition worse.

♦ If he is unconscious but breathing, place

IN AN EMERGENCY!

CALL 911 FOR AN AMBULANCE if:

♦ you think your child has swallowed poison; amounts of drugs, vitamins, and alcohol too small to affect an adult can have serious effects on babies and children.

DO NOT make your child vomit unless told to do so by the Poison Center.

him in the recovery position (see page 269).

♦ If your child is unconscious and not breathing, follow the ABC of resuscitation (see pages 268–269). Before you begin rescue breathing, wipe his face with a damp cloth to prevent you from contacting any of the poison.

electric shock

Even safe electrical appliances and sockets can turn into lethal objects if a child pokes fingers or metal objects into them. Electric shocks range from a mild brief tingling sensation to burns and severe shocks that can stop your child's breathing and heartbeat.

SYMPTOMS

- crying from fright
- burns, often small
- muscle spasm
- unconsciousness
- no breathing

What can I do?

- If your child is still in contact with the electricity, the first thing to do is to break the contact between him and the current. Switch the electricity off at the main circuit or pull the plug out. **CALL 911**.

- If you can't do this, stand on some insulating material, such as a pile of newspapers, a telephone directory, or a rubber car mat. Using a dry, non-conducting object, such as a wooden broom handle, very carefully push the electrical source away from your child. Never touch the child until contact is broken.

- If he is unconscious, check his breathing and start Rescue Breathing and CPR if necessary. **CALL 911 FOR AN AMBULANCE.**

- If you find any burns on your child,

CALL 911 FOR AN AMBULANCE. Electrical burns can occur where your child touched the electrical source, but they can also appear on any part of the body that was in contact with the ground. These burns do not always appear serious at first glance, but they can be very deep and always require urgent medical attention.

burns and scalds

The goal is to cool the area as quickly as possible. A burn can be superficial, partial thickness, full thickness, or a combination. Young children often panic if they suffer a burn, and may run around and cry or scream.

A superficial burn involves the outermost layer of skin and is painful. It looks red, but heals well. A partial thickness burn involves the whole of the outer layer and is red, raw, and blistered. A full-thickness burn affects all of the skin layers and can actually be painless because nerve endings are damaged. It may lead to scarring later.

Burns are serious for a child because dehydration and shock can result. For all burns, seek medical help.

What can I do?

- Run cool water over the burn for about 10 minutes. For burns on the trunk, put your child in the bathtub and use a shower, but don't let him get cold because he could develop hypothermia (see page 275). Keep your child warm.
- Do not remove clothing that is stuck to the affected area. It doesn't matter if clothes get wet. If necessary, carefully cut around any clothing that is stuck to the skin.
- Cover the burn with a non-fluffy, sterile dressing. Do not apply adhesive dressings, ointments, gels, butter, fats, Vasoline, etc.
- Get medical help.

SYMPTOMS

- a superficial burn will be red, swollen, and tender
- a partial-thickness burn will be red, blistered, raw, and very painful
- a full-thickness burn often looks white or waxy, or dark and charred; it may be painless

BURNING CLOTHES

- If your child's clothes catch fire, keep him from moving. Don't let him run around even though he may want to.
- Lie him down so the flames cannot burn his face and airway.
- Dowse the flames with water.
- Alternatively, wrap him in a non-flammable (wool or cotton) coat or blanket and roll him on the ground to smother the flames.

Call 911 for an ambulance, even if your child seems well.

seizures

These are caused by temporary electrical overactivity or irregularity in the brain. In young children, the most common cause is a high fever (see pages 224 and 226–227); this causes seizures known as febrile seizures. Other causes of a seizure are a recent head injury, tumors, certain illnesses, poisoning, infection, or congenital brain defects. Seizures are usually isolated events, but children with epilepsy have repeated attacks (see page 261).

SYMPTOMS

♦ noisy breathing or breath holding
♦ sudden loss of consciousness
♦ rigid muscles, followed by jerking limbs
♦ temporary loss of control over bodily functions; for instance, your child may wet or soil herself
♦ possible frothing at the mouth; bloodstained if she has bitten her tongue

What can I do?

DO NOT attempt to restrain your child in any way. Your initial reaction is often to try to prevent your child from flailing, but you must let the seizure run its course. The only reason for ever moving her during a seizure is to keep her from getting hurt, for instance, by moving her from the path of an oncoming car.

♦ Clear a space around your child to stop her from hurting herself on surrounding objects.
♦ Note the seizure's start and finish times.
♦ Stay with your child to reassure her when the attack is over.
♦ If she has a fever and is awake, try to bring down her temperature (see pages 224 and 226).
♦ If your child is unconscious after the seizure, check breathing. If she is breathing, put her in the recovery position (see page 269) and summon help. If she is not breathing, begin rescue breathing and CPR if necessary (see pages 268–269).

IN AN EMERGENCY!

CALL 911 FOR AN AMBULANCE if:
♦ your child has not had a seizure before
♦ she has had a recent head injury
♦ the attack lasts for more than 10 minutes.
If you are unsure what to do, call the doctor.

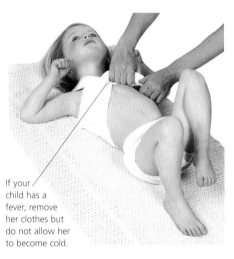

If your child has a fever, remove her clothes but do not allow her to become cold.

anaphylactic shock

This is a rare, severe allergic reaction to particular stings, foods (especially nuts), or drugs causing constriction of the air passages. Symptoms may develop within a few minutes of the child ingesting the food or drug or being stung. The face and neck can swell during a reaction, and this increases the risk of suffocation.

SYMPTOMS

♦ red, blotchy rash all over the body
♦ puffy eyelids or face
♦ rapid, shallow breathing
♦ rapid or weak pulse
♦ clammy skin
♦ anxiety or confusion
♦ wheezing or difficulty breathing
♦ unconsciousness

What can I do?

CALL 911 FOR AN AMBULANCE.
♦ Help your child into the position that best enables her to breathe and loosen any tight clothing.

♦ Reassure her while you wait for the ambulance to arrive. Check her breathing and pulse every few minutes.
♦ If your child loses consciousness, assess her condition and check to see if she is breathing. If she is breathing, put her in the recovery position and wait for help.

IN AN EMERGENCY!

CALL 911 FOR AN AMBULANCE if:
♦ you suspect your child is suffering an anaphylactic shock.

♦ If she stops breathing, begin rescue breathing immediately (see pages 268–269).
♦ If your child has a known allergy, she may have medication to take in case of an attack: use this as soon as possible after exposure or as soon as the attack starts.

Put your child in the recovery position while you wait for the ambulance.

fractures, sprains, and dislocations

Young children's bones are more flexible than an adult's, so broken bones are unusual in this age group. Until the diagnosis of a break, sprain, or dislocation has been confirmed by a doctor, you should treat the injury in the way described below. Partial breaks, known as greenstick fractures, mend easily. Sprains, where the ligaments are damaged, cause symptoms similar to a broken bone, but usually are less severe. If one or more bones slip out of place, the joint is dislocated.

IN AN EMERGENCY!

CALL 911 FOR AN AMBULANCE if:
♦ you can't support the injured part while you take your child to the hospital yourself
♦ you suspect an injury to the spine.

SYMPTOMS
♦ severe pain and tenderness
♦ swelling
♦ deformity of the affected area, for instance a limb may look misshapen or shorter than the other
♦ inability or reluctance to use the injured part

What can I do?
♦ Do not move your child unless absolutely necessary. Remove any clothing that is constricting the injured area.
♦ Immobilize the injured limb by strapping it to an uninjured part of the body. Support an injured arm in a sling, but do not attempt to bend an injured elbow. If you suspect a neck or spine injury, DO NOT move the child or lift her head. Immobilize her by placing padding around her, and then **CALL 911 FOR AN AMBULANCE.**
♦ Do not give your child anything to eat or drink since broken bones and dislocations may require sedation.

Arm slings support the arm or wrist, or take the weight off the shoulder.

Elevation slings are used to reduce bleeding, pain or swelling.

finger and toe injuries

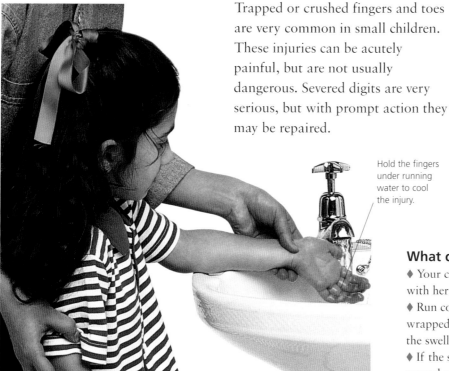

Trapped or crushed fingers and toes are very common in small children. These injuries can be acutely painful, but are not usually dangerous. Severed digits are very serious, but with prompt action they may be repaired.

Hold the fingers under running water to cool the injury.

IN AN EMERGENCY!

CALL 911 FOR AN AMBULANCE if:
♦ a finger or toe is severed.
Put the severed part in a plastic bag and wrap the bag in a cloth for protection. Place the bag in a container filled with ice and label with the name of your child and the time of the incident. Apply pressure to the limb to stop the bleeding.

What can I do?
♦ Your child may be frightened and in pain, so stay with her and reassure her.
♦ Run cool water over the injured part or apply ice, wrapped in a clean cloth, or an ice pack to reduce the swelling.
♦ If the skin is broken, apply direct pressure over the wound and raise the limb. Apply a clean dressing.

head injury

Children often bump their heads, and fortunately most incidents are not serious. Any cut to the scalp or forehead will bleed profusely, which is distressing for both parent and child. Severe blows to the head can result in compression of the brain. A child may not show symptoms until several hours after the injury, so it is important to be able to spot them.

What can I do?

♦ If your child's head is bruised, apply a cold compress to the bruised area. This can be a cloth wrung out in cold water or an ice pack wrapped in a clean, damp cloth.

♦ Keep checking the bruise.

♦ If there is bleeding, place a clean cloth over the injury and press on the wound.

♦ Check for any unusual symptoms for up to 24 hours (see *In an Emergency!*, right).

♦ If your child is unconscious or the bump is severe:
CALL 911 FOR AN AMBULANCE.

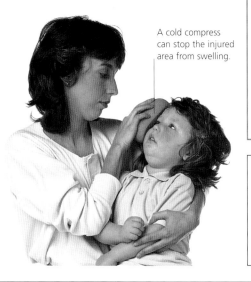

A cold compress can stop the injured area from swelling.

IN AN EMERGENCY!

CALL 911 FOR AN AMBULANCE if your child displays any unusual behavior or any of the following symptoms up to 24 hours after receiving a head injury:
♦ unconsciousness (even if very brief)
♦ vomiting
♦ noisy breathing or unusual snoring
♦ double vision
♦ drowsiness or loss of coordination
♦ dislike of bright light or headache
♦ discharge from the nose or ear
♦ unusual crying.

UNCONSCIOUSNESS

If your child loses consciousness, check breathing. If he's not breathing, send a helper to call an ambulance and start Rescue Breathing. If he is breathing, put him in the recovery position, then call an ambulance.

drowning

Even very shallow water can be a hazard to babies and children, so never leave a young child alone in or near water. Drowning can kill because inhaled water stops air from getting into the lungs. It can also stop breathing by causing a spasm of the throat. In addition, cold water can bring on hypothermia (see opposite).

What can I do?

♦ If you can do so safely, pull your child out of the water. Be very careful if there is any chance that he might have injured his neck or back.

♦ Do not endanger your own life trying to rescue a child from drowning. If you cannot reach the child safely unaided, summon help.

♦ **If your child is conscious,** give him comfort and reassurance. He is at risk of hypothermia so keep him warm, but don't heat him up too quickly.
CALL 911 FOR AN AMBULANCE.

♦ **If your child is unconscious but breathing,** place him in the recovery position and **CALL 911 FOR AN AMBULANCE.** If he is coughing, choking, or vomiting, he is breathing.

Cover your child with a blanket, towel, or coat to prevent hypothermia.

♦ **If your child is unconscious** and is not breathing, clear any debris you can see from his mouth and begin Rescue Breathing and CPR if necessary (see pages 268–269).
CALL 911 FOR AN AMBULANCE

IN AN EMERGENCY!

CALL 911 FOR AN AMBULANCE even if your child seems to have recovered now. This is because the airway can swell up later.

and continue CPR until help arrives or he begins breathing. If he begins breathing, put him in the recovery position and keep him warm.

Cover your child with a towel or blanket to keep him warm.

hypothermia

This happens when the body temperature becomes dangerously low, causing body functions to slow down and eventually stop. Babies can develop it very easily (see box right), but in older children, it is most likely to occur after playing outside in very cold conditions or falling into cold water.

SYMPTOMS

♦ shivering
♦ very cold, pale skin
♦ weakening pulse
♦ listlessness
♦ slow, shallow breathing
♦ decreasing consciousness

What can I do?

♦ The most important thing is to warm your child gradually. Do not put a source of direct heat, such as a hot water bottle, next to your child's skin.

♦ Change his wet clothes for dry ones. Wrap him in warm towels or blankets, or dress him in warm clothes, including a hat, and put him to bed in a warm room.

Help your child to sip a warm drink.

IN AN EMERGENCY!

CALL 911 FOR AN AMBULANCE if your child loses consciousness. Begin the ABC of resuscitation (see pages 268–269).

♦ Give him a warm drink and some high-energy food. Do not leave your child alone.
CALL THE DOCTOR.

HYPOTHERMIA IN BABIES

Temperature regulation is not fully developed in the very young, so babies may lose warmth rapidly and can even develop hypothermia in a cold room.

Symptoms include:
♦ pink, healthy-looking skin that feels cold
♦ limp, unusually quiet baby
♦ refusal to feed.

Increase your baby's temperature GRADUALLY in a warm room:
♦ replace any wet or damp clothes
♦ put a hat on his head
♦ wrap him in a blanket
♦ use your body heat to warm him by cuddling him against your body.
CALL THE DOCTOR.

heat exhaustion and heatstroke

These happen when the body becomes severely overheated. Both heat exhaustion and heatstroke usually occur in hot weather. Heat exhaustion is due to loss of body salts and water due to excessive sweating. Heatstroke is a failure of the body's temperature-control system.

SYMPTOMS

Heat exhaustion
♦ headache and dizziness
♦ cramplike pains in limbs or abdomen
♦ pale, clammy skin and sweating
♦ rapid, weak pulse

Heatstroke
♦ hot, flushed dry skin
♦ temperature above 104°F (40°C)
♦ rapid loss of consciousness

What can I do?

For heat exhaustion
Lay your child down in a cool place and remove his outer clothing. Use a folded towel or pillow to raise his legs. Reassure your child and give him sips of water.

For heatstroke
Heatstroke strikes quickly and your child may lose consciousness. To help prevent this, lay him down somewhere cool and remove his clothes. Cover him with a cool,

IN AN EMERGENCY!

CALL 911 FOR AN AMBULANCE if:
♦ your child loses consciousness or fails to improve
♦ your baby is under a year old.
Open the airway, check breathing, and be ready to start Rescue Breathing (see pages 268–269). If he is breathing, put him in the recovery position.

wet sheet and fan him. Alternatively, you can sponge him down with tepid (not cold) water until his temperature drops to about 100.4°F (38°C) (see page 227).

insect bites and stings

These can be very upsetting and painful for a young child, but most bites and stings are not serious. Some people do develop a severe allergic reaction, known as anaphylactic shock, and while this is rare, it is important to be able to spot the warning signs (see page 272).

SYMPTOMS

♦ your child may be panicking or crying after a sting
♦ the area stung may be red, often with a central white area and a tiny hole, or punctum, showing the site of the sting
♦ alternatively, the stinger may still be visible
♦ insect bites are usually bigger than stings, especially horsefly bites, which are ragged

What can I do?

♦ Bites and stings can be frightening, so it is important to calm your child down and reassure her that she'll be all right.
♦ Keep her as still as possible so you can look at the sting or bite. If the stinger is still in the skin, scrape it off using your fingernail or the back of a knife or a credit card.
♦ Hold a cloth wrung out in ice-cold water or a bag filled with icecubes and wrapped in a towel over the area to ease the pain and swelling. See the doctor if a sting or bite gets worse in a few hours or days.

Use a fingernail or blunt edge to brush the stinger off.

♦ If your child has been stung in the mouth, give her a cold drink or a Popsicle to suck, then take her straight to the hospital. If she has trouble breathing, don't give her anything to drink.
♦ If your child collapses, she may be suffering an allergic reaction to the sting (see *anaphylactic shock*, page 272).

IN AN EMERGENCY!

CALL 911 FOR AN AMBULANCE if:
♦ your child has difficulty breathing
♦ she has been stung in the mouth or throat
♦ she has been bitten by a snake, spider, or scorpion, or has a severe jellyfish sting
♦ she feels dizzy or faints
♦ she develops a widespread rash.

POISON IVY

The rashes of poison ivy, poison sumac, and poison oak are caused by plant resins. Sensitivity to the resin varies. After exposure, remove the resin with soap and cool water or use rubbing alcohol as a solvent. To soothe the itching, dab the rash with calamine lotion, or bathe the area with Aveeno oatmeal in one cup of tepid water.

If the rash is widespread, **CALL THE DOCTOR**.

cuts, grazes, and bleeding

Cuts and grazes are common in childhood and can usually be treated at home as long as they are not dirty or infected, but severe bleeding is serious and requires swift action.

What can I do?

Cuts and grazes

♦ Wash your hands. Rinse the wound or wipe around it with an antiseptic wipe or cotton ball and warm water.
♦ Remove any particles of dirt or gravel. DO NOT remove any embedded objects.
♦ Put a dressing over the wound and change daily.
♦ If an object is embedded call the doctor.

Severe bleeding

♦ If there is severe bleeding, apply direct pressure to the wound and raise the limb above the level of your child's heart.

Raise the injured part above the heart to reduce the bleeding.

IN AN EMERGENCY!

GO TO THE HOSPITAL if:
♦ your child has a large, deep, or jagged cut
♦ she has severe bleeding
♦ she has a bad cut on the face
♦ she has a cut or graze that is very dirty
♦ she has a puncture wound caused by something dirty
♦ she has something embedded in the wound.

♦ Dress the wound with a clean, non-fluffy pad secured with a bandage.
♦ Lay your child down if you suspect shock, keeping the injured part raised, then **CALL 911 FOR AN AMBULANCE**.

foreign bodies in the ears, eyes, or nose

Young children often push items such as pieces of food, small beads, or marbles into their ears or noses. It is very important to supervise young children and not allow them to play with small items such as these until they are old enough to understand the danger they can pose.

What can I do?

♦ Reassure your child. She may be afraid that you'll be angry with her.

♦ If the object is in your child's nose, ask her to gently blow her nose (if she is old enough to understand). Otherwise, or if this does not work, calmly reassure your child, tell her to breathe through her mouth

and then **GO TO THE HOSPITAL**.

♦ Do not attempt to remove the object yourself because you may inadvertently push it farther in.

♦ If the object is in her ear, do not attempt to remove it yourself. Try to find out what the object is. Reassure her and **GO TO THE HOSPITAL**.

IN AN EMERGENCY!

GO TO THE HOSPITAL if:
♦ your child cannot remove a foreign object from her nose by blowing it
♦ your child has pushed an object into her ear
♦ you are unable to dislodge an object from her eye by washing it
♦ the object is on the colored part of the eye
♦ the eye is bleeding.

FOREIGN OBJECT IN THE EYE

Particles of dirt and eyelashes often get into the eye, but they can usually be removed fairly easily.

♦ Pain, blurred vision, or a red, watering eye may indicate a foreign object lodged in the eye and your child may rub her eye.

♦ If the eye is irritated, but you cannot actually see the object, take her to a doctor because she may have an eye infection, or the foreign object could be hidden under the eyelid.

♦ Reassure your child and try to stop her from rubbing the eye.

♦ If you can see the object on the white of the eye, pour clean, cold water over the eye. Tilt her head and aim the water over the inner corner so that water will wash over the eye toward the outer corner.

♦ If this does not work, try to remove the object using a clean cotton swab moistened with water.

♦ **DO NOT** touch the colored part of the eye or the pupil; both of these are covered with a thin layer of cornea, which is very easily scratched, even with a cotton ball.

If you are still unable to dislodge the object or it is on the pupil or colored part of the eye, **GO TO THE HOSPITAL**.

Aim the water over the inner corner so that it washes the eye.

nosebleeds

Nosebleeds are very common in childhood and can be the result of rough play, nosepicking, or excessive nose blowing. Some children are prone to nosebleeds.

What can I do?

♦ Help your child to sit upright, leaning slightly forward.

♦ Pinch the nostrils together below the bridge of the nose for 10 minutes. Don't release them during this time just to see if the bleeding has stopped.

♦ Encourage your child to breathe through her mouth and spit out the

Pinch the nostrils firmly together.

IN AN EMERGENCY!

GET MEDICAL HELP if:
♦ your child's nose is still bleeding after 30 minutes.

blood rather than swallow it.

♦ If her nose is still bleeding after 10 minutes, reapply pressure for two more 10-minute periods. If the nose is still bleeding, get medical help.

♦ Speak to your doctor if your child has frequent or very heavy nosebleeds.

useful addresses

pregnancy and birth

Canadian Association of Midwives

Website: http://members.rogers.com/
canadianmidwives

Canadian Council for Tobacco Control

75 Albert Street
Suite 508
Ottawa, ON
K1P 5E7
Tel: (800) 267-5234
Website: www.cctc.ca
National organization providing support
to help stop smoking

Canadian Medical Association

1867 Alta Vista Drive
Ottawa, ON
K1G 3Y6
Tel: (613) 731-9331
Website: www.cma.ca

Canadian Women's Health Network

419 Graham Avenue
Suite 203
Winnipeg, MB
R3C 0M3
Tel: (204) 942-5500
Website: www.cwhn.ca

College of Family Physicians of Canada

2630 Skymark Avenue
Mississauga, ON
L4W 5A4
Tel: (905) 629-0900
Website: www.cfpc.ca

Dieticians of Canada

408 University Avenue
Suite 604
Toronto, ON
M5G 1V2
Tel: (416) 596-0603
Website: www.dieticians.ca
An association of food and nutrition
professionals committed to the health and
well-being of Canadians

Doula CARE (Canadian Association Registry and Education)

Maple Grove Village
PO Box 61058
Oakville, ON
L6J 6X0
Tel: (888) 879-3199

Infertility Awareness Association of Canada

PO Box 23025
Ottawa, ON
K2A 4E2
Tel: (800) 263-2929
Website: www.iaac.ca
A national charitable organization
providing awareness, education and
support to those with infertility concerns

Motherisk Program

Hospital for Sick Children
555 University Avenue
Toronto, ON
M5G 1X8
Tel: (416) 813-6780
Website: www.motherisk.org
Information on prescription and over-the-
counter medications and their effects on
pregnancy and breastfeeding

Multiple Births Canada

PO Box 432
Wasaga Beach, ON
L0L 2P0
Tel: (866) 228-8824
Website: www.multiplebirthscanada.org
Provides support to multiple birth
individuals and their families

Multiple Birth Families Association

PO Box 5532
Station F
Ottawa, ON
K2C 3M1
Tel: (613) 860-6565
Website: www.mbfa.ca

National Institute of Nutrition

408 Queen Street
3rd Floor
Ottawa, ON
K1R 5A7
Tel: (613) 235-7032
Website: www.nin.ca
Provides nutrition advice and has a
find-a-dietician directory

Sidelines Canada

31 Iona Street
Ottawa ON
K1Y 3L6
Tel: (877) 271-7433
Website: www.sidelinescanada.org
A non-profit prenatal support network
for women experiencing complicated
pregnancies

Society of Obstetricians & Gynaecologists of Canada

780 Echo Drive
Ottawa, ON
K1S 5R7
Tel: (800) 561-2416
Website: http://sogc.medical.org

baby and childcare

La Leche League of Canada Breastfeeding Referral Service

18c Industrial Drive
PO Box 29
Chesterville, ON
K0C 1H0
Tel: (800) 665-4324
Website: www.lalecheleaguecanada.org
Support, advice, and help for breastfeeding

PASS-CAN – Postpartum Adjustment Support Services Canada
PO Box 7282
Station Main
3–460 Woody Road
Oakville, ON
Tel: (905) 844-9009

development

Canadian Association of Family Resource Programs
707–331 Cooper Street
Ottawa, ON
K2P 0G5
Tel: (613) 237-7667
Website: www.frp.ca

Canadian Child Care Federation
383 Parkdale Avenue
Ottawa, ON
K1Y 4R4
Tel: (800) 858-1412
Website: www.cccf-fcsge.ca

Canadian Parents Online
45 Coulter Avenue
St Thomas, ON
N5R 5A5
Tel: (519) 637-7342
Website: www.canadianparents.com

Dads Can
St Joseph's Health Care
268 Grosvenor Street
PO Box 34
London, ON
N6A 4V2
Tel: (888) 323-7226
Website: www.dadscan.org
Provides support for fathers and offers links to sites for dads

health

Autism Society Canada
PO Box 65
Orangeville, ON
Tel: (519) 942-8720
Website: www.autismsocietycanada.ca

Bereaved Families of Ontario
36 Eglinton Avenue West
Suite 206
Toronto, ON
M4R 1A1
Tel: (416) 440-0290
Website: www.bereavedfamilies.net
Each province may have its own bereavement services

Canada Safety Council
1020 Thomas Spratt Place
Ottawa, ON
K1G 5L5
Tel: (613) 739-1535
Website: www.safety-council.org

Canadian Association of the Deaf
251 Bank Street
Suite 203
Ottawa, ON
K2P 1X3
Tel: (613) 565-2882
Website: www.cad.ca

Canadian Association of Speech-Language Pathologists and Audiologists
401–200 Elgin Street
Ottawa, ON
K2P 1L5
Tel: (800) 259-8519
Website: www.caslpa.org

Canadian Cystic Fibrosis Foundation
2221 Yonge Street
Suite 601
Toronto, ON
M4S 2B4
Tel: (800) 378-2233
Website: www.cysticfibrosis.ca

Canadian Down Syndrome Society
811–14th Street NW
Calgary, AB
T2N 2A4
Tel: (800) 883-5608
Website: www.cdss.ca

Canadian Foundation for the Study of Infant Death
586 Eglinton Avenue East
Suite 308
Toronto, ON
M4P 1P2
Tel: (416) 488-3260
Website: www.sidscanada.org

Canadian Immunization Awareness Program
Canadian Public Health Association
400–1565 Carling Avenue
Ottawa, ON
K1Z 8R1
Tel: (613) 725-3769
Website: www.immunize.cpha.ca

Canadian Institute of Child Health
384 Bank Street
Suite 300
Ottawa, ON
K2P 1Y4
Tel: (613) 230-8838
Website: www.cich.ca

Canadian Mental Health Association
8 King Street East
Suite 810
Toronto, ON
M5C 1B5
Tel: (416) 484-7750
Website: www.cmha.ca

Canadian Pediatric Society
2204 Walkley Road
Suite 100
Ottawa, ON
K1G 4GS
Tel: (613) 526-9397
Website: www.cps.ca

Canadian Red Cross
170 Metcalfe Street
Ottawa, ON
K2P 2P2
Tel: (613) 740-1900
Website: www.redcross.ca

Children's Aid Societies
Website: www.childwelfare.ca

**Children's Safety Association
of Canada**
385 The West Mall
Suite 250
Etobicoke, ON
M9C 1E7
Tel: (416) 620-1584
Website: www.safekid.org

Children's Wish Foundation
95 Bayly Street
Suite 404
Ajax, ON
L1S 7K8
Tel: (800) 700-4437
Website: www.childrenswish.ca

**Heart and Stroke Foundation
of Canada**
222 Queen Street
Suite 1402
Ottawa, ON
K1P 5V9
Tel: (613) 569-4361
Website: www.heartandstroke.ca

Juvenile Diabetes Foundation
7100 Woodbine Avenue
Suite 311
Markham, ON
L3R 5J2
Tel: (877) 287-3533
Website: www.jdrf.ca

**Learning Disabilities Association
of Canada**
323 Chapel Street
Ottawa, ON
K1N 7Z2
Tel: (800) 238-5721
Website: www.ldac-taac.ca

**Muscular Dystrophy Association
of Canada**
2345 Yonge Street
Suite 900
Toronto, ON
M4P 2E5
Tel: (800) 567-2873
Website: www.mdac.ca

**Spina Bifida and Hydrocephalus
Association of Canada**
977–167 Lombard Avenue
Winnipeg, MB
R3B 0V3
Tel: (204) 925-3650
Website: www.sbhac.ca

**Parent Help Line
Kids Help Phone National Office**
439 University Avenue
Suite 300
Toronto, ON
M5G 1Y8
Tel: (416) 586-5437
Website: www.parentsinfo.sympatico.ca

Safe Kids Canada
180 Dundas Street West
Toronto, ON
M5G 1Z8
Tel: (888) 723-3847
Website: www.safekidscanada.org

notes
immunization record and important milestones

index

acknowledgments

Dr. Carol Cooper would like to thank her agent Catherine Clarke, Anna Davidson and her team at DK, Alison Pottle of the cardiology department at Harefield Hospital, and Maria Buckingham of Chorleywood Health Centre.

Dorling Kindersley would like to thank the following writers:
Pregnancy: Joanna Moorhead
Baby and child care: Tracey Godridge
Development: 0–6 months Katy Holland; 6–12 months Tracey Godridge; 12–24 months and 24–36 months Harriet Griffey

Dorling Kindersley would also like to thank Tracey Ward, Nicola Rodway, Caroline Buckingham, Jennifer Crake, Madeleine Jennings and Salima Hirani for their contributions to this book.

Medical consultants Georgia Rose, CNM, MS; Catherine A. Hansen, MD; Laurie Solomon, MD
Americanizer Aviva Schein, MD
Proofreader Lucas Mansell
Indexer Nanette Cardon

Illustrators Debbie Maizels and Philip Wilson
Models Whippersnappers Day Nursery, Felstead, Essex; Kasey Berhardsen and Simon Alpin with Lowell, Tracey Townsend, Mark, Sally, Harvey, and Sidney Barron; Arucha with Eya Choudhury, Esmari with Jeanri Burger, Fiona with Beatrice and Tabitha Ashley-Norman, Anne, and Roland with Callum Nightingale, Danny with Violet Mermelstein, Mark and Lupia with Sasha Noor, Beej with Ria Shah, Chris Nunn and Julia Nicholls with Lauren, Erin with Gabriel Sorensen, Darren and Louise with Inca Rix, Alison with Leo and Evie Dolon, Julia Harris and Colin with Mari Short, Doug, Tali, Noa, Ella, and Gil Krikler, Joe Ejiofor and Anne Stenett with Lauren, Jeanette and Paul with Daisy Copperwaite, Famoush Bikdeli with Dara Adjudani, Lorna with Rhys and Bethan Holland, Mr. and Mrs. Stennett, Colin and Veronique with baby Bozunga, Beth and Biraj with Emma Parma, Sarah and baby Broome, Jo with Jade Salliger, Jason with Kasia Wall, Linda with Mackenzie Quick, Simon with Oban Murrell, Rachana with Arianna Shah, Penny with Anastasia Stephens, Thimmie with Emily Pickering, Andrea with Joel Peters, Rachel with Zoe Nayani, Rachel with baby Best, Isabelle with Carla Wicker-Jourdan, Alison with Phoebe Lee, Tali with Gil Krikler, Denise with Kymani and Kymarley Woodstock, Helen with Joseph Jack and Leo Stiles, Mulki with Wyse Ali, Janis and Maureen Lopatkin with Mia Lopatkin, Mr. & Mrs. Kiyomura with Eri, Michelle with Charlie Terras, Ivor with Ruby Baddiel, Rachel with Zoe Nayani, Maria with Jasmine Leitch, Lilian with Gregory Maya, Tracey with James Coleman-Ward, Faith Knight with her dad, Janis and Maureen Lopatkin with Mia Lopatkin, Mrs. Sugiya with Nana and sister, Lina with Anna Maria Sheridan, Shelley with Sadie Goswell, Penny with Evie McCann, Kay with Ben Whiteley, Lynn with Esme Spencer, Carol with Hannah Tennant, Nicki with Max Riggall, Tina with Lewis Oakey, Fiona with Ellie Messer, Sarah with Phoebe Berman, Simon with Lauren Murrell, Deborah with Aaron Bright, Mr. and Mrs. Perez, George with Sophia Sirius, Tony with Christina and Louise Aquino, Sima and Tim with Danielle and Tal Randall, Gaynor with Oliver Benveniste, Sue with Anya Dziewulski, Deborah with Sadie Seitler, Meena with Shaun MacNamara, Jane with Luke Rimell, Cheryl and John with Yasmin Weekes, Orlean with Ethan Stennett, Sibel with Lara Peck, Teresa with Isabelle.
Hair and makeup Tracy Townsend

Picture researcher Samantha Nunn
Picture librarians Hayley Smith and Sarah Mills

Picture credits
Dorling Kindersley would like to thank the following for their kind permission to reproduce their photographs: (Abbreviations key: t=top, b=bottom, r=right, l=left, c=center)
17: Stone/Getty Images (bl); 20: Mother & Baby Picture Library/emap esprit; 21: Mother & Baby Picture Library/emap esprit/Ian Hooton (tr); 29: Mother & Baby Picture Library/emap esprit (br); 33: Mother & Baby Picture Library/emap esprit (tl); 35: Stone/Getty Images (tr); 39: SPL (bl), SPL/Neil Bromhall/Genesis Films (tr); 43: SPL/Mike Bluestone (b); 47: SPL/Ruth Jenkinson/ Midirs (t); 49: SPL/Joseph Nettis (b); 51: SPL/Petit Format/Nestle (bl); 53: TCL/Getty Images (br); 63: Art Directors & TRIP/Helene Rogers (tr); 65: Mother & Baby Picture Library/emap esprit/Ruth Jenkinson; 73: Mother & Baby Picture Library/emap esprit (t); Mother & Baby Picture Library/emap esprit/Mampta Kapoor (bl); 75: Mother & Baby Picture Library/emap esprit/Frances Tout (b); 76: Mother & Baby Picture Library/emap esprit (bc), Mother & Baby Picture Library/emap esprit/Eddie Lawrence (br); 77: Mother & Baby Picture Library/emap esprit (bc), Mother & Baby Picture Library/emap esprit/Eddie Lawrence (bl), SPL/Joseph Nettis (tc); 91: Corbis Stock Market/Jon Feingersh; 114: Stone/Getty Images; 116: TCL/Getty Images; 117: Corbis Stock Market/David Raymer; 125: Art Directors & TRIP/Helene Rogers; 145: Stone/Getty Images; 149: Robert Harding Picture Library/Caroline Wood/Int'l Stock (b); 169: Corbis Stock Market/Steve Prezant (tr); 216: Stone/Getty Images; 219: SPL/Medical Illustration, St. Bartholomew's Hospital (tr); SPL/Tricia Reid (tl); 232: Stone/Getty Images; 234: Corbis Stock Market/LWA-Dann Tardif; 235: SPL/Antonia Reeve; 244: Meningitis Research Foundation (tr); 252: SPL/Dr P. Marazzi; 253: SPL/Dr P. Marazzi (cr); 257: SPL/Hattie Young; 258: The Image Bank/Getty Images; 259: SPL/Dr P. Marazzi (br); 260: SPL/Gary Parker (cr); 261: SPL/Will & Deni McIntyre (tr); 265: Garden Picture Library/Juliet Greene.
All other images © Dorling Kindersley.
For further information see: www.dkimages.com